HAND
133
AUN
AF245563

JGSMI
5/19/14

Jewish Life in Philadelphia
1830–1940

Edited by
Murray Friedman

HOLOCAUST MEMORIAL CENTER
28123 Orchard Lake Road
Farmington Hills, MI 43334-3738

ISHI PUBLICATIONS
Institute for the Study of Human Issues
Philadelphia

Copyright © 1983 by the Philadelphia chapter of
The American Jewish Committee
All Rights Reserved

No part of this book may be reproduced in any form or by any
electronic or mechanical means including information storage
and retrieval systems without permission in writing from the
publisher, except by a reviewer who may quote brief passages
in a review.

Manufactured in the United States of America

2 3 4 5 6 7 8 90 89 88 87 86 85 84 83

Library of Congress Cataloging in Publication Data
Main entry under title:
Jewish life in Philadelphia, 1830–1940.

Includes bibliographical references and index.
1. Jews—Pennsylvania—Philadelphia—History—
Addresses, essays, lectures. 2. Philadelphia (Pa.)—
Ethnic relations—Addresses, essays, lectures.
I. Friedman, Murray, 1926–
F158.9.J5J525   1983   974.8'11004924   83-10763
ISBN 0-89727-050-9

For information, write:

Director of Publications
ISHI
3401 Science Center
Philadelphia, Pennsylvania 19104
U.S.A.

Front endpaper: Children playing in South Street, 1901.
Courtesy of the Philadelphia Jewish Archives Center.

Back endpaper: Jewish Publication Society 25th Anniversary
Banquet, 1913. *Courtesy of the Library Company of Philadelphia.*

Contributors

E. Digby Baltzell is Professor of Sociology at the University of Pennsylvania and author of *Philadelphia Gentlemen, Protestant Establishment* and *Puritan Boston and Quaker Philadelphia.*

Evelyn Bodek is Associate Professor of History at Community College of Philadelphia. She is a founding member of the Greater Philadelphia Consortium for Women's Studies and since 1980 has served on the Board of Directors of the *Jewish Exponent.*

Dennis Clark is Executive Director of the Samuel S. Fels Fund and the author of several books on race relations and urban history, including *Cities in Crisis, The Ghetto Game, The Irish in Philadelphia* and *The Irish Relations.*

Joseph Eckhardt is Associate Professor of History at Montgomery County Community College and a member of the American Film Institute and the Pennsylvania Academy of the Fine Arts.

Sandra Featherman is Assistant Professor of Political Science at Temple University, co-author of *Jews, Blacks and Ethnics* and author of the forthcoming *Environmental Policy: An Ethical/Political Approach.*

Murray Friedman is Middle Atlantic States Director of the American Jewish Committee and a lecturer on minority problems and American Jewish life at La Salle College. A frequent contributor to *Commentary, The New Republic* and *The Progressive,* he is also the author of *Overcoming Middle Class Rage* and co-author of *Moving Up: Ethnic Succession in America* and *New Perspectives on School Integration.*

Allen Glicksman is a doctoral candidate in sociology at the University of Pennsylvania. He has taught at Penn and the Netsky Institute of Gratz College and has developed and toured with a multi-media program on the history of Jewish immigration to the United States.

Diane King is Assistant Professor of Education at Gratz College. She is the co-author of an original series for the teaching of Hebrew and Jewish cultural history, produced by Gratz College and the Philadelphia Board of Jewish Education.

LINDA KOWALL is a freelance writer with a special interest in motion picture and theater history. A former magazine editor, she is a member of the Theater Historical Society and the American Film Institute.

JACQUELYN LITT is a doctoral candidate in sociology at the University of Pennsylvania. She is writing her dissertation on women and medical education.

PHILIP ROSEN is an historian and veteran developer of Holocaust studies for area public schools. His book, *The Neglected Dimension*, which dealt with Philadelphia's ethnic groups, appeared in 1979.

DAN ROTTENBERG is Editor of the *Welcomat* and a regular contributor to the *Philadelphia Inquirer* as well as to *Town & Country* and *Chicago* magazines. He is the author of *Finding Our Fathers: A Guidebook to Jewish Genealogy*.

MALCOLM STERN, former Assistant Rabbi of Reform Congregation Keneseth Israel, is Genealogist of the American Jewish Archives. Founder and first Director of the Reform Rabbinic Placement Commission, he is also an honorary vice-president of the American Jewish Historical Society and has published widely in Jewish history, genealogy and music.

ROBERT TABAK, a graduate of Reconstructionist Rabbinical College and a doctoral candidate in history at Temple University, currently serves as Rabbi of Temple Beth Am in Henrietta, New York.

MAXWELL WHITEMAN is Archivist-Historian of The Union League of Philadelphia and senior appointed member of the Pennsylvania Historical and Museum Commission. The author of numerous books and articles in social history and bibliography, he is the co-author of *A History of the Jews of Philadelphia* and has lectured on American history at Dropsie University and Hebrew Union College.

EDWIN WOLF 2ND is Librarian of the Library Company of Philadelphia and former president of the National Foundation for Jewish Culture. He is the author of *Philadelphia: Portrait of an American City* and co-author of *Rosenbach: A Biography* and *A History of the Jews of Philadelphia*.

Contents

(1)

Introduction:
The Making of a
National Jewish Community

Murray Friedman

It may come as a surprise that there are no critical studies of the three largest Jewish immigrant cities outside of New York—Chicago, Philadelphia and Boston. The only history of Philadelphia Jewry now in print is the volume by Edwin Wolf 2nd and Maxwell Whiteman, and it covers the period up to the Age of Jackson when there were only a few Jews here and others had been absorbed by the broader society.[1] If the histories of these communities were better known, it has been suggested, we would have a deeper understanding of the development of American Jewish life.[2]

The tercentenary of the founding of Philadelphia by William Penn in 1682 has provided such an opportunity. With some 295,000 Jews living here, it is the third largest Jewish community in the United States, the fifth largest in the world. Only New York, Los Angeles, Paris and Tel Aviv-Jaffa exceed it in size.[3] More significant than the inattention of historians is the fact that the city has been a center of Jewish life in this country. Here major national institutions, including the Conservative movement, the Jewish Theological Seminary, the Jewish Publication Society, Dropsie and Gratz Colleges and the American Jewish Historical Society, were conceived or founded; here the first sermon in English was preached and the first English-Jewish newspaper was published; here the author of Hatikvah, the Israeli national anthem, lived and here the hymn Adon Olom was composed. The community has produced or directly influenced some of American Jewry's most interesting and significant leaders—men and women such as Isaac Leeser, Rebecca Gratz, Judge Mayer Sulzberger, Cyrus Alder, key business figures like Samuel and Joseph Fels, Siegmund Lubin and

1

Albert M. Greenfield, to name just a few. A number of important writers, scholars and artists, including Clifford Odets, Samuel Grafton, Marc Blitzstein, David Riesman, I. F. Stone, and Noam Chomsky grew up and honed their early talents, often in rebellion against the second-generation world they found here.

In 1830, when Wolf and Whiteman leave off in their telling of "the Philadelphia story," there was no coherent Jewish community in the United States. Immigration had brought a small number of individuals and families to these shores, but they were lost among their neighbors. There were 500 Jews living in New York and between 500 and 1000 in Philadelphia.[4] What Jewish life there was existed within single Jewish congregations. Philadelphia had two by this time—Mikveh Israel and Rodeph Shalom. The Jewish community of America "was small, its future uncertain; the environment . . . was too cramped for either great ideas or great organizations."[5]

By 1836, however, economic conditions in Central Europe were deteriorating. What had been a mere trickle of Jewish immigrants in the eighteenth and early nineteenth centuries now became a mass migration of entire Jewish communities. In 1840, American Jewry numbered some 15,000; ten years later it was 50,000. From a group hugging a number of communities along the Atlantic coast, Jewish settlers had spread across the country, reaching even to San Francisco in the Gold Rush of 1849. On the eve of the Civil War there were 150,000 Jews living in the United States.

Philadelphia shared significantly in this growth. By 1846, Isaac Leeser, hazan of the Sephardic congregation, Mikveh Israel, noted that there were three congregations in the city, numbering about "1500 to 1800 souls." A dozen years later there were perhaps 8000. At mid-century the city's most prominent Jewish leaders carried German names like Gans, Hackenberg, Binswanger, and Wolf rather than those of founding Mikveh Israel families.

The study of Jewish life in this country revolves around the transformation of a colonial single, synagogue-oriented community into nationally organized bodies representing hundreds of independent congregations, benevolent societies, philanthropic and educational institutions. The coming of the German Jews marks the beginning of these developments. Shocked by what seemed to them the watered-down "Jewishness" of the Jews they found here, many were anxious to shore up traditional forms of Judaism as they went about the business of establishing themselves.[6] The growth of a Jewish resident population made it possible to begin the process of building the infrastructure of Jewish communal life and activity. It required Jewish Americans to deal with internal divisions and relate to other communities and groups in an increasingly pluralistic society.

Philadelphia took a leading role in this transformation. Rarely can events of such magnitude be traced to a single individual. Just such a figure, however, was Isaac Leeser, an immigrant from Westphalia who was ultimately selected hazan of Congregation Mikveh Israel in 1829. Daniel J.

Immigrant Station, Swanson Street south of Washington Avenue, 1913. *Courtesy of the Philadelphia City Archives.*

Elazar has described him as "the great creative force of nineteenth-century Jewry."[7] Indeed, it is no exaggeration to speak of this period as "the Age of Leeser."

The essence of Leeser's contribution, as Maxwell Whiteman notes in his contribution, lay in his recognition of the character of this Jewish community coming into being and the need to develop institutional and other forms that would insure its unity and coherence. Leeser was the first American rabbi to travel extensively around the country in an effort to pull together the isolated Jewish communities. He sought to combine "traditionalism with a moderate and conciliatory approach to the modern world." Traditional himself, Leeser was in a sense one of the "founding fathers" of what would later become the Conservative movement in the United States.[8] He founded the *Occident and American Jewish Advocate* in 1843, the nation's first English-Jewish publication, which was as eagerly read in the mining settlements and Gold Rush camps in the West as in the industrial cities of the East. In its pages, Leeser called for union among the established congregations as well as united benevolence so that the business of the Jewish community could be carried on more effectively. When Isaac Mayer Wise, the founder of Reform Judaism in this country sought to reach American Jews with his call for a national conference to deal with the disorder in modern Jewish life, he did so in the pages of the *Occident.* (It was an indication of the importance of Leeser and Philadelphia at this time that Wise urged "the place of assembly" to be Philadelphia, "it being nearly the center of the Jews living in North America.") It was Leeser who introduced the English sermon into the synagogue ritual, who made an original, English translation of the Hebrew scriptures, who developed the program for the Board of Delegates of American Israelites, the earliest Jewish "defense" agency, amdestablished the first Jewish Publication Society. A number of these institutions were short-lived, given the undeveloped form of Jewish communal life, but Leeser had clearly charted the course that life would take.

Isaac Leeser was not alone in conceiving and developing the early structures of Philadelphia Jewish life. As Evelyn Bodek points out, the redoubtable Rebecca Gratz initiated the Hebrew Sunday School Society of Philadelphia, an idea quickly picked up by Jewish women in New York and Charleston. Along with other women from Mikveh Israel and the ubiquitous Leeser, she helped organize the Jewish Foster Home and Orphan Asylum, more recently the Association for Jewish Children. Her brother, Hyman, included a codicil in his will in 1857, calling for "establishment and support of a college for the education of Jews residing in the city and county of Philadelphia." Later in the century, this provision resulted in the founding of Gratz College, the first Hebrew teacher training school in the country. In the creation of Jewish books and liturgical music the city had no match at this time, largely owing to the efforts of Leeser (who contributed more than 150 books and articles) and the publisher Abraham Hart.

Following an abortive attempt by New York Jews to set up an institution of higher learning, a group of Philadelphians that included Hart, Moses A. Dropsie, Isidore Binswanger, and Rabbis Sabato Morais and Marcus Jastrow joined with Leeser, the Board of Delegates and the Hebrew Educational Society to found Maimonides College in 1864, the first training seminary for rabbis in the United States. Hart, who was president of the Board of Delegates, headed it and Mayer Sulzberger served as secretary. And although the Reform movement was the creation of Wise, his disciples ignored his *Minhag America,* as Malcolm Stern notes, and adopted the prayerbook developed by David Einhorn, then rabbi at Philadelphia's Keneseth Israel.

Why did Philadelphia become a focal point of Jewish religious, intellectual and cultural life in America? Boston Jewry, as E. Digby Baltzell suggests, was still too young and too small to play such a role. New York might have done so, but it had as yet no dominant personalities, certainly none who possessed Leeser's determination and drive. New York's Jewish population may simply have been too big, too diverse and too anarchic, as Bertram Korn suggests. As early as 1840 it was divided into a number of hostile camps. In contrast, Philadelphia Jewry possessed a stronger sense of com-

The 700 block of Race Street, 1915. *(Philadelphia City Archives) Reproduced by courtesy of the Museum of American Jewish History.*

munity. Accordingly, Philadelphia became the "ideal experimental center of American Jewish creativity."[10]

Unlike Puritan Boston, which sent its first known Jew back to England, Quaker Philadelphia welcomed Jews from the outset. They were among the original subscribers to the exclusive Dancing Assembly when it was formed in 1748, and when Mikveh Israel found itself in serious financial straits and appealed for funds, its subscription list included such non-Jewish dignitaries as Benjamin Franklin, then President of the Executive Council of Pennsylvania, as well as David Rittenhouse, William Bradford and Charles Biddle.[11] During the Mexican War, Hyman Gratz, a respected merchant, was named temporary president of the prestigious Philadelphia Club when its head was on active duty, and a few years later the Democratic party hurriedly divested itself of a man nominated for County Treasurer when his anti-Jewish feelings became known.[12] So far had this process of acceptance proceeded that most of the descendants of the early Jewish families had disappeared.

Cultural congruence accounted in large degree for the ease of relationships. John Lukacs has pointed out that the city's leaders were patrician rather than aristocratic. "Solidly bourgeois" distinctions of birth existed, but these arose out of "consanguinity of families with high civic reputations and not from noble ancestors."[13] In a society in which sober business habits, business success, and close family ties were more important than bloodlines, German-Jewish families could more easily take their place alongside their neighbors.

The treatment of Jews differed markedly from that accorded other social or ethnic outsiders. As Dennis Clark notes, large numbers of poverty-stricken Irish poured into the city in the 1830s and 1840s and were greeted with violence by Protestant workers who viewed them as economic rivals and "papists," while the city's patrician leaders looked on with indifference or tacit approval. (Philadelphia Jews stayed clear of these struggles, not unlike many Southern Jews in the school desegregation struggles in the 1950s. Leeser believed that the Jewish community was simply too small to get involved.[14]) In turn the newly arrived Irish clashed with the old and well-established community of free blacks with whom they competed for jobs. As a result of the rioting that took place, many blacks were driven from the city and the black population actually decreased from 1840 to 1850.[15]

While Jews in Philadelphia were not free from antisemitism, especially as they became more visible,[16] there is reason to believe that they faced less animosity here than did Jews in New York and other cities.[17] When New York's Union League began to proscribe Jews at the turn of the century, Philadelphia's Union League already had some 40 members, including Judge Mayer Sulzberger and the Orthodox Rabbi Sabato Morais, Leeser's successor at Mikveh Israel. Nor did participation in the full range of the city's activity require any lessening of Jewish identity or efforts, as the careers of the "Philadelphia Group" clearly reveal. Indeed, when the 1881 "Christmas Massacre" in Warsaw began the major exodus of Jews to these shores—the first shipload landed in Philadelphia in March 1882—the city's most distinguished civic, religious and governmental leaders, headed by John Wanamaker, participated with Jews in a mass rally at the Academy of Music in protest.[18]

Thus on the eve of a massive new wave of immigration, the Jewish community of Philadelphia was well integrated and relatively homogeneous. A U.S. Census report in 1890 included a profile of American Jews, one that likely reflected the state of Philadelphia Jewry. Some 15 percent were bankers, brokers and wholesale merchants. Another 35 percent were retail dealers. Accountants, bookkeepers and clerks numbered some 17 percent, while 5 percent were professionals and 12 percent were skilled workers.[19] More successful Jews were already beginning to carve out specialized economic niches such as the manufacture of soap (Fels & Company) and the running of department stores (Lit Brothers, Snellenburgs and Gimbels), in contrast with the Irish, who, as Clark points out, found the construction business closer to their experience and cultural style.

One indication of the success and integration of the German-Jewish families was their movement, in the 1890s, into the fashionable area north of Market Street. Roughly about the time the newly wealthy Gentiles were beginning their move from North Philadelphia to the area around Old York Road, a Jewish neighborhood was forming from North 17th to Broad between Spring Garden and Diamond Streets. Members of Gerstley, Gimbel, Wolf, Fleisher and Binswanger families moved there in the nineties. By 1895, Rodeph Shalom and Keneseth Israel had built large and impressive synagogues on North Broad Street. In the same year, the Mercantile Club constructed an imposing structure midway between the two congregations. A few members of the Jewish upper class began to move out to the suburbs, primarily to the Old York Road area. One symbol of the social standing of the German elite was the founding by the Gimbels, Snellenburgs and Loebs of the Philmont Country Club, the most exclusive Jewish retreat in the city.[20]

Religiously, the Reform movement, led by Wise, had triumphed despite Leeser's strong defense of traditional Judaism. The religious reformers of the West had already attacked Maimonides College, condemned Philadelphia's traditional or Orthodox rabbinate, and quarreled with the city's leading Jewish figure, Judge Sulzberger. (The latter, in turn, referred to Wise coolly as the "wise D.D. of Cincinnati."[21]) As Lucy S. Dawidowicz has observed, "There were no venerable institutions of Jewish learning in the United States and no great Talmudists who commanded sufficient authority to retard if they could not altogether halt, the pace of Reform." Indeed, the absence of "traditional brakes" facilitated Reform's headlong rush into radical change. It placed its emphasis on moral law alone. Kashruth was cast aside along with the concept that Jews constituted a nation. These changes were incorporated in a declaration of principles adopted in 1885 by a group of Reform rabbis in Pittsburgh.[22] It was the coming of Jews from Poland, Russia and other parts of Eastern Europe—the Russian Jews as they came to be called—that was to alter profoundly the character and status of Philadelphia and American Jewry.

Beginning slowly in the 1870s and then more rapidly in subsequent years, the somewhat staid community began to receive increasingly larger numbers of Russian Jews. The estimated 12,000 to 15,000 living here in 1875 grew to 75,000 by 1900, a figure larger than the number of blacks living in the city. At the time of America's entry into World War I, when immigration virtually ceased, there were 200,000.[23] The thousands of Jews who streamed off boats that docked at the foot of Washington Avenue in South Philadelphia settled in blind, bandbox alleys with hydrants and cisterns in the courtyards along Fourth and Fifth Streets, south of Pine, a small area that was to become Philadelphia's equivalent of New York's Lower East

Side. Here the vast majority were to remain until after World War II. Despite the squalidness of their surroundings, they were spared tenement living as a result of the city's pattern of row houses.

It was not only the large numbers who came here and their poverty that was to change the Philadelphia Jewish community. They were different kinds of Jews. In addition to being poor, they dressed differently and spoke a strange language—Yiddish. In 1894, Henry Morais noted the "peculiarity of Jeudisch Deutsh." "Even operatic and theatrical companies," he noted, "gave their performances in this mixture."[24] That these scruffy looking immigrants would soon be attending such entertainment should have surprised him even more. Many practiced, also, what to the older families living here seemed a primitive form of Judaism in ramshackle Orthodox synagogues created in the midst of their poverty. Between 1880 and 1890, more synagogues were founded than the city could boast in its entire history. It was true, of course, that the services conducted were in Hebrew and they shared a common liturgy with elite and Orthodox Mikveh Israel, but there the similarity ended. The pronunciation and intonation of the prayers were different, the service more personal, less inhibited and, to many, quite indecorous.

Most of all the older elite worried about how the Russian Jews would affect their own standing in the community. Part of the reason for their movement north and west of Broad Street was to get away from the "blight" that had hit the Street in the form of a "diaspora from the ghetto." Philip Goodman, who wrote these words, was still able to smile. "To hear us talk and protest," he wrote, "you might have thought that we were Americans by right of our pure Mohawk blood."[25] After a visit in 1894 with Count Leo Tolstoy, who told him that dispersing Jews would spread "a good name for your people throughout the land," Rabbi Joseph Krauskopf of Keneseth Israel went home and started the National Farm School in Doylestown, just north of Philadelphia.[26] There is some indication that very early in the flow of immigrants here, the local leadership sought to limit it even as they bent their efforts increasingly in philanthropic activities to relieve the suffering of new arrivals and help them to adjust to American life.[27]

From the point of view of the newcomers, however, the Jews and the broader community they found here were no less strange. The Reform movement articulated principles of social justice that might have found reverberations among Jews working in clothing factories and other manufacturing establishments. However, this had gotten mixed up somehow with "Social Gospel" Protestantism which seemed only rarely to have touched the sweatshops in which they labored. They found themselves in conflict, too, with German-Jewish bosses. Disastrous strikes took place in 1889 and 1890. Their employers did not look with favor on trade union activities, insisting, as one clothing manufacturer declared, "the Lord will punish such conduct."[28] The anarchists, who took the lead in organizing early strikes, were quick to point out that the patrons and directors of the United Hebrew Charities who found work for the immigrants in the factories were also owners of the run-down housing in which they lived. The central philanthropic bodies took no official position in the particularly harsh strike of 800 Jewish clothing workers in 1890, probably contributing significantly to the conflict of working and lower-middle-class Jews with the "Establishment" that endures, albeit less harshly, down to the present day.

Conditions did not improve materially when newcomers rose to become "bosses." Moreover, older labor organizations in the city did not initially welcome Jewish members while the socialist movement here, unlike New York's, was weak and ineffective. In the process of testing the industrial structure through trial and error, the "greenhorns" managed nevertheless to develop a new sophistication as members of a growing working class. This permitted them ultimately to join with the Italians and Irish in unions like the International Ladies Garment Workers and the Amalgamated Clothing Workers to confront many of the harsher forms of exploitation and indifference they found here.

Along with the enervating effect of their occupations, the very openness of American society weakened traditional religious habits and culture. Unlike in the old country, there was no established leadership on whom they could count to provide guidance. Israel Sachs, a forceful speaker and Talmudist who might have provided that leadership, died before he could stand the test. He had sought to counter those elements that tore Jews away from ritual and religious customs. Even though he possessed some influence, he was no match for the eroding effects of a new industrial society.[29]

In spite of the limitations of background and the difficulties of adjustment, the newcomers possessed "total commitment to Jewish identity, complete faith in the American promise and an almost inexhaustible source of psychic energy which had been repressed for so long."[30] Indeed, they began almost immediately to remake the Jewish community they found here. A number of the synagogues had Hebrew schools connected to them, but the Russian Jews introduced their own Hebrew schools, the heder, in little rooms in blind alleys, often unheated in winter. The melamed traveled through these bleak areas, bringing Jewish education to homes for fifty cents a week.

A rich and vital cultural life flourished in Hebrew and Yiddish. As Whiteman notes, a lively Jewish press soon emerged to provide the newcomers with news about their community and their brethren all over the world. The immigrants and their children had an insatiable desire for learning. They attended lectures in English and Hebrew in the uptown YMHA, the Hebrew Literary Society founded in 1885 at Third and Catherine Streets, and at Touro Hall, and patronized the Jewish Theater on Arch Street where Jacob Adler and Boris Thomashevsky starred. Animated debates rocked the community as radicals battled anarchists to the dismay of

Market Street, looking east from Ninth Street, 1910. *Courtesy of the Philadelphia City Archives.*

the established leadership. One group made up primarily of physicians—Jews were beginning to enter the medical profession here by the 1890s—decided to deride Yom Kippur and were promptly arrested, although later released.

The *Jewish Exponent*, created by the older elite in 1887 to help in the Americanizing process, proved to be a useful means by which the immigrants and their children could test their English skills. Here they could read articles by such figures as Mayer Sulzberger, Sabato and Henry Morais, Joseph Krauskopf, David Werner Amram, Cyrus Adler, Horace Stern, Simon Wolf, Oscar Straus, Solomon Schechter and Benjamin L. Gordin, whose autobiography, *Between Two Worlds*, along with Abraham Cahan's novel, *The Rise of David Levinsky*, are among the best descriptions of immigrant Jewish life. The *Exponent* also ran Israel Zangwill's *King of the Schnorers.*[31]

Organizational life in the city took on a new vigor. The 1900 volume of the *American Jewish Yearbook* reported some 150 organizations that included sisterhoods and various study groups, without even counting B'nai

B'rith or branches of national bodies. Major new business enterprises came into being. Siegmund Lubin pioneered in the development of the film industry, becoming as Joseph Eckhardt and Linda Kowall suggest, "The Movies' First Mogul." Sam Paley built a major cigar business, eventually selling it for $30 million before the Great Depression, and encouraging his son, William, to purchase a fledgling New York radio network which ultimately became CBS.[32] Albert M. Greenfield amassed a vast business empire encompassing real estate, retail stores, banks, hotels and transportation companies.

From the very outset, despite feelings of distaste, the older German elite came to feel an oblication to assist their poor cousins. The United Hebrew Charities increased its relief from $12,000 in 1880 to $42,000 a dozen years later. Soon filled to capacity, the Jewish Foster Home built a new wing and by 1892 had doubled its size. A year earlier the Hebrew Education Society opened its headquarters in Touro Hall at Tenth and Carpenter Streets, in the very heart of the immigrant settlement. The contributions here by Edwin Wolf 2nd, Philip Rosen and Evelyn Bodek describe these efforts. Dr. Bodek explores the special role played by upper-class women: "Communal philanthropy utilized the 'Ladies' as an auxiliary force, almost an 'army' to socialize and acculturate the poor, the ignorant, the destitute with their superior 'weapons' of domesticity, piety, and moral motherhood."

There is no mistaking the patronizing quality of much of this work. Yet it was accompanied by a deep sense of empathy among many of Philadelphia's religiously traditional and upper-class leaders. As early as 1886, Wolf notes, the Association of Jewish Immigrants of Philadelphia, headed by Louis Edward Levy, sharply criticized the wealthy New Yorkers in the United Hebrew Charities for attempting to stem the tide of Russian immigrants. Much to the dismay of the clothing manufacturers, Sabato Morais worked hard to settle the terrible cloakmakers' strike in 1890, with justice for the workers. "We are all bourgeois and those of us who have the fortune to be rich are generally newly rich," Judge Sulzberger thundered some years later against those who had not paid their welfare fund pledges. "They mistake their narrowness for superiority to another man who may be a Shakespeare in his own language but is ignorant of English."[33] Philadelphia's upper class recognized that the Russian Jews were destined, in the words of Henry Morais, to be "representative of the race of Israel in the United States."[34]

There was still another factor that drew older residents' efforts to assist the newcomers. This was the sense of common peril growing out of a rising tide of antisemitism. The small Jewish community had tended to minimize hostility and restrictive barriers, but during the Gilded Age the general struggle for place and privilege upset the pattern of urban life. The emergence of a Jewish *nouveau riche* only exacerbated anxieties in this socially competitive period.[35] While there is some indication that Philadelphia was slower than other communities to raise up barriers—probably because Jews here were an old and well-established community and their economic rise was not as sudden as in New York—it was not long before fears arose. In 1914 the native Philadelphian Elizabeth Robbins Pennell wrote, "the Jew and alien are forcing their way into society."[36] Many prominent Jewish families, accustomed to spending summers in such proper Philadelphia resorts as Cape May, soon found that they were no longer welcome there as well as in elite clubs and certain favored neighborhoods.[37] Unlike New York, where social barriers sometimes erupted in highly publicized episodes such as the exclusion of Joseph Seligman from the Grand Union Hotel in Saratoga, Philadelphia's Protestant establishment, in a cooler, patrician manner, built an inviolable caste system. Upper-class and seemingly well-integrated German Jews learned the painful lesson that to their Gentile peers a Jew remained a Jew and as such an outsider.

These social and psychological changes propelled the Philadelphia Jewish elite into its most creative period of community development in the period before World War I. The limited amount of study devoted to Philadelphia Jewry and the absence of full-scale biographies of its leaders have tended to obscure the significant role they were now to play in developing many of the major institutions of Jewish life.[38] Philadelphia's traditional leaders were deeply disturbed about what was happening to the masses of Jews who had recently come here. They saw the latter as becoming atomized and drawn to secular pursuits and to radical activities. Radical Reform Judaism, they knew, offered no countervailing force since it was foreign to the life of the newcomers. Proud of their heritage, the Jewish elite of New York and Philadelphia, along with leading Jews throughout the United States, sought ways to reach the newcomers and attach them to Jewish life.

The leadership groups of the two major Jewish communities were linked along class lines, but there were important differences between them. Gotham's Jews were businessmen and lawyers, whereas the "Philadelphia Group" was predominantly intellectuals and scholars. Men like Jacob Schiff, James Warburg, Adolph S. Ochs, Oscar S. Straus, and Jesse Seligman possessed wealth and ability, as well as deep commitment, but Sabato Morais, Cyrus Adler, Solomon Solis-Cohen, and Mayer Sulzberger were richer in ideas. (In his biography of Solomon Schechter, Norman Bentwich has described Sulzberger as "the Maecenas of learning and the 'Nathan der Wise' of American Jewry."[39]) Many of the Philadelphians were traditional or Orthodox Jews, members of Mikveh Israel, whereas the New Yorkers belonged to Reform congregations. Among the key Philadelphians only Rabbi Krauskopf was a Reform Jew.

Decision-making was a shared activity, but the Jewish leadership in Philadelphia was looked to increasingly for guidance in this critical period. In the matter of the negotiations involving abrogation by the U.S. govern-

The outdoor market at Fourth and Fitzwater Streets, 1914. *Courtesy of the Philadelphia City Archives.*

ment of the Russian-American trade agreement, Justice Julian Mack of the Illinois Appellate Court wrote Sulzberger, "I am inclined to think your statement to Straus and Schiff . . . would be heeded more than anyone else's," while Solomon Schechter, who was being wooed primarily by the Philadelphians to come to the United States and take over the Jewish Theological Seminary, looked to Sulzberger and Adler for approval. "When you give the matter your blessing, I will answer Amen," he wrote to the latter at one point.[40]

The Philadelphia Group recognized the centrality of New York in the evolving pattern of the Jewish community of America and were often willing to work through the New Yorkers. The American Jewish Historical Society was "wholly the child" of Adler's creation but at its founding in 1892, Adler, who was serving as temporary chairman, nominated Straus as chairman and accepted the less conspicuous role of secretary. When Straus stepped down six years later, Adler and Abraham S.W. Rosenbach, both Philadelphians, headed the organization for the next 50 years.[41]

The Philadelphia Group turned aside from their regular scholarly and intellectual pursuits and, together with their friends and colleagues in New York, bent their efforts toward developing many of the major institutions of

American Jewish life, including the Jewish Theological Seminary, the American Jewish Committee, Gratz and Dropsie Colleges, the Jewish Publication Society, Jewish Chautauqua, and the Baron de Hirsch Fund. The path taken by the Philadelphians had been laid out by Leeser and the small number of Jews here who shared a common set of values and goals. In his book, *The Protestant Establishment,* Baltzell has suggested that orderly progress in society rather than revolutionary change "depends to a very great extent on the maintenance of a continuity of cultural traditions."[42] Philadelphia Jewry was clearly such a community and Philadelphia was such a city. Although it covered an area larger than London, it was a "town" of families and neighborhoods, old-fashioned and not a little stodgy. By the time of the arrival of the Russian Jews, as Wolf notes, everyone was related to or at least knew everyone else, and this organic connection was expressed through philanthropic activity. Sulzberger was a protégé of Leeser. On the latter's death, Sulzberger edited the *Occident* for a brief period and read law in the office of Moses Dropsie. In turn, Adler, who as a child was carried playfully on the backs of the students at Maimonides College, and was a cousin of Sulzberger, became the latter's protégé and successor.

In his autobiography, *I Have Considered the Days,* Cyrus Adler observes that New York had important figures like Schiff, Straus and Marshall, but he found to his surprise that "most of these men had no contacts outside of those they had in the common business of life."[43] Many were newcomers to the city from Europe or other parts of the country. (Schiff had been born in Frankfurt-am-Main; Marshall came to New York from Syracuse in 1894; and Adolph S. Ochs arrived two years later from Chattanooga to purchase the *New York Times*.)[44] Adler suggested to Schiff that an informal organization in New York modeled on an English group, "The Maccabeans," might be useful. Through Schiff he helped organize "The Wanderers" which, he later wrote, "made good friends of men who had been only acquaintances."[45]

The formation and early days of the American Jewish Committee illustrate the unusual partnership between the New York and Philadelphia leadership. The idea for the formation of an authoritative body to speak for American Jewry on national and international affairs was first discussed at a meeting of "The Wanderers." Spurred by these deliberations, Adler introduced the idea in a letter to the *American Hebrew* in January 1906. He served on the organization committee and when the group was unable to agree, he broke the deadlock. Judge Sulzberger became its first president, although he continued to live in Philadelphia. He ran it by sending directives from his home, while Adler, who was less reluctant to travel, handled the routine and worked closely with the organization's secretary. Sulzberger was succeeded by Louis Marshall, widely judged the outstanding Jewish leader of his time. On Marshall's death, Adler was elected to take his place.[46] Presiding over an organization at this time was a functional activity since a "Jewish civil service" had not yet fully developed. Nor was the idea of running a national organization in New York from Philadelphia considered unusual. Morais had presided earlier over the Jewish Theological Seminary, Adler headed several simultaneously, and the antiquarian bookseller, A. S. W. Rosenbach, was for decades president of the American Jewish Historical Society and American Friends of Hebrew University.

Close consultation and common action on behalf of Jews between the "unofficial oligarchies" of Philadelphia and New York was the norm in the decade prior to and following the turn of the century. Straus, then Secretary of Commerce and Labor, persuaded Adler to take over the presidency of Dropsie College in Philadelphia and when the latter went on to head the American Jewish Committee, Felix Warburg proposed Horace Stern of Philadelphia to head its Executive Committee. Adler, who spearheaded Philadelphia's brief attempt at a Kehilla, attended meetings of the New York Kehilla. While Philadelphia's upper-class elite worked with their social counterparts in New York, Rabbi Bernard Levinthal, the unofficial chief rabbi of Philadelphia Orthodoxy, helped found Agudat Harabanim in 1902, later serving as its president, and led the embattled East European rabbis across the United States and Canada in efforts to strengthen kashruth, sabbath observance and religious education.[47] The Philadelphians opposed the suggestion of Schiff in 1894 that the Baron de Hirsch School of Agriculture in Woodbine, New Jersey, be closed because "Jewish boys are not willing to do what we want them to do," and the school limped along until 1918.[48]

After the Pittsburgh conference formulated the radical Reform platform and more traditional Jews felt the need to found a rabbinical training institution—Maimonides College having closed in 1873—the gentle yet forceful Dr. Morais of Mikveh Israel took the lead in calling a meeting of Conservative Jewry attended by rabbis and laymen from eastern states. He was named president of the Association of the Jewish Theological Seminary in America when it was formed in New York in 1886. The movement, however, did not prosper and with the death of Morais and his successor, New York Jews wanted to move the Seminary to Philadelphia. Sulzberger and other Jewish leaders here rejected the idea. In the 1901 reorganization that brought Solomon Schechter to this country to revive the Seminary, Solomon Solis-Cohen, Sulzberger and Adler played critical roles. They knew that financial support was necessary. In a letter to Schechter, Sulzberger noted, "I have discussed the matter with Schiff, who is *the* Yehudi of New York and we have agreed that to render the plan assured a friend of mine, Louis Marshall, should be the President. With him at the head, things would be perfectly safe." As the project moved toward completion, Sulzberger wanted Adler to be president of the board of trustees, to which Schechter responded with pleasure, comparing his relationship with Adler to that which existed in ancient Babylon between the Masi and the Gaon. Schechter and the JTS proved to be powerful forces in the growth of Conservative

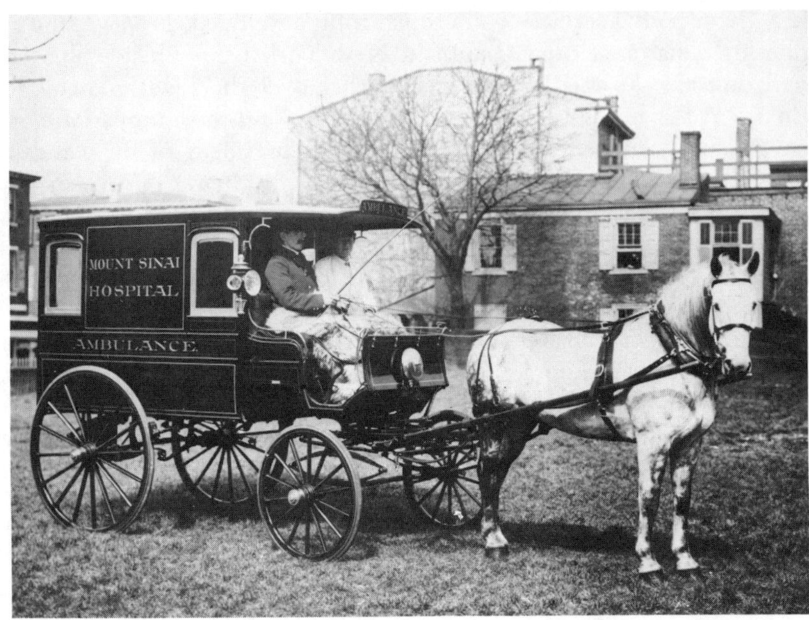

Mt. Sinai Hospital's horse-drawn ambulance, about 1910. *Courtesy of Albert Einstein Medical Center.*

Judaism, which later served as a bridge over which many of the children of immigrants passed into an association with Jewish life based on a combination of "tradition and change."[49] Upon Schechter's death in 1915, Adler succeeded him.

In the period between the wars, the older German-Jewish families continued to be the dominant group in the city, but the new immigration was now one and two generations old. Many of the newcomers had moved out of working-class occupations into white-collar jobs and businesses of their own, aided by informal institutions like the Mastbaum Loan System created by wealthy German-Jewish businessmen. By this time, a number of them resided in Logan, Strawberry Mansion and West Philadelphia. There was also a rapid growth of new synagogues, largely English-speaking and Conservative, although the lines between Orthodox and Conservative were not clearly drawn. The three large and several small Conservative synagogues of 1919 grew to 25 by 1945. Formal Jewish religious education expanded through communal, afternoon Talmud Torahs and the growth of congregational Sunday Schools. Secular schools were begun by the Workmen's Circle in 1921. After 1928 they had competition from the communist Yiddish schools of the International Workers Order. A new English-language weekly, the *Jewish Times,* began publication in 1926, seeking to reach English-speaking Jews of Eastern European origin as a challenge to the *Jewish*

Exponent, published by the German-dominated Federation of Jewish Charities.[50]

Since status in the Jewish community is conferred through the democracy of money expended in communal or civic activities, business success led inexorably to the creation of a special network of philanthropic institutions by Russian Jews. The annual reports of the Federation, as Philip Rosen notes, started listing names like Bayuk and Paley (cigars), Publicker (whiskey) and Schorr (law). The movement of these men into Jewish communal life was sometimes assisted by older German leaders who were not indifferent to their business success. Judge Sulzberger had led the way by befriending Bernard Levinthal. Sulzberger sponsored Rabbi Levinthal's membership in the American Jewish Committee in New York, and the latter served as one of the AJC delegates with Cyrus Adler at the Paris Peace Conference in 1919. Albert M. Greenfield headed the annual welfare fund drive in 1923, and at about the same time became one of the first two members of the Mercantile Club who were not of German origin.[51] By World War II, Greenfield and Jews of Russian origin were elected to the Philmont Country Club and Center City's Locust Club.

By this time, too, the pattern of antisemitism and social discrimination that had begun to develop here and in other parts of the country at the turn of the century had become intensified among the city's older-stock elite. The upward mobility, particularly of the "foreign" Russian Jews, fulfilled the worst patrician fears. New immigrant entrepreneurs such as Greenfield and the film pioneer Siegmund Lubin were outsiders in every way. They refused to do business in the traditional Philadelphia manner. They were speculators, quick to spot new trends and opportunities and none too fastidious in their methods. When the Philadelphia business and social elite met on December 19, 1930, at the height of the Great Depression, and decided not to bail out Greenfield's floundering Bankers Trust Company, they were expressing a very real anxiety about the Jewish "invasion" of the corridors of power that had always been their special preserve.

This fear was felt most deeply in the practice of law, perhaps the city's most prestigious occupation. While the bar had grown by 21 percent between 1920 and 1930, the number of foreign-born lawyers, many of them Jews, increased by 72 percent. "Overcrowding" became the euphemism to describe the "problem" posed to an increasingly castelike Protestant establishment. Henry S. Drinker, whose name graced one of the city's leading firms and who chaired the Philadelphia Law Association grievance committee, described those who having come "up out of the gutter . . . were merely following the methods their fathers had been using in selling shoestrings and other merchandise. . . ." The head of another patrician law firm, Robert McCracken, later president of the Pennsylvania Bar Association, explained to New York lawyers how the state had handled "the question of the social origins of the men." Before a character examination was instituted, 76 percent of the applicants were immigrants, predominantly Russian Jews. Within a few years, he added with satisfaction, the proportion had slipped to 60 percent. Summing up the situation, Jerald Auerbach has written, "Ethnic hostility so blatant in the profession in New York and Chicago became almost subdued by contrast with the Pennsylvania experience."[52] Jews were painfully aware as well that restrictions existed against their admission to medical and dental schools.

The developing Jewish community worried proper Philadelphians in other ways. The older German-Jewish elite tended to be safely conservative in a city that remained Republican after Alfred E. Smith and Franklin D. Roosevelt had changed the political patterns of the country. By the mid-1930s, however, as Sandra Featherman observes, Jews were moving into the Democratic party. Not the least of Albert M. Greenfield's transgressions, Dan Rottenberg notes, was that he left the GOP to support Roosevelt in 1936 and, in fact, became the vice chairman of the Democratic National Finance Committee. In addition he had backed J. David Stern, publisher of the liberal Philadelphia *Record,* a thorn in the side of the city's elite. In the process of climbing Philadelphia's social ladder, Rottenberg concludes, Greenfield "and other Jews of his generation did more than adapt to the city's way of doing things; they changed the city so that, in many ways, the old rules no longer applied."

By 1940, members of the Jewish upper class were socially isolated. Indeed, according to Baltzell, two parallel, upper-class structures existed in the city. Only one Jew, David Riesman Sr., father of the distinguished author of *The Lonely Crowd* and a member of the German-Jewish elite, was listed in the *Social Register,* while Howard Loeb, chairman of the Tradesmen's National Bank, was the only Jew employed in a significant role in a Gentile institution. Segregation extended to the University of Pennsylvania campus. The 40 undergraduate fraternities were divided into 28 "A" or Gentile houses and 12 "B" or Jewish houses.[53] Looking back at his youth and college career at Penn and Johns Hopkins, Adler wrote sadly, but with typical Philadelphia restraint, "I always mingled freely with all friends and students without regard to their creed or origin, or their color . . . I feel sure that our America was much broader, and much more liberal, much freer from prejudice than it is today."[54]

Most Jews, however, were not connected with the WASP upper class or, for that matter, with the German-Jewish elite. Working- or lower-middle-class Jews were naturally segregated from both. The world of their fathers was the Arbeiter Ring or the Workmens Circle, not clubs of the Jewish or Protestant establishments. Moreover, the full weight of the Great Depression came to be felt by the great mass of Jews. By 1929, the boom of the twenties had collapsed and lines of unemployed were forming in the offices of the Jewish Welfare Society. In 1930, during the administration of Lessing J. Rosenwald, the Federation ran a $320,000 deficit. The following year, the city's business, labor, government and philanthropic leaders got together to consider how to avert the worst of the catastrophe. The two major city-wide agencies of philanthropy were the Federation and the Welfare Federation of Protestant and nonsectarian organizations. The two groups joined together for purposes of local fund-raising. Ultimately, this alliance became the basis for the United Way.[55]

The Depression coincided, as well, with the rise of Nazism in Germany. This produced an influx into Philadelphia of disoriented refugees requiring broad assistance. Charitable and overseas services now had to be expanded. The Employment and Vocational Bureau (later the Jewish Employment and Vocational Services) was established initially to aid refugees.[56] Since Federation and its partner groups around the country were geared primarily to provide local health and welfare services in tandem with the overall city welfare effort and there was now a need for overseas rescue operations, the Allied Jewish Appeal was created side by side with Federation in 1937. The threat posed by Hitler at home and abroad brought forth not only large sums of money, but significant growth in the numbers of contributors. Allied had 7000 in its first fund-raising drive, and 48,000 in 1939. Practically every Jewish family in the city was involved. Most of them gave under $25—usually $10 or less. As a result, the base of Jewish giving expanded enormously, laying the groundwork for the postwar drives for Israel. Philanthropy was no longer an exclusive function of the Jewish upper classes. In World War II, for the first time, money raised for overseas relief was greater than that raised for local needs.

Although Morris Wolf, a member of the German-Jewish group, served as Allied's first president and the older leadership continued to occupy key posts for some years, Allied became the prime interest of Russian Jews and their children and of Zionist-oriented groups that were increasingly undertaking major roles as contributors and community leaders. As the threat of Nazism increased, philanthropy which just a few years earlier had been assimilated into the broader community effort, was returned to the Jewish community. There now existed "two separate central communal structures," according to Donald B. Hurwitz, later head of the combined effort, "operating sometimes cooperatively but often competitively and in conflict."[57]

The rise of Hitler in Europe together with the trauma of the Depression created an atmosphere in which Jews found themselves increasingly the targets of broader antisemitic attacks. The improvement of the position of Jews in the United States following World War II has obscured for new generations the fearful nature of the situation in 1940. In the six years following the assumption of power by the Nazis in Germany, some 121 right-wing, antisemitic organizations, including the Christian Front and the German-American Bund, came into existence in the United States. The Sunday afternoon radio broadcasts of Father Charles Coughlin, which attracted a national audience of millions, grew increasingly more strident in its attacks on Jews. By 1938 his antisemitism had become blatant. He charged that Communism was a Jewish plot, that capitalism was a Jewish scheme to control the finances of the world, and that Jews were involved in international intrigue.[58]

In Philadelphia a segment of the Irish community became attracted to Coughlin. Older citizens today recall families sitting out on their stoops in the summer, listening to the broadcasts. Although there were cordial relations among many individual Catholics and Jews—one Irish radio station owner flatly refused to carry the Coughlin broadcasts—tensions existed in the neighborhoods which sometimes erupted in attacks on Jewish merchants and children. Jews and Catholics tended to have somewhat different foreign concerns: Jews wanted to fight fascism and Hitler, while many Catholics saw Communism and Stalin as the greater evil. This was evident especially during the Spanish Civil War in the late 1930s. Cardinal Dougherty mounted a boycott of Stern's Philadelphia *Record* when it editorialized against Franco. The boycott ended only with an apology by Stern, published in the *Catholic Standard and Times,* the archdiocesan newspaper.[59]

The German-American Bund, under the leadership of Gerhardt Wilhelm Kunze, was built into a powerful organization here, perhaps stronger than its counterparts in other cities. Although small in numbers, it had many supporters and it backed the newly founded *Weckruf und Beobachter,* a bilingual newspaper subsidized and controlled by the German propaganda machine. When national Nazi leader Fritz Kuhn was imprisoned in 1939 for embezzlement, Kunze succeeded him. Dressed in stormtrooper uniforms, Bund members joined in marches with supporters of Father Coughlin, shouting anti-Jewish slogans and hawking copies of Coughlin's newspaper, *Social Justice.*[60]

The need to respond to these threats was recognized by Maurice B. Fagin, a young insurance executive of Russian origin. On January 30, 1939, Fagin founded and became director of the Philadelphia Anti-Defamation Council, with offices provided free of charge by Greenfield. Leon Solis-Cohen, son of Solomon Solis-Cohen, served briefly as president and was succeeded by Jerome Rothschild, an attorney and member of the German-Jewish group, continuing the older pattern of Jewish communal leadership. Support quickly came from the Allied Jewish Appeal, and the Council expanded its work to include 17 city-wide Jewish agencies, becoming in 1944 the Jewish Community Relations Council. Hostility toward blacks also was rampant at this time. Recognizing the close relationship between racial and religious bigotry and the need to enlist the total community in the battle against prejudice, Fagin created the Fellowship Commission, an umbrella organization consisting of the Anti-Defamation Council, the Friends

Committee on Race Relations and the Philadelphia Council of Churches. In succeeding years the Jewish Community Relations Council and the Fellowship Commission, both run by Fagin, would stand at the center, not only of civil rights and intergroup relations activities, but also of liberal reform efforts in the city.

As the battle against antisemitism merged imperceptibly with civil rights and other efforts to create a more just society, liberal politics became the central, secular passion of the Jewish community. It was not surprising that working-class Jews, many of whom came out of a socialist tradition, would enlist in efforts to remake society. However, virtually all segments of the Jewish community were involved. Joseph and Samuel S. Fels had been in the forefront of every reform effort. The former organized the Fels Fund (later the Samuel S. Fels Fund) to collect contributions for these efforts, while the latter, in his 1933 book, *This Changing World—As I See Its Trend and Purposes,* advocated a system of unemployment insurance tied in with opportunities for adult education and organization of a Federal Trade system.[61] Greenfield was among the first businessmen in the city to employ blacks and women in his operations. A small number of the first American-born generation of Eastern European Jews joined the Communist Party. Indeed, one study estimates that they were the predominant group here.[62] Jews, however, were not Communists and chose the usual political processes. By the mid-thirties, as Sandra Featherman points out, Jews had deserted the Republican Party and enthusiastically enlisted in the New Deal coalition.

The zeal for social change merged, as well with the powerful cultural ferment among many of the children of the immigrants. Much of this centered in the late twenties and early thirties in the home of Morris Vladimir Leof, who lived in a brownstone building at 322 South 16th Street. Here gathered the young intelligentsia in rebellion against parents who were illiterate and ran chicken stores and fruit stands. "Papa," as Leof was called, was in fact a born dissident who valued Jewish traditions of intellectualism, humanitarian service and the "oneness of humanity." The young playwright Clifford Odets, who lived in West Oak Lane, looked upon him as a surrogate father, as did the composer Marc Blitzstein. Into the Leof home streamed a steady procession of extraordinary visitors to Philadelphia, including Sholem Asch and the Jewish tragedian Jacob Adler, as well as locals like I.F. "Izzy" Stone, then an editorial writer on the Philadelphia *Record,* and the millionaire blueblood John Frederick Lewis. The latter would lend Leof the Academy of Music from time to time for a liberal benefit.[63] Idealistic young Jewish intellectuals, unable to make it to Greenwich Village and with fantasies of "salvation in Moscow," would climb the steep stairs to the amphitheater section of the Academy on Saturday night for the concerts of the Philadelphia Orchestra and then repair to Horn and Hardart across the

The Marshall Street market, 1925. *Courtesy of the Philadelphia City Archives.*

street (now the Bains restaurant) for heated discussions of current political and aesthetic issues. Blitzstein's 1937 musical, "The Cradle Will Rock," and other works reflected this atmosphere.

If "defense," liberal reform and cultural rebelliousness were major expressions of Jewish social consciousness at this time and responses, in some measure, to being viewed as outsiders, then Zionism—the movement to create a Jewish state and homeland—was another. Philadelphia had been a center of Zionist activity even before the turn of the century. The concept had been brought here by Russian Jews. Publication of Herzl's *Der Judenstaat* aroused much interest here and this excitement led to the founding, in June 1897, of the first official Zionist organization in Philadelphia, Ohavei Zion (Lovers of Zion), some two months before the first Zionist Congress in Basle, Switzerland. Within the year a member of the group traveled to New York to help form the Federation of American Zionists.

Here as elsewhere, the movement was caught in the ideological crosscurrents of Jewish life. Many within the German-Jewish and Reform group viewed their Zion as being in America. They feared that support of a Jewish state would open up the question of "dual loyalty" even as they exerted their efforts, through the Jewish Agency and in other ways, to upbuild the land there.[64] Adler wished the Zionists would give up a "theory" and unite with other forces that advocated colonization projects, while Rabbi Krauskopf held Zionism to be an "empty dream." Opposition came also from elements of the Orthodox community, although less vocally, and from the socialists and communists whose goals, of course, were the eclipse of capitalism and the creation of a new society which Jews would share with all peoples. In turn Zionists here were critical of Krauskopf's Farm School. *Zion's Friend*, the official publication of Ohavei Zion, thought that the money used for this and other projects could be better employed by Palestine colonists. The tensions between the "Yehudim"—rich, assimilationist Jews—and the "Yidden" were noted in a first anniversary editiorial in *Zion's Friend*. "The uptowners have dubbed us Russians and in the eyes of the downtowners we are Germans. But we are neither Germans nor Russians. We are Jews and Zionists."[65]

Ten years after the founding of the movement, however, Zionism had become a firm part of the institutional life of Philadelphia's Jewish community. Rabbi Levinthal, an ardent Zionist, and his two sons helped to diminish the opposition, as did the efforts of the *Jewish Exponent*, then a private newspaper, which became in effect a spokesman for the Zionist movement. Before long all manner of Jews came to support the idea of a Jewish state, including those on the Left, Orthodox Jews, businessmen and even anarchists. Philadelphia became an increasingly important part of the Zionist movement in this country despite the lack of major figures of national stature like Louis Brandeis or Rabbi Abba Hillel Silver. The Poale Zion, Labor Zionism, issued its first call for a formal organization from Philadelphia, while Judge Louis E. Levinthal became national president of the Zionist Organization of America in 1941, declaring in his "Credo" the postwar goal of "Zionizing the bulk of American Jewry" and "winning over sympathy and support of Christian America" for "a homeland in Palestine." By 1935, even the Central Conference of American Rabbis, the arm of Reform Judaism, which had been opposed to political Zionism, reversed its stand. Meeting on the last day of 1942, the CCAR called for establishing a "Jewish army."[66]

The CCAR's call was the last straw for a number of Jews opposed to a nationalist solution to the "Jewish problem." At a meeting convened by non-Zionist members of the CCAR in Atlantic City, which Rabbis William Fineshriber of Keneseth Israel and Louis Wolsey of Rodeph Shalom organized with New York leaders, it was decided to develop an anti-Zionist movement of "practical and prestigious laymen" as well as religious leaders. Lessing Rosenwald, who had earlier fought the merger of the United Jewish Appeal and Joint Distribution Committee, was asked to serve as president of the new American Council for Judaism. Rabbi Elmer Berger took a leave of absence from his pulpit in Flint, Michigan, to move to Philadelphia, where he established his office in Rosenwald's neighborhood and began pulling together the organization and its program. The latter held that

Judaism was a religious and not a national or racial identification, called for free immigration to Palestine after the war on a humanitarian basis and sought the creation of a democratic structure in Palestine of all elements of the population.[67] It is ironic that Philadelphia leadership, which earlier had helped to forge so many of the major institutions in American Jewish life, should now play a leading part once more in the creation of an organization that would be so much at variance with what was to become its focus in the years ahead.

The development of the ACJ, however, carries us beyond the scope of this discussion. Its founding was a direct response to the desperate state of American Jewry on the eve of World War II. Clearly, this was the darkest hour of American Jewry. Still ahead lay what some would call its "Golden Age." Following the war, the children and grandchildren of the earlier waves of immigrants found education, careers, and affluence that their fathers could only dream of. They moved out of areas of first and second settlement to the verdant suburbs of the Main Line and the Great Northeast. In the mid-sixties, large Gentile law firms, banks, and industrial organizations began to hire and promote Jews, and by the seventies they had once more become a firm part of the civic life of the community. But this still lay ahead.

The fact is that by the time of World War I, Philadelphia Jewry had ceased to play a leading role in the development of Jewish life in America. New York had simply overwhelmed it both in numbers and magnitude of influence. The distinguished editor of the *Jewish Daily Forward*, Abraham Cahan, had landed in Philadelphia before going on to New York, as did Clifford Odets, who found the city "a sad place" filled with "broken middle-class" lives. Symbolically, too, the death in 1940 of Cyrus Adler, who personified so much of what the extraordinary "Philadelphia Group" had accomplished in institution building, marked the end of an era.

*   *   *

In closing I would like to express appreciation to those who have made this book possible. Edwin Wolf 2nd interrupted his busy schedule not only to contribute his essay, but also to serve as a source of information and wise counsel. I have also profited greatly from the friendship and insights of Professor E. Digby Baltzell. From time to time I sought advice from Henry Feingold, who never hesitated to provide it, along with much encouragement. The contributors, of course, share responsibility with me for the basic contents of this book. The project has been a true collaboration from the outset. It was undertaken following an initial meeting to discuss how the Jewish community could observe the tercentenary of the founding of Philadelphia. It was decided that the Philadelphia Chapter of the American Jewish Committee would sponsor a series of lectures and then present a fuller treatment of these in book form. While there has been consultation among the contributors, each has pursued an independent course.

I am greatly in debt to the trustees of the Leon C. Sunstein Foundation for funding this project. One of the central theses that has emerged from these essays is the active role played by Philadelphia families in the development of so many of the structures of Philadelphia and American Jewish life. This was illustrated in the work of the late Leon C. Sunstein Sr., who served as president of the Allied Jewish Appeal from 1939 to 1945, and helped bridge the gap between the German and Russian communities. This sense of communal and civic responsibility has been maintained by his children, who have played and continue to play an important role in all aspects of this city's life.

Sincere appreciation is due to those who gave of their time and expertise in helping to secure illustrations for this book: Lee Leopold of the Philadelphia Jewish Archives Center, Milton Mustin of the Philadelphia City Archives, Fredric Miller of the Temple University Urban Archives, Shelley Benedict of Albert Einstein Medical Center, Joseph Anderson and Pat Proscino of the Balch Institute, Peter Parker and Bruce Laverty of the Historical Society of Pennsylvania, Dina Loeb of the Museum of American Jewish History, Robin Fogel of *Inside* magazine, Kenneth Finkel of the Library Company of Philadelphia, and architectural photo researchers Allen Meyers and Michael Gillikin.

I am deeply indebted to my editor, Brad Fisher, and the staff at ISHI for their patience, skill and unfailing resourcefulness throughout the many months it took to prepare and produce *Jewish Life in Philadelphia*.

My special thanks, finally, go to Maxwell Whiteman. In addition to writing the trail-blazing *History of the Jews of Philadelphia* with Edwin Wolf 2nd, and four of the essays included here, it was he who originally suggested this project and format. He made himself available to the other contributors for advice and assistance which only he could provide. The community is deeply in his debt for his prodigious labors over the years in bringing to life the world of Philadelphia Jewry and other aspects of the American Jewish experience.

(2)

The Legacy of
Isaac Leeser

Maxwell Whiteman

The Jewish townsfolk of Neuenkirchen, in Westphalia, where Isaac Leeser was born in 1806, would never have believed that he was destined to become a religious leader of remarkable importance on the distant American Jewish scene. Leeser was orphaned at an early age, but relatives were eager to see that he would receive a proper Jewish education, one that the schools of Neuenkirchen could not offer. He was sent to the Jewish Institute at Münster where he acquired a rabbinic and classical education. Before he could complete his studies he was beckoned by an uncle, Zalma Rehina of Richmond, to come to the United States.

When Leeser arrived in Richmond at the age of eighteen in 1824, he found a closely knit group of Jews of diverse background. Many were descendants of colonials and a few were old soldiers of the Revolution. Perhaps the least number had emigrated from central Europe, among them, his uncle, a resident of Richmond since 1789.

From his uncle's provincial shop, where Leeser went to work, he had the opportunity to see at first hand the black slaves of Virginia and the fringes of their plantation life. Life in a country store did not quell his constant pursuit of learning, and his spare hours were spent in the Richmond Library, or using his newly acquired English to teach in the local Jewish Sunday school.[1]

There was a severe shortage of Jewish books and though Leeser's personal library was adequate, most of the Jewish literature that came his way was imported from London and Amsterdam. Of general literature there was a constant supply, and young Leeser discovered a new world in American letters which had a pronounced influence on his thinking and writing.

He was also fortunate in making the acquaintance of John Hampden Pleasants, editor of the Richmond *Whig,* who introduced him to American

26

journalism. Pleasants encouraged him to contribute to the *Whig*, but Leeser had no interest in writing on topics of general interest. When he submitted some comments on the state of Jews in America, he was politely chastised by friends for being too forward in the public press. Toward the end of 1828, a significant episode in Anglo-American journalism changed the course of his life.

In the widely circulated *London Quarterly Review*, an article disparaging the beliefs of Jews, called for a response, in Leeser's view, particularly since it was reprinted in a number of American papers. The editor of the *Whig* encouraged Leeser to prepare a reply for publication. It was done over the objections of Leeser's warmest Richmond friends. When the series, defending the beliefs of Jews, appeared in the winter of 1828, it immediately attracted considerable attention.[2]

At the same time Philadelphia's Congregation Mikveh Israel was in search of a Hebrew reader and one who could minister to its spiritual affairs. Much against his will Leeser was urged to apply for the post. There was no question about his qualifications. In Richmond he had learned to read the prayers according to the Spanish-Portuguese rite. He had mastered English and enjoyed a proper Hebrew background. But at 23, Leeser questioned his own lack of experience. His uncle encouraged him and Richmond's elder Jewish statesman, Jacob Mordecai, virtually insisted that the young man apply for the position. After a preliminary visit to the northern city, Leeser took up his new post in the fall of 1829.[3]

The Jewish population of the United States in 1830 was estimated at 3000. In Philadelphia it was believed to be slightly over 300. From New York to Savannah there was not a city whose Jewish population exceeded 1000. With the exception of Cincinnati there were few inland Jewish communities. Although each was compact and held together by religious bonds, many Jews lived in isolated areas east of the Mississippi River. A national tie did not exist. Nor, as Leeser later observed, was an attempt made to develop a religious organization to bring Jews under a common canopy. Protestant denominations struggled to cope with the same problem. Their sense of recognition came earlier. A brief, short-lived attempt to change the existing religious order was made by the Jews of Charleston. In the face of overwhelming circumstances it failed. Throughout the 1830s Leeser identified the major problems and needs confronting Jews and mustered all of his intellectual energies to challenge these obvious weaknesses. A rapid increase in immigration during the same decade confounded the possibility of an easy solution. Abandoning religious life for secular pursuits, Jews entered a period of transformation that was not uncommon among many immigrants.

What Leeser recognized as a national problem he witnessed first in his own congregation. The traditional aims of Jewish education were weak and flabby. Methods of teaching Hebrew and biblical literature were haphazard and inadequate. Texts were nonexistent, there was no English Bible for

Mikveh Israel, Cherry Street between Third and Fourth, about
1830. *Courtesy of Dropsie University Library and Allen Meyers.*

Jews, and nearly all prayer books were imported. Belles lettres were not
even considered. A program to write, publish and distribute such materials
did not intrigue the mind of American Jewry.

With an unmeasured zeal and a sense of uncontained urgency Leeser set
forth with plans that could not keep pace with the needs of the day. What is
remarkable is that in the decade that followed he accomplished more than
had any other individual.

The books that were so sorely needed he wrote, edited and published.
His first work in book form was a translation from the Hebrew and German
of Yosef Yohlson's *Alumay Yosef (Instruction in the Mosaic Religion)*, which
appeared in 1830. It was followed three years later by *The Jews and the
Mosaic Law*, a collected version of the articles that were originally published
in the Richmond *Whig* by Pleasants. Meanwhile Pleasants became embroiled
in a war of words with a competing Richmond editor and like two Virginia
gentlemen, they surrendered their pens for the sword. Pleasants lost his life
on the field of honor. Leeser was dismayed. Pleasants was to have served as a
distributor for his books in the South. Fortunately, Leeser was befriended
by Abraham Hart, a young publisher associated with Edward L. Carey and
a member of Mikveh Israel, who aided him in distributing his books.[4]

Disappointment over the death of Pleasants was minor by comparison
to the problems that struck him personally. The one woman for whom he
showed affection, Rachel Peixotto, was forbidden to see him by her father.
Following this blow Leeser was afflicted by smallpox. His younger brother,
who only recently arrived in Richmond, came to Philadelphia to nurse him

Interior of Mikveh Israel, about 1830. *Courtesy of Maxwell Whiteman.*

and was infected by the disease and died. To add to this series of woes, the congregation looked askance at his taking quarters in the home of a Gentile woman.[5]

At the age of 28, heavily pockmarked and slightly bent by his ordeal, Leeser resumed his former labors. For two years he worked on a full translation of the Sephardic prayer book in order to make available an English Hebrew edition. He failed to anticipate the difficulty of obtaining Hebrew type, the lack of Hebrew typesetters, the typographical problems and the absence of Hebrew proofreaders. Once Leeser was able to overcome the problem of type, he trained typesetters, but proofreading was entirely his own responsibility. When the work finally appeared in 1837—*The Form of Prayers According to the Custom of the Spanish and Portuguese Jews* in six royal octavo volumes—it was recognized at once as a milestone in American Jewish liturgical literature. His *Hebrew Reader* of 1838 was credited as the first juvenile speller for Jews in the United States, and the following year saw publication of the *Catechism for Younger Children.*[6]

Leeser had meanwhile set up a network of book agents in the major American communities where Jews lived in addition to the island communities of Kingston, Jamaica, and St. Thomas in the Virgin Islands. Before the close of the decade his reputation as author, editor and translator was solidly established in the English-speaking world.

The making of Jewish books was a basic educational concept. To broaden its scope locally Leeser identified the English-language sermon as a necessity in the synagogue. Preaching in the vernacular was not only uncommon but frowned upon. The regular English sermon, a commonplace in the modern American synagogue, was introduced by Leeser on June 2, 1830, before he had served a full year at Mikveh Israel. It aroused congregational opposition and on each occasion that he preached permission had to be obtained from the president of Mikveh Israel who had sole authority to grant or reject it. Thirteen years later Leeser received final approval for his sermons. The struggle to preach had not been without acrimony, but Leeser made sure that it was an educational experience for all.[7]

Through the sermon were funneled the seminal ideas that were later to govern a major segment of Jewish life in the United States. From the pulpit of Mikveh Israel he advocated the establishment of a home for widows and orphans and stressed the need for hospitals under Jewish auspices long before the concept of denominational hospitals became popular. Personal charity and institutionalized philanthropy were frequently a subject for discussion. These topics alone have become major configurations in modern Jewish life. But in Leeser's day no one else had either probed or articulated their importance, to say nothing of the fact that sermons made the service more attractive.

His traditional interpretation of the Bible and of biblical literature revealed his careful orthodox discipline, a knowledge of Talmud and Midrash and an extensive familiarity with Jewish life in all periods. While he was occupied in preparing the new prayer books he collected all of his sermons delivered prior to 1836. They appeared in an edition of three volumes. The ten volumes of Leeser's religious discourses appearing during his lifetime form a body of nineteenth-century sermonic literature unequaled for its thought, content and well-reasoned presentation of the historical role of Judaism.

To launch an educational program Leeser first advocated a school beyond the confines of a single congregation "where the children might acquire a knowledge of the Hebrew, together with a thorough English education." He was not satisfied with the *Alumay Yosef* that appeared in 1830, and though it instituted a first step it was not an academic sensation. His ultimate plan was a well-defined, long-range program that went beyond the synagogue, beyond local limits, to reach a vast body of students.

In the midst of his recovery from smallpox, and mourning over his brother's death, Leeser issued the first proposal for an all-day Jewish school in America. "A school like the one herewith proposed, is very much needed in this country, since there is not one in any city of this extensive land, where a Jewish child can obtain a knowledge of its religious duties." With the aid of Rebecca Gratz and the Female Hebrew Benevolent Society, a warm advocate of the proposal, the idea evolved into the first Jewish Sunday School. In 1838 Rebecca Gratz became superintendent of the school. The texts were made available by Leeser. Before long the system was extended to other cities. But it was only a half measure for it lacked the element of

Hebrew as well as qualified teachers. Leeser was content with each advance even though he recognized the inadequacy of the Sunday School system. However, it enabled him to argue urgently for the need to broaden the scope of higher Jewish education and raise it from its elementary and provincial status.[8] But the intrusion of other issues took precedence over his educational plans.

A major episode in the history of nineteenth-century Jewry—one in a long series of blind, unfounded accusations—occurred in Damascus, then part of the old Turkish empire, where members of the Christian community charged local Jews with killing Christian children to obtain their blood for use in the preparation of the Passover matzot. News of these frightening accusations first appeared in the Philadelphia press on October 23, 1840. The charge of ritual murder, political in context and supported by the local Franciscan order, led to the torture, imprisonment and death of a number of Jews. However, before any organization or public protest was heard from American Jewry, the U.S. State Department condemned the barbarous treatment of innocent Jews in an official document.

The reaction to the blood accusations was mixed with indignation and confusion. In 1840 the synagogue was still the spokesman for Jewry but America's oldest, leading congregation, Shearith Israel of New York, failed to raise its voice; in Philadelphia Mikveh Israel undertook to organize a national protest which never took place. Public meetings were held in many cities, and national interest was aroused, but the sinews of unity were absent. American Jewry clearly lacked vitality and the organization to be effective. This undoubtedly had the greatest impact on world Jewry as well. The absence of a national American leadership to which Jewish congregations could turn was now an undeniable fact. Combined with a growing religious dissent and the weaknesses that Leeser belabored for a decade, the first national step was taken to overcome this serious void.

As a first step Philadelphia's three congregations issued a circular in the summer of 1841, containing Leeser's plan for a national ecclesiastical authority, a system of education and a union of American Jewish congregations. It was an ambitious program. In it may be found the elements from which rabbinical organizations derive their origin. Before the summer had ended, a powerful but dignified protest was received from Abraham Moise of Charleston, South Carolina, denying the need of an ecclesiastical authority. Other congregations, or their spokesmen, hesitated to respond.[10]

It was not merely pride and prestige that restrained older congregations, or that poorer congregations could not afford to maintain themselves, but also opposition to an ecclesiastical authority. Only the Philadelphians recognized the need for immediate organization. For whatever reasons the response was so poor that the plan was set aside and revived again later in the decade.

If the first call for union was a failure it by no means reduced the

Isaac Leeser. *(Library of Congress) Reproduced by courtesy of the Museum of American Jewish History.*

lingering impact of the "Damascus Affair." Western Jewry had been aroused, sensitized by the fact that countries like France, Germany and England, as well as the island communities of the Carribean, had no public voice. It inspired the rise of European Jewish journalism, which in turn had its impact on Leeser's thinking.

With the failure of the call for union Leeser joined the pioneer journalists by announcing in Germany and England that if he could attract a sufficient number of subscribers he would launch a journal for the Jews of the United States. Within a year, in April of 1843, the first issue of *The Occident, and American Jewish Advocate* made its appearance. Leeser solicited all of his correspondents in a prospectus that initially reached 15 states and almost 50 cities and towns. To the north, in Canada, he obtained subscribers in Montreal, Quebec and Three Rivers, and in the islands he reached St. Thomas, Barbados, Grenada and Jamaica. In South America Leeser found subscribers in the tiny Jewish community of Porto Cabello in Venezuela. His English friends responded from London, Liverpool and Hackney.[11]

The *Occident*'s broad aim and purpose was "to give circulation to everything which can be interesting to the Jewish inhabitants in the western hemisphere . . . we shall not hestitate resorting to publications which are not generally accessible, or furnish translations from Hebrew, French and German works." Leeser invited contributions on various aspects of Jewish literature, history and contemporary events. He asked for "controversial articles . . . written temperately and candidly." The pages of the *Occident* also were open as a medium of Jewish news. "We also request the respective presidents and secretaries of our American congregations especially to send us a condensed account of their first establishment and of anything of interest connected with them." And with an eye to the future he added: "Such a regular series would serve as the best history of the American Jews. . . ."

The *Occident* appeared monthly in octavo format, not unlike most literary and religious publications in antebellum America. It was well printed, bound in decorative printed wrappers and had an immediate appeal. For six years it was the only Jewish publication in the United States, and for eleven years it was free of national competition. Beginning with the first number an advertising section was included which published only items of Jewish interest. All of the work devolved on the editor-publisher who also assumed the responsibility of seeing the journal through the press as well as reaching subscribers. And so it continued until Leeser's last issue in January 1868, a month before he died. Leeser's life as editor, journalist and bookseller and his ministerial career form a separate chapter of the middle decades of the nineteenth-century Jewry.[12]

The content of the journal, in a sense an intellectual autobiography, is of consummate importance. It informed Jews of the states and territories of their activities and constantly advocated the idea of organization and the building of institutions. For a record of Jewish thought it is unequaled, and for the period prior to the Civil War it is the outstanding source for the study of American Jewry.

Leeser encouraged the publication of the history of the older communities; hence the first accounts, beginning with the colonial settlements of Charleston and Savannah, appeared in the *Occident*. He appealed to women writers to contribute to his journal and was the first editor to introduce the popular Anglo-Jewish writer Grace Agular in the United States. The opportunity for American women writers followed. An avenue for Jewish self-expression which confined women to charitable activities now invited them to publish in a national journal.

The scope of the *Occident* is revealed by the inclusion of articles on rabbinics, Hebrew grammar, sermonic literature, and conversionist societies. As an educational instrument its views were broad and liberal, and moved toward the accommodation of traditional Judaism to American society without interfering with basic tenets. Leeser saw America as the open door for the growth and nurturing of Judaism: "in nearly all other countries there are antagonizing principles . . . which prevent a fusion of the elements in one homogenous mass . . . here we are in very truth in a new position; for freed on the one hand from governmental interference, and uninfluenced on the other by rights vested in rabbinical courts and in the consistories which have elsewhere the supervision in church matters . . . we are enabled . . . to deliberate upon the best interests of our people. . . ." But American Jews were in a disjointed state: "Some are natives, others newcomers; some wealthy, others poor; some professing love for the German Minhag, others again for the Polish or Portuguese; some have reform ideas, whilst others at last refuse even the smallest concession to the changed state. . . ." Leeser argued that a community of feeling and spirit could indeed produce a community of action and unity. He chastised American Jews, intoxicated by their new freedom, for failing to use this freedom to further the traditional beliefs of Judaism. Page after page and year after year the *Occident* presented this unswerving argument long before any other editor or journalist dreamt of a united Jewry.

Max Lilienthal, a man of great experience, and later Isaac Mayer Wise, hitherto unknown, arrived in the United States after Leeser's first call for union, familiarized themselves with these independent statements and recognized their national appeal. They in turn proposed to organize a *Beth Din,* or rabbinical court, that would serve the nation. This effort also failed. Calling on the *Occident* for support, Lilienthal and Wise proposed another convention to organize American Jewry. Pleased with this fresh burst of energy, Leeser opened the pages of the *Occident* to the new call. In his appraisal of this new effort, a modified form of his original idea, Leeser reintroduced an earlier proposal for a hospital founded on Jewish principles.[13] In a spirit of liberality Leeser devoted the pages of his journal to all viewpoints on the impending organization, publishing accusations about orthodox aggrandizement, the fear of reform domination and trickery on the part of certain rabbis.

In its early years the *Occident* was described by some readers as flat and uninteresting. It lacked controversy, which was considered a failing. Critics were many, supporters were few. Later his repeated attempts to organize the American Jewish community were thwarted by a fresh band of critics. Those like Wise and Lilienthal who as newcomers sought his assistance and advice soon heaped scorn upon him.

In 1845, before his future opponents had shed their foreign accents or mastered the English language, Lesser completed the first American translation of the Pentateuch as a bilingual, vocalized text, a project he had begun in 1838. Lesser lamented the lack of Jewish compositors, and the great difficulties in setting the Hebrew text with vowel points, and adding the musical accents necessary for a proper rendition and pronunciation. The exhausting task of proofreading was undertaken by Leeser himself, and despite some English critics he produced a readable, annotated translation. The additional readings for the Sabbath and festivals were designed to be read by those observing either the Portuguese or German rites. This too was a pioneer achievement. It was a handsome, clearly printed work of which Lesser was especially proud.[14]

Initially Lesser feared that the number of subscribers would be too few to guarantee the success of the Pentateuch. But it met with greater approval than he had anticipated. As a matter of fact, shortly after its publication, a pirated edition appeared in Germany and was sold in England.

Jewish Bible translation, which later occupied the energies of generations of American scholars, did not yet meet popular needs and still attracted more attention among Christian scholars than it did among Jews. It was this difference that struck Lesser when he accurately observed: "The various Christian and political sects understand this principle quite well, and daily you see the notices of Bible societies, Sunday School unions, tract societies, book concerns, boards for education, domestic and foreign missions [and] prayer book societies. . . ."

Why then should not Jews have a similar society of their own? Convinced that a society equal in scope was necessary to provide Jews with a real appreciation of their history and religion, Leeser launched a new program. Since no publisher had as yet risked one cent on any of Lesser's translations or other literary ventures there was little chance that a change would suddenly take place. Instead he believed that a publication program under Jewish auspices with a formal board could meet such an undertaking. Accordingly, a provisional committee was set up in January 1845, chaired by Abraham Hart, publisher and president of Mikveh Israel.

The new organization, known as the American Jewish Publication Society, began modestly by reprinting *Caleb Asher* from the London-based "Cheap Jewish Library." The American edition was published in a pocket format in both paper and cloth. *Caleb Asher* was chosen over other titles because it was expected to counteract "some flagrant violations against our sacred faith." A second title, Hyman Hurwitz' *Hebrew Tales,* was a more popular choice. A friend of Coleridge and an expositor of Talmud and Midrash, its introduction found favor among American readers. Of the 14 titles published, one met popular acceptance—Grace Aguilar's *Spirit of Judaism.* Leeser had introduced her to the American public in 1842. The Hurwitz volume was later reprinted with a new introduction by Crosby's of Boston, and Appleton of New York presented Aguilar to a wider American audience in 1850, keeping her books in print for almost half a century. Lesser had indirectly influenced both publishers in the choice of Jewish authors.[15]

The American Jewish Publication Society, although not successful in reaching a mass of readers, was sophisticated by the standards of the day, especially when compared to the publications of Christian societies. Their output was enormous and well organized; their books were also drawn from the works of English and continental writers, and their resources and support were superior. In spite of its ambitious program the Society may have expanded its scope and encouraged an American Jewish literature. However, it did not reckon with an intense, mobile, German-speaking immigrant population. Furthermore, it was doomed to failure when a disastrous fire destroyed its stock of books and melted down its printing plates in 1851. No attempt was made to revive the society until after the death of Leeser.

Failure here did not deter Leeser from his course. His boundless energy and determination to fulfill a great need impelled him to other projects. After the appearance of the Pentateuch he continued to work on his translation of the Twenty-Four Books of the Bible, as well as issuing a vocalized text of the whole Bible. This too was the first of its kind in American biblical publishing. It appeared in 1848, running to three editions and superseding the pioneer effort of Jonathan Horwitz, whose unvocalized Bible appeared in Philadelphia in 1814.[16]

These milestones in Bible publishing represented the epitome of Jewish literature so central in the history of Judaism. The English translation, on which Leeser labored daily, was still six years away. Meanwhile Leeser was immersed in his pastoral obligations, editing the *Occident*, promoting a series of communal activities, reviving old programs to serve the national interest and furthering the aims of education. All of this was done against a growing confrontation with Congregation Mikveh Israel.

Leeser's zeal and advocacy for a sound educational system that went beyond the doors of the synagogue were undoubtedly major irritants to some members of his board. One of the points stressed in the 1841 plan for union was religious education. The Jewish Sunday School, influenced by Protestant practice, evolved with the aid of Rebecca Gratz. Ten years later, in 1848, a more comprehensive plan emerged when the Hebrew Education Society was founded. The decade witnessed a series of publications, first introduced for Philadelphians and later adopted nationally. Primers, cathechisms and various elementary readers were either written or inspired by Leeser's friend and student, Simha C. Peixotto, and a third by Mrs. Eleazer Pyke. Peixotto's volume, *Elementary Introduction to the Scriptures*, acknowledged that it was modeled roughly after the American Sunday School Union's *Child's Scripture Question Book*. Pedagogic innovations in the teaching of Hebrew with biblical texts were occasionally patterned after those used by English Jews. In addition Emma Mordecai of Richmond submitted prayers to be recited at Sunday Schools which Leeser published. Moses N. Nathans of St. Thomas added to the American market his *Road of Faith*.

Gradually the Sunday School system became a basis for the broader needs of a growing population. It was deficient, however, in failing to provide for a more advanced education. Leeser's intense and continuous editorials in the *Occident* decrying the absence of a higher general education finally convinced a number of communal leaders to support such a school. Support meant commitment to the idea as well as providing the funds for a schoolhouse, furnishings and teachers. Leeser provided the leadership, spelled out a program and helped choose a board that believed in the new educational undertaking. At no time did he seek to become a presiding officer of the new educational society. Although the Hebrew Education Society was focused locally, its officers and supporters were associated with other aspects of Jewish education. Among them were Moses A. Dropsie, Hyman Gratz and Mayer Sulzberger, each of whom, at a much later date, was responsible for or involved in a distinctive school of Jewish learning.

Leeser's most important consideration in drawing up the charter for the Society was a provision for the eventual establishment of a seminary.[17] In 1849 he wrote:

> To our mind, the whole of the system of distributing charity is defective and wrong in principle. The amount given may suffice to relieve immediate want, but no more. Perhaps under existing circumstances, this is all that can be done; but might not a union of all the charity funds raised in any one city be effected, and they be placed under the control of a central board?

The principle of union, which Leeser had advocated to improve the religious standing among American Jews, was now being proposed for an effective system of philanthropy. "United benevolence" was a national requisite and the idea had already found expression in the pages of the *Occident*. As soon as Leeser could envision it as a functional part of the broader aspect of union, he urged communal responsibility for the care of the sick and impoverished, the immigrant, the orphan, and the aged. In the spring of 1856 a committee of Jews, spurred perhaps by the efforts of the City of Philadelphia, which was then planning to consolidate its charities, took steps to campaign for a formal consolidation of the Jewish charities. Three years later the Jews of New York merged two of their own. The concept of merger, consolidation and the federation of Jewish agencies was planted in fertile soil.[18]

In a sermon preached in New York's Congregation Shearith Israel on December 15, 1836, Leeser emphasized the need for a widows' and orphans' home. But the establishment of such institutions in New York did not come about until much later. A national appeal for the same purpose was made by Leeser in 1850 when he added his views to those of Rebecca Gratz, who urged the establishment of a local foster home. Nothing came of it on a national basis until years later, but in 1855 the Philadelphians established a foster home of their own.

The Jewish hospital idea, a sanctuary for the care of the old and sick, embraced the practice of dietary laws and provided the comfort of dying without the intrusion of the zealous Christian conversionist. In February 1849, this prospect was advocated as a part of the combination of Jewish charitable resources.

Seventeen years after the idea was proposed nationally, a Jewish hospital was founded in Philadelphia. Meanwhile hospitals were founded by Jews in Cincinnati, New York and New Orleans, and other attempts were made in Charleston and Chicago. Once a program of medical care was instituted in Philadelphia, it spread across the nation, and hospitals under Jewish sponsorship appeared in many major American communities.[19]

Within the synagogue, Leeser lamented the irregular attendance and the decline of decorum. The sermon helped make the service more attractive, but the system of offerings remained a source of disagreement. Leeser recommended a change in making offerings amidst the reading of the Torah. He made proposals concerning a modification of the rite of priestly blessings. He opposed those customs whose origins he believed to rest in superstition, but he clung to formal traditional practice. If the old ways could endure so long and produce a rich culture, how could new ways, untried and unknown, survive when subjected to a devouring non-Jewish environment? Leeser's words were not a feeble cry in the dark. They offended a few and were ineffective among some, but they influenced many. Alongside this striving to maintain the old, traces of German Reform appeared in Philadelphia.

As a pioneer advocate of Jewish religious reform, Julius Stern has escaped the attention of historians. Stern was a resident of Philadelphia since 1837 and first appears as a seat-holder and contributor to Mikveh Israel. It may have been he who led the movement in 1837 to start Beth Israel, Philadelphia's third congregation. As the head of an independent group which expressed interest in religious change, he was privately criticized by fellow members of the new congregation and was subject to censure. Beth Israel's secession is an example of the spliting away from the central congregation which expressed the independence and development of the American synagogue. The organization of Beth Israel had little effect upon the strength or prestige of the parent congregation, and Beth Israel withstood Stern's dissenting views. Leeser, unsure of Stern's motives and critical of his religious tendencies, still encouraged Stern's short-lived pioneer German journal, *The Israelite*, which appeared in the summer of 1843. Stern forged ahead, helped organize Keneseth Israel and later participated in transforming it into the city's first Reform congregation.[20]

While this appears to be purely local in character, it is typical of the ferment in American Jewish life of the 1840s. Congregations in New York, Baltimore and Charleston were making strides in the direction of Reform. Its relevance comes into focus when viewed against the rise in strength of a German immigrant group and the influence of American political institutions that allowed full independence in religious expression.

A new era had begun: the struggle between Reform and the traditionalism espoused by Leeser, and the efforts to achieve unity in American Jewish life. The years between 1840 and the death of Leeser were strife-ridden as rabbis and congregations vied for individual power. The westward expansion brought about competitive centers of Jewish activity, and the fear of dual loyalty to Jewish American institutions expressed itself in defensive terms. Each congregation, if it was at all vocal, added its voice of protest, dissent or disagreement on the conduct of Jewish life and its inability to reach a state of unity. Jewish controversies, though not as deep, paralleled those which troubled Protestant denominations and filled their press with biting criticism.

Timothy Flint later observed, "Nine pulpits in ten in our country are occupied chiefly in the denunciation of other sects." Because Jews as a group were neither plantation owners in the South nor abolitionists in the North, they were spared the difficulties arising from the slavery controversy. Protestant denominations were split along geographic lines, and Jewish congregations, involved in a different type of factionalism, became "feeble fragments," each widely differing from the other.[21]

In 1845, when Leeser was busying himself with the new Jewish Publication Society, he turned again to the theme of union, summarizing what had taken place since 1841 and appealing for "Union for the sake of Judaism."

> The history of the confusion of the last few years speaks a language not to be misunderstood—the necessity of a more perfect understanding among us than has been hitherto witnessed. Every little while, we speak now of America, some division takes place among the established congregations, and there start up a few feeble and useless corporations from the ruins of a powerful, well-organized body."[22]

A second call in 1849 which involved the support of Wise and Lilienthal was no more successful than the first, but the idea had attracted attention, and while it retreated into dormancy, it was to be revived twice in the years prior to the Civil War.

The long-simmering controversy between Leeser and his congregation, whose intrigue had been hidden from the public eye, now erupted fully. A clause introduced in his contract of 1850 clearly indicated what was on the minds of his opponents when they insisted that "in all things he would act by Jewish laws." Was Leeser, the great advocate of the basic tenets of Judaism, conducting himself by Jewish laws? Not according to Isaac J. Phillips and Joseph L. Moss, who had quickly spread the canard, later published in an anonymous brochure in Germany, that Leeser's mode of living in the household of a Christian widow was a biblical abomination. Leeser refused to sign a contract with such a stipulation. In a lengthy letter Leeser defended his personal life and his local and national position, but to no avail. No compromise was reached and he was censured. The congregation was wracked by dispute. Leeser fulfilled his function as a reader until the close of the cycle of high holy days for the year 1850, when, after reciting the lengthy morning prayers and singing the hosannas with fervor and passion, he stepped down from the reader's desk, never again to return. The unspoken resentment that was harbored in the hearts of his opponents spilled into print in a series of pamphlets and anonymous articles. Internal dissention continued within the congregation for a number of years in the cause célèbre that finally led to the secession of Leeser's supporters from Mikveh Israel. The conflict, which has not been historically appraised, rested on contractual arrangements and Leeser's refusal to be dominated by an inflexible system.[23]

The agony of this experience was softened only by Leeser's completion and publication of the translation of Joseph Schwartz's *Tebuoth haeretz* under the title, *A Descriptive Geography and Brief Historical Sketch of Palestine*. The publisher Abraham Hart was one of Leeser's key supporters in the conflict at Mikveh Israel. It was the first of his books to be published by a commercial publisher and of all his works the most beautifully printed. Leeser wrote with pride that with the exception of the cartographer, the designer, the engraver and the binder, all were Jewish.

Joseph Schwartz had emigrated to Jerusalem from Floss, Bavaria, in the late 1820s and wrote not only of the geography of Palestine, but also of its flora and fauna. In 1849, he came to the United States on a mission to raise funds for the Jews of Safed, Hebron and Jerusalem and to arrange for an English translation of a major work, one of the first to be published in Jerusalem. Its real significance was in introducing Palestine, Israel and the Holy Land to American readers and to refute an increasing number of non-Jewish publications which fostered the image of a fallen Jewry in the ancient dismembered state, who could only be redeemed by a Christian Messiah.[24]

This was not Leeser's first contact with the Jews of Palestine. He had befriended Warder Cresson, the Quaker convert to Judaism who was responsible for many innovations in nineteenth-century agriculture. Brought to trial in Philadelphia for his conversion to Judaism and charged with insanity—for only an insane person of his wealth and position would convert to Judaism—Cresson was legally vindicated and finally made Jerusalem his home until his death in 1862.[25]

Cresson was exceptional. American Jews showed their eagerness to support the poor and indigent of the Palestinian Jewish centers, but only rarely ventured to immigrate. However, Leeser's ideas on eliminating the need for personal messengers to make the long journey to raise funds led to the organization of a national body. In 1853 the North American Relief Society for the Indigent Jews in Jerusalem was founded with the aid of New Yorkers and Philadelphians.

Although no formal plan was ever expressed by Leeser that was comparable to latter-day Zionism, his emphasis on agriculture, commerce and small industries to turn Jews into mechanics and farmers paralleled his immutable, traditional beliefs in the restoration of the Holy Land and in the concept of a modern Jewish commonwealth.

To bring "the ancient wasted fields again under cultivation" became a major issue in Leeser's lengthy editorials in the *Occident*. The theme was repeated in issue after issue, and it awakened a strong interest in the colonization of Palestine. One of Leeser's correspondents wrote of an agricultural colony in St. Louis where Jews could be trained and use their knowledge to redeem the ancient homeland. Little came of this project, but more became convinced that Palestine was the Jewish land of the future.

Leeser lamented with contempt the apostate Jews of the Holy Land who engaged in trading bread for souls, but he added a positive note on the news that cargoes of timber from Georgia were sent to Jerusalem "to build up the cities which are now desolate and would perhaps have to remain so from the want of trees. . . ." "Are we not right in hoping that commerce will be the natural miracle and the forerunner of the miraculous accomplishment of the divine promise?" In brief he was a model Zionist with a religious mission.[26]

Following his release from ministerial duties, Leeser spent a number of months hard at work on the English translation of the Twenty-Four Books. In November 1851 he began a journey of "nearly sixteen weeks, during which we traveled upwards of 5200 miles and visited at least 25 settlements or congregations of Israelites from the Shores of Lake Erie to the Gulf of Mexico." He was without doubt the best traveled Jew in antebellum America. His numerous prior visits throughout Virginia to New Orleans and New York had established for him an influential reputation. On this major trip his lectures and sermons added to his reputation. His impressions and observations, eventually published in the *Occident,* provide an unequaled panorama of Jewish life. In the 41 days he resumed contact with correspondents, increased the circulation of the *Occident* and spread the Jewish word. In Cleveland he defended the local authority in a major rabbinic dispute involving a case of divorce. When he later published the Hebrew documents of the case, he made public for the first time a knowledge of rabbinic data unappreciated up to that time.

From Cincinnati, Leeser wrote of the undeveloped and limited state of Jewish education, and from Indianapolis of the small but devout number of Jews. He participated in the dedication of Louisville's Adath Israel before he left Kentucky on his way to St. Louis where he was detained because of the freezing weather. This gave him the opportunity to acquire details of the economic life in addition to the religious growth of a population that exceeded 1000. Leeser went further south through Alabama, stopping in Mobile and Montgomery and learning of the smaller settlements at Claiborne, Selma, Wetumpka and Tuscumbia where Jews were unknown at the time of his arrival in Richmond in 1829.

In Georgia stops were made in Atlanta and Augusta, and meetings were held with friends in nearby towns. From there Leeser proceeded through the Carolinas, and the towns he knew so well in Virginia before he finally returned to Philadelphia. Weary from weeks of travel by coach, by rail and over American waterways, Leeser returned to his Bible translation and prepared a double number of the *Occident*.[27]

Although, Leeser never neglected the *Occident* or his other literary engagements, all of his efforts were concentrated on the Bible, seeing it through the press and planning for its distribution. In September 1853 he wrote the introduction while the thick quarto Bible was in preparation. By December, after long months of proofreading 1011 pages, copies of the great Bible, the first in the English language for Jews by an American, were ready for delivery. It extended the name of Leeser to every Jewish home where the Bible was read.

The Bible was a grand success. The quarto edition, read from the pulpit, went into three editions. Pocket-size editions quickly followed. By all standards of translation, it is still useful and quite readable; for Leeser it fulfilled a 25-year dream and 18 years of ponderous labor.

Within months of the appearance of the great Leeser Bible what Leeser anticipated in his western travels found voice as the scene shifted from East to West. Isaac Mayer Wise, with a sense of competitiveness and defiance, had moved to Cincinnati where he resolved to publish a newspaper of his own and advocate a program he acquired from Leeser. Nevertheless, his program for a union of American Jews was based on ideas that controverted traditional beliefs and practices. Wise, once an admirer of Leeser, whom he considered his best friend in a world of "flattery and falsehood," became a hostile opponent of the founder of American Jewish journalism.

Wise's removal to Cincinnati, a city with a rapidly growing Jewish population, gave him a potential seat of power. He had by this time thoroughly absorbed Leeser's idea of union. The voluntary attitude toward religion, which already characterized Protestant thought, had a considerable influence on Jews. This attitude fortified the arguments of the reformers in advocating changes that could be adapted to the daily religious practices of Jews and appeal likewise to those who might look upon religion indifferently. With these matters uppermost in the minds of many, Wise arranged for a conference in Cleveland in 1855. For a while it appeared as if the established Orthodox tenets, strict adherence to the Bible and the authority of the Talmud were favored by the participating rabbinate and lay members. According to Wise, "It was considered a peaceful solution of the difficult problem." However, when Leeser subsequently learned that Wise reversed the agreement, all hope for a religious union involving divergent views faded. The Cleveland conference gave birth to a midwestern sectionalism, repelled the eastern reformers such as David Einhorn, and irrevocably drove Leeser away.[28]

What all the intellectual efforts, appeals and persuasions could not do to bring about a unification of Jewish forces was accomplished by the pressures of antisemitism and persecution. Just as the blood accusations of Damascus

Isaac Mayer Wise. *(Library of Congress) Reproduced by courtesy of the Museum of American Jewish History.*

prompted action in 1841, a series of similar events brought the Board of Delegates of American Israelites into existence. The Russian Ukase of 1844 removing Jews to the interior; the Swiss Treaty of 1850, banning American Jews from Swiss cantons; the massacre of Moroccan Jews in 1853 and 1859, creating a mass refugee problem; and the unexpected kidnapping and forced conversion of Edgar Mortara by Papal authorities aroused an unorganized community into action. The first major step in the direction of organization was again taken by the Philadelphians when the *Occident* published the resolutions of their Mortara committee, recommending that "the different congregations throughout the Union take into consideration the propriety of electing delegates to represent them in the future, so as to form a body similar to the Board of Deputies of British Jews in London. For united we can accomplish almost everything, otherwise nothing."

The anti-Jewish events had been compounded with such force as to compel congregations from all over the country to take action. On November 27, 1859, 46 delegates representing 25 congregations in 13 cities met in New York to form the first functional organization representing American Jewry. The Board of Delegates of American Israelites was the name it adopted. Its program embodied Leeser's proposals: the gathering of Jewish statistics, the encouragement of education, the promotion of Jewish literature, philanthropic activity and a system of arbitration of congregational disputes. The new Board received the backing of lay and religious functionaries, but they veered away from religious organization and excluded Leeser's attempt to set up a religious authority. The defeat of this measure came from the Orthodox leaders, hoping to avoid a controversy, and not from the reformers who stood aloof. The reformers, as a matter of fact, were not represented on the Board. They opposed the Board because they feared it would obstruct the growth of Reform. Wise first fought the Board with silence and then attacked it publicly because it was in the East where his influence was weak. David Einhorn distrusted it and rejected it. In New York, Temple Emanu-El argued against it, appealing to the congregations of the land not to join the Board on the grounds that it would only add problems to Jewish life. It would revive the "obsolete idea of galuth [exile]"; it would interfere with the independence of each congregation and would be superfluous in the field of benevolence and charity. What it feared most was the possible accusation of dual loyalty to Judaism and American institutions.

Despite this opposition, the Board received sufficient support to carry on its work. During the trying years of the Civil War its activity was curtailed, but it continued to meet and publish occasional reports, to study a program of Jewish statistics, to encourage an Army chaplaincy program and to seek action on the Swiss Treaty and other affairs that affected the civil and religious rights of Jews.[29]

The Philadelphians contributed a president in the nationally prominent Abraham Hart; Leeser was a vice-president and after the war, Isidore Binswanger, one of Philadelphia's most eminent laymen, served in the same office. He was succeeded by William B. Hackenburg, who kept alive the Board's program of statistics. Among the members of its Executive Board was a young newcomer, Mayer Sulzberger, a student of Leeser's who was about to embark on a career in the law and who was to project Leeser's ideas into the twentieth century.

The Board was successful in many of its undertakings, tardy in some, uncertain in others, but it grew from year to year. At the time of Leeser's death in 1868, almost one-third of the nation's 180 congregations had joined its ranks. In spite of its growth and activity, the object of a religious union was not achieved, but the first step in implementing the principle of union had been made.

In the midst of launching the Board of Delegates, Leeser decided to turn his monthly *Occident* into a weekly newspaper. The weekly had become a popular segment of the American Jewish news media. The Jewish press had spread from New York to California, from Chicago to New Orleans. German newspapers for Jews rivaled those appearing in English. Leeser doggedly stuck to English despite an occasional German column or even a page. This was consistent with his views of Americanization. On the other hand, Isaac Mayer Wise, who held the same views, recognized the need of a broad, German-reading public and therefore launched, in addition to the *Israelite,* a weekly German newspaper, *Die Deborah.* Contrary to common belief, it did not replicate the content of the *Israelite.* The success of the weekly *Occident,* begun on March 31, 1859, was immediate, but the outbreak of the War Between the States wreaked havoc for American journalists, especially its Jewish members. Perhaps the most faithful and devout subscribers were Southern Jews, who became warm supporters of the new Confederacy. Wise lost heavily. Leeser discontinued his weekly and resumed his monthly journal. Jews of the South were denied a source of Jewish information. Leeser was silent on the issues of the war and spoke only when the fate of Jews was involved.

Shortly before war erupted, his old friends and supporters of Mikveh Israel—who found no fault with Leeser's successor, Sabato Morais—seceded in numbers large enough to form a new congregation for the sole purpose of providing a pulpit for Leeser.[30]

Once more Leeser's voice rang from the pulpit, but now it came from Congregation Beth El Emeth. Again and again old programs were revived. The clamor for higher Jewish education and earlier failures at unity were reminders that no more time could be lost. He condemned arguments that distracted attention from the central theme and particularly on the use of German.

> Is it nothing to have a ministry trained on the spot, who can speak the language of the country with all the elegance and correctness that are customary in other societies? Must our pulpit always remain German? Must natives of this country learn foreign languages first before they can receive religious instruction in the synagogue? We know well enough, that in so speaking we shall be charged with committing treason to our native land, as we are German ourselves, and have whatever information we have, brought it over with us when we crossed the Atlantic . . . But after all is nothing due to the *native* population who cannot speak German? Or do our Germanists expect to maintain the Teutonic tongue for more than two generations in the large cities, unless it be done by excluding Israelites from a general intercourse with society?[31]

Leeser was not opposed to a milieu that kept its records in German, that preached in German or to a German press. A vast amount of his correspondence was in his mother tongue. But he was against its perpetuation in a land where English was the major language. Throughout the war, when he visited wounded Jewish soldiers in the Philadelphia hospitals, a knowledge of German was essential. The war-torn nation, the agony between North and South, left its mark on Philadelphia. Leeser carefully avoided political comment but did not refrain from discussing its impact on Jews. The summer of 1864 revealed the fatigue of two determined armies. The hospital experiences were sufficient for him to revive the old idea, especially in the face of a growing number of denominational hospitals. Jews moved cautiously in sponsoring one of their own. A hospital had been established in Cincinnati and one in New York at whose dedication Leeser was present. The time had come to move swiftly in his home city. During the summer a bilingual leaflet was circulated throughout the city, announcing the intention of organizing a hospital on Jewish principles. To expedite the idea for which Leeser had argued so long, B'nai B'rith, through Leeser's local devotees, gave its name and support. The plans moved swiftly and successfully. A year later a site was acquired in West Philadelphia, and on August 6, 1866, after two years of preparation, the hospital opened its doors. In a spirit of equality still uncommon in medical institutions, it was "dedicated to the relief of the sick and wounded without regard to creed, color or nationality." Leeser regretted that the minutes of the hospital were entered in German, but was gratified with what had been accomplished. The new hospital was the forerunner of the present Albert Einstein Medical Center.[32]

Three months later a meeting of equal importance was held with the purpose of establishing a college of Jewish learning. Its object was to establish a rabbinical school where American rabbis could receive training in Bible, rabbinics and secular studies. The Jewish pulpit called for ministers who spoke the language of the land. Feeble efforts were made in Cincinnati and New York, emulating aspects of Leeser's progam. Both failed for want of support. B'nai B'rith, the most influential Jewish fraternal society in the United States, which gave its name to the Philadelphia hospital movement, withdrew its name from the support of an institution similar in purpose to the one that was now advocated.

Leeser attracted the city's leading and most influential laymen as well as younger men to participate in the new action. His old friend and occasional publisher, Abraham Hart, was the president of the Board of Delegates of American Israelites; Moses A. Dropsie, lawyer and traction magnate; and Isidore Binswanger, a prominent merchant, were confirmed in the belief that such a school could no longer be deferred.

Initial support was obtained from the Board of Delegates after two years of unenthusiastic fund raising. When the Board finally agreed to join in the undertaking, it was to be on the basis of a partnership with the Hebrew Education Society, which had earned a good local reputation. A year later, in 1867, the Board meeting in Philadelphia gave its unanimous ratification. The trustees included three New Yorkers and four Philadelphians. A faculty was chosen, Leeser was named provost and the institution was named Maimonides College. But students were few; in its brief existence it graduated three rabbis in the course of six years.[33]

At the time Maimonides College was launched, Isaac Leeser completed a ten-volume edition of his sermons, discourses and prayers, the first detailed collection delivered and published by an American Jew. He was still envisioning a grand program for Maimonides College and the fulfillment of other incomplete projects. But his frail body was harassed by a chronic throat ailment. His last sermon was delivered on behalf of the Jewish Hospital Association. Young Mayer Sulzberger, who had just completed reading law in the offices of Moses Dropsie, aided him in editing the *Occident*. Leeser had four months to live and requested of young Sulzberger that he continue the *Occident* for at least one year after his death. In February 1868, Isaac Leeser, the greatest Jewish thinker and proponent of Judaism in America, ended his earthly efforts.

What must be remembered in discussing Leeser is his relation to his age and to his particular sense of a Jewish world undergoing a major transformation. When one considers the history of the immigration of Jews from western and central Europe in quest of economic freedom and civil liberties, his role is revealed with increasing clarity.

The immigration of Jews from Germany coincided with American expansion. The process of adaptation and accommodation, grasping the spirit of American democracy and the remarkable opportunities offered here, were truly intoxicating. When Leeser assailed the race for riches, he was not attacking wealth, but lamenting the neglect and abandonment of Jewish life and its religious culture, lost in the course of time. To stem this tide of indifference and a rising mid-nineteenth-century secularism, he sought a program of institutional organization, a system of education and an American Jewish literature.

Of more than a hundred books and pamphlets, and a journal that reached the new state of Texas, and crossed the Rocky Mountains and the gold fields of California, Isaac Leeser's English translation of the Bible, his prayer books and general literature were the most significant. As a journalist he had no peer in his lifetime. Wherever there was a frontier there were Jews, and wherever there were Jews, his publications followed them.

In the course of almost 39 years, Isaac Leeser's frenzied energies were devoted not to reversing the old order, but to maintaining the traditional conduct which was the substance of Jewish life and history. His personal world was lonely, a mere handful of the laity supported him, and the clergy was unable to keep pace with his constant plea to instill a traditionalism compatible with the American scene. Yet most of his plans were adopted in less than a half century after his death. The Jewish Publication Society, the Jewish theological seminaries, the congregational and rabbinical associations and the Jewish civil rights societies—none of which bear their founder's name—are Isaac Leeser's greatest tribute.

(3)

Orthodox Judaism in Transition

Robert Tabak

The structure and social composition of Philadelphia Jewry were greatly changed, as was American Jewry in general, by the waves of Eastern European immigration that began on a large scale in the 1880s. The vast increase in Jewish population—in Philadelphia from an estimated 15,000 Jews in 1880 to 70,000 in 1904 and 200,000 in 1920—changed not only the size but the norms of Jewish expression, including religious expression.[1]

Conventional wisdom has had it that almost all Yiddish-speaking immigrants were Orthodox. Recent studies, however, suggest that most of the nominally Orthodox immigrants to the United States between 1880 and 1924 possessed primarily an ethnic commitment to elements of Jewish tradition rather than a religious commitment.[2]

Though there was no organized Reform Judaism in Eastern Europe, traditional Judaism was being eroded by the impact of the *haskalah* (Jewish enlightenment) and economic forces that affected all of the region. Some Jews were secularists of socialist or anarchist persuasions before coming to America. There is some evidence that especially before 1905, Jewish immigrants to the United States may have been less traditional than the general population they left. Certainly as a group immigrants were younger, and perhaps more adventuresome.[3]

A more accurate description of Eastern European Jewish immigrants would be that their folk religion was traditional—in American terms what came to be called Orthodox. While only a minority had clear theological definitions of Judaism, the synagogues they went to, their way of eating,

Research for this chapter was supported in part by a grant from the Abe and Libbie Pruce Memorial Scholarship Fund and by a summer research grant from Temple University.

48

their patterns of holiday and life cycle observance, like their language, tied them to traditional Judaism.

To understand traditional Judaism, even among American immigrants, one should not focus only on such formal patterns as synagogues. For example, many folk beliefs continued in Philadelphia, including the sale of amulets to protect women in childbirth. Jewish folk healers *(opshprekhers)* functioned in South Philadelphia in the 1920s alongside modern medical doctors. The difference between kosher food and Jewish food generally may have been clear to the Orthodox rabbinate but not so clear to the Jewish consumer.

Many of these folk practices were not essential to an ideologically orthodox Judaism. However, because Judaism was based on a folk religion, it seems probable that the idea of kosher Chinese food would have been far more alien to most Philadelphia Jewish immigrants, even those who kept kosher, than the possibility of eating a traditional Jewish chicken soup made with a non-kosher chicken purchased from a Jewish butcher.

In the earliest years of Jewish life in Philadelphia, all the synagogues were "Orthodox," though the term was not used. The oldest, Mikveh Israel, formally founded in 1782, followed the Sephardic rite, though the majority of its members were not Sephardic. The earliest Ashkenazic synagogue in the country, Rodeph Shalom, began as an Orthodox congregation and maintained very traditional patterns through mid-century. By the end of the nineteenth century this congregation was decidedly Reform, as was its younger counterpart, Keneseth Israel. Most of the other Ashkenazic synagogues in existence by 1880 had evolved a pattern of at least moderate reforms in liturgy and practice, such as decorum, a sermon in English or German, a choir, and often mixed seating. These patterns would be identified later as Reform or Conservative—in Philadelphia, particularly the latter.[4] However, these synagogues did not describe themselves in general as belonging to some formal group delineated from traditional or "Orthodox" Judaism.

Philadelphia was a center for the Americanized traditionalism that later became the basis of conservative Judaism. Figures such as Isaac Leeser, Sabato Morais, Marcus Jastrow, and Cyrus Adler had national as well as local impact. Their models of traditional Judaism probably influenced the local elite and later immigrants.

In many cases the practice of those Jews who attended the older synagogues existing in the late nineteenth century was not "orthodox" as that term came to be used in the twentieth century. Some attended particular synagogues for family, social, or sentimental reasons. Individual Jews followed some traditional customs and not others.

The role of Mikveh Israel is unique among those institutions that can be considered Orthodox. As the oldest synagogue in the city, and one of the oldest in the country, it was also among the most prestigious. It was the only synagogue in Philadelphia after 1894 using the ritual of the Spanish and Portuguese Jews, and thus somewhat alien to Eastern European Jews. Among its members were leaders of the Jewish social, business, and professional elite, many from German Jewish families. Very few Eastern European Jews joined Mikveh Israel. Although this synagogue's ritual was (and still is) Orthodox, cultural and class distinctions made its contact with Eastern European Jews relatively rare, except through social welfare activities.

Jews from Eastern Europe began arriving in Philadelphia in noticeable numbers in the 1870s. The earliest settlement of any size was in the Port Richmond area, near Kensington. Although this district was called "Jewtown," it did not become a major center of settlement.

By the early 1880s, Eastern European Jews began settling in the Society Hill area, first around Fourth and South Streets and gradually spreading southward. This district was not far from Independence Hall, in a slum area, several miles from Port Richmond, The inconvenience of traveling such a long distance for holidays and sabbath services, when traditional Jews do not ride, was a factor in the organization of the first Russian Jewish congregation, B'nai Abraham, in 1883. Conflict may have played a role too. Moses Freeman reports that the refusal of the German Jews to allow the burial of an Eastern European Jew was a factor behind this synagogue's formation. This story cannot be confirmed, and while possible has a certain unlikely quality. Regardless of the role of conflict, the *Russishe shul,* B'nai Abraham, emerged to provide a religious home for Yiddish-speaking Jews in the area.[5]

B'nai Abraham occupied temporary quarters at first but within a few years acquired its own structure. This congregation had a certain prestige as the oldest and one of the largest Eastern European congregations in the area of largest Jewish immigrant concentration.

This congregation, in cooperation with three others, brought from Lithuania to the United States as its third leader Rabbi Bernard L. Levinthal after the death of his predecessor, Levinthal's father-in-law, Rabbi Eleazar Kleinberg in 1891. Rabbi Levinthal, who played a key role in the leadership of Philadelphia Orthodox Jewry, was formally rabbi of B'nai Abraham congregation throughout his sixty-year rabbinic career in Philadelphia. This meant that he was the congregation's recognized religious authority, not primarily a paid functionary. By the early decades of the twentieth century, Rabbi Levinthal was a frequent speaker throughout the city and was at this synagogue only occaisionally, as on major holidays.

The establishment of B'nai Abraham by Russian Jews was indicative of the patterns of most of the early synagogues founded by immigrants. Many of these synagogues were founded in the same period that fraternal landsmanshaftn were established to aid those who were sick, to provide death benefits, and to provide a formal social network for those from one area. Among the early landsmanshaft synagogues were the Hungarian synagogue, Emunath Israel; the Rumanian synagogue, or Chodosh (both founded by the

South Fifth Street, 1915. *Courtesy of the Philadelphia City Archives.*

mid-nineties) and the Neziner synagogue, opened in 1889. The latter indicates an important pattern. All of these synagogues were in Society Hill. Since a "Russian" synagogue already existed, this new group was one of the first to define itself on the basis of a locality of origin rather than a region. It further defined itself on the basis of a liturgical variation: this congregation was to follow the Nusach Ha-ari, named after sixteenth-century mystic Isaac Luria and followed by a number of Jews, including but not limited to many Hasidim. The full name of the Neziner synagogue was Ahavas Achim Anshei Nezhin Nusach Ho-ari, literally "Brotherly Love Men of Nezhin, liturgy of Ha-Ari (Luria)." It is also noteworthy that this was the first synagogue to be named after a town, this one Nezhin in the Ukraine. In 1897 Nezhin had a population of about 28,000 of whom about a quarter were Jews. Preliminary data indicate that a large minority of Philadelphia Jews came from the Ukraine in general and from Kiev province and immediately adjoining areas in particular. Jews from these areas and other parts of Europe continued establishing landsmanshaft synagogues after the turn of the century, and in a very few cases even in the 1920s.

Before World War I, the major basis of synagogue organization was geographic origin. By then, however, some Orthodox synagogues were

B'nai Abraham, Fifth and Lombard Streets. *Photograph by Allen Meyers.*

organized on a neighborhood basis. In addition, the significance of geographic origin was breaking down by that period, at least among immigrants who had been in America for decades and among those raised in this country.

The pattern of neighborhood synagogues was particularly true as Jews began to move from the original areas of settlement such as Society Hill and Northern Liberties. For example, in South Philadelphia the large Orthodox synagogues, Shaari Eli at Eighth and Porter and Shaari Israel at Fourth and Porter, were built in 1912 and 1913 respectively. This area was geographically contiguous to Society Hill and also had many landsmanshaft synagogues.

In districts geographically separated from the original immigrant districts, large Orthodox synagogues, small ones, and conservative ones were the pattern. While areas such as Strawberry Mansion and West Philadelphia were growing before immigration was restricted, few landsmanshaft synagogues moved to, or were founded, in these areas. The first major synagogue in Strawberry Mansion was Kerem Israel, Orthodox throughout its existence and founded at about the same time as the Porter Street congregations. (Kerem Israel was located at 32nd and Montgomery.)

By 1920, large and small Orthodox synagogues existed in West Philadelphia as well, as did several major Orthodox congregations in Parkside. Congregations were founded in Logan in the 1920s. These newer and often larger synagogues, though orthodox in liturgy and Yiddish-speaking, drawing members from within walking distance, were more likely by the 1930s to have auxiliary activities, particularly Jewish education for the young, women's groups, and in some cases special services and activities for English-speaking young adults. Unlike other cities, no strongly Orthodox English-speaking congregations, such as those of the Young Israel movement, developed in Philadelphia before World War II.

Education has been regarded as a religious obligation in Judaism, at least for males, since ancient times. New patterns of Jewish education became a major factor in the transformation of orthodoxy in Philadelphia. The education of the young was conducted in a noncentralized fashion before the end of World War I. A variety of private teachers offered tutoring, classes *(hadarim)*, and some community-supported Talmud Torahs (Hebrew schools). The Hebrew Sunday School Society (HSSS), established in 1838, afforded a modicum of Jewish education, particularly for girls.

An attempt to organize a community-sponsored Talmud Torah network under the auspices of the Jewish Community of Philadelphia (the Philadelphia *Kehillah* which existed from 1912 until the early 1920s) failed in 1915. In 1919, under the influence of Rabbi Levinthal and other community leaders, the Associated Talmud Torahs (ATT) was established, promising a traditionally oriented education after school hours and on Sundays, under the direction of a professional staff. In contrast to traditional Jewish education, but in keeping with American practice, girls also could study at these schools. This group was able to get funding from the Federation of Jewish Charities.

The Associated Talmud Torahs were not explicitly Orthodox, but their curricula appealed to traditionally oriented families. Bible, Hebrew, prayers, and holidays were among the topics emphasized. In emphasizing Hebrew, the ATT moved away from Yiddish. Some Yiddish was used but was not formally taught until the late 1930s. Then it was taught only as an elective, and only reading and writing were included. Knowledge of spoken Yiddish could be assumed for the majority of ATT students, even in the mid-1930s. The introduction of some formal Yiddish may have been an influence of competing secular schools, particularly those of the socialist Workmen's Circle and the communist International Workers Order. In both those systems Yiddish was the major classroom language.[6]

ATT attempted to recruit teachers with formal training and develop modern teaching methods. Unlike traditional schools, these classes were coeducational. ATT schools, mostly on the elementary and junior high level, did not teach Talmud, the mainstay of traditional education for boys. Through the mid-1930s, the largest number of children receiving a Jewish education in Philadelphia attended the four- to five-day-a-week ATT classes. The next largest number attended the one-day-a-week program of the HSSS.[7]

Though exact figures have not been found, it seems the ATT had more boys than girls, and HSSS more girls than boys. Thus many more girls than boys received no formal Jewish education or tutoring at home. This reflected the traditional patterns of assuming that formal religious education, including bar mitzvah preparation, was more necessary for boys than girls.

For some the ATT's program of Jewish education was not intensive enough. An elite set of Talmud Torahs and a yeshiva had been established, also as supplementary schools, to provide education for Orthodox children. The earliest one, established by Rabbi Levinthal in 1892, was the Central Talmud Torah. Leading community figures such as Cyrus Adler and Mayer Sulzberger also played a role in organizing one of the first religious schools for Eastern European children. Girls also attended the Central Talmud Torah. Interestingly, this institution, more directly under the supervision of Levinthal, did not merge with the ATT when that group was founded in 1919. Under Levinthal's influence a yeshiva for boys over 13, Yeshiva Mishkan Israel, was founded in 1903. These institutions shared a building at Third and Catherine Streets, and were formally merged in 1924. By the mid-1930s a teacher's preparatory course for female high school students was being offered. In the 1920s another yeshiva, Ohel Moshe, opened in Strawberry Mansion and in the 1930s still another began in West Philadelphia.

The Central Talmud Torah and Yeshiva Mishkan Israel were basically Talmud Torah programs with a greater emphasis on traditional texts, including Talmud at the higher levels. These schools were on a somewhat more intense level than the ATT schools, and prepared some of their graduates for Yeshiva College or other Orthodox seminaries. They did not grant semicha (Orthodox ordination) themselves.[8]

These institutions were not supported by the Federation of Jewish Charities in the period before World War II. They depended on voluntary appeals in addition to modest tuitions. Thus their financial condition was even more precarious than some other Jewish institutions in the Depression. At one point in August 1933, the Strawberry Mansion Yeshiva was faced with closure and a sheriff's sale for non-payment of rent. An urgent appeal netted only $300, though this seems to have staved off the immediate threat.

The continuation of more intense elite schools (Levinthal sometimes personally taught at Yeshiva Mishkan Israel), centered on traditional texts, is noteworthy. These institutions existed side by side with the mass-participation ATT which could not be considered explicitly non-Orthodox, but whose religious position was built into the program. Although Rabbi Levinthal had a part in the formation of the Associated Talmud Torahs and remained on the board throughout this period, he played a largely pro forma role. On the other hand, he personally participated at times in teaching, and issued regular appeals for the Central Talmud Torah, Yeshiva Mishkan Israel, and the Strawberry Mansion Yeshiva, Ohel Moshe. In 1932, Levinthal proposed a 1 cent tax on all kosher chickens sold in the city to benefit the Central Talmud Torah and the two yeshivahs. This "tax" was denounced both because of its cost to consumers and because it would benefit only some schools. Eventually direct appeals were insufficient, and the yeshivahs began to receive some financial support from the Allied Jewish Appeal in the late 1930s.[9] In 1952, the decline of communal schools generally and the opening of Orthodox day schools led to a merger between the Associated Talmud Torahs and the Yeshiva Mishkan Israel, forming the United Hebrew Schools and Yeshivos.

In traditional Judaism, women's roles in formal religious observances outside the home were severely limited. Orthodox institutions (and before World War II almost all Conservative synagogues) maintained this pattern in terms of formal liturgy and ritual. However, the increased importance of women as organizers and supporters of Jewish life was given formal recognition through the development of ladies' auxiliaries or sisterhoods. In some of the older synagogues (non-Orthodox by and large) such groups functioned before World War I, but in immigrant Orthodox synagogues women's groups were widely organized in the 1920s.[10]

Although formal synagogue roles were not often granted to women, new rituals for women were organized in many Orthodox synagogues during the 1930s. A woman was often chosen by her peers as "Mother of the Year," frequently on Mother's Day. In a ritual more clearly created from Jewish motifs, one woman would be honored and crowned as "Queen Esther" not for her beauty but for her personal qualities and service. Both these rituals are still carried on in some Philadelphia synagogues largely populated by the children of Eastern European immigrants.

A development that paralleled the growth of activities within Orthodox synagogues for women was the increase in activities for young adults. The recognition of youth as a distinct stage of life was part of Jewish culture from the 1920s on. As more and more young Jews began to finish their formal education and enter the work force and the Jewish community, a number of synagogues and other institutions developed young people's services or congregations. These were oriented to people in their late teens, twenties, and early thirties. Besides synagogues, the YM-YWHA at Broad and Pine Streets and the Associated Talmud Torahs at their Jewish Educational Centers in South Philadelphia sponsored religious services oriented toward young adults.

Worship was often led by young men in their twenties. These groups were likely to include some stylistic modifications: a late Friday night service; guest lecturers in English; some readings in English; a more decorous service; at times a choir; and usually mixed seating of men and women. Except for the latter and a mixed choir, none of these innovations could be considered a violation of halacha (Jewish law). Still they represented changes in the patterns of folk orthodoxy and were typical of the major liturgical patterns of Conservatism in the prewar era.

Some of the young people's congregations, begun as arms of an Orthodox synagogue, eventually took over the original congregation or split to form independent congregations. The Neziner synagogue had a young people's service, drama groups, boy and girl scouts and other activities beginning in about 1927. It came to be identified as Conservative by the mid-1930s, though it never formally affiliated with the Conservative United Synagogue.

Not until the late 1930s were activist Orthodox youth groups organized, largely under Zionist auspices. In 1937 the West Philadelphia Young Israel-Poale Mizrachi group sponsored a third seder at congregation Lenas Hazedek, led by that congregations's Rabbi David Swiren. The third seder, a nontraditional communal Passover meal, shows the inroads of the American Jewish environment on this Orthodox group. This seder was attended by over 200. The group also sponsored beginning Hebrew and Yiddish classes. It is noteworthy that these activities took place in a synagogue whose rabbi though Orthodox, was more involved in the wider Jewish community than most of his Orthodox colleagues.[11]

While the Orthodox rabbinic leadership insisted on the distinction between Orthodoxy and Conservatism, popular blurring encouraged the growth of the latter. For most Philadelphia Jews a more "modern" service meant "Conservative," without any clear understanding of the ideologies that were beginning to divide the two groups.

The distinctions between Orthodoxy and Conservatism were somewhat more clear to movement leaders than to Jewish laypersons. The choice of a rabbi from the Jewish Theological Seminary (Conservative) or Yeshiva College (Orthodox) was a factor in influencing the ultimate direction of individual congregations. At least 20 graduates of JTS served in Philadelphia in the twenties and thirties (not all simultaneously), while only a handful of graduates of American Orthodox seminaries served here, most of them late in the period mentioned. Many of the JTS graduates were quite traditional in practice. A number had studied at Yeshiva College before ordination at JTS; others were sons of Orthodox rabbis. However, these men had ties to an institution that was gradually being defined as other than Orthodox.

The attempt to maintain clearly defined Orthodox pattern of life inside and outside the synagogue was a primary function of the rabbinic leadership in Philadelphia. The major leaders of Orthodoxy in the city before World War II were European-born and trained, though some had long careers in America. Chief among them was Rabbi Bernard L. Levinthal (1862–1952) who served in Philadelphia from 1891 until his death. Rabbi Levinthal's role was singular among local Orthodox leaders of this period. He achieved not only national stature and a great deal of power within the local Orthodox

The Neziner Synagogue, South Second Street. *Photograph by Allen Meyers.*

community, but he also held a position of prominence and influence in the Philadelphia Jewish community at large.

Rabbi Levinthal's involvement with national Jewish affairs included being one of the founders of the Union of Orthodox Rabbis in 1902. He played a role in the plans for Yeshiva College and its development, particularly through the close relationship he had with Dov (Bernard) Revel, the college's president from its founding in 1928 until his death in 1940. Revel came to Philadelphia to study under Levinthal and to serve as his assistant in 1907 and 1908. Revel's biographer describes Levinthal's home and office:

> The home [at 716 Pine Street] was a four-story house with very large rooms which always seemed to be filled with people. The young rabbi joined the master in the dining room where Rabbi Levinthal dealt with representatives of Talmud Torahs, shohatim, and charitable institutions. There were also the lay people who came to ask for the rabbi's advice regarding business venture or to complain that their children were no longer religious.[12]

Under Levinthal's influence Revel studied law at Temple University and the University of Pennsylvania. Interestingly, Levinthal played a key role in opposing the merger of Yeshiva College and the Jewish Theological Seminary in 1927. Among other differences, Levinthal did not support JTS's requirement of a secular college education as a prerequisite for the rabbinate.[13]

Levinthal's long-term goal was the creation of frameworks for Jewish action that would transcend the narrow interests of individual landsmanshaftn and shuls. This is particularly evident in his attempts to create networks in the fields of Jewish education and kashrut. Levinthal shared his philosophy on the difference between American and European communities with many of the younger rabbis he met:

> In Europe the rabbi is needed by the community (kehillah); in America the community is needed by the rabbi. In Europe there are kehillot (communities) and they have Jews who need a rabbi. But in America the community does not yet exist. It needs to be created. It is necessary to form the need and urgent necessity for a rabbi.[14]

As a national rabbinic leader, Levinthal was frequently in contact with government officials. He was the only rabbi among a delegation of American Jews at the Paris peace talks after World War I. During Prohibition he furnished the Treasury Department with a national list of orthodox rabbis who were authorized to distribute wine for religious purposes.[15] In the early days of World War II he was called upon to secure a meeting with State Department officials for a delegation of Orthodox rabbis attempting to secure visas for a group of Jewish scholars stranded in the Far East.[16]

Though he formally held the post of rabbi of B'nai Abraham, Levinthal was a community rabbi. It appears that the majority of his income came from supervision of kashrut, including meat, various processed foods and cleaning supplies, and special supervision at Passover. Although he performed dozens of divorces and hundreds of marriages, his primary work was in Jewish legal matters. In essence Levinthal was the dean of the Philadelphia Orthodox rabbinate for the first half of this century—the unelected chief rabbi of Philadelphia.[17]

Rabbi Levinthal was an always visible figure representing traditional Judaism. When new synagogues were dedicated in the 1920s—including the West Philadelphia Jewish Community Center and B'nai Jeshurun in Strawberry Mansion—he was present as a speaker. He wrote annual letters to the mayor, postmaster, and head of the Philadelphia Rapid Transit company to secure leaves of absence for Jewish employees on the high holy days. He headed appeals for financial support for yeshivahs in Philadelphia and Palestine. During World War II he helped the Orthodox rescue committee, Vaad Hahatzala, raise money in Philadelphia. Although in his eighties, he appeared with other leading community figures at rallies for the Jewish Committee for Russian War Relief.[18]

Though he was less personally involved as his age advanced, Levinthal had a major local role as well as his national role in the Union of Orthodox Rabbis (Agudat Ha-rabbanim), the Orthodox Zionist Mizrachi, and Yeshiva College. His personal popularity and recognition in Philadelpha can be measured by the elections held in late June 1938 for delegates to the

American Jewish Congress. In Philadelphia, 45,000 Jews were eligible to vote at neighborhood polling places. Over 50 delegates were running for 20 seats. Although the turnout was low, only one delegate received an absolute majority of those voting—Rabbi Bernard Levinthal.[19] Rabbi Levinthal's personal popularity among the Eastern European Jews who were most of the voters in the 1938 election far exceeded the general support for Orthodox candidates.

The provision of kosher food has been an important and sometimes controversial concern of Orthodox leaders. Shortly after his arrival in Philadelphia, Levinthal began to organize the chaotic situation regarding kosher meat supervision in Philadelphia. He attempted to centralize control by banning "imported" kosher meat produced in other cities. Meat from other cities would not be under Levinthal's supervision, nor would the meat packers contribute to the expenses, including salaries, of the Philadelphia Vaad Hakashruth (meat supervision board). This ban, imposed in 1907, remained in force with considerable effectiveness through World War II. It became ineffective through changes in the distribution of kosher meat. The decline in the number of local packing houses corresponded with a trend toward regional and national kosher meat processing. The number of kosher slaughterhouses appears to have gradually declined during the Depression years and World War II.[20]

By the 1920s the Vaad Hakashruth, under Rabbi Levinthal's leadership, had a supervised system of monitoring cattle slaughterhouses. The owners, sometimes reluctantly, contributed $10 to $20 a week or a fee per head of sheep or cattle slaughtered. Since the kosher trade represented a substantial part of their business, the threat of removal of certification was a significant instrument of power. There were, however, conflicts over the amount to be paid to the Vaad. Rabbi Levinthal reported that he sometimes made up shortfalls out of his own pocket.

The control of local butcher shops proved more difficult, in part because there were so many of them. The careful consumer relied on the certification of the Vaad Hakashruth which was displayed in each kosher butcher shop. Unlike the case of a few abattoirs, the constant personal supervision by a few recognized agents was not possible. The reliability of sources of supply and of the butchers themselves was important. One continuing problem was the deliberate selling of non-kosher meat to kosher butchers by the wagons and agents of kosher meat distributors, who could legitimately sell also to the *non-kosher* trade parts of animals not allowed for kosher distribution, as well as animals not ritually slaughtered and never intended for kosher use.[21]

An additional area of meat production, chicken slaughtering, was not completely controlled by the central Vaad. Dozens of neighborhood slaughterers *(shochtim)* received a few cents per live chicken killed. If the question of the kashrut of a particular bird arose, the neighborhood Orthodox rabbi

was consulted and the evidence set before him. The chicken *shochtim* were
chronically underpaid; their attempts to raise the price charged per chicken
provoked outcries since this was a major source of meat in the Jewish diet.
(Evidence from New York suggests that in the 1930s Jews, then about a
quarter of the population, consumed a majority of the poultry sold in the
city.) Eventually the Vaad Hakashruth attempted to demand a kosher tag, or
plumba, on all authorized fowl. Circulars in Yiddish (with a few lines in
English) distributed by the city's Orthodox rabbis in 1935, indicate that this
was hardly being observed.[22]

A major problem that went beyond providing reliable kosher supplies
of meat was the presence of Jewish butcher shops that were not kosher.
Rabbi Levinthal, aware of the impact of radio advertising, attempted to
suppress the Yiddish advertising of a non-kosher butcher on the radio—not
on the grounds that it falsely claimed to be kosher (apparently it did not) but
because the advertisement in Yiddish would lead the unwary to assume that
the meat was kosher.[23] This again indicates the power of folk beliefs—the
popular sense that a "Jewish" chicken and a kosher chicken were identical,
without any deliberate attempt at misrepresentation.

While an organized supervision of kosher food was necessary for a
traditionally observant life, controversies between sellers, producers, and
occasionally rival rabbis were all too frequent. Such conflicts were among
the factors in two attempts to establish a democratic kehillah in Philadelphia.

Rabbi Levinthal supported the attempts of Cyrus Adler and others to
form a Jewish Community of Philadelphia, modeled on the one attempted
in New York. He supported efforts that would include all the religious
elements of the city, and apparently felt that the Community would recognize and strengthen his control of kashrut. This turned out to be an area
where the kehillah made little progress. Although a United Orthodox Congregations of Philadelphia was formed in the 1920s, confirming Levinthal's
authority, it had little impact or visible activity.[24]

In 1928, a large meeting attended by hundreds of immigrants and Eastern European Jews, many of them Orthodox, attempted to establish a kehillah.[25] Perhaps indicating the base of support, the Anglo-Jewish press was
more skeptical of the attempt than was the Yiddish press. Though widely
representative of Eastern European Jews, the organizing committee of 70,
under the chairmanship of Judge William Lewis, was unable to provide a
functioning organization. Shortly after the organizing meeting, the kosher
chicken *shochtim* raised their fees from 7 to 10 cents per chicken. They acted
unilaterally despite the plea of Judge Lewis to wait until the new organization could study their claims for a better pay scale.

Levinthal strongly opposed the 1928 attempt, in seeming contradiction
to his commitment to community institutions. (Curiously, the proposed
Vaad Hair, the governing council of the proposed kehillah, reportedly
promised him a "fixed and honorable income.") Levinthal apparently be-

lieved that rather than reinforcing his authority, a democratic mass organization would undermine it. Unfortunately, the available sources do not completely illuminate the reasons for this opposition. The new group refused to submit to Levinthal's authority, and his opposition may have been one reason for its failure.

At least one other attempt was made to achieve some control of kashrut outside of Levinthal's Vaad Hakashruth. This effort was encouraged by a series of front-page editorials and "exposés" of kashrut problems in the Orthodox Yiddish daily *Morgen Zhurnal,* which had a Philadelphia edition. A planning meeting attracted representatives of 30 synagogues. In August 1933 a "new Philadelphia kehillah" was proclaimed, and a new "chief rabbi" *(rav kollel),* Raphael M. Barishanski, was brought from Washington. Barishanski was former rabbi of Gomel, Belorussia. Editorials in the *Morgen Zhurnal* made clear that this was a direct attack on Levinthal's authority. The fact that this new kehillah was endorsed by the chicken shochet's union indicates internal conflicts behind this effort. The attempt was short-lived and seems to have drawn little attention outside the newspaper that promoted it and a brief note in the *Jewish Exponent.* The relatively tight control of meat slaughtering and distribution by a committee headed by a highly visible figure was a deterrent to outside attempts to gain control. However, central control of chicken slaughtering was never fully achieved.[26]

Since the maintenance of kosher eating patterns is important to Orthodox Judaism, it is of some interest to attempt to learn the reasons for the decline in kashrut observance. Though this decline was due in part to a lessening of concern with formal religious observance, it was more the result of changes in food consumption habits. The rise of supermarkets with meat departments and the sale of precleaned chickens were more of an attraction than the appeal of forbidden food. A large majority of the meat sold to Jews for home consumption on the eve of World War II was undoubtedly kosher, though statistics are hard to come by. The Jewish folk culture was strongly supportive to buying kosher meat for home use. On the other hand, the number of Jews meticulously observing kashrut outside the home was modest, and perhaps never was very large. Outside the home, kashrut was usually a part of formal catered observances such as weddings. The meals of many Jewish agencies, including the heavily German-Jewish Federation of Jewish Charities, were seldom kosher-catered in the prewar era. While many, perhaps most, of those of the Eastern European elite would eat non-kosher food, this reinforced the sense of cultural gap between the two groups.

Levinthal was not an "isolationist" and served on the boards of a number of Jewish community organizations. His children received secular educations as well as Jewish ones. Two of his sons were leaders of Conservative Judaism. Louis E. Levinthal, a graduate of the University of Pennsylvania, became a prominent Philadelphia judge. Louis served as President of the Philadelphia Branch of United Synagogue of America. Israel Levinthal, a graduate of the Jewish Theological Seminary, became rabbi of the Brooklyn Jewish Center, a major Conservative synagogue.

Despite these different versions of traditioanal Judaism, the elder Levinthal maintained good relationships with his children. His first wife died in 1929, and when Rabbi Levinthal remarried six years later (in a private ceremony performed at the home of his friend Rabbi Nathan Riff in Camden), his son Israel performed the ceremony. Levinthal's third son, Abraham, was eventually a Philadelphia city attorney, and his son-in-law, Hyman Ehrlich (married to daughter Lena), served as kashrut administrator. (The fourth and youngest son was named Cyrus.)

Levinthal had friendly relations with a number of non-Orthodox rabbis. He invited Joseph Krauskopf, a leading Reform rabbi, to one son's bar mitzvah and to a dinner to celebrate his twenty-fifth year in Philadelphia. He frequently met with C. David Matt, a JTS graduate and rabbi of the West Philadelphia Jewish Community Center. Matt's father, Isaac, had served as Levinthal's *shamash* (aide) for many years.

The Orthodox leadership, following Levinthal's example, generally declined formal ties with non-Orthodox religious leaders, except on specific projects. Rabbi Levinthal and Conservative Rabbi Max Klein were both involved in securing the first kosher kitchen at Philadelphia's Mt. Sinai Hospital in 1930.[27] However, Rabbi Levinthal did not join the Board of Jewish Ministers, predecessor of the Board of Rabbis, as he did not recognize their rabbinic legitimacy. Most of the other Orthodox rabbis followed his lead.

Perhaps because New York was so large, no single leading figure emerged from Orthodoxy in the interwar period. Other cities had rabbis recognized as head of the Orthodox community (as were Rabbi David Novoseller and Rabbi Ephraim Yolles following Levinthal's death), but few had a truly national influence. Levinthal, a man of strict orthodoxy, was able to carry his voice to the Jewish masses even if he could not always influence them to follow in his path.

Levinthal left an ambiguous heritage. He was willing to cooperate for the advancement of Jewish education and other priorities with Jews whose beliefs he could not endorse. His door was open, and he was a visible figure of strength to the Yiddish-speaking community in general as well as to Orthodox Jews specifically. But he did not develop another generation of local orthodox leadership. No educational institutions beyond the secondary level were created. The appeal of Orthodoxy was diminishing, and few American-raised Jews were fully committed to it. There is not much suggestion that Levinthal encouraged activities in an Orthodox pattern for English-speaking Jews. His pervasive role left one model of leadership. This was an essential part of the particular weakness of Philadelphia Orthodoxy by the era of World War II, and its decline thereafter. Rabbi Moshe Shapiro wrote of Levinthal and the Orthodox community, "he lit the way for them until no matter was undertaken in Philadelphia Jewry except by the initiative, assistance, or support of Rabbi Levinthal."[28] This observation, written in praise, contains as well a critique of the power of the "Chief Rabbi of Philadelphia."

Out of the Sweatshop

Maxwell Whiteman

If the conditions of the Jewish immigrant workers did not improve after the disastrous strikes of 1889 and 1890, their recognition of—and response to—the new world of toil was sharpened. In the decades that followed, their energies were honed for the struggles, deceits and frustrations yet to come.[1]

The initial clash between Jewish workers from eastern Europe and their employers, Jews of German background, was an internal affair. Differences in religious practice, political radicalization, dissention over education and condescending philantropic aid were among the trappings of a new confrontation that permeated other levels of Jewish life. Those who had obtained a firm foothold in America found themselves in competition with those groping to find a foothold in fertile American soil. As long as Jews of German background were major employers in the clothing trade and allied industries, no accommodation existed between the two groups. Some of these attitudes crumbled when many of the sweatshop workers of the eighties and even some of their radical leaders became the bosses of the twentieth century.[2] But mutual social contempt was to linger for a long time after the events that inspired these feelings were forgotten. Jewish immigrant workers discovered that their plight did not improve when some of their former associates were drawn into manufacturing.

Another factor which divided the descendants of older immigrants from the newcomers was an absence of union or other leadership in contrast to the rising number of manufacturer's associations. In the strike of 1890, rabbis had taken a position which disturbed the old order. After the death of Rabbis Sabato Morais and Marcus Jastrow, men who belonged to the older community and acted independently, there was no friendly communal voice or a recognized spokesman, except when a specific issue arose affecting all Jews. The new unionists were completely on their own. In this sense they had joined the ranks of the American working class and allied themselves with other immigrants who were attracted to the clothing trades. In doing so they no longer were a union of immigrant Jews. Many Italians had been drawn to the trades once dominated by Jews, and they were slowly followed by a lesser number of Lithuanians and Poles, while some of the specialty trades were closely tied in with ethnic Germans.[3]

One of the few sources of independent and acceptable leadership came from former members of the Bund, the Jewish Social Democrats, who emigrated in large numbers after 1905. They introduced a fresh intellectual strain although they failed to offset the flamboyant tactics of local anarchists.

At the beginning of the century the immigrant survivors of the great disillusionment of the nineties were again prepared to march along the rocky road of unionization. They were still untutored in organizational skills, constantly faced with uncertainties, and inner Jewish conflicts blotched with antisemitism added to their state of confusion.

To escape the stench and pollution of the sweatshop, many of the workers drifted into independent occupations. Others, although few in number, fled the trades and were quickly replaced by new immigrants happy to find immediate employment. At once they became the focus of the unionists who would rise for a brief hour of victory to again face defeat.

Unions also provided young immigrant women their first opportunity to work together other than in charitable societies or in domestic occupations. Here their role as officers and organizers enabled them to express a position which other women workers could not. The history of the original Waist, Silk Suit and Children's Dressmaker's Union, Local 15 of the ILGWU, is the history of a woman's union.[4]

Jewish immigrant workers dominated other trades as well, but never to the degree in which they were involved in the apparel industry. The Salespeople and Clerks Protective Union, Local 5 of the United Hebrew Trades, the reorganized Silk, Waist and Dressmakers' Union, the Paperhangers' Union, the Bakers' Union, the Cloak and Shirtmakers' Union and numerous others represent groups that have long since vanished, taking with them their sparse records, but their inconsistencies in victory and success, failure and frustration, are a classic account of immigrants who rose from pitiful ignorance of unionism to a group of men and women capable of articulating their demands.

The industry of which they were a part attracted attention in the ornate clothing catalogs of the mail-order houses which sprung up throughout the East and Midwest. But the industry also attracted attention as a national health hazard when cases of smallpox in the Midwest were traced to clothing made in the East. Then measures were taken to investigate the sweatshop system.

On December 21, 1892, Charles F. Reichers, general secretary of the United Garment Workers of America, testified before a committee of Congress that Philadelphia suffered from the worst conditions of any city in the trade. The workers were not just underpaid, which was true of many industries supplied by cheap labor, nor were they alone in working long hours, but they lived a life of intolerable filth, pestilence and disease. The scathing Congressional report emphasized that the clothing trade was the most unsanitary industry in the nation. In spite of overwhelming testimony and documented evidence supporting these findings, no serious action was taken. Government inspection of contractors' shops was ludicrously inadequate and municipal inspectors were indifferent to the health standards in the clothing trade so long as they could be confined.[5]

Before the sweatshop disappeared, bitter strikes were fought, unions sprung up and withered under the pressure of the manufacturers until finally the immigrant Jewish clothing worker was transformed from a bewildered novice of the garment trade to a sophisticated trade unionist. Many of the immigrants also moved forward to become manufacturers and jobbers controlling a broad segment of the clothing industry, taking on the full character of their predecessors against whom they once fought so vigorously.[6] Many more deserted the industry to take advantage of the professions closed to them in Russia, and by the time the United States entered the First World War they only vaguely recalled the *katerinka*, the sewing machine, that was slung over their youthful shoulders.

The early success of the Jewish capmakers was due in part to the history of a trade somewhat more sophisticated when it suffered losses or enjoyed victories. Its evolution from a home to a shop industry was completed by the time east European Jews entered it. A series of strikes during the 1870s in New York, Boston and Philadelphia brought a common awareness to the cutters, blockers and finishers that one union was necessary to serve the various branches of the trade. Adaptations of the sewing machine to the manufacture of hats and caps reduced the number of hand finishers who were replaced by operators in the early eighties. Operators quickly became central to the trade. At this juncture Russian Jews entered the trade in which many manufacturers were Jews from Germany and employees were Irish, American-born and Jews of the earlier German immigration. The new Russian Jewish immigrants attracted to cap- and hat-making brought a new zeal to the wavering unions. In Philadelphia they called the first organizational meeting for a joint union in September 1891 and affiliated themselves with the Knights of Labor. Toward the end of 1895, when Daniel DeLeon's Socialist Trade and Labor Alliance was founded, the 56 unionized Jewish capmakers became part of the new Alliance. In four years they organized eight of the city's ten shops. Although they faced conditions equal to or worse than those in the general garment trade—a twelve-hour, seven-day work week and irregular pay, or at best payment once a month—the diverse unions viewed their membership skeptically. A national union affiliation was hard to achieve. In their early years the United Hebrew Trades denied

Russian-Jewish shoemakers in South Philadelphia. *Courtesy of Maxwell Whiteman.*

them support and guidance, and the United Hatters of Philadelphia stood aloof from the Jewish cap- and hatmakers. A temporary affiliation with the United German Trades enabled them to attain their first successful footing. During 1898 they faced a major test of strength in a nine-month lockout and strike.[7]

Throughout this crucial period the survival of the union was imperiled. Their leaders were blackballed. One major firm retired from business; others instituted costly litigation with the object of eliminating the union from the scene. Financial support from the New York hatters and cloak-makers, and particularly the United German Trades, rescued the hatters and capmakers from disaster. Socialists and anarchists increasingly vied for their attention, and emerging labor leaders like Ella Reeve Bloor, later a leader of the Communist Party, painted glowing pictures of working class strength in the flowing oratory for which she was to become known. The strikers were successful in two ways, their union survived the crisis and furthermore won an independent victory in eliminating monthly wage payments by instituting a system of weekly wages. Two years later, at the end of another strike, another forward step was made in the reduction of the work week to 59 hours. In the period between 1901 and the First World War five major strikes were fought before Local 6 of the Cloth, Hat, Cap and Millinery Workers firmly rooted itself in trade union society.

If the workers in the Philadelphia-dominated kimono and wrapper trade employing Jews exclusively were only half as successful as the cap-makers their future might have been different. Those among them who argued for better conditions were mocked by their fellows, and those who planned to bring them into a union wandered from shop to shop like lost sheep in search of a field to graze. A volcanic eruption among the workers at the opening of the fall season of 1898 coincided with the prolonged capmak-ers' strike and ended abruptly. And though nothing was immediately ac-complished, the first seeds were sown by a new group of recently arrived immigrants who, unlike those of the eighties and nineties, heralded the new social consciousness of twentieth-century unionism among the Jewish im-migrants.

At the end of two years of secret meetings and private agitation, 25 of the more than 2000 men in the trade formed a nucleus for the Wrapper and Kimono Makers' Union of Philadelphia. In 1900 the infant union, Local 23, obtained a charter from the newly organized, New York-based Interna-tional Ladies Garment Workers Union. But they received no support or direction from the New York office. Meanwhile the shop owners reacted swiftly by blackballing the first organizers of the local, forcing them into retreat by long periods of unemployment. Appeals for guidance from the ILGWU went unanswered or were met apathetically. The International was content with the fact that it issued a charter to the Philadelphians, noting that it was too occupied with other problems. Local 23 was instructed to be patient.[8]

But patience made daily stresses a burden impossible to accept. Unpaid union organizers were forced to find other employment or flee the city. The trade underwent a major transformation when the manufacture of wrappers and kimonos shifted to New York City. It was replaced by the production of cheap waists, dresses and childrens' clothing, and in their production Philadelphia ranked second between 1901 and 1904. Under these conditions leadership vanished and the union perished.

The men's ready-to-wear industry did not fare much better. It had affiliated itself with the United Garment Workers of America, chartered by the American Federation of Labor. Its craft union principles and unrelated locals created difficulties in achieving unity in the men's ready-made cloth-ing industry. As a result the cutters of this trade held supremacy over the tailors, who by far outnumbered other branches of the industry. Craft divisions made progress extremely difficult among the immigrant tailors.[9]

At the beginning of the twentieth century, events in Russia forged a new Jew in the political and economic crisis of the land. The counter-czarist movement, malicious antisemitism and human carnage spurred an immigration that exceeded that of the nineteenth century and an enlightened, politically minded new group of arrivals outnumbered the inexperienced handful that previously attempted to organize Philadelphia's thriving clothing industry. The intellectually minded men and women of the early 1900's who also went from ship to shop were like a fresh wind that blew through the stench-ridden sweatshops.[10]

Previously unarticulated themes were now publicly voiced—piecework, prices per garment, reasonable overtime and sanitation—themes that were made public more than a decade earlier by a congressional committee investigation. They were flesh-and-blood issues to which were added ideologies that were strange to the older immigrants, labor and capital, exploiter and exploited, self-determination in the shops and Jewish nationalism as a unifying ingredient among the workers.

The Yiddish press, still struggling for survival but no longer confined to its cradle, became a volatile exponent of the rights of Jewish labor. Even the Orthodox rabbinate bestirred itself on the side of the sweatshop worker, confining its resolutions to those who were compelled to work on the Sabbath. While the *Jewish Exponent,* within the bounds of editorial respectability, slapped the wrists of employers, it also ascribed an ultra-radicalism to those immigrants espousing nonconformist philosophies.

Restlessness swept the entire trade. Each passing day deepened the dissatisfaction of the workers. Those who helped dig a grave for the first union by rejecting it, revised their thinking. An awakening of self-interest and a greater trust in the future were evident.

Union spokesmen were heavily concentrated in the city's major shops. They issued a special appeal that roused the apathetic and impressed the cynical in demanding the removal of charges for steam, belts, needles and normal operation breakage. This drive originated completely with the Philadelphians; the ILGWU from its New York seat continued to remain aloof. In the eyes of the International, Philadelphia's waist and children's dressmakers were upstart stepchildren. And still, unyielding manufacturers remained impervious to the demands of their workers.[11]

What the advocates of unionism were unable to accomplish was unexpectedly sparked by a minor incident that brought unforeseen unity to the trade, attracting the attention of those who were consistent in their reluctance to associate with any union movement. With new hope and freshly spun dreams it was resolved to reorganize the union of waist and dressmakers. A more experienced executive board was elected and given the power to reach all of the shops. Weekly meetings were held at the downtown Hebrew Literature Society, and once the excitement of organization had subsided, members insisted that their grievances receive attention.

The first item was to eliminate charges for parts. Demands to strike out these provisions were made in one shop and quickly rejected. Carefully the union bided its moves until finally it decided to call a general strike with the main issue resting on charges and breakages. In 1905, as the summer season began, the strike was called. To the delight of the union, some of the shops yielded at once; others agreed to meet with the union and discuss their grievances. At this meeting charges for parts and breakages were eliminated from the trade and the right to organize was granted.[12]

It was a tremendous victory, although it added little to the wages of the dress and waistmaker. Union men and women were not blackballed, and the speed with which a settlement was reached was gratifying. For the first time those who stood on the sidelines instead of the picket line looked upon the union with respect.

In an ironic outcome to Philadelphia's first gain in the clothing trade, the ILGWU revoked the old charter of the dressmakers' union because the original local had been suspended for nonpayment of its per capita dues. A new charter was issued under the designation of Local 15 of the Shirt and Waistmakers Union of Philadelphia. By the time the union received its new charter it was no longer a blooming organization. Typical of immigrant unionist response, there was a decline in interest following the victory. Determined leaders managed to hold the union together, but in measuring their accomplishments they were unaware that their success was to be short-lived, and in a few months their leaders would be crushed and their union shattered as if it had never existed.

The hard-pressed shirt workers with whom they were affiliated called their first major strike in 1906. By the provisions of their joint charter the waist and dressmakers joined in sympathy and struck the two largest firms in Philadelphia. One of the manufacturers, Tutelman Brothers and Fagen, determined to rid themselves of the union and prepared to use every means to do so. That they planned for a strike of long duration, that they engaged non-union labor and employed strikebreakers were customary practices familiar to the immigrants. That non-union workers were "green" immigrants who in their ignorance became scabs, was frowned upon but also taken for granted. This time the scabs were non-Jews. Yet when Tutelman and Fagen were reported to have told the English-language press that the "Jewish workers had gone on strike because they were opposed to working with Gentiles," a serious street battle was provoked between Jews and non-Jews. The outpouring of antisemitic agitation and rabble-rousing in the Philadelphia press approached unprecedented heights.[13]

Unsuspecting minds naively believed that the manufacturers were misquoted by the press who seized upon the incident and fully exploited it. When the firm was asked to deny the statement or issue a retraction, they remained silent. The reaction of most of the Jewish community was swift; not only were the strikers proscribed by the charge of the manufacturers, but all of the city's Jews were thereby proscribed. A mass meeting was called at the New Columbia Theater in Northern Liberties to condemn the manufacturers and the antisemitic outbursts. Diverse and normally opposed groups publicly denounced Tutelman Brothers and Fagen. Bernard Levinthal, the city's leading Orthodox rabbi, spoke first. He was followed by radical thinkers and representatives of conservative Jewish quarters criticizing the unconscionable tactics of the clothing firm. And if Tutelman and Fagen failed to reverse themselves, an embarrassed press quickly changed its position and attacked what it had helped fulminate.[14]

The Yiddish press was especially obligated to its readers, and the Philadelphia edition of the *Forward* vigorously inveighed against the clothing bosses. The most caustic statement came from David B. Tierkel, the Hebrew poet and Yiddish journalist. Tierkel described the Tutelman brothers and Fagen as men "who still had in their nostrils the stench of the steerage," men who themselves had risen from the miserable sweatshops to become manufacturers and who had taken all the worst from their past with them. For once the entire Jewish community arrayed itself on the side of the strikers, if only in a position of defense rather than in a forthright approval of the immigrant workers' struggle for dignity.[15] The *Jewish Exponent* editorialized benignly: "We have no means of determining whether their alleged grievances existed in fact or were merely unreasonable demands without merit or substantial basis." It was opposed to violence and criticized the police department for the speed with which the arrested strike-breaking rowdies were released, while Jewish strikers were charged with an unfounded threat to burn the factory and dynamite it if necessary.

In spite of the city-wide reaction to the new antisemitic flare, little was done to support the strikers. A committee composed of Rabbi Levinthal, Dr. Aaron Brav, Bernard Harris and five others undertook to arbitrate on behalf of the strikers, but they lacked the tenacity of Sabato Morais in his efforts among the cloakmakers in 1890. Perhaps because of the condemnation of downtown Jewish spokesmen, Tutelman Brothers and Fagen finally issued a statement disclaiming responsibility for the antisemitic charges. But they used it also to denounce the union as a band of petty, quarrelsome people, disgusting in their actions and rejected by the International Shirtmakers Union with whom they could not meet under any conditions.

The strikers' funds were rapidly exhausted and their strength accordingly diminished. The New York office of the ILGWU, involved with its own problems, continued in its aloofness. So embittered were the Philadelphia Waist Makers toward the International that at the 1906 convention they moved that the New York group dissolve "as having accomplished nothing." Those who were permitted to return to their jobs did so. Meanwhile Tutelman Brothers and Fagen shut down their two factories north of Market Street and moved to country plants in New Jersey and Delaware. Only the factory at Eighth and Snyder Streets, the scene of the rioting in 1906, was kept working at full strength.[16]

A sense of failure spread throughout the immigrant needle trades. Union meetings went unattended, dues went unpaid, and spirits were broken.

However, a handful of devoted union people remained impervious to the scabs, the beatings and the defeat. They had survived czarist terror and uprooted themselves to come to the United States, and they were not ready to surrender to the new economic difficulties.

Six months later the nation was swept by an economic depression that added fresh misery to the garment and apparel trade. Wages of the shirt and dressmakers were cut; the cloak and capmakers were in the same corner and there was little that the weakened unions could do. Yet they persisted in attempts to bargain with the manufacturers who just as stubbornly refused to yield.

The depressed economic conditions were particularly destructive to the fledgling clothing trade unions. Without a firm foothold, without leadership and with a generally high rate of unemployment, the manufacturers were in a superior position to control the clothing trade as they saw fit. Philadelphia's workers were pressed against a wall. Immigrant workers were severely tested at a time when immigration to the city reached one of its highest peaks.

It was an opportune time for the revival of radical thought by the numerous groups who had agitated among the immigrants for better living conditions, for recognized unions, and for an equalization of the social forces that benefited only a few. But the immigrants who sought to live from day to day, who hungered for bread and not philosophy, desperately snatched at crumbs of old and new ideologies.

Hidden away in the streets of South Philadelphia was the burgeoning Italian community, younger than its Jewish neighbor, but held in the same contempt. More and more they were entering the clothing trade, battling illiteracy, accommodating themselves to urban growth and becoming an object of radical focus. Italian tailors entered the clothing trade slowly and two European peoples of diverse immigrant backgrounds began to merge under the common canopy of a work force that was never before anticipated. Manufacture was depressed; 18,000 of the 28,000 textile workers were unemployed; the clothing trade had come to a standstill and the accumulated bitterness was turned into a mass protest in which Jews, Italians and a small segment of Lithuanians and blacks joined forces.[17]

The New Auditorium Hall at 747-53 South Third Street, in the heart of the Jewish quarter, could not contain the crowd that responded to a bilingual circular calling for a meeting there. Four major addresses were to be given on the causes of unemployment and the cure for industrial stagnation.

The main speaker was Voltairine de Cleyre, a local idol of philosophical anarchism. Educated in a Canadian convent, she later returned to her home in Grand Rapids, Michigan, where she became imbued with the concepts of Free Thought. When she later moved to Philadelphia in 1900 and taught music and language to immigrants, she was so impressed by her Jewish students that she took up the study of Yiddish, mastering it well enough to command a literary use of the language. This position gave her rapport with immigrant Jews, and likewise her study of Italian earned her similar attention.[18]

De Cleyre was followed to the podium by George Brown; both of them spoke in English. When Brown concluded, an unidentified Italian socialist was introduced. The *Public Ledger* commented: "While he spoke the Jewish element sat in open-mouthed wonder. The Italians shouted and danced their approval. It was apparently easy to work the Latins into a frenzy."[19]

The Italian socialist was followed by Hyman Weinberg, a cigar maker who addressed the audience in Yiddish, emphasizing the same themes of demanding jobs and decent pay. He accused the employers of deliberate conspiracy to curtail production.[20]

According to newspaper allegations—for no formal record of the meeting exists—one of the speakers cried out to march on City Hall, smash the mayor's windows and commit as much mayhem as possible. What started out as a peaceful protest and a demand for employment turned into a scene of pandemonium.

When the marchers reached Broad and Walnut Streets—after allegedly overturning the carts of Irish draymen, waving knives and pistols and maltreating bystanders—squads of policemen were descending from all quarters of the city. At this important intersection a pitched battle took place. "Good, clean-cut Irish policemen," it was reported, "seemed to have done their duty" against the "swarthy Italians" who were maltreating the only Negro policeman of Philadelphia's entire force. And ironically the only motorcycle policeman, Israel Cohen, led a thundering troop of mounted police in what was described as a cavalry charge in the area between the Union League and the Academy of Music. Scores of men and women were dispersed by the mounted police, their heads battered by swinging clubs, their bodies trampled by the mounted police. Thousands fled through nearby streets and alleyways, returning to their homes in the Society Hill area. The march was broken and when a group of wounded, bandaged men was brought before Mayor Reyburn, he agreed that the police had "trimmed" their men well.[21]

A series of arrests followed. Defiant Voltairine de Cleyre, who was held responsible for a frenzied and inciting speech—which most of the Jews and Italians did not understand—was again arrested, as was Hyman Weinberg. Many of the Italian socialists were charged with being anarchists.

Weinberg was one of a number of immigrants introduced to the cigar trade in Durham, North Carolina, and expelled from the city for his attempts to organize a union. Together with Max Staller, Benjamin Gordon and Isadore Prenner—none of whom worked in the clothing trades— Weinberg was deeply involved in bringing together the butchers and bakers, the paperhangers and cigarmakers on behalf of the clothing workers, the trade in which the immigrant workers were a dominating factor.[22]

By this time there was little sympathy for Weinberg and for the clothing workers, regardless of their immigrant background. The unfortunate episode was to be repeated again and again, as the clothing trade had strengthened the hand of the manufacturers, and united the diverse immigrant group in a common cause.

Under the circumstances—widespread unemployment and wages whittled below subsistence level—appeals were made to the manufacturers not to introduce further wage cuts. The appeals were rejected. On July 10, 1908, Tutelman Brothers and Fagen, using the ploy of anarchist influence in the weakened unions, dismissed their workers and closed their shops.

Within three weeks it became known that the shops were manned by scabs working at considerably lower wages. Exasperated by this unexpected device, the workers declared a strike against the firm that locked them out. A fierce battle ensued. The scabs were not Jewish and the union made every effort to avoid the violent clashes of 1906. Tutelman Brothers and Fagen, impervious to the strikers, lost none of their determination in smashing another strike.

In an outburst of nativism they declared that they would no longer employ foreigners, for foreigners were troublemakers bent on ruining their business. Since they employed only Jews, the implication was clear. The *Jewish American*, a conservative Yiddish weekly, noted that the most rabid antisemite in Philadelphia would have hesitated to make such a pronouncement, especially after the previous provocation. But the sweatshop moguls unhesitatingly stood by their ignominy.[23]

This time there was no public outcry, no communal support, and no rabbinical protest. Prominent Jewish leaders, busily concerned with immigration restrictions, illiteracy tests and anti-foreignism, curiously remained silent. Only the Yiddish press condemned the manufacturers. After 16 weeks almost 2000 striking shirtmakers were forced to retreat in total defeat.

In the years prior to America's entry into the First World War, innumerable strikes were waged in every branch of the garment industry. In the same period the transformation of undisciplined, inexperienced unionists took place and the groundwork was laid for four strong unions. The ILGWU, after a series of hard-won victories, finally turned its attention to the notoriously anti-union conditions in Philadelphia. It was a matter of securing its own gains by concentrating on the city that was second only to New York in the production of garments in the United States.

The great uprising among the waistmakers of New York in 1909—the famous Triangle Strike—resulted in work being shipped to Philadelphia. Philadelphia unionists were unaware of their sudden good fortune which turned them into strikebreakers. When the New Yorkers learned of the increase in manufacture and the sharp rise of employment in Philadelphia, they were convinced that each shop was endangering the success of New York's general strike. The only answer was to send its representatives to call a general strike in Philadelphia. But the rank and file, suspicious of the aloof New Yorkers, were not easily convinced. Their memories were full of defeat, and their union was fragmented by unemployment and depression. Ardent pleas by the New Yorkers failed to assure them that another strike would bring a victory. In desperation the New York representatives proceeded to agitate the trade on their own initiative.[24]

Mass meetings were called. Prominent New Yorkers such as Rose Pastor Stokes addressed the reluctant Philadelphians. The executive board of the Philadelphia union remained adamant in its opposition to a general strike, but the workers of the waist and dress industry, carried away by a sense of despair, outvoted their leaders and issued a call for a general strike. Without publicizing their demands, informing or consulting with the manufacturers, the workers struck suddenly on December 20, 1909. Jewish, German and Italian members of the reorganized union all responded immediately. Only a small number of native-born workers remained at their benches and machines. So spectacular was the response that the most optimistic union leaders were surprised. Paralysis struck the trade instantly.

Equally surprising, however, was the spontaneous reaction of the manufacturers. They reactivated their old association with the common purpose of not yielding one mite. Within days the strikers began to question a general strike that was unsupported by funds, lacked guidance and was led by men unfamiliar with the conservative Philadelphia scene. These disturbing questions were traced to the executive board's initial opposition to the unprepared call for a general strike.[25]

Meanwhile the manufacturers launched a public advertising campaign and rapidly filled their shops with scabs. There was little satisfaction in the knowledge that the scabs were novices to the trade. To guarantee production the angered manufacturers utilized all the resources at their command for open warfare. Split heads, bloodied streets and arrests were a daily occurrence. Each side refused to yield, and each side fanatically insisted on total victory.

After weeks of mutual violence the manufacturers submitted to an overture for arbitration. Local union leadership, still unable to comprehend the precise definition of arbitration, confused the intent with compromise and rejected the terms on which it was based. By the time the strike reached its eighth week, the scabs had become experienced hands. Seasonal goods were completed on time and the spirit of the strikers was so undermined that the manufacturers were in an ideal position to maneuver. Only then did it dawn upon the strike leaders that they had erred in rejecting arbitration. Instinctively, the manufacturers knew that they had discredited the union and believed that in a return to artitration they controlled any possible settlement. Instead of being the leading actors in the drama of strife and hunger, union representatives were pawns easily manipulated by the clothiers.

Philadelphia's waist and dress shops were fully manned. To return the

Interior of a Philadelphia sweatshop, this one manufacturing bedspreads, about 1915. *Courtesy of the Museum of American Jewish History.*

strikers to their former benches was impossible. The manufacturers agreed to permit the workers to return 30 days after an agreement was signed. Vocal supporters of the union, devoted pickets, socialist spokesmen and others characterized by the manufacturers as workers inharmonious to the trade were not considered acceptable. The first general strike in the Philadelphia apparel trade was an abysmal failure.

For the clothing workers it was a day of sadness mixed with gall. The leaders, it was believed, sacrificed the workers at the altar of inexperience. Not a word was heard of the New York leaders who led them blindly to a defeat that exceeded in depth all previous losses for Philadelphia's clothing trade. The New Yorkers also had failed in their first general strike, and whatever gains they previously made were completely lost. Further acrimony came from the conservative Yiddish press in its charge that Abraham Cahan's *Forward*, the New York socialist newspaper, undermined the position of Philadelphia's clothing workers. So confused and embittered were the strikers that they deserted the union, denouncing it with the same hatred they held for the manufacturers. Demoralization was unprecedented. The International in New York, still unable to comprehend conditions in Philadelphia, thoughtlessly complained about the failure of a bankrupt, virtually memberless Local in not remitting its per capita tax. A sepulchral lull briefly settled over the dress and waistmaking trade in Philadelphia.[26]

The New York office of the ILGWU, beset by numerous difficulties, among them claims and charges of the United Hebrew Trades as to the Union's ineptness and particularly its organizational tactics, reviewed its unhappy experience and intensified its plans for a new general strike. It was carefully planned and called in the early summer of 1910. The strike lasted nine weeks and was a major turning point in the history of the clothing trade and the ILGWU. Its settlement, based on the arbitration proposal of Louis D. Brandeis, A. Lincoln Filene, Louis Marshall and men of equal prominence, brought about the "Protocol of Peace." The historic "Protocol," which won recognition of the union shop, the abolition of contract work and other provisions, paved the way for the ILGWU to spread its activity beyond New York. Before 1910 the union had a membership slightly over 2000. Following the great strike, membership soared to 67,000, and the jurisdiction of the union became widespread. It was in sharp contrast to the defeat in Philadelphia where outstanding leaders of the Jewish community, except for Sabato Morais in 1890, never became involved. Four years later, however, a similar principle was accepted by the manufacturers and cloakmakers after a disastrous strike of 26 weeks.[27]

By 1914 the workers in the waist and dress trade recouped a nucleus of determined but impoverished leaders. Again they appealed to the ILGWU at its twelfth convention in Cleveland. Too poor to raise funds for a delegate, their simple request for aid was hand-delivered by a member of the local cloakmakers. It was an important juncture in the history of the Philadelphia trade. A full-time union organizer, familiar with the city's problems, launched a new campaign based on the New York experience. Independent action, detailed planning and a fresh educational program were prepared for the difficult battles that faced the clothing trade in the decade following the First World War.

The leadership which was present in all areas of the city's Jewish life was noticeably absent in the field of unionism. For almost a quarter century all of the attempts at unionization in industries where Jews were most prominent had failed. The anarchists failed because they were too busy condemning capitalist society. Their slogan of bread and freedom, which excited the imagination, failed to go beyond words. The socialists were ineffective because they were divided; the few dominant figures among them were unable to reach the more sophisticated immigrant workers. Only former Bundists had a conception of the need for a united labor organization. But they produced no leaders.

It was not until the New York-based unions developed a formula of organization, lost their provincial approach and measured their own success that their effects were felt in Philadelphia. Organizers were sent into the city. This was initially done to protect the New York-based unions. A strike in New York had repercussions in Philadelphia for the nearby city with its vast manufacturing facilities received the work of the New York manufacturers, turning the Philadelphians into strikebreakers. To eliminate this condition wherever possible, the unions were determined to send skilled men to Philadelphia and launch a full unionization program.

During the summer months of 1914, when the nations of Europe were torn asunder by war, the two unions that best represented the extensive clothing trade made a grand debut in Philadelphia. The ILGWU was now in a position to give the city the attention it warranted. And in December of the same year the tailors of the United Garment Workers seceded from the union to found the Amalgamated Clothing Workers of America.

For the first time the predominantly Jewish cutters, pants- and coatmakers, buttonhole and pocketmakers and finishers were enabled to join in a common goal. By June 1915, seven locals were brought together under the leadership of Sam Silverman and August Bellanca. Of the 12,000 unorganized workers in the trade less than 700 responded to the union call in two years. The leaderless ad hoc unions were an episode of the past. The new union was constructed on a pattern of systematic education with a program for a 54-hour week, the elimination of the old sweatshop practice and wage increases commensurate with the trade. All of this was dependent on a devoted professional leadership.

American industry thrived when the United States entered the European war in the spring of 1917. War meant uniforms and full employment. The manufacturers, in their zeal and competition with one another, again resorted to sweatshops, homework and child labor. However, the conditions of the war permitted the Amalgamated to appeal to the newly created War Labor Board in protest against the resumption of the old order. If labor standards could not be upheld in other areas of the apparel industry, they were protected where Army and other government contracts were in force. Furthermore, it was a step toward attaining a 48-hour week. The right to unionize was still a matter of dispute, and when the war ended, some of the gains were reversed. But a method of discussing grievances and the wider use of arbitration to adjust differences was a lasting achievement.

One of the major contributions made by the ILGWU and the Amalgamated was the recognition of women as officers in their respective locals. A district library was established in the heart of the garment trade; regular outings with professional performers in attendance helped attract many reluctant workers, and those who experienced years of disillusionment slowly yielded when a variety of benefits improved their lives.

The Italian members of the union developed a kinship with Jews on a scale far above any other immigrant groups. By 1918 their participation and leadership had risen to considerable proportions and provided a working relationship that helped solidify the union through the difficult decades of the twenties and thirties. Without a conscious realization of their mutual influence, this combination also tempered the residual hostilities toward the manufacturers as Jews of German ethnic origin. Manufacturers and contractors arose from diverse backgrounds that included former sweatshop workers and former radical advocates as well as Jews and Italians of different social origins.

The unharnessed energy released in the twenties was temporarily suppressed in the thirties. The lingering sweatshop system was finally erased, and the last foul oders vanished from the numerous trades over which they had hung like a dark, immovable cloud.

On the third anniversary of the ILGWU in 1918, the Waist, Silk and Children's Dressmakers, Local 15, published the first and only account of its struggles. Edited and written by Abe Silver, it included some of the earlier writings of the well-known Yiddishists Sholom Asch, Abraham Reizen, Charney Vladeck and many others. Its pages sing with the idealism of youth in a history that was more an autobiography of a union expressing the yearnings of immigrant men and women and their confrontation with the economic and industrial life of a new world. Its freshness and lack of sophistication provide a statement different from the numerous accounts of the clothing trade by New Yorkers. Written in Yiddish with English supplements, the history better served unionism than the repetitive generalizations that poured forth from the Yiddish writers of New York City. The earlier provincialism which characterized the adolescent tactics of the largest supplier of clothing in the United States crept into their writings and completely ignored Philadelphia, the second largest supplier. In addition Philadelphia's account, whatever its literary weakness, gave full recognition to its Italian and Lithuanian members. An Italian summary was contemplated but is not known to have been published. It is a particular tribute to Local 15 for producing a record of its early struggle to unionize without which this first English account would not have been possible.

The Fiddlers Rejected: Jewish Immigrant Expression in Philadelphia

Maxwell Whiteman

Yiddish, like a hoop of steel, bound the immigrants together. Like a magnet transplanted from the *shtetl,* it drew them to a common area of settlement. It united them at home in observing the traditions they best understood and voiced their feelings in the synagogue, at union meetings, social clubs and *landsmanshaftn.* Yiddish was the voice of the ultra-orthodox, the Zionist, and the ultra-radical, and as such it introduced the immigrants to life in the New World.

No matter how qualified the immigrants were in biblical or modern Hebrew letters, Yiddish was the conduit through which ideas flowed back and forth to the east European mass. The Russified intellectual, the assimilated Lithuanian, the Polish scholar and the Ukrainian villager shared a common language base with the Rumanian, Galician and Austro-Hungarian. Few could escape it. Its subdialects and various pronunciations identified the Rumanian and marked the Galician. Diversity within Yiddish evolved from Slavic provincialisms and numerous Hebraisms drawn from Bible and rabbinic literature. Linguistic flexibility altered and influenced Yiddish syntax, enriched its nuances and shaped its colorful idiom. Whatever differences resulted from the incorporation of localisms, its identification with the new immigrant was of major importance. Embodied in the language lay the core of the *shtetl.*

To Philadelphians in particular Yiddish was nothing new. In the decades before and after the American revolution, it spread itself across the internal correspondence of the small community. Colonial Jews from Germany and central Europe brought with them a Germanized Yiddish. It was the mother tongue of the Silesian Gratzes, Posen-born Haym Salomon, and Joseph Wolf Carpeles of Prague who drafted complex rabbinic inquiries on Jewish life in Philadelphia which were forwarded to Europe for response. The patriotic sentiments of Jonas Phillips were expressed in Yiddish and so were the land transactions of Aaron Levy of Aaronsburg. For Jacob I. Cohen, a resident of Elfreth's Alley, it was the spoken tongue of the street and it docketed the margins of his retained correspondence with such men as Daniel Boone.[1]

In the half century prior to the mass exodus from the Russian empire, immigrant Jewish settlers from Germany and a few from Holland, the Mailerts, Hynemans, Mastbaums, Sulzbergers and Dropsies wrote and spoke a Yiddish that smacked of nineteenth-century German. It was enriched by unique Hebrew phrases that blended smoothly with medieval German nuance. Men like Abraham Sulzberger also entered it in neat cursive script on the formal records of the synagogue.

Although its spelling was undisciplined and varied considerably from East European usage, and its use began to wither among the children and grandchildren of the colonials who favored German, Yiddish absorbed and yielded to the overwhelming power of Hebrew and was newly revitalized by the fresh cycle of immigrants from Russia.

Lacking formal structure, Yiddish was slow to achieve literary recognition. It was demeaned as jargon, a vulgar and contemptible corruption of German. But the transition from jargon to Yiddish, according to Simon Dubnow, was in process before Jews had begun to move westward. Its transformation to a stylized, literary medium is evident in the fiction, poetry, drama, and historical and scientific works that were published in unbelievable quantity on both sides of the Atlantic. New York City emerged as the great center of the Yiddish word and produced its own talent. It was the heart of the publishing community and from its presses came the pamphlets, books and newspapers designed to satisfy every possible reading taste. It overwhelmed the Philadelphians at once. But Yiddish-speaking Philadelphians had no intention of surrendering their independence to the growing Yiddish metropolis. At first they vied unsuccessfully with New Yorkers in establishing local publishing houses. Eventually, and with great difficulty, a Yiddish milieu arose with presses that filled the needs of lodges and synagogues, satisfied the wants of literary societies and published the books of those too stubborn to turn to New York.

One of the most precious items found in the belongings of the immigrant when he left home was the pocket-size Yiddish-Hebrew calendar. If it contained the prayers for a long voyage it became his guide and mentor. It alerted him to the precise time to begin the Sabbath on shipboard, told him of the setting of the sun and the holy days that awaited him. It was a convenient record for ticking off the passing days on a seemingly endless journey. The calendar, or *luach*, found a ready market on American soil and was among the first items printed for Yiddish readers. English was quickly added to the text supplemented by a western calendar. Its popularity attracted every printer with fonts of Hebrew type. Supporters for this publication were found among individuals happy to announce their reestablishment in Philadelphia as booksellers and bookbinders, marriage performers, cantors and circumcisers. Purveyors of ritual food, Hebrew scribes and newly opened shops specializing in liturgical wares and prayer books looked upon the calendar as a popular advertising medium. Its instantaneous success attracted Jewish and non-Jewish steamship agencies and immigrant ticket companies to underwrite whole editions. Booksellers in particular made use of it. The almanacs of Joseph Magilnitsky (Magil) appeared annually for more than half a century. Another notable example was the imprint of Philadelphia's oldest banking institution, the Pennsylvania Company, one of whose earlier presidents, Hyman Gratz, was raised in the Yiddish milieu of late-eighteenth-century Philadelphia.[2]

However popular the calendar or almanac, it could not meet the needs of a growing immigrant population eager to devour anything printed in Yiddish. Reading matter poured in from New York, but a source of local news and opinion did not exist. To overcome this void a small group of Lithuanian and Ukrainian Jews met in the winter of 1888 to launch a local newspaper.

In their home towns, even in many urban communities, newspapers were scarce. In most areas they were not published. The ephemeral Hebrew or Russian journals for Jews were limited in circulation. Hunger for news was intense. Zalman Shneour, in one of his stories, describes the meaning of the press to the Jews of Sklov: "although the reading of Yiddish newspapers had now become a necessity in Sklov, the reading of newspapers in the Russian language still remained a luxury, a caste mark of the intelligentsia, a symbol of importance tantamount, for instance, to stopping the inspector of police on the street for a chat. You could even read a Russian newspaper upside down, if you liked—it did not really matter." But Philadelphians had no local Yiddish newspaper, nor were most of the immigrants able to read an English newspaper upside down or rightside up.[3]

The talents of the men who came from these backgrounds to start a newspaper were as diverse as their interests. Moses Freeman in whose Lombard street home the meeting was called, was a member of the *Am Olam* movement, the Eternal People so named, desirous of tilling the soil and laboring to dispel the image of the Jew as petty tradesmen. His associates, also members of the *Am Olam,* were the physician Charles Spivak and the *maskil,* Moses Herder, both of whom had settled in the New Jersey agricultural colonies. Disillusioned with their failure in tilling the sandy soil of New Jersey they went to work in the woolen mills of Lisbon Falls, near Lewiston, Maine. Yearning for Jewish association which could not be found in the Maine mills, they returned to Philadelphia to enter the sweatshops and the petty trade they were so eager to escape. Chairing the meeting was Getzel (George) Selikovitch, a contributor of popular articles to the New York *Yiddishe Folks-tsaitung*. Selikovitch was formerly literary editor of *Hamelitz*, a Hebrew journal of considerable note published in St. Petersburg. His association with Lord Wolsey and Lord Kitchener as interpreter of Arabic and Sudanese dialects during the British expedition to relieve General Gordon at Khartoum, qualified him to lecture in Near Eastern Orientalia and Egyptology at the University of Pennsylvania. At the time he was working on a Yiddish translation of the Declaration of Independence and the Constitution of the United States which was not published till four years later. Selikovitch was an accomplished linguist who wrote in six languages. S. S. Blum, an ardent Hebraist and later an active Zionist, guaranteed the financial resources and support for the newspaper. Selikovitch was named editor. About the same time his post as lecturer at the University was severed for undetermined reasons. The Philadelphia vista quickly narrowed and Selikovitch was lured by brighter prospects to New York. Before one issue of the projected Yiddish newspaper was published the grand idea was abandoned.[4]

Three years later, in 1891, Freeman made a second attempt to publish a newspaper. By circularizing the Yiddish-speaking community with a statement that Philadelphia lagged behind the smaller cities of Baltimore and Pittsburgh in publishing a peoples' journal, Freeman attracted the necessary financial support. Responding to his call was Morris Rosenbaum, a successful owner of an immigrant steamship agency and money exchange office. Rabbi Nehemiah Mosessohn was chosen as editor and Philadelphia's first Yiddish newspaper, *Dos licht*, an eight-page weekly appeared in October. Its conservative policy eliminated editorial content. Instead, an exegetical interpretation of the complementary weekly reading of the Pentateuch was included. Contributions were sent in from New York by Selikovitch and others. The following July Rosenbaum unexpectedly withdrew his support and the paper abruptly ceased publication.

The dramatic expiration of *Dos licht* did not prevent Freeman, the zealous Yiddishist, from making a third effort. In August 1892, *Di Yudishe presse* under Freeman's private tutelage was begun with John Paley as editor. Barely out of his teens, Paley's stated purpose was to provide news of the institutional life of the immigrants and their emerging role in Philadelphia. The new venture was more successful in attracting local literary aspirants. Dr. Charles Spivak, Joseph S. Prenowitz, Moshe Herder, Aaron H. Frankel Ozer (Oscar) Smolenskin and other minor Yiddish luminaries made their first appearance in the *Presse*. From New York came poems from the pen of Morris Rosenfeld and his colleagues struggling to break into print. Added prestige came in the translated articles of Sabato Morais of Congregation Mikveh Israel. Great promise was associated with the new newspaper and it quickly expanded from four to eight pages.

The progress of the *Presse* was interupted when Paley left without notice to join *Der Folks-vechter* which stepped onto the narrow stage of Yiddish journalism in the summer of 1893. Later Paley was associated with the New York *Varheit* and the venal journalism which affected the Yiddish press. Freeman was left without an editor. In desperation he left for New York City in search of one. He found an editor in the unknown youthful Bowery candy vendor, Israel Joseph Zevin, a genial spirit later known by the name of *Tashrak,* a humorist whose early writings failed to attract New York publishers. His satirical critiques of Jewish communal workers, bountiful uptown ladies, which failed in New York, met with immediate success in Philadelphia. His delighful vignette on the hole in the bagel, its origin and fate found its way into English when translation from Yiddish was still a novelty.

Competition from another newspaper seeking the same writers and appealing to the same audience imposed additional hardship upon Freeman. Besides, the *Folks-vechter* was believed to be supported by two prominent Jews of German background, Mayer Sulzberger and Simon Muhr, thereby raising its status among the uptowners and distrust from some of the downtowners. The severity of the depression of 1893 imposed new hardships upon Freeman and his limited resources were unable to cope with a sweeping tide of financial problems. Soup kitchens, breadlines and sporadic strikes in the needle trades engulfed the economically disoriented immigrant settlements and the penny or two readers paid for a newspaper could better be spent for bread. The struggle by the press for economic survival was increased by competition. Undaunted by these difficult circumstances, a third and fourth paper entered Philadelphia's Yiddish world. In the belief that financial problems could be avoided *Di Filadelfier shtodt-tsaitung* was organized as a cooperative enterprise in which the editor worked with and shared whatever was earned with his colleagues. European writers were introduced for the first time in Philadelphia. Stories and poems by Sholom Aleichem, Shimon Frug and Abraham Reisen added luster to the local press. An experiment by the publisher in printing Yiddish in Roman characters defies evaluation because the paper was shortlived and copies are unlocated. In its brief career Leon Kobrin's early sketches were published with those of Prenowitz, Max Barber and other Philadelphians. In March 1894, the *Presse* expired without a sigh but with a number of debts; four months later *Der Folks-vechter* vanished while the *Shtodt-tsaitung* lingered on for 83 issues. The less ambitious *Folks-zhurnal,* a monthly edited by the former anarchist Max Gilles, ceased after an undetermined number of issues of which only one has been located.

In the two decades that followed, 16 newspapers and journals were published representing as many points of view. Their life span extended from a single issue *(Filadelfia Yiddishe presse)* to the three-year-old *Gegenvart.* With the rise of modern Zionism, there appeared in 1898 the annual

Immigrant quarters, South Philadelphia. *Courtesy of the Philadelphia City Archives.*

Zion's Fraint in newspaper format. It provided a yearly summary of Zionist news and propaganda and sought financial aid for the support of local Zionist societies. With the appearance of the eighth and last issue of *Zion's Fraint*, the first major Zionist journal published in the United States in Yiddish, *Der Yiddisher kemfer* made its debut. Under the editorship of Kalman Marmor, the *Kemfer* thrived at once. An array of young, outstanding writers appeared in its columns, including David Pinski, Kobrin, and Yehoash (Solomon Bloomgarten). No sooner did the *Kemfer* show signs of success when its editorial seat was moved to New York. The Yiddish metropolis devoured one effort after another, capturing the best local talent and snatching up any journal that suggested promise. Before the *Kemfer* departed, the Zionist territorialist *Dos Folk*, a weekly, and the bilingual *Der Shtern*, an annual, came forth with their own ideological interpretation of Zionism and the potential of a future Jewish state. And to add to local publishing difficulties, the established press of New York—the *Forward*, *Der Tog*, and the *Morgen-zhurnal*—issued local supplements directed to Philadelphia readers. For almost a half-century the Philadelphia supplements of the New York Yiddish press vied for Philadelphia readers, appealing to their religious sentiments and political ideologies.

Unlike the Hearst press in New York, which established a Yiddish paper, or a similar attempt by Louis Marshall to test the vast potential of Yiddish readers, Philadelphians avoided these disastrous pitfalls. One newspaper, the *North American,* did issue front page news in Yiddish during election years to seek support for the candidates they endorsed. To counteract outside influence, to liberate Philadelphia from the persistent hegemony of the New Yorkers, Jacob Ginzberg and William B. Leaf, both of whom had considerable experience with the New York press, formed a partnership which led to the founding of *Di Yiddishe velt (The Jewish World).* Economic conditions were still severe but with suffcent financial resources and an overwhelming determination to publish a daily newspaper that reflected every aspect of its Yiddish-reading population, the publishers proceeded. They were faithful to their promise and published everything from daily news to the views of the ultra-orthodox and the ultra-radical. Its aim and purpose was to become a paper for the people of Philadelphia. One contemporary commentator exclaimed that no longer will the Yiddish-speaking Jews of Philadelphia be a "colony" of the "Crown" in New York which determined what was newsworthy for Philadelphians.

On February 1, 1914, a bitterly cold day when few people ventured forth to buy anything, *Di Yiddishe velt* published the first issue of its daily paper. Its editor, Moshe Katz, shared a career that was not untypical of contemporary Yiddish journalists. He was the editor of the libertarian *Fraye arbeter shtime,* a benign philosophical anarchist who cast aside these ideals for the Zionism that lured some of the journalists. Gradually he identified with the resurgent nationalism of the East Europeans and finally moved into the more conservative, nonpartisan, and at times tradition-oriented *Yiddishe velt.* He was one of the few New Yorkers who came to work and stay in Philadelphia.

Katz's literary and journalistic connections were significant. They enabled him to attract an array of writers and contributors who imbued spirit to the infant press. The poets Morris Rosenfeld, Israel Ravitch and Israel Lutzki were regularly featured. Such diverse writers as Zisi Weinper, Moshe Nadir and Shmuel Niger enhanced the literary columns without reprinting what they wrote for the New York press. Reaching into the competitive world of New York journalism was not an easy task, but Katz did so successfully.

In addition to a host of Philadelphia Yiddishists hungering to publish in a local journal, an English section was introduced to which Dr. Julius Greenstone, an antiquarian bookseller as well as a fine Hebrew scholar, contributed regularly. Rabbi Bernard Levinthal wrote both in Hebrew and Yiddish. Dr. Ben Zion Halpern, an authority on the Cairo *Fustat genizah* and Phineas Mordell also contributed in Hebrew. Fragments of Levinthal's memoirs appeared in Yiddish and essays in economic thought came from the pen of David Lasson.

As a source for the study of immigrant societies and their activities, *Di Yiddishe velt* is unequaled. What its sister newspaper, the *Jewish Exponent,* often failed to print, *Di Yiddishe velt* published. Its appeal to a broad base of Yiddish readers was much different than the aims of the press of New York which was either conservative or orthodox, socialist or ultra-radical. With the field to itself, *Di Yiddishe velt* had only to compete with the single approaches of each of the New York papers.

Although it sidestepped controversy, it could not avoid the imbroglio over kosher meats. Meat which was alleged to be ritually fit turned out to be unacceptable, and this controversy which involved the rabbinate and leaders of the community remains unstudied.

Katz, who achieved the local honor of a "captain of the literary pen," was far from being an armchair journalist. At the conclusion of the Russian revolution he joined his friend Israel Friedlaender in a visit to Russia to witness at first hand the circumstances confronting Jews, especially in the Ukraine. Friedlaender had just completed his translation of Simon Dubnow's *History of the Jews in Russia and Poland.* During their travels Friedlaender "was murdered under the most revolting circumstances." Katz barely escaped the Ukrainian *pogromshchiks* and returned to his Philadelphia post. Katz was succeeded as editor in 1934 by Nathan Fleisher. *Di Yiddishe velt,* having struggled through the Depression, finally succumbed in 1941. Once again what had survived of the New York press, seized the opportunity to refurbish its Philadelphia offices and regain some of its former readers, but it recaptured little of its former glory.[5]

A competitive associate of Katz was David B. Tierkel. He was one of the Philadelphians whose life time was spent promoting the Yiddish press and as a representative of the Philadelphia edition of *Der Tog.* Although his first love was Hebrew poetry, most of his career was identified with Yiddish. With the exception of the radical journals he contributed to all of the early papers, and during 1908 and 1909 he was editor of the *Filadefia American.* His pioneering articles on the areas of immigrant settlement, Zionism, Hebrew and orthodoxy are accurate and well-written. He was an astute bibliophile, given to collecting Yiddish newspapers, as well as the historian of Philadelphia's Yiddish theatre and the Hebrew Literature Society.[6]

With all the bombastic rhetoric of the Yiddish anarchists, their one short-lived newspaper *Broit un Freiheit* had no impact on the local community. Its editing was as amateurish as its propaganda was fiery. It contained little of local interest, and it spent its energies on non-Jewish notables such as Johann Most, Voltairine de Cleyre and Francisco Ferrar. It disappeared without a whimper in 1906.

To the men associated with the press, New York was irresistible. Journalists and novelists, poets and playwriters made it their permanent home. Abe Cahan arrived in Philadelphia and left for New York the following day. Most biographical accounts make no mention of Selikovitch's Philadelphia residence. The novelist Leon Kobrin moved to New York after a short stay and others followed the trail to East Broadway, the American haven of the Yiddish word.

Many of the rootless writers, disillusioned by the promise of New York, returned to Philadelphia in the belief that within a smaller population the opportunity for success was greater. Among these was the erratic, unpredictable Hebrew poet, Naftali Herz Imber, author of the *Hatikvah*, a poem later set to music and adopted as the Israeli national anthem. Interestingly, Imber's first published appearance in the United States was neither in Hebrew nor in Yiddish. Shortly after he arrived in 1891, Imber published a series of articles in English in the Philadelphia *Jewish Exponent*, parodying himself and tilting pens with the darling of the Anglo-Jewish novel, Israel Zangwill. More than a decade later, in 1904, after wandering across the United States, Imber became a co-editor of the ill-fated *Filadelfia yiddishe presse* to which he contributed a single Hebrew poem to the only issue published. His reputation as a hard drinker competed with his reputation as a literary talent. Without the direct and indirect support of Judge Mayer Sulzberger, Imber's peripatetic career may have been further shortened. Today few recall the name of the author of the *Hatikvah*.[7]

At no time did the journalists confine their efforts to the newspaper press. Whenever they could find funds and wherever they could induce a publisher to print their stories, essays, poetry or solutions to world problems, they were ready to break into print. Seldom was writing a livelihood; it was a sacrosanct passion, a religious mission, fulfilled when turned to type.

Among the first faithful contributors to the Yiddish press was the Ukrainian-born Ozer Smolenskin. Steeped in Bible and rabbinics, a master of Russian and Yiddish literary style, his passion for poetry flowered with the first Yiddish translations of Keats and Shelly. Smolenskin rejected the religious influences of the pietists and *hasidim* of his youth, recalling later that the turning point in his life came with the secret reading of Joel Linetzki's forbidden satiric novel, *Dos poilishe yingel*. But the influences of the rabbinic life he rejected imbued his writing and shaped the nuances of a graceful style. For a livelihood he had to depend on teaching and the earnings derived as a part-time real estate agent, an occupation he detested.[8]

Unlike Smolenskin, Joseph Solomon Prenowitz, arriving in the United States in 1888, went to work as a laundryman, became a sweatshop menial, drifted into peddling and then worked as a general factotum in a number of trades. While he was groping for a livelihood, he regularly submitted verse to the Yiddish press in New York. In 1895 he settled in Philadelphia where he mingled in the current of the Yiddish intelligentsia, determined upon a career in literature and journalism. He became a local correspondent of Abe Cahan's *Forward* and eventually editor of its Philadelphia page. A constant contributor to other papers, to Yiddish *festshriften* and memorial volumes, his collected verse and short stories fill three volumes.[9]

Varying little from Prenowitz's experiences but considerably from his socialist philosophy and embittered outlook was Moses Herder. It was not the common experience of disillusion with the *Am Olam* movement, tilling the soil or working in a sweatshop that Herder chose for his first book, but the cultural resources of Judaism and the Jewish religion. In his *Sefer teshuba l'epikursim (Response to Unbelievers)* which appeared in 1911, he discussed the problems of youth and age, and challenged the findings and views of Darwin and Haeckel by upholding the Bible as immutable truth.

Many of the regular contributors to the press were intrigued by the secular life of their new-found freedom. The philosophies of the vegetarians and libertarians, Zionists and educators, attached themselves to the ambitious Yiddishists who poured their own ideas into print. Aaron H. Frankel, among them, choose to do his four-part tract on vegetarian thought, *Thou Shalt Not Kill*, in English, and then presented his work in a Yiddish translation. It attracted sufficient attention to appear in two editions. His novel, *In Gold We Trust*, in spite of patronizing comments by non-Jewish reviewers, is a stilted, pedestrian tale of immigrant life in New York.[10] The economic life and its social impact is clearly revealed in the poetry of Aaron Kurtz and David Lasson contributors to *Di Yiddishe velt*, who wrote on the potential of workers becoming shareholders in the shops, factories and utilities which employed them. Such a policy was adopted by the former Philadelphia Rapid Transportation Company, the city's first consolidated traction line. In his slim volume, *Di Velt*, David Lazarson wrote in the same spirit. His quasi-utopian novel of 1902 included a journey to Mars and advocated an improved economy and better housing. L. Cresskoff, a shopkeeper-turned-novelist, lamented on the problems of the small businessman in *Der soher*, which he claimed to be the first novel picturing the problems and disillusionment of the shopkeeper and petty merchant. Finally appearing in 1927, it attracted little attention.

In addition to Ozer Smolenskin, who brought to Yiddish Philadelphia both classical English and Russian poetry, Oscar Dubin undertook to translate all the works of the Indian poet Rabindranath Tagore. Two years after Tagore was awarded the Nobel Prize in 1913, Dubin completed *The Gardener, Kitra* and *Gitanjali*, all of which were popularly received.

Simon S. Skidelsky, equally skilled in Russian, Yiddish and English, was responsible for a number of translations from Russian into English. He too was a regular contributor to the Jewish and secular press. His association with Nathaniel Haskel Dole of Harvard's Slavic department led to the collaboration of a number of works, the most significant being Nicolai G. Chernishevsky's influential novel, *A Vital Question: What Is To Be Done?*[11] Of lesser importance as a Russian translator was Dr. David A. Modell, an

1893 graduate of the Medico-Chirurgical College. Modell's energies were devoted to the spread of Prince Kropotkin's anarchist works in the United States.

The extensive knowledge of Russian among East European Jews made it possible to establish a Russian press in the United States devoted to language, literature and politics. Up to this time few Americans were acquainted with Russian. Although Russian publication was confined to New York City, a number of contributors were Philadelphians. The Russian Jewish periodical press of the old world also attracted contributors from Philadelphia, but most writers found it more convenient to write in Yiddish if they hoped to reach a wider audience.

Prior to the coming of the East Europeans, Hebrew was confined almost exclusively to the prayer book. The new enlightenment of Hebrew letters did not reach American Jews from Germany, but for one major exception. To Isaac Leeser, publisher of the *Occident* from 1843 to 1868, belongs the credit for publishing the first rabbinic correspondence in his journal and later Henry Vidavers' pioneering translations of the poetry of Alexander Pope and Thomas Hood. It was a remarkable beginning for Hebrew letters prior to the Civil War, not only in Philadelphia but, owing to the *Occident's* national circulation, for the whole country.

Among the first to utilize non-rabbinic Hebrew in Philadelphia was Rabbi Moses Weinberger, a Hungarian from Sborow. Weinberger arrived in New York in 1880, removed to Scranton, Pennsylvania, 10 years later to accept a pulpit there, and a year later came to Philadelphia where he was elected rabbi of the Hungarian synagogue, Emunath Israel, at Fifth and Gaskill Streets. By this time he had published two books on the American scene, *Haperaim be-erets ha-hadasha (The Aborigines in America)* and *Ha-Yehudim veha Yahadut b'Nu York (Jews and Judaism in New York)*, a sharp criticism of traditional Judaism. He was a prolific contributor to the Hebrew journals of Europe and America, many of which rose and fell overnight.[12] Although not a rabbi, Hilel Malachovsky in his 1902 work, *Ketuvim b'sefer (Sketches and Letters of Jewish Life in America)*, took the same critical view of Jewish life in the new urban world.

Yiddishists beginning their literary careers frequently chose Hebrew only to learn that their published work found too small an audience. David B. Tierkel, author of *Shirei David*, decried this poor response as did Manahem M. Dolitsky, the Zionist poet whose stay in Philadelphia was brief. Imber, however, managed to find funds for the publication of the first Hebrew translation of the Rubaiyat of Omar Khayyam, which he presented in a "Hebrew cage" to his benefactor, Judge Mayer Sulzberger. A second work, the ephemeral and delightful *L'haivriya (To the Hebrew Language)*, was published in Philadelphia on one of Imber's frenzied trips from New York to seek money from Sulzberger.[13]

Hebrew fiction was in its infancy. The only Hebrew novelist of impor-

Kater Street. *Courtesy of Temple University Urban Archives.*

tance, Samuel L. Blank, did not appear on the scene until the close of this period. Works in nonrabbinic Hebrew were few in number. Fascinated by mathematics and mystical literature, the Hebrew teacher Phineas Mordell, father of the literary critic and of the mathematician, delved into cabbalistic literature and the *Sefer yetzira,* producing two small works on the same subject. Moses Klein, the first agent of the Association for the Protection of Jewish Immigrants, relied on Hebrew to reveal the contemporary scene. In *Migdal zophim (The Watch Tower),* Klein discusses the potential of Palestine as an agricultural colony—he visited there in 1869—and the promise and pitfalls of the New Jersey colonies where the imigrants labored desperately to survive. Portions of the Hebrew and English sections of the book were reprinted or translated from letters Klein had sent to *Hamagid* in Prussia and *Hamelitz* in St. Petersburg in the mid-1880s, cautioning immigrants on the problems that faced them in the New Jersey colonies.[14]

Forgotten as a Philadelphia figure was Henry (Zvi) Gershoni. A highly capable Hebraist, trained in the yeshivot of his native Vilna, he converted to the Greek Orthodox Church at an early age. Although Gershoni publicly repented and won the support of eminent rabbis upon his return to Judaism, the stain of conversion lingered throughout his life. He was present in

Philadelphia at the founding of the Association for the Protection of Jewish Immigrants in 1884. In addition to his works in Yiddish, German and English, Gershoni was a regular contributor to the Hebrew press in Russia where he published numerous articles on America. His last article *"Ha-Yehudim veha Yahadut b'Amerika"* appeared in *Hashiloach* shortly before his death in 1897. Gershoni wrote scornfully and with undisguised sarcasm on the state of Jewish education of the United States, accusing Rabbi Krauskopf of Reform Congregation Keneseth Israel of reducing to dust the spirit of Judaism. By lusting after strange ceremonies and introducing non-Jewish customs into worship, he charged, the reformers were taking steps that ultimately would lead to the conversion of their flock. Furthermore, Gershoni wrote, they devoted more time to the teachings of Islam and Christianity than they did to Judaism. Whatever influence Gershoni's writings may have had on Jewish thought is unmeasured, but at his death he was lamented by the world of modern Hebrew letters.[15]

Unlamented and deservedly unnoticed were the conversionist tracts that appeared in Yiddish, the effort of local missionaries. Editions of the New Testament, more closely resembling German than the tongue of the *shtetl*, were distributed to anyone with an open hand. The text borrowed from European editions because of the difficulty in obtaining willing translators in Philadelphia. So small was the number of Yiddish-speaking converts that if it were not for the single exception of one full-length book, *The Jewish Question and the Key to Its Solution*, discussion would be unwarranted. The converted author, Dr. Max Green, subdued his arguments for the Christian Messiah in a pedestrian Germanic Yiddish. But even this is unimportant; his ultimate return to Judaism took place quietly and with as little impact as his "Key" that failed to open any doors.[16]

Interest in Hebrew books and journals was confined to a small audience. American authors seldom exhausted a complete edition of their works, and the infant state of modern Hebrew was constantly in peril. Like the Yiddishists, Philadelphia Hebraists looked to New York. Daniel Persky and Kalman Whiteman, variously involved in promoting Hebrew education and in the founding of a number of ill-fated journals, spent too little time in Philadelphia to be associated with its Jewish literary history. At best modern Hebrew made only a minor impression on a city that had numerous cadres of Hebraists. Perhaps the joint work of Charles Spivak and Yehoash (Solomon Bloomgarten) may be considered an exception. Their Yiddish philological dictionary had an appeal sufficient for two editions.[17]

Rabbinical and theological literature fared no better than modern Hebrew. It was not innovative and followed strict European patterns of biblical exegesis, casuistry and the publication of special sermons. To this list belongs the works of Rabbis Bernard Levinthal of South Philadelphia, Nathan Brenner of "Jewtown" (the Richmond section of Philadelphia), Yosef Zev Kaufman, Moshe Lipschutz, and Moshe Bayuk, among others. Although little of the philosophical and literary glory was added to the wealth of east European rabbinics, there was a need to publish, to exhibit the product of the rabbinic mind. It was unimportant if buyers and readers were few. Whole editions ended unsold on the shelves of the Jewish booksellers until their stocks were liquidated in the mid-twentieth century.

In 1888, six years after the first mass arrival of Russian Jews in Philadelphia, the present Jewish Publication Society was founded. Its purpose was to introduce the best in Jewish literature to an English-reading American public. It drew upon the established Anglo-Jewish writers, translated outstanding works from the German and reacted to the Russian turmoil by reprinting widely circulated accounts of Czarist persecution. The life of the immigrant as seen through his own literature was remote from the mind of the publication committee.[18] A lone exception was Judge Mayer Sulzberger, the Society's dominating intellectual force. Sulzberger's intense and fanatical devotion to the Jewish book led him to probe every possible source at home and abroad for publishable manuscripts.

Word spread throughout the immigrant community that an endorsement from Sulzberger was an assurance of publication. And if this failed, he had a purse open for the Yiddishists and Hebraists to turn their unpublished manuscripts into print. Envisioned as a benefactor and maecenas, a classical statesman and patron of literature and the arts, his fame spread among the Jewish literati of Eastern Europe. At home he was besieged by imploring letters begging for aid, and immigrant writers, scribblers and men of talent virtually camped on the doorstep of his Girard Avenue home in the hope of being admitted even for only a brief interview.

Leading a host of others was the aggressive, peripatetic poet-author of the *Hatikvah*, Naftali Herz Imber. Imber's American debut, on the front page of the *Jewish Exponent*, made possible by Sulzberger, brought him close enough to a publisher hungering for fresh manuscripts, but like so many of Imber's endeavors, both the author and a projected manuscript on the Kabbalah vanished. All the efforts of the Society's literary editor to burnish his colorful and awkward English failed, and all that remained of the Sulzberger-Imber link depended on a stipend that was transmitted through the librarian of New York Public Library's Jewish Division.

A host of Zionist poets and prose writers of the school of Menahem Mendel Dolitski and Gershon Rosenzweig obtained support for the publication of their Hebrew verse from Sulzberger. Philadelphia's Hilel Malachovsky found his favor and the pitiful, half-starved mystic, Solomon J. Silberstein, also received his support. Neoclassical Hebraists of Warsaw, Vilna and Odessa learned of Sulzberger in the Russian Hebrew press, inscribed their books to the Philadelphian, sent them across the sea and implored for funds to publish others.

Sulzberger, however, was attracted to the socialist journalist Abraham Cahan whose first English novel, *Yekl,* had caught his eye. The precise circumstances of their meeting have not been determined, but the two men, worlds apart socially and politically, entered into a brief and pointed correspondence. Sulzberger invited Cahan to do a novel for the Society and for a brief moment Cahan yielded to the suggestion: "a novel—a love story—of life in the fast dwindling world of Talmudic Judaism. But then I am not sure that fiction would be acceptable to the Jewish Publication Society. The story would be laid partly in New York and partly in Russia." To Sulzberger's questioning but favorable response, Cahan gave his views on the structure of the proposed novel: "You speak of imagined situations, while what I meant was a novel based on a situation which I find on every turn and which grows out of the essence of the world under my observation. As to 'selecting ugliness as the ideal,' I can't think of a single instance in the entire range of recognized literature where this has been done. We all know of masters who have painted ugliness in order to show that it is anything but the human ideal; we also have great works of art where the effect is to disabuse our minds, to free them from old prejudices, by calling attention to men we are accustomed to hate who really deserve our sympathy and affection."

In the spring of 1901, Sulzberger and Cahan met briefly in New York, reviewing the possibility of an immigrant novel. A few days later Cahan wrote that he could not provide a synopsis or theme for the Jewish Publication Society. "Frankly speaking it would give me pleasure to submit any manuscript to you personally, in your private capacity. I have heard how much good you have done as head of the Society. In the present case, however, the gulf between the tastes and views of your organization and my own seems impassable." Cahan grasped the conservative views of the young Society and believed that the immigrant themes with which he was grappling would be unacceptable. They were later incorporated in the Yiddish and English novels that were published elsewhere.[19]

In an effort to introduce a knowledge of Yiddish literature to the readers of the Jewish Publication Society, Leo Wiener, Professor of Russian Literature at Harvard College, was invited to prepare a history of contemporary European and the new American Yiddish literature. Wiener zealously approached the task. The still inadequate bibliographical resources in the United States required him to go to England and Russia, visit their libraries and booksellers, and return to Harvard with thousands of rare and obscure Yiddish works. By the end of 1898 his manuscript and bibliography of *A History of Yiddish Literature in the Nineteenth Century* was in the hands of the publisher. For reasons that cannot be determined but are suggested in the twenty-fifth annual report, the manuscript was rejected. Wiener reacted furiously, placed the manuscript in the hands of Scribners, who published it promptly. When Scribners offered the Publication Society the opportunity to acquire a small portion of the edition, the offer was not accepted. The Yiddish collection was acquired by Harvard, and Wiener made no further attempt to pursue the history of a literature that was less

Arch Street Theater program for Max Gabel in "Her Mother's Wedding Gown." *Courtesy of the Museum of American Jewish History.*

known in the United States than that of the Gypsies. The Philadelphia-dominated Jewish Publication Society had lost a second important round in making the Yiddish milieu better known to its readers.[20] Wiener must be acknowledged as the first American historian of Yiddish and the first to introduce the word *Yiddish* to formal literary history.

Yet the quest and interest for Yiddish in English translation was unabated. Sulzberger who heard the brilliant Yiddish orator Zvi Hirsh Masliansky speak on one of his Philadelphia engagements suggested a volume of his sermons and orations. But Masliansky, an extemporaneous speaker, seldom put his addresses down on paper. There also was some doubt as to whether "his sermons will sound well when poured over from the loamy pot of the Jargon into the golden bowl of the English." As far as the Society was concerned the bowl remained empty.[21]

However, the Society was strongly attracted by the fiction on Russian immigrant life in England by Israel Zangwill and Samuel Gordon, two English novelists. It published Milton Goldsmith's novel *Rabbi and Priest,* which used for its background the first mass immigration to Philadelphia in 1882, and the essays of Solomon Schechter and Israel Abrahams, both of whose studies included material on East European social life and literature. Not until 1906 did a work of Yiddish literature, *Stories and Pictures* by Isaac Loeb Perez (Peretz), appear in translation under the Society's imprint. It was undertaken by a non-Jew, Helena Frank of London. The translation was heralded as "admirable in preserving to a remarkable degree the atmosphere of the original, with all of its unique phrasing and idiomatic expression. . . ." The translation, however, was not unexceptionable and the book was pushed through by Henrietta Szold to meet the publisher's schedule. As an afterthought, Peretz' permission to translate was obtained when the book was already in galley sheets.[22]

Peretz found yet another translator in the Catholic-born anarchist, Voltairine de Cleyre. Her involvement with Yiddish-speaking immigrants to whom she taught English brought her into the Yiddish orbit. Voltairine de Cleyre mastered Yiddish to the point of fluency and wrote in a clear, cursive script. She was a regular reader of the *Fraye arbeter shtime* and the local Yiddish press as well. In the April 1906 issue of Emma Goldman's *Mother Earth* she contributed her translation of "Hofenung un Shrek" ("Hope and Fear") by Peretz. She was the English teacher, among others, of Joseph J. Cohen, the Yiddish anarchist journalist who later wrote *Di Yidish-anarkhistishe bevegung in amerike.*[23]

Voltairine de Cleyre and Helena Frank were not isolated examples of women of non-Jewish background who learned Yiddish for literary or for other purposes. Social workers coming into South Philadelphia felt ill equipped without a knowledge of the immigrants' mother tongue. In her application to the Presbyterian Board of Foreign Missions, Emily Wayland Dinwiddie, the author of an important work on Philadelphia housing, stated that she had learned Yiddish sufficiently well to pursue her social work career among Philadelphia's immigrant Jews.[24]

The acceptance of Peretz by an American audience did not guarantee the translation of other Yiddish story tellers. The grandfather of Yiddish literature, Mendele Mocher Seforim, remained unknown and untouched among American readers. Although Mendele and Sholom Aleichem found their way into German, and the youthful Sholom Asch was early recognized in continental literature, both were politely rejected by the Jewish Publication Society—except for the stories later anthologized by Frank—owing to the lack of "any particular merit in their stories, or any grace of style apparent in the German translations. . . ." In spite of such reports, Dr. Solomon Solis-Cohen, who read German versions of the Yiddish, thought it might be "a matter of policy, with a view to pleasing an important element in the community."

To satisfy this "important element" of English-reading subscribers, the Society offered the first anthology of Yiddish literature in the United States six years after the appearance of the Peretz translation. The new book, *Yiddish Tales,* was a success. Perhaps it was the result of Israel Abraham's brief essay on Helena Frank or her own essay on the importance of Yiddish literature in the Western world.

Behind the literary scene, hesitation toward Yiddish translation was evident. The taint of "jargon" was widespread. The use of Hebrew printed characters for Yiddish was condemned by East European pietists, but their feeble voice had little impact on the Philadelphia-dominated Society. On the other hand, the clamor of American reformers was loud, articulate and influential. Yiddish was associated with Zionism, the two forming a twin evil. Its authors were believed to be hampering the spread of English among immigrants, hindering the process of Americanization by its use and perpetuating the language of the old European ghetto. The Hebraist, no less antagonistic, struck it down in favor of spreading the use of Hebrew. With such diverse reactions and influences the Society found it difficult during the years of mass immigration to pierce the thick curtain that obscured a new genre of writing discovered more than a generation later, only to be exploited and even vulgarized. The first "Fiddlers" of Yiddish literature were rejected.

If the mass of Yiddish-speaking Philadelphians were aware of these circumstances, they showed little evidence of it. In fact they throbbed in the rich offerings of their mother tongue. Local publishers, numerous bookshops, a lively theatre and a number of literary societies fulfilled the yearnings of a curious spectrum of the immigrant population.

In an ironic twist the Connecticut Daughters of the American Revolution published a *Yiddish Guide to the United States for the Jewish Immigrant*. The Daughters viewed the native tongue of the immigrant as the door that opened upon American life. Although it originated with the Connecticut Society and was published in New York, the *Guide* was widely distributed in Philadelphia. The book was so popular that it went into two editions before being translated into English as an incentive to study the language of the new world. The Philadelphia *Jewish Exponent* wrote editorially that the *Guide* was "full of indispensable information couched in a most sympathetic tone."[25]

Yiddish in Philadelphia approached its nadir in the early 1920s. A decade of postwar prosperity assured its growth. The appearance of avant-garde "little" magazines, an increase in the daily circulation of the New York and local press, and an overwhelming crop of new writers suggested a Yiddish renaissance on American soil. There were no established publishing houses, but numerous printers issued a variety of subsidized publications. Books were sponsored by anniversary and jubilee committees, by friends of the author, or by *landsmanshaftn*. There were six prominent Yiddish booksellers who sold these literary wares to the public, but frequently the author was his own bookseller.

At the same time the number of bilingual publications increased. Pages or sections in English were added to the daily press and photographs carried English subtitles. Union literature was increasingly monolingual, and the general press of the city no longer appealed to Jewish readers with blazing Yiddish headlines and political broadsides. Like other Americans, Jews were gradually becoming monolingual, and like the descendants of other foreign-speaking immigrants they were not encouraged to pursue their parents' tongue. The number of Jews who learned Yiddish beyond a corrupt, fragmented street and home parlance were few. American-born Jews are not known to have become supporters of the Yiddish press or the world of Yiddish books. The use of Yiddish was almost exclusively confined to the immigrant generation.

Philadelphia's polyglot immigrant libraries flourished for almost half a century. The Hebrew Literature Society, founded in 1885, was the largest and most popular, and it became a major cultural center. While the libraries of the immigrant societies rose and fell, the established Jewish institutions disregarded Yiddish as studiously as the immigrants clung to it.

In a little more than one generation the publisher of the first Yiddish newspaper, Moses Freeman, busied himself writing about the pioneer press. The first Jewish unions in the garment industry also produced their histories in Yiddish, making them valuable documents in the absence of other records. Bibliographical data on the press was accumulated and published in part by David B. Tirkel.

Were Philadelphians of the immigrant generation sensing their own decline, their waning influence in Yiddish letters, or were they continuously overwhelmed by the New York Yiddish "Mecca"? The Depression dealt the *Yidishe velt* a severe blow as it did the press in New York. Writers and journalists were seeking greener fields, but the fields were as dry as winter grass. Leivick's adage on the fate of Yiddish was constantly invoked: *Ihk bren un ihk bren un ihk ver nit farbrent* ("I burn and I burn but I am not consumed"). Leivick could not have anticipated the fate and future of his mother tongue, uprooted from its native land, burned out of the soil of Europe, languishing in the United States, and exiled in Israel.

The Movies' First Mogul

Joseph Eckhardt and Linda Kowall

On September 14, 1923, in a small Jewish cemetery near Atlantic City, Siegmund Lubin of Philadelphia, the first movie mogul, was laid to rest. The *New York Times* and motion picture trade publications briefly noted the passing of a "pioneer."

Thomas Edison, the bitter rival who eventually became Lubin's colleague during the formation of the motion picture industry, had long since turned his attentions away from moving pictures. On that September day in 1923, trying to produce a substitute for rubber from milkweed preoccupied the ailing "Wizard of Menlo Park." Celebrated director Henry King, who had entered the movies as an actor with Lubin's West Coast studio, was in Rome directing Lillian Gish and Ronald Coleman in *The White Sister* for MGM. For Oliver Hardy, who had served his motion picture apprenticeship at Lubin's Jacksonville, Florida studio, an historic teaming with Stan Laurel still lay in the future. Cecil B. DeMille, who would always credit Lubin with saving his career, was wagering that career and over $1 million of Paramount Pictures' money on a modest little film called *The Ten Commandments.* From the industry Lubin had helped to create, only his friend, Adolph Zukor, traveled to Atlantic City to pay his last respects.

Siegmund Lubin's colorful personality and even more colorful career were too early to have been chronicled by the Hollywood writers whose stories of the powerful heads of the large studios would blend into our popular stereotype of the movie "mogul": a middle-aged, balding, well-dressed, cigar-smoking, diamond-flashing, shrewd and eccentric Jewish businessman, part cutthroat and part sentimental father figure. Lubin had already retired from the industry when the term "movie mogul" was just coming into common usage. As his career was nearing its height, a contributor to *Who's Who in the Motion Picture World* wrote, "Lubin will always be remembered as the man who combined dramatic power with the wizardry of finance and made it possible to commercialize the film industry. . . ."[1] Yet at his death a mere 13 years later, Lubin's name was all but forgotten by members of the industry he had done so much to create.

Lubin was well remembered, however, by a small but very influential band of men—Jewish immigrants like himself—who all shared his energy, his commercial sense, his gambler's instinct, and his chutzpah. These were the movie moguls whose names have become part of Hollywood mythology: Louis B. Mayer, Adolph Zukor, Samuel Goldwyn, the Warner Brothers. Some had wined and dined with Lubin, some had learned from him, some sought help from him and, whether consciously or unconsciously, all followed the pattern he had set.

Men who would later be described as "part splendid emperors, part barbarian invaders,"[2] the moguls were all immigrants or sons of immigrants who had fled the economic hardships and antisemitic pressures of Eastern Europe. Their rapid rise to power as heads of major studios has often been traced to their Jewish roots, to backgrounds and experiences which made them uniquely sensitive to the wants and needs of the masses and uniquely skilled at adapting to meet those needs. These men who had dealt with the man in the street as glove salesmen, junk collectors, and purveyors of herring, saw the emerging popularity of the movies as a golden opportunity and seized upon it when no one else could or would. In many ways, the story of the moguls' rise and assimilation into their adopted culture is a paradigm of the movies themselves. An amusement dismissed by most as a flash-in-the-pan, movies rapidly expanded into a multi-million-dollar industry that catered to and eventually helped to shape the tastes of the original storefront audiences which were soon absorbed into the American middle class. As the moguls helped to shape America, it slowly reshaped them. By the end of their lives, the Jewish moguls had become decidedly non-Jewish. Moving away from their religious and cultural heritage, they assimilated themselves thoroughly into the American way of life. As writer and critic Ben Hecht once observed, "Samuel Goldwyn, Louis B. Mayer, the Warner Brothers, the Schenck Brothers, Adolph Zukor, Harry Cohn, Irving Thalberg, Carl Laemmle, Jesse Lasky, B. P. Schulberg, and their *mispochas* were conducting a Semitic renaissance, sans rabbis and Talmud."[3]

The moguls' tale is a classic example of the "immigrant-makes-good" chapter in the epic of the American Dream. Young enough to have been Lubin's sons, they were still the children of impoverished Jews living in urban ghettos in 1897 when Lubin's career in "Life Motion Pictures" began, and the word "movies" had not yet been coined.

"This is the story of the King of the Movies," wrote the *Philadelphia Ledger* in 1913 as Lubin was approaching the height of his career. "It is a story of hard work, inventive genius, pluck and perseverence. It tells of the rise of Siegmund Lubin from a little optician's store on Eighth Street . . . to the head of the Lubin Manufacturing Company in 18 years."[4] The story of Lubin's rise, from an itinerant peddler of optical wares to a multi-millionaire feted by American dignitaries and foreign royalty, is the basic theme upon which the second generation of film pioneers, the moguls of Hollywood's golden age, would weave their own variations.

The motion picture industry and the fortunes of its moguls were built on a series of gambles: Louis B. Mayer's first "high-class" nickelodeon; Goldwyn, Lasky and DeMille's first feature film; Harry Warner's legendary gamble on talking pictures in 1927. But perhaps the most daring gamble of all was Lubin's gamble in 1897 on the "flickers."

The very first movies were far more primitive than most people today realize. The first "Life Motion Photographs" projected on bedsheets in churches, halls, and vacant storerooms were as crude and pathetic as man's first attempts to fly. The image jumped and flickered in a way that caused headaches and upset stomachs. Only their brevity—most lasting only a few minutes—offered some relief from the assault they made on the optic nerves. The image blurred and streaked, and depending on the skill of the operator, moved too fast or too slowly. Brief as they were, the presentations were often interrupted as scratched and peeling footage clogged the machine, as the film broke and flew off the sprockets, or caught fire with spectacular—and occasionally disastrous—results. The projectionist who could crank a whole reel of 50 feet through the projector without any mishap was either extremely skilled or extremely lucky. The projectors were heavy and cumbersome; they were hand-cranked and, in an age when electricity was not readily available, the illumination was provided by open flames. The equipment used to produce calcium or acetylene gas for light was awkward and dangerous.

Small wonder that when Lubin, an obscure Philadelphia optician, suddenly began to throw large sums of money into making these clumsy films and the equipment to produce and project them, and then threw additional money into extensive and sophisticated advertising to sell them, most of his friends thought he was crazy. "They all laughed at me when I showed my first movies," he would recall at the end of his remarkable career. "They said I could never make them go."[5]

But as primitive as they were, those early films attracted audiences when exhibited. These audiences were almost exclusively lower-class factory workers and immigrants, the wretched refuse of America's teeming urban neighborhoods. Paradoxically, the greatest potential for profit lay in the major industrial cities where moving pictures held a great appeal for the urban poor. To go to the movies required no clean clothes, no presentable appearance, no knowledge of the English language, no sobriety, no prior arrangements. It also required virtually no free time and very little money.

Siegmund Lubin, aged 30, in 1881. *Courtesy of the Lubin Archive, Free Library of Philadelphia.*

With 20 minutes and five cents to spare, a customer could be on his way back home or back to work after having seen something truly remarkable—a picture that moved.

In the earliest days that was enough and Lubin knew it. Among the men who would soon be acknowledged as the film pioneers—men like Thomas Edison, J. Stuart Blackton, Albert Smith, and William T. Rock—Lubin was the only one who shared the immigrant experience of the motion pictures' first patrons. Like them he had once been a stranger in a strange land himself.

Historians generally designate 1881 as the dividing line between the "old" and "new" immigration and, most particularly, between the old immigration of culturally elite Sephardic and German Jews as opposed to the new immigration of lower class Eastern European Jews. While members of the old immigration—David Belasco, Daniel Frohman, and Florenz Ziegfeld—would carve out theatrical empires by catering to the carriage trade, the new immigrants—like L. B. Mayer, Adolph Zukor, Carl Laemmle, and Samuel Goldfish—would found their fortunes on the nickels and dimes of the unlettered and unwashed.

Lubin defies such easy categorization for he successfully combined many of the traits commonly attributed to both. He was unique in this regard: he shared the experiences that enabled him to understand the movies' first audiences and had the education and technical expertise that enabled him to supply their needs. Siegmund Lubin, more than anyone else, had both the vision and the skill to develop the early motion pictures from a lower class amusement into a respected industry.

'What does one do here for a livelihood?' asked an immigrant in the 1880s who had been a *maskil*, or learned man, in Russia. 'You do what everyone does,' came the reply, 'You become a peddler.'[6] Lubin, a learned man who possessed considerable technical skills, an extensive knowledge of chemistry and optics, and a degree from Heidelberg, was no exception.[7] He became a peddler too. This man who would frequently be referred to as "Professor," spent most of his early years in America as an itinerant peddler traveling across the country, selling a variety of wares to a vast assortment of people. In addition to the jewelry he is alleged to have sold to the Indians, Lubin peddled his own spectacles "with hooks" and a metal polish he called Putzpommade (it cleaned everything).[8]

In 1882, after years of peddling, Lubin and his wife settled in Philadelphia and opened his shop—an optical store at 237 North Eighth Street, just up the block from Keith's Bijou Theater. By 1890, he had moved the shop to 21 South Eighth Street, and it was from here that "S. Lubin, Manufacturing Optician" would become "LUBIN, World's Largest Manufacturer of Life Motion Picture Machines and Films."

When Lubin's motion picture business eventually succeeded beyond anyone's wildest dreams, the optical shop became a symbol of success to other immigrants in Philadelphia. Mark Dintenfass, a film pioneer and, with Carl Laemmle, one of the founders of the Universal Film Company, once told a companion of a conversation he had had with his mother: "Mamma! Sometimes she thinks I should need the old optical shop!" Lubin was worth $11,000,000 at the time.[9]

Lubin and his wife would always have a special attachment to the Eighth Street shop. As Lubin expanded to bigger, more sophisticated studios at 912 Arch Street, followed by 926 Market Street, 20th and Indiana and, finally, the great studio-estate at Betzwood in Montgomery County, he would always keep the optical shop for what he described as "sentimental reasons." It was for such sentimental reasons that another film magnate, William Fox, would always keep a reproduction of "LeBrun and Child" which he and his wife had gotten by saving Babbit's Soap coupons. For the Lubins and the Foxes, the optical shop and the picture served as links to their beginnings and, perhaps, as reminders of their early struggles.[10]

Whether he was prompted by an occasional tinge of *Wanderlust* or a commercial opportunity too good to pass up, Lubin still left the optical shop from time to time to peddle his wares in other cities. The year 1896 found him in New Orleans, peddling smoked glasses to Mardi Gras visitors wishing to view the eclipse. It was here that, according to film historian Terry Ramsaye, Lubin met William T. "Pop" Rock and first conceived the notion of entering the moving picture business:

> The pompous 'Pop' Rock, with his massive gold watch chain across his vest and his diamond handshake and richly genial manner, was to the hopeful Lubin a very personification of that American success and prosperity which he desired to overtake. Lubin pursued Rock for a clue to his method. Lubin watched the Vitascope with profound interest. This was something to get into. . . .[11]

This questionable account of Lubin's inspiration to enter the motion picture business is by no means the whole story.

Lubin's knowledge of optics led, quite naturally, to an interest in photography and, for anyone interested in photography, nineteenth-century Philadelphia was the place to be. From the 1840s on, many of the most significant advances in photographic technology were made in Philadelphia by men like Robert Cornelius, Frederick Gutekunst, and William and Frederick Langenheim. Philadelphia became a center for the manufacturing of stereopticon slides and it's not surprising that by 1895, and probably earlier, Lubin had also begun to manufacture stereopticon slides and then to produce the illustrated song slides which were quite popular in vaudeville houses as a visual accompaniment to sing-alongs and as a means of plugging the popular ballads of the day.[12]

From 1885 to 1893, Eadweard Muybridge was at the University of Pennsylvania, conducting more of the animal locomotion studies which were a major step toward solving the problem of photographically reproducing the illusion of motion. It was from Muybridge that Lubin claimed to have gotten his first ideas about motion pictures. "He showed a horse walking by stereopticon pictures, shown rapidly one after the other. I started to experiment then," Lubin said, "It was in the nineties."[13] Lubin's technical curiosity, whetted by the Muybridge studies, was further excited by Francis Jenkins' demonstration of the Projecting Phantoscope at the Franklin Institute on December 18, 1895. Not long after this demonstration, which was the first motion picture exhibition using flexible film ever presented before an American scientific body, Lubin entered the motion picture field with equipment purchased from this same Francis Jenkins.[14]

The motion picture's commercial possibilities were also beginning to make themselves manifest and could not have gone unnoticed by Lubin. On December 25, 1895, Major Woodville Latham's Eidoloscope was shown at Keith's Bijou Theater, right up the street from Lubin's first shop. On May 25, 1896, Edison's Vitascope made its Philadelphia debut at Keith's Bijou, and there, on July 27, the Lumiere cinematographe began a five-month run in Philadelphia.[15]

Philadelphia offered still another advantage to a man about to enter the moving picture business. By 1882, the year Lubin settled in Philadelphia, the city was becoming a major port of entry for the second wave of European immigrants, the same people who would soon provide eager audiences for his first films.

The elements were all assembled—the technical resources, a large untapped audience starved for a cheap and undemanding form of entertainment, and a man with the commercial instinct to see the money-making potential in a scientific curiosity, the experience to promote it, and the skill to satisfy the unprecedented demand he would create. The conjunction of these elements would result in the transformation of the movie business into a mass medium and an industry.

This conjunction was announced bravely, but rather inauspiciously, in the back pages of the *New York Clipper*, sandwiched between advertisements for "Mlle. Rosina Venus, queen of the invisible and dancing tight-wire" and "Professor Kriesel's Trained Dogs."[16] Amid a barrage of announcements for "Buffalo Foot Cycles" and "Cuticura Cure for Salt Rheum," perusers of the *Clipper* ads of 1897 and 1898 encountered regular advertisements for something called Lubin's Cineograph, "the latest development of the Vitascope and all projecting machines." By February 13, 1897, a mere month after its first appearance in the *Clipper*, the Cineograph was to become the "New Improved" Cineograph and, three weeks later, the "Most Improved." This "lightest, cheapest, and most perfect of projecting machines on the market" was quickly rendered obsolete by the introduction of an 1898 model, "the Greatest Machine of the Age," which, in turn, was soon outmoded by a 1900 model, "the only practical Professional moving picture machine in the world." The 1901 model was "A Marvel of the 20th Century," and the 1902 model became "The Only Perfect Life Motion Picture Machine Ever Made."

Siegmund Lubin was not the first to patent motion picture equipment, nor was he by any means the only source of films and machinery. By 1898 would-be exhibitors could order an "animated film outfit" from the Sears catalogue. For $160.50 he would receive an Edison projector, film, posters, tickets, and rubber stamp. However, Lubin pioneered the mass marketing of motion picture machinery and films with an eye toward creating a demand. In his imaginative use of advertising, his exploitation of the movies as a mass entertainment, and his painstaking creation and cultivation of a network of exhibitors ready to buy whatever he could produce, Lubin opened up the field and set a pattern which others would quickly follow.[17]

Beginning with his first *Clipper* ads of 1897 and 1898, Lubin hit the ground running. In their size, their frequency, their placement (usually at the top of the page), and their bold, eye-catching use of illustrations and all the tricks of the typesetter's trade, Lubin's ads for the Cineograph and for his films completely overshadowed the modest, unremarkable ads of a sleeping giant—the Edison Manufacturing Company.

While Thomas Edison's ads matter-of-factly stated that the company had a product—projectors and films—for sale, the Lubin ads exhorted, cajoled and enticed would-be exhibitors with the "Greatest chance ever offered . . . make a small fortune in a short time . . . Every One who has bought Lubin's Passion Play is coining money . . . You can make a barrel of money . . . Strike While the Iron is Hot . . . Don't wait for the next new thing. . . ."

Within two short years, Lubin applied most of the techniques still used by modern advertising to the promotion of motion picture machinery and films. In addition to the free trial offer, he introduced the money back guarantee, the limited time offer, special package deals, and price reductions due to factory enlargement to motion picture advertising. Lubin worked to impress potential customers with the idea that they were buying the latest state of the art technology by constantly stressing his "latest development," a "new process," or specialties such as "lenses ground under my personal supervision. . . ." This potent concoction was then accompanied by eye-catching illustrations (the first illustrated motion picture ads), a string of superlatives and those mainstays of the patent remedy salesmen—testimonials. In response the Edison Company ads remained the same, week after week, for nearly a year.

This sharp contrast between the early advertising styles of Lubin and Edison reflected a far more profound difference separating the two titans. Theirs was a difference between two cultures, between the Protestant ethic and the pleasure principle, between order and spontaneity, in short, the difference between a rigid, single-minded vision and a flexible, all-embracing *Weltanschauung.* This difference would soon engender a bitter and protracted clash between Lubin and Edison over the motion picture industry and would, in the end, be the underlying reason why it was Lubin, an immigrant, and not the native-born Edison who commercialized America's motion picture industry. The difference was firmly rooted in their basic attitudes toward the motion picture, what it was and what it could become.

Edison first viewed the motion picture business as a market for machines, not recognizing that the films were far more important than the machines that showed them. After developing his Kinetoscope or "peep show" machine, Edison resisted the clamor for "screen machines" because projected pictures would, he thought, mean the need for fewer machines.[18] Once he had given in, reluctantly, to the public's demand for projected pictures, Edison was then faced with producing a supply of films for them. This was becoming a nuisance.

Norman C. Raff, who handled Edison's motion picture merchandising, had other problems besides Edison's reluctance to give the public what it wanted. Raff had come from the world of banking and tried to conduct Edison's motion picture business in the same orderly fashion.[19] Rather than selling Edison projectors and films outright, he sold exclusive territorial rights to exhibit to the comparatively small number of entrepreneurs able to raise the rather large amounts of capital needed for such an investment.[20]

As a result of the Edison Company's inability to produce enough films to meet the demand and the problems inherent in the exclusive rights approach to film marketing, letters from disgruntled exhibitors began to pour in. William T. Rock complained about the shortage of films, the poor quality of Edison's prints, and the sleep-inducing nature of the subjects. He also had to contend with competition in spite of his so-called "exclusive" rights for which he had paid $1500.[21] From Philadelphia, a Mr. Kiefaber sent another letter: "It is ridiculous, the few films I bought from your place yesterday. There are not two good scenes in the whole lot . . . You folks will certainly have to get a hurry up on business or I will not give much for the chances on the Vitascope.[22]

Into this vacuum stepped Lubin. With his first *Clipper* ad on January 16, 1897, he launched a campaign that blew the motion picture business wide open to all comers. Instead of the sizeable investment—sometimes running as high as $20,000 for prime territories[23]—required to obtain exclusive territorial rights from Edison, Lubin was offering his Cineograph to any would-be exhibitors "On trial, FREE." Anyone wishing to keep the machine could buy it—no strings attached—for $150, complete with films. What is more, the Cineograph became cheaper—$125 by March—and cheaper—$90 by May—and still cheaper—$70 by September of 1897. Arthur Hotaling, who joined Lubin in 1897, recalled that "people of all sorts bought machines in those days . . . A man would come off the farm to make his fortune as an exhibitor, and he did not have to sell the farm either. For $75 he could get a head and a lamp, a handful of carbons, four or five fifty-foot films, a sheet, some tickets and a few lantern slides. All he needed was the location."[24]

Beginning with his first *Clipper* ad, Lubin established a practice of courting new exhibitors and, in so doing, built up a network of loyal customers who would provide a steadily growing market for the motion picture equipment and films he would produce. In October 1897, in an ad announcing the "GREATEST BARGAIN EVER OFFERED," Lubin went on to say, "my intention being to lend all possible assistance to prospective showmen, I will sell one dozen Cineographs in different states as an inducement for one week only." Five years later, Lubin would still be offering bargain priced machinery with the explanation that "We do this as a mode of advertising in order to secure permanent customers for Films and Slides."

In a sense Lubin's first customers—the first motion picture exhibitors—were itinerant peddlers just as he had once been. Before the rate of film production grew fast enough to provide permanent theaters with even a weekly change of pictures, exhibitors traveled from town to town showing their films and, when the novelty wore off, moving on. In addition to

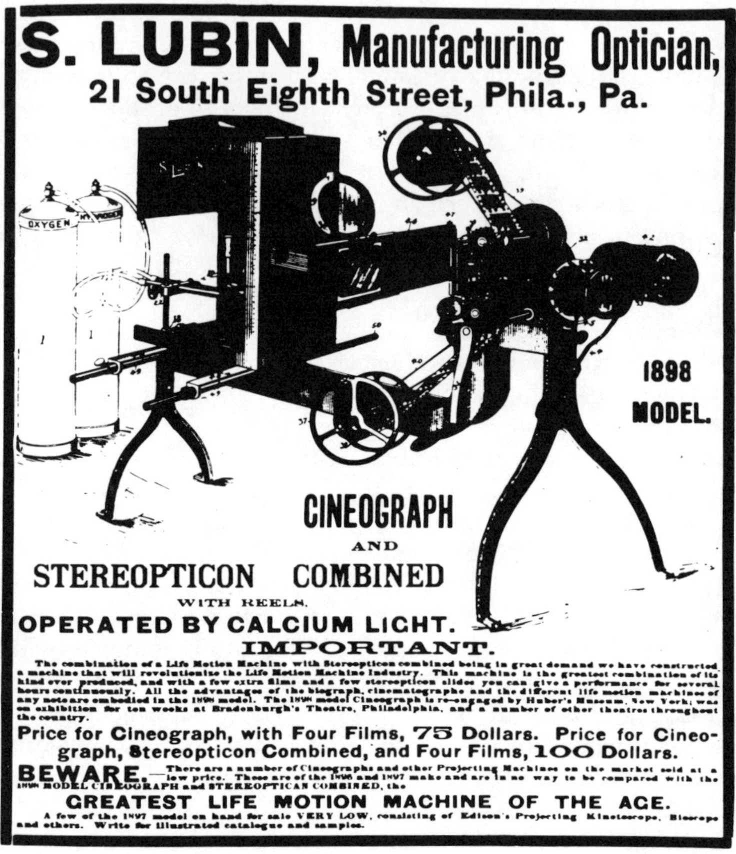

An early Lubin advertisement in the *New York Clipper. Courtesy of the Lubin Archive, Free Library of Philadelphia.*

providing affordable equipment, Lubin, who had spent many years on the road himself, was able to provide them with projectors and films better suited to their particular needs. The Cineograph was light (less than 50 pounds), small and portable, and ready for the road. It was not dependent— as Edison's first models were—on electricity which was still in short supply. It was hand-cranked and exhibitors had the option of electric, acetylene gas or calcium lights for illumination. By 1904, Lubin was offering them a most interesting package: a Cineograph, complete with attachments, two films, two Monarch records to provide background accompaniment, and a free Victor Talking Machine—all for $99.[25]

Lubin himself took the natural step from production into motion picture exhibition, a step which the film moguls like Fox, Laemmle, Zukor and L. B. Mayer would take a decade later—but in reverse—as they branched out from film exhibition and distribution into production. The end result was the same as these men all combined motion picture production and exhibition to accomplish the vertical integration of the motion picture industry. The theater Lubin built at the National Export Exposition of 1899 in West Philadelphia and which he claimed to be the first structure in America built expressly for showing motion pictures, proved to be one of the Exposition's most popular attractions.[26] By 1908, Lubin had four theaters in Philadelphia—the Auditorium, Palace, Victoria, and Savoy—and a string of theaters along the East coast, including what could very well have been the world's first triple-cinema complex in Baltimore.[27] Well before the first movie palaces were opened in New York City, Lubin employed architect Franz Keenig to build some of the country's first ornamental motion picture theaters.[28]

In sharp contrast to the Edison Company, which accused Lubin of "trying to straddle two horses or eat the cake from both ends" and then boasted, "WE ARE NOT, AND NEVER HAVE BEEN EXHIBITORS. Our business is MANUFACTURING and SELLING the finest motion picture film," Lubin built upon the rapport he had established with his fellow exhibitors. By offering to make a free colored stereopticon slide of every exhibitor who sent him a photograph, and by running a half-page ad in 1906 that wished his exhibitors a "Merry Christmas and a Prosperous New Year, Lubin added the personal touch to his business relationships. Lubin ran a photograph of himself in his 1906 Christmas ad. The only "personal" touch to appear in any of Thomas Edison's *Clipper* ads was his signature at the base of ads headlined "Warning."

It's easy to understand why the first motion picture exhibitors would have felt more comfortable dealing with a man like Lubin. Most were Jewish or Mediterranean immigrants and, like L. B. Mayer, who referred to reserved people as "Kalte Zähne" (cold teeth),[29] they were distrustful of detachment and coldness. To these men the Lubin and Edison companies must have presented images as different as the gulf between your friendly neighborhood grocery and the dignified but forbidding impersonality of a large bank.

Besides approachability and "special terms to the Profession," Lubin offered his customers much more. Unlike those first unhappy Edison exhibitors like "Pop" Rock and Mr. Kiefaber who flooded the company with letters of complaint, Lubin's exhibitors never had to worry about a shortage of films or a lack of interesting subjects. At a time when the lights were threatening to go out on the flickers because film supply wasn't keeping up with demand, Lubin stepped in and changed the course of motion picture history.

In February 1897, Lubin was already offering 250 film titles; in September he was able to furnish "every known film made, either American or foreign," and by October he was advertising "At least 1,000 films constantly on hand." By the summer of 1898, Lubin had added at least 70 films of the Spanish American War and a Passion Play in 28 episodes "taken expressly for us at the expense of several thousand dollars." By April 1899, he was able to say, "Being the largest manufacturer, we have the most select list to choose from." On that select list it was not unusual to see "UNVEILING OF THE GRANT MONUMENT AT PHILADELPHIA" offered with "RAID OF A NEW YORK BOWERY SALOON." Lubin's offering for the week of January 14, 1899, not only suggests the wide variety of films he was making available—truly something for everyone—but also tempts one to wonder if that week saw the exhibition of the world's most eclectic program:

NEW COUCHEE DANCE (Dance a la Francaise)
LADY CONTORTIONIST (See Her Do Her Famous Act, the Split)
NEW LIPMAN DANCE (Very Spicy)
SANTA CLAUS
CHRISTMAS MORNING
PASSION PLAY
CORBETT AND SHARKEY FIGHT

Lubin employed a variety of methods in building up this repertory of films. Some he produced himself, some he copied scene for scene using his own actors, and the rest he simply ran through an optical printer and "duped."[30] To sell them he used testimonials from newspapers and theater owners, including Philadelphia's Jules Mastbaum and C. A. Bradenburg of Bradenburg's Dime Museum, and endorsements from the popular fighters who were portrayed or actually appeared in his fight films. In what was probably the *ne plus ultra* of endorsements, Lubin even ran an ad proclaiming, "THE PRESIDENT ENTERTAINED. By special request, we gave one of our unexcelled Life Motion Picture Exhibitions . . . His Excellency pronounced it THE BEST LIFE MOTION PICTURE ENTERTAINMENT EVER WITNESSED."

To this formidable display of salesmanship Lubin added another surefire technique—bribery. Recalling his first meeting with Lubin, Arthur Hotaling told of one summer day in Atlantic City in 1897 when a man came to him with some films to sell. "At first glance I saw they were copies and said so. . . .He did not argue, but as he turned away, he slipped something into my hand with a request to buy a drink when I was not so busy. I looked at a five-dollar bill and called after him to come around next morning when I could look at them more carefully. . . . As we needed a change of program we bought some of the best."[31]

Lubin's first big hit was his recreation of the Corbett-Fitzsimmons fight. A group of filmmakers calling themselves the Veriscope Company filmed the actual Corbett-Fitzsimmons fight in Carson City, Nevada, on March 17, 1897. After great effort and expense—including the percentages promised the fighters and their trainers, the cost of bribing Nevada officials to allow the fight to take place, and the cost of travel and production—the Veriscope Company advertised that their films would be ready by May 15. At considerably less expense, Lubin hired a couple of freight handlers and, on the roof of 912 Arch Street, filmed a recreation of the fight,[32] which he proceeded to advertise one month before Veriscope's films would be ready to deliver. Exhibitors and their patrons were pleased with the Lubin facsimile. Veriscope was less enthusiastic. It warned against the "unprincipled parties" (namely Lubin) who "are advertising that they have films for sale in imitation of this great contest," adding that, "anyone buying these bogus films will not be permitted to exhibit them." But before Veriscope could get its own films on the street, Lubin countered with the announcement that he had just received a copyright for his Corbett-Fitzsimmons imitation and therefore, exhibitors were protected. This little sparring match with Veriscope was but a prelude to the main event—a ten-round fight between Lubin and Edison that was slugged out in the courts and on the pages of the *Clipper*.

It began in the courts on January 10, 1898, when Edison filed suit against Lubin to bar him from manufacturing motion picture equipment and films.[33] It spread to the pages of the *Clipper* over the Spanish American War and Passion Play films. Edison warned, "I propose to prosecute, under my patents, anyone showing an unauthorized version of the Passion Play. Yours Very Truly, Thomas A. Edison." In reply to Lubin's ad for war films headlined, "REMEMBER THE MAINE," Edison's agent warned "REMEMBER THE PATENT (EDISON'S) Also that Infringers Are Being Proceeded Against Right and Left." Edison warned again, "BEWARE OF PIRATES." Immediately below it on the same page, Lubin replied, "PASSION PLAY—FILMS—PASSION PLAY—A forfeit of $500 if these films are not Original."

In the response to the example Edison made of Eberhard Schneider, a hapless exhibitor who was fined for showing, among others, Lubin films, Lubin countered with "DON'T BE SCARED BY NEWSPAPER BLUFF" and then proceeded to dispense some legal advice to the exhibitors before concluding with a dare of "$5000 TO ANYBODY who can prove that our show was ever stopped or interfered with." Lubin followed with another dare, this one clearly directed at Edison, "If anyone can prove their sole right to make films let them stop us." Edison did, for a while. In July 1901, he announced, "WE HAVE WON. . .The Only Right to Manufacture Motion Pictures and Films." Lubin was against the ropes, but by March 1902, he came back to proclaim, "LUBIN IS VICTORIOUS." The Court of Appeals had decided in Lubin's favor.

Edison continued to file other actions and remained on the legal offensive, but commercially he was waging a defensive war. The American Mutoscope and Biograph Company, with its equipment specially designed to circumvent Edison's patents, posed the most serious legal threat to Edison's claim to the sole right to manufacture motion picture machines and films.[34] It was Lubin, however, who posed the clearest commercial challenge to Edison's supremacy in the motion picture field.

By May 1899, Lubin was already claiming to be "At least five years ahead of our competitors," and in a full-page ad on the back cover of the *Clipper*'s Christmas edition—an ad totally without precedent in the short history of motion picture advertising—Lubin was, again, "ALWAYS IN THE LEAD." Correcting for a great deal of hyperbole, there was still much truth in these claims. With his mass production and wide dispersion of motion picture machinery and films, Lubin completely undermined Edison's exclusive rights approach to film marketing within a matter of months and proved to others, like Biograph and Vitagraph, that the commercial waters were just fine. With his saturation ad campaigns, Lubin also led the way for others to follow. By 1902, ads for Biograph and Vitagraph began to appear more frequently and Lubin catchphrases even began to creep into the Edison ads which were starting to offer Mt. Pelee films that were "simply coining money" and *Life of an American Fireman* which was "A Money Getter." Following Lubin's lead, Edison was also forced to offer updated models of his projectors every year or run the risk of appearing to offer antiquated equipment, but when Edison offered an Exhibition Model projector for $115 and a Universal Model for $75, Lubin bested him again by offering *his* Exhibition Model for $75 and his Universal Model for $50.

To make matters worse for Edison, Lubin inaugurated a price war on films be telling exhibitors, "don't buy inferior goods for $7.50 when you can get the best for six dollars." Edison retaliated with, "We have no cheap films to offer," adding that his were "films worth owning that will cultivate the public's taste for motion picture shows instead of disgusting them."

In the field of film duping, where Lubin also led, others, including Edison, quickly followed. "It required little intelligence to know that this was shady business," Fred Balshofer recalled, "but Mr. Lubin carried on the practice as if it were perfectly ordinary and completely legitimate." In a now-classic story, Balshofer described the day he screened a dupe of *A Trip to the Moon,* one of Georges Melies' best pictures, for a prospective customer: "Suddenly he jumped from his chair . . . and shouted . . . 'you want me to buy that film? . . . I made that picture! I am Georges Melies from Paris! Lubin glared at him and . . . brazenly began telling Melies what a hard time he had had blocking out the trademark." Melies was speechless with rage, but as Balshofer recalled, "Lubin seemed to consider the incident a joke. . . ."[35] By October 1902, *A Voyage to the Moon* could be had from Edison, Melies' *Trip to the Moon* was available from Biograph, and *Trip to the Moon* was being offered by Lubin. To add to the confusion, Lubin, who had offered his own *Trip to the Moon* in 1899, retitled his Melies dupe *A Trip to Mars.* Edison's nice orderly motion picture sideline to his more important work had degenerated into a confusing, chaotic, and creative free-for-all.

At the eye of this hurricane, exhibitors were benefiting from a cheaper and more plentiful supply of films, and their patrons were benefiting from the incredible variety of subjects being unreeled before them.

By flooding the market with his own popular fight films, Passion Play pictures, and dupes of films which otherwise might have been in short supply, by setting an example for other competitors to follow, and by lowering the cost of motion picture machinery and films, Lubin was instrumental in placing motion pictures within the reach of anyone, no matter how remote or how poor. By broadening the market and demand for films through his advertising and mass marketing, and by stepping up supply and competition to meet those demands, Lubin created a context which enabled all of the earliest motion pictures to receive the maximum distribution and exposure. While Edison tried to control and restrict motion picture production and exhibition, Lubin unlocked the gates and made it possible for the movies to become a mass medium.

For the immigrants, many of whom were illiterate, nickelodeon documentary footage—genuine or faked—was their only source of news and information. Besides the Spanish-American War films, they could see films of the Paris Exposition, films of striking mine workers, *Russian Anti-Semitic Atrocities, The Revolution in Odessa,* and films of the Olympic Games in Athens "where the Americans outclassed all other nations of the world."[36] In addition Lubin was already exporting films—little glimpses of America— and, "For a long time, while thousands flocked to see his pictures in the great capitals of the world, Mr. Lubin had the field to himself." As Lubin, the only American film pioneer for whom English was a second language, himself told an interviewer, "Pictures speak all languages. The title can . . . be written in Chinese in China, or Russian in Russia, and then the picture becomes of that nationality."[37]

In addition to pursuing Lubin and the other infringers in the courts, the Edison Company resorted to hiring husky spies to follow the outlaw film crews on location in hopes of catching them in the act of using illegal cameras. Lubin deftly evaded them by sending out decoy crews with dummy cameras to lure Edison's men on a wild goose chase through Fairmount Park. The real crew with the real cameras would then leave for a day's filming at one of Lubin's many "secret" locations outside Philadelphia.[38] Addingham and Garrett's Ford in Eastern Delaware County were two favorite locations which provided Lubin crews with scenery and sanctuary for a number of years.[39]

Edison's endless attempts to thwart Lubin and his fellow infringers became increasingly expensive and exasperating. Finally a truce was declared. On December 18, 1908, a treaty was signed by the exhausted combatants—Edison, Lubin, Biograph, Vitagraph, Kleine, Selig, Essanay,

Melies and Pathe—and, the following evening, a dinner to celebrate the formation of the Motion Picture Patents Company was held in the great library at the Edison labs in East Orange, New Jersey.

After more than ten years as adversaries, one can only guess at what went through the minds of Lubin and Edison that evening in the library. The ways of business had always been unintelligible to Edison,[40] and now he found himself allied with the consummate businessman who had almost succeeded in stealing the motion picture business away from him. Besides that, Lubin was a Jew, and perhaps the very man Edison was referring to when he made his now infamous remark that his idea of a good invention was "something so practical that even a little Polish Jew would buy it."[41]

As for Lubin, the only Jew among this exclusively WASP organization of motion picture pioneers, it must have felt strange to now be accepted as an insider, a member of the establishment, after so many years as a "pirate." To compensate for whatever awkwardness he might have felt, however, membership in this elite monopoly offered Lubin undreamed of wealth and social prestige.

As the film industry now entered a period of explosive growth, the Lubin Manufacturing Company quickly mushroomed into a motion picture empire with studios in Jacksonville, Florida; Los Angeles and Coronado, California; Phoenix, Arizona; Newport, Rhode Island; and even Berlin in addition to the company's two giant flagship studios at 20th Street and Indiana Avenue in Philadelphia and at Betzwood. As this motion picture empire flourished, so did Lubin and, for a brief period after the formation of the Patents Company, he puckishly adopted his initials—"S" and "L" intertwined to form a dollar-sign—as the new Lubin trademark. He also adopted a shamelessly extravagant and complicated lifestyle and, in the process, emerged as a new phenomenon in the movie industry. Although the term would not come into common usage until near the end of his career,[42] Lubin became the movies' first "mogul," a complex role composed of many parts.

Lubin's earlier roles as immigrant peddler, inventor, optician, shopkeeper, showman, theater owner and even "pirate" now gave way to the more demanding and, at times, seemingly paradoxical roles of business titan and friend of labor, land baron and benevolent patriarch, philanthropist and bon vivant, medical researcher and raconteur, patriotic American and cosmopolitan world traveller. Like MGM's L. B. Mayer, whose wife was to say her husband had been many men,[43] Lubin had the ability to be all things to all people. His incredible adaptability, a particularly Jewish quality painfully acquired through centuries of being the outsider, is the one overriding quality that encompasses Lubin's complexity and links him most firmly with the legendary Jewish moguls of Hollywood's golden age. For these men, the ability to be social chameleons was the prerequisite for success on a grand scale in such a rapidly changing public industry as the motion picture business.

"A stage Lew Fields in real life" is how one reporter described Lubin. Others who knew him have said that with his colorful way of mangling the "King's English," he could have made a good living as a stage comedian. Like L. B. Mayer, who routinely gave Academy Award-worthy performances in order to coax recalcitrant employees into parts or out of raises, Lubin was a natural showman.[44] He held his companions at the Hotel Vendig spellbound for hours with his stories and anecdotes. His tales were about his early days in the movie business and were typically self-deprecating in the style of the Jewish vaudeville comedians of the day. They also served, however, to remind the listeners that he had been there at the birth of the industry he now led. The image still persists of Lubin as the man who provided Motion Picture Patents Company meetings with comic relief and, like Sam Goldwyn whose celebrated Goldwynisms followed him to the end of his days, Lubin's popular image was greatly at odds with the many accomplishments of this remarkably shrewd and surprisingly cultured man.[45]

Beyond the image was another Lubin, the Lubin once described as "the Rockefeller of the movies." In the eyes of veteran film historian Charles Tarbox, this title was well deserved: "In terms of finance, organization, salesmanship, not to mention technical devices in the studios, recruitment of writers, directors, actors . . . Mr. Lubin achieved . . . what Vanderbilt and Gould and Hill did in building and running railroads where there had been nothing except barren land, or what others did in steel and commerce."[46]

Lubin's elevation to the role of empire-builder and industrial patriarch began with the building of a large, glass-enclosed studio at 20th Street and Indiana Avenue with his share of the enormous profits accruing to the Motion Picture Patents Company. In the days when motion pictures were regarded as a product with no attempt to justify them as art—as evidence by the fact that the major film companies were still listed as "manufacturing" companies—the Lubin Manufacturing Company's new plant was located in a heavily industrialized part of Philadelphia and in a neighborhood community referred to as "Stifftown" because of the grimly visible traces of activity frequently left behind by the Black Hand.[47] Except for the glass roof and walls, the Lubin plant looked much like any other manufacturing company—from the outside, that it. Inside was another story. The manner of operation in this factory was as different from that of other turn of the century factories as the product—moving picture fantasies—it manufactured.

In an age when working conditions were often extremely harsh, pay was poor, and benefits were nonexistent, Lubin employees were treated like members of the family. "Injury and ill-health did not stop pay. Lubin footed doctor and hospital bills. Lubin sent sufferers to better climes. Lubin took care of his 'children' " is how the *Philadelphia Evening Ledger* described the treatment of Lubin employees.[48] Such consideration for his workers drew a

Interior of the studio at 20th and Indiana. While filming was in progress, no one was permitted to smoke because the haze might cloud the image on the film. *Courtesy of the Lubin Archive, Free Library of Philadelphia.*

special commendation from the newly founded *United Labor Journal* in 1915, and inspired 565 employees to endorse an unusual metrical tribute to "Herr Siegmund Lubin," who "made our lives a happiness and our labor a joy."[49] Former employees still make a special point of mentioning Lubin's kindness, accessibility, readiness to offer encouragement, and the free lunches he provided at the company's cafeterias. It was the same sense of shared experience that had once enabled Lubin to identify with the first moviegoers and to recognize what would appeal to the masses which now enabled him to identify with his own employees. "I am the friend of all these people," Lubin told reporter Stephen Bush. "I have myself risen from the depths of poverty. I can feel just as they feel and I know that the bond of loyalty between us will last while I live."[50]

   "People that have worked for me seldom want to leave me," Lubin once said. In adding "I want them to feel we are all one family,"[51] he unconsciously pinpointed the characteristic that set him apart from most of the other industrialists of his day, but which he shared with the Hollywood moguls—his sense of *Mispocha*, or extended family. *Mispocha* was a new concept in industrial management, a concept which set the Hollywood studio system of the Jewish moguls apart from the impersonality of the emerging corporations which viewed workers as interchangeable parts.

Around the studios of Hollywood's Jewish moguls there was a saying that "the son-in-law also rises."[52] Lubin set the motion picture industry's first precedent by naming his sons-in-law Ira Lowry and Ferdinand Singhi as general managers of his studios.[53] In addition to this the 20th and Indiana studio, or Lubinville as it was popularly called, was in a very real sense a community of families. Many Lubin actresses were married to their directors, sometimes entire families—like the Hacketts and the Carrs—acted in Lubin films, and many of the technicians had at least one brother, sister, or brother-in-law among the host of Lubin employees. Lubin presided over this "family" like a benevolent patriarch, but even he was surprised when a disaster demonstrated his employees' tremendous *esprit de corps*. "My people here looked as if they were so sorry for me and many of them said they wanted no more wages until I felt I wanted to pay them again," Lubin recalled after a film-vault explosion destroyed all the company's films in 1914. "It made me feel that they loved me as much as I love them."[54] "Love" was hardly a word commonly used to describe labor relations of the time; it's a word usually reserved for family and one can't help being struck by the resemblance group photos of the Lubin employees—all assembled around Siegmund "Pop" Lubin—bear to family portraits.

Other moguls—"Uncle" Carl Laemmle, Adolph Zukor, and L. B. Mayer whose MGM studio was jokingly called "Mayer's-Ganz-Mispocher"[55]—would translate the traditional Jewish reverence for the all-powerful family patriarch to their roles as studio heads. Their studio families responded to the patriarchal rule with varying degress of respect, rebellion, sometimes hate, often bewilderment, but almost never love. In that Lubin would remain a motion picture patriarch without peer.

Amid an endless procession of banquets, charitable affairs, parties and meetings, Lubin's role as a patriarch expanded beyond the walls of 20th and Indiana. "Siegmund Lubin has made a present of a fine moving picture machine to the Northwest Business Men's Association, through Benjamin Schwartz, Secretary to Congressman R. O. Moon. . . ."[56] "Siegmund Lubin, the photoplay film manufacturer, was the guest of honor . . . at the Progress Club, Philadelphia. Many appreciative speeches were made. . . ."[57] "The San Diego Exposition has set aside Saturday, September 25 as Lubin Day in honor of Siegmund Lubin. . . . Not only the city of San Diego and its officials but the governor of the state will be there to welcome him. . . ."[58] Such were the myriad of personal contacts and appearances that greased the gears of Lubin's motion picture industry and kept it turning. No one was better suited to meeting those demands than the outgoing, expressive Siegmund Lubin of whom it was said "Prize fights, one-steps, a good story, a pretty girl and the click of the chips in a good game of cards delight the heart of this rare man-about-town and huge liver."[59] Like an earlier Jewish statesman of a different sort, Benjamin Disraeli, Lubin was amply endowed with wit and charm and knew exactly how to use it.

As his role as a motion picture statesman expanded, Lubin's view of the role of motion pictures also expanded. Business merged with his sense of patriotism and his philanthropic instincts evolved into a sense of *noblesse oblige.* In 1908, as the motion picture industry was slowly struggling toward legitimacy, Lubin instituted a series of patriotic films and began to run ads stating, "OUR FILMS TEACH A MORAL . . . OUR PICTURES DRIVE HOME A LESSON." In May 1908, Lubin became a pioneer in the use of motion pictures to dramatize philanthropy when at the annual meeting of the relatively new Federation of Jewish Charities, he showed a film depicting the work of the agencies comprising the Federation.[60] September of that year saw the release of a Lubin film showing presidential candidate William Jennings Bryan at work on his farm and in his study. Long before Mogul William Fox would install his movietone process in a Chicago hospital to record a surgical operation or envision the use of films in schools as a valuable teaching aid,[61] Lubin was quoted as saying, "There are unlimited ways in which the Cinematograph working in cooperation with science may become a public benefactor in educating the masses to a true knowledge of health, sanitation, and hygiene. . . ."[62] To this end he committed moving pictures—and the resources of his studio and his own considerable technical skills—to furthering the causes of education and medicine. As early as 1910 he placed 20th and Indiana at the disposal of several Philadelphia medical specialists for the making of films to be used in the training of medical students. In 1912 Dr. Theodore Weisenberg, a noted specialist in neurology and neuro-pathology at Philadelphia's Medico-Chirurgical Hospital, made a special motion picture study of the effects of nervous disorders with Lubin's help. In collaboration with other specialists such as Dr. Francis X. Dercum of Jefferson Medical College and Dr. Charles D. Mills of the University of Pennsylvania, Lubin also filmed through a microscope to take some of the world's first motion pictures of the movement of microbes in milk and changes in nerve cells. By 1912, he was working on a camera which he hoped would be capable of producing moving x-ray films. Dr. Joseph F. Neff, Director of Public Health and Charities in Philadelphia praised Lubin for these services which he provided entirely at his own expense,[63] services which were, perhaps, in keeping with the example set by the Jewish community in his native Berlin[64] and the German-Jewish community in Philadelphia, both of which were known for their charitable works.

Lubin's many philanthropies were truly, to quote one observer, "curious and nonsectarian." He arranged an annual outing for the residents of the Presbyterian Old Ladies' Home[65] and in the spring of 1915 presented "Lubin Hall" to the alumni of Philadelphia's Congregation Keneseth Israel. Lubin director Joseph Smiley opened the hall and the series of talks on science by lecturing on "The Making of Moving Pictures."[66]

It's tempting to speculate on what link, if any, existed between Lubin and Joseph Krauskopf, rabbi of Keneseth Israel and a strong advocate of Americanization at the expense of the Yiddish language and some Jewish customs. What did Krauskopf, who worried about the unassimilated Jews of Eastern Europe crowding into South Philadelphia,[67] think of Lubin's movies which were giving many of these people their first taste of American dress, customs and even language? And what did the Rabbi think when the Lubin Company advertised in *The Jewish World* one Friday in 1915 for "Jewish gentlemen with flowing beards" to act as extras in a film about Russia?[68]

Consciously or unconsciously, Lubin, with his gift for being all things to all people, was the embodiment of Rabbi Krauskopf's belief that "It must be the supreme duty of every Jew to be like unto those among whom he lives."[69] However, Lubin went much farther and assimilated himself much more thoroughly than anything Krauskopf intended. Lubin's daughters were educated in Quaker schools and both eventually became practicing Roman Catholics[70] while their father made some of his first big money in motion pictures with a Passion Play depicting "the life and sufferings of our Lord Jesus Christ." Long before the Jewish moguls of Hollywood's golden era produced *White Christmas, Miracle on 34th Street,* and *It's a Wonderful Life,* or gave audiences Bing Crosby, Ingrid Bergman and Jennifer Jones playing a host of priests, nuns and saints, Lubin made a series of children's Christmas movies and was suggesting to Protestant ministers the uplifting possibilities of cinema in his "Call to the Clergy for Silent Sermons to the Many Millions."[71]

For Lubin, a world traveler and the most cosmopolitan of the early film pioneers, motion pictures played an important part in his *Weltanschauung.* After the outbreak of World War I, Lubin expressed his hopes for the future by telling an interviewer that "the camera is dispensing more happiness than guns, and will be an institution when the Krupp is silenced and the ships of the nations are free to dance over the waters again. . . ."[72] In this interview Lubin's characteristically Jewish sense of internationalism, which had originally enabled him to know what was needed to entertain the peoples of all nations—both within America's immigrant neighborhoods and abroad—was still prompting him to view motion pictures as an international commodity with a worldwide market and worldwide influence. This motion picture *Weltanschauung*—so unlike anything expressed by his fellow Patents Company members—was something Lubin would share with the Hollywood moguls whose movies exported the American Dream.

Lubin's motion picture business expanded to an industry and then, finally, to an empire. Most prominent among the many farflung studios in this empire was Betzwood, the 500-acre studio complex in the Philadelphia suburbs near Valley Forge. It was hailed as "Betzwood the Great" . . . "the greatest plant for the perfect production of motion pictures," "More than a factory—it is an institution." It was "a small city in itself . . . the largest outdoor studio in the world." For its general manager, Ira Lowry, it was "a director's paradise."[73] For Lubin it was all this and much, much more; Betzwood was his baronial estate.

Originally built by fellow German immigrant, millionaire brewer John F. Betz, the huge Betzwood estate fronted for two miles along the banks of the Schuylkill River and included farms, woods, extensive gardens and a conservatory, and exotic imported trees. As if describing a mythical kingdom, one reporter wrote, "Thus it came to pass that a sort of Paradise grew up on the confines of the counties of Philadelphia and Montgomery. . . . There were ponds and breaks, miniature gorges and canyons. Some called it the Switzerland of Eastern Pennsylvania." Above it all rose "a many-towered mansion with great rooms and paneled halls and carved staircases which could be duplicated only in a European chateau."[74] Situated on the highest point of the estate, it afforded Lubin an incomparable view of all that he *beherrscht* or lorded over.

Just as it had been for Gerson Bleichröder, Bismarck's personal banker who had helped to finance the unification of the Germany of Lubin's youth, the purchase of a great estate signified the capstone of Jewish success and rise to social prominence.[75] Betzwood was at once an anachronism and a look into the future, a studio-estate that included both a European castle and laboratories with the world's most sophisticated motion picture technology. It was the ultimate extension of the concept of mispocha where, "in effect the Lubin Company when quartered here will be one large family having a common interest."[76] Here Lubin's employees could not only work, but live. Betzwood was a medieval fiefdom whose lord opened the grounds on Sundays and took great pride in welcoming the crowds of sightseers who came to wander the gardens, conservatory, and deer park.[77]

The paradoxes represented by Betzwood reflected the essential paradoxes in the story of Lubin's rise and the character of the man himself: the Doctor who became a peddler; the man deferred to as "Professor" Lubin who spent Monday nights ringside at the prizefights. The film baron who guided businessmen, politicians, and social luminaries—from Mary Pickford to Prince Henry of Prussia—on grand tours of his fief also liked to quietly sneak into a little dive of a theater in Norristown to see how his latest productions were going over with the crowds.[78] The ultimate paradox manifested itself during a triumphal visit Lubin made in 1913 to his native Berlin. Upon hearing that his friend was in Berlin, Prince Henry of Prussia placed his carriage, driver and footmen at Lubin's disposal while sarcastic Berliners told him: "Mr. Lubin, we don't believe in your Indians; we think they're a lot of Polish Jews."[79]

As Betzwood moved into high gear, three thousand miles away another Jewish immigrant—and friend of Lubin—Carl Laemmle was building Universal City.[80] When Universal City was opened in 1915, it had all the

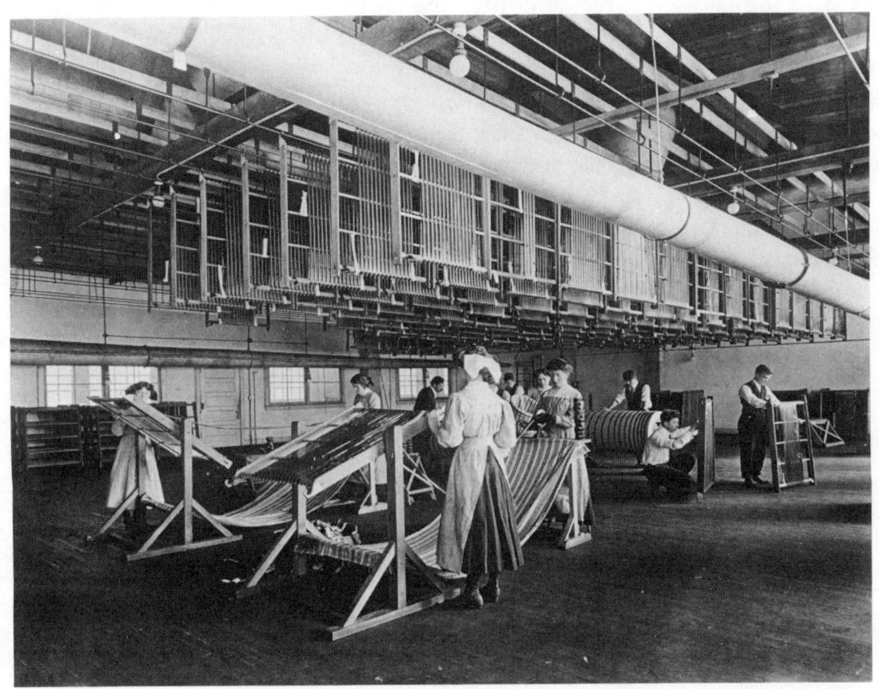

The drying room at the Betzwood studio in 1914. Humidity and temperature were automatically controlled throughout the huge plant. *Courtesy of the Lubin Archive, Free Library of Philadelphia.*

features of Betzwood, but on a smaller scale. Yet, ironically, whereas Laemmle's Universal City represented the beginning of a new era in the motion picture industry, Betzwood, Lubin's greatest triumph, also marked the beginning of the end of his film empire. Betzwood's final paradox was that it was an elaborate structure supported by Lubin's membership in the Motion Picture Patent Company, a once-powerful but now shaky film trust which had failed to take into account the fighting spirit of the independent exchangemen, exhibitors and film producers, most of whom were Jewish.[81]

For Lubin, acceptance as a member of the backward-looking Patents Company—a WASP organization attempting to root out the competition now coming mostly from his fellow Jews—posed a commercial and personal dilemma that in many ways paralleled the trauma of assimilation experienced by the successful Jews of his native Berlin.[82] After years of dodging Edison's detectives and thugs himself, it is not difficult to understand the sympathy Lubin now felt for these fellow "outlaws." The aid he gave to them would have far-reaching consequences.

In 1913, when Jesse Lasky, Samuel Goldfish (Goldwyn), and Cecil B. DeMille joined their forces and their savings to produce a feature-length film of the popular play, *The Squaw Man,* their first serious problem was fending off the Patents Company's attempts to sabotage the film and even maim or kill members of the crew. Overcoming these odds, the filmmakers faced what looked like the ultimate disaster. *The Squaw Man* was impossible to view; the images jumped and moved around on the screen. They faced financial ruin. "That night was the longest I can remember," Samuel Goldwyn later recalled. "I lay awake telling myself that this was the end, that it was back to the glove business for me. I made up my mind to exercise some courage. I would take the problem to Sigismund Lubin of Philadelphia, a great technical expert who was a member of the Film Trust and one of our arch-enemies." Recalling the day he was ushered into Lubin's office, Goldwyn continued, "I told him what my troubles were, and that it had taken all the courage I possessed to come to him for aid. He laughed and said that such an attitude as mine deserved to be rewarded. He looked at my film and quickly spotted the trouble. . . . When this was corrected, *The Squaw Man* went on to become one of the landmarks in motion picture history."[83]

In exchange for saving the first major American-made feature film—not to mention the careers of Goldwyn, Lasky and DeMille—Lubin acquired the exclusive contract to print all distribution copies of *The Squaw Man* at Betzwood.[84]

The irony of Lubin, a Patents Company member, not only saving an "outlaw" film, but also processing the release prints of the film whose success would greatly undermine the Patents Company, is less surprising when several factors are taken into consideration. Lubin saw Goldwyn and Lasky as *Landsmen* and "outlaws" with whom he, a former "outlaw" himself, could easily identify. Furthermore, they were not the first renegade filmmakers Lubin had helped. Years earlier, independent producer Mark Dintenfass had found sanctuary from the Patents Company in a most unlikely place—Lubin's Arch Street studio. There is also evidence that other independent film producers were already sending their films to the Lubin labs for processing.[85] The chance to get a sneak preview of *The Squaw Man* which had by now become a *cause celebre,* offered Lubin an opportunity to see first-hand what promise, if any, these new feature films might offer. "It's no coincidence that after the *Squaw Man* episode, Lubin would be the first of the Patents Company members to enter the field of full-length feature film production.[86]

In many ways, Lubin was as stifled as the independents by the conservative restrictions imposed by the Patents Company on film production, restrictions which ran contrary to his own commercial instincts. During his first seven years in the motion picture industry, Lubin had offered an incredible array of innovations. As a member of the Patents Company, the money was pouring in but Lubin's role as a dynamic commercial innovator

Lubin at the height of his career in 1913. All of his formal portraits were of his left profile to avoid showing his blind right eye. *Courtesy of the Lubin Archive, Free Library of Philadelphia.*

was drawing to a close. He was now told what kinds of films to make, to whom he could sell them, and for how much. The Patents Company quietly torpedoed the introduction of color film technology to the United States and resisted the dreaded feature film because such new developments were expensive and required producers to take risks.[87] Reluctantly for Lubin—who had never been afraid to take risks—"don't rock the boat" became the order of the day. The future of the motion picture would, he knew, rest with the young independents, his fellow Jews, who had not lost their willingness to take the risks he himself once took. California would become the new motion picture promised land and these men would take the movies there. Lubin would not be able to make the trip with them, but when they came to him for help, he gladly provided it.

At the height of his career Lubin's empire was estimated to be worth $11 million. The motion picture business he had created quickly took on a life of its own and, by 1913, he was to remark: "The business has grown to such vast proportions, I feel sometimes as if it was getting beyond me."[88] It had indeed. The great Lubin Manufacturing Company had always been a family business with Lubin himself as the sole owner and authority. Like Lewis J. Selznick, William Fox, and Carl Laemmle who followed him, Lubin's natural inclination to expand infinitely had resulted in the overextension of his energy and his empire. When World War I cut off the foreign market for his films, antitrust suits against the Patents Company cost him millions, and ill health robbed him of energy when he needed it the most, the empire collapsed.

By the end of 1916, Lubin was left with the family home in Atlantic City and the old optical shop in Philadelphia.[89] The first movie mogul spent his last years in relative obscurity. "I've lost a lot of money," he said without much regret in his voice. "I didn't care so much for a great lot."[90] Like so many of his fellow *Landsmen* whom life had given a particularly keen awareness of their vulnerability to forces beyond their control, Lubin was philosophical about his losses. With mogul Lewis J. Selznick, who would also make and lose a fortune, Lubin would definitely have agreed that "we get a million dollars worth of laughs they'll never take away from us."[91]

The German-Jewish Influence in Philadelphia's Jewish Charities

Edwin Wolf 2nd

On February 23, 1882, the *S.S. Illinois* sailed up the Delaware River and landed in Philadelphia. Abroad were 225 Jews who had fled from the anti-semitic pogroms initiated by Czar Alexander II of Russia. Reports of the outrages had preceded the immigrants to America. The ship was met by state and municipal authorities; $20,000 was raised from the citizenry at large to help settle them; a meeting protesting the pogroms was held in the Academy of Music.[1] Little did anyone then realize that the trickle of Eastern European immigrants would turn into a flood.[2]

In the four decades before the mass Eastern European immigration the Jewish community of Philadelphia, numbering perhaps 15,000, had developed a well-rounded, if—by today's standards—small philanthropic network, almost entirely managed and financed by German Jews who had come and flourished a generation or more earlier.[3] By the 1860s most of the members of the Sephardic congregation of Mikveh Israel were of German-Jewish, or at least Ashkenazic, origin. It was more a matter of social upward mobility than adherence to a preferred ritual; it was throughout Europe more fashionable to be "Portuguese" than "German." It it interesting that the same social impetus took most of the German-Jewish members of Mikveh Israel into the Reform congregations of Keneseth Israel and Rodeph Shalom by the end of the century. To be sure, the magnetism of Isaac Leeser, the German-born rabbi of Mikveh Israel, had attracted many of them. He had had as well the support of the descendants of old colonial families few of whom, however, by the Civil War had maintained an active and supportive interest in the city-wide charities. And very few of them were of true Sephardic origins.[4]

Five major Jewish charities had evolved in Philadelphia before the *Illinois* docked. The Hebrew Education Society, founded in 1848 at the urgent insistence of Isaac Leeser, was chartered by the Commonwealth to teach "the elementary branches of education, together with the sciences, and modern and ancient languages, always in combination with instruction in Hebrew language, literature and religion."[5] It was the first Jewish day school.

Leeser also backed the effort of Abraham Sulzberger and District Grand Lodge No. 3 of B'nai B'rith in 1864 to found a Jewish hospital. Such hospitals had already been established in New York and Cincinnati; it was a matter of pride for the Philadelphians to do what others had successfully done. Furthermore, the hospital was established out of a desire to take care of one's own; a resolution calling for the establishment of the Jewish Hospital noted that "Within the last six months three Israelites of this city have died in Christian Hospitals, without having enjoyed the privilege of hearing the watchword of their faith and nation."[6] Its first building, at Fisher's Avenue and Haverford Road, was dedicated in 1867. Three of the four rabbis who spoke at that ceremony delivered addresses in German.[7]

Many of the men who were responsible for the founding and continuing support of the school and the hospital participated in 1869 in the merger of the relief agencies—the United Hebrew Beneficent Society, United Hebrew Relief Association, United Hebrew Fuel and Saving Society, German Ladies' Hebrew Benevolent Society and Ladies Sewing Society.[8] According to the prevailing methods of dispensing charity to the worthy needy, these charities gave coal, food and clothing to the poor and loans to the struggling but honest. In a more efficient way the consolidated United Hebrew Charities continued the work.[9]

Although the Jewish Foster Home had been founded as early as 1855 by a group of women from Mikveh Israel, it struggled through its early years on a small scale with limited finances. In 1874 the management was transferred to a board consisting of men who thereupon expanded its operation and gave it a solid base of support. "Orphan Asylum" was added to its title and responsibilities, and in 1881 a large property on Mill Street in Germantown was purchased.[10]

The last of the major local institutions to be founded was the Young Men's Hebrew Association. A meeting chaired by Mayer Sulzberger in the spring of 1875 resulted in the formation of what was in its early days a club for the social intercourse and self-education of the intellectually inclined. It was, perhaps, the most democratic of the Jewish organizations. As its historian, William L. Langfeld, wrote: "The Mercantile Club existed for a restricted group, the congregations had a certain life of their own, but there was no general organization for personal social contact where everyone might mingle."[11] It remained, until the new building at Broad and Pine Streets was completed in 1924, a small-town friendly organization where the young men engaged in low-key athletics, relaxed and good-fun dramatics, and high-brow lectures series.

The first major attempt at joint fund raising was the first Charity Dinner, brought into being by the needs of the Hebrew Education Society, held on February 23, 1853. It was attended by 350 guests including the former vice-president of the United States, George M. Dallas, Mayor Charles Gilpin and other local non-Jewish celebrities. The dinner grossed over $5,000. Two-thirds of the proceeds went to the Hebrew Education Society, one-third to the United Hebrew Fuel Society. The second year the number of beneficiaries was increased by the addition of the Ladies' Hebrew Sewing Society and the United Hebrew Beneficent Society. Soon it was decided to have a ball instead of a dinner, and the Hebrew Charity Ball came into existence.[12] It became Philadelphia Jewry's principal social event and the only cooperative fund-raising medium until the emergence of the federation of Jewish Charities in 1901.

Among the many men and women who were active in the management of these charitable endeavors some names occur again and again as officers or on the boards of several agencies. It is fascinating how closely linked most of them were by business connections or family relationships. The post-Civil War era was one in which the comparatively open American society began to crystallize, to become exclusionary and to establish clubs and societies basing membership on circumstances of birth.[13] The Jewish community coalesced in much the same manner, but its aristocracy was created by philanthropic generosity and service rather than bloodlines. It was this aristocracy, overwhelmingly German in origin, that in 1853 founded the Mercantile Club. The social peak in the Philadelphia Jewish community was to belong to the Mercantile Club and to be chosen a manager of the Charity Ball, just as in the non-Jewish community it was to be a member of the Philadelphia Club and a manager of the Assembly Ball.

The presiding officer of the 1853 dinner was Abraham Hart, for many years a creative influence in the development of Jewish philanthropy. His father had come from Hanover; Abraham was born in Philadelphia in 1810. As a partner in the nationally successful publishing firm of Carey and Hart, he was as ubiquitous in the world of books as in Jewish communal enterprises. He was the first president of the first Jewish Publication Society, founded in 1845. Among Hart's many other responsibilities were those of treasurer of the Hebrew Education Society from 1848 to 1875, president of the Jewish Foster Home during 1874, president of the short-lived Maimonides College, and president of the Board of Delegates of American Israelites. It was Hart who, commanding the high respect of his fellows, chaired the meeting to consider the move of the Jewish Hospital to Broad and Tabor and the one that led to the founding of the YMHA. Hart, born of a German father and a Dutch mother, was president of Sephardic Mikveh

A Charity Ball at the Academy of Music, March 14, 1865, from *Frank Leslie's Illustrated Newspaper. (Library of Congress) Reproduced by courtesy of the Museum of American Jewish History.*

Israel for over 32 years, one of the more interesting manifestations of the nineteenth-century German-Jewish presence in Philadelphia.[14]

The real promoter of the Charity Dinner and the subsequent Hebrew Charity Ball was Isidore Binswanger. He was Bavarian-born, and he, too, was a member of Mikveh Israel. In 1846, at the age of 26, he settled in Philadelphia and went into the wholesale notions business with his brother-in-law, David Eger. They did well and opened a branch in St. Louis—a mistake, for the defalcation of an associate there brought Binswanger to the brink of bankruptcy. He did better with a Richmond granite company.[15] At the peak of his success in 1864, he was recorded as having a taxable income of $65,143. As with many men who flourished early in the war, Binswanger's income tailed off; in 1865, it was $40,820 and the following year only $13,050. Another Jew active in community affairs, the clothing magnate, Solomon Gans, reported an 1864 income of $69,819.[16]

Binswanger was elected to the first board of the Hebrew Education

Society in 1848, only two years after he arrived in Philadelphia, and he served as president from 1870 to 1878. He was also the first vice-president of the Jewish Hospital and the second vice-president of the United Hebrew Charities. As one of the men who assumed responsibility for the financial survival of the Jewish Foster Home, he served as its president from 1875 until 1890. It was a further measure of the esteem in which he was held that for almost twelve years he was reelected president of the Mercantile Club. Before he died in 1890, Binswanger established bequests from his estate to aid Russian Jews.[17] Another of his legacies was the ongoing interest of his descendants, who have remained among the comparatively few representatives of old German-Jewish families still active in Jewish communal life.

Binswanger's brother-in-law, Abraham Simon Wolf, was equally faithful as a community servant. Born in Virginia in 1809, he came to Philadelphia in 1838 and went first into the dry goods and then into the clothing business. Financial success on a larger scale came with his investment in coal lands. The offices he held read like entries in a Philadelphia Jewish *Who's Who*. Wolf was on the board of the Hebrew Education Society from 1848 to 1876, vice-president from 1849 until 1854, and president from 1854 to 1862. He was president of the United Hebrew Benevolent Society when it was merged into the United Hebrew Charities. His main interest, however, was the Jewish Hospital of which he was a founder. Wolf's contribution of $500 was the largest of the initial subscriptions. During the financial panic of 1873 he gave $1500 in an emergency campaign. From 1871 to 1878 Wolf was the hospital's president.[18]

The spider's web of connections continues, a reflection of a time when the Jewish community was small and everyone really did know everyone else's business. The first president of the United Hebrew Charities was Wolf's nephew and partner in the clothing business, Simon W. Arnold. His father, Mayer, had come from Ebenhausen and in 1822 married Fanny, Abraham S. Wolf's sister.[19] It is fascinating to note that a typographical error made Arnold the richest man in Philadelphia in 1864; the published statistics showed his annual income as an incredible $616,817![20] He was, nonetheless, well-off and generous, and he served on the board of the Jewish Hospital for a number of years.

The man who started the movement that resulted in the founding of the Jewish Hospital was Abraham Sulzberger who had emigrated from Heidelsheim in 1849. His son, Mayer—destined to be the most prominent and influential Philadelphia Jew of his generation, and in 1894 the first Jew sit as a judge of the local Court of Common Pleas—was brought to the city as an infant. Young Sulzberger was fortunate to enter the legal profession by clerking in the office nof Moses A. Dropsie. Mayer early became involved in Jewish education; while studying law he taught at the Hebrew Education Society. The institution was the main interest of his legal mentor, Dropsie, who was an officer or board member continuously from 1848 until 1892, twice occupying the office of president. Sulzberger also played a leading role in the Society.[21]

When the Jewish Hospital was founded, Mayer Sulzberger was chosen its first secretary and thereafter remained a member of the board. He was instrumental in bringing about the move from West Philadelphia to its present site at Broad Street and Tabor Avenue, and was an energetic fund-raiser on the hospital's behalf. In many ways he succeeded German-born Isaac Leeser as a national leader. As a young man Sulzberger edited the 26th volume of the most influential Jewish periodical, *The Occident,* which Leeser had begun publishing in 1843—coincidentally the year of Sulzberger's birth. In his memorial address on Sulzberger, referring to his taking over *The Occident,* Dr. Solomon Solis-Cohen observed, "Thus did Elijah cast his mantle upon Elisha."[22] On that same occasion in 1923, the recognized spokesman for American Jewry, Louis Marshall, summarized Sulzberger's career:

> Through him the Jewish Publication Society became a possibility. . . . He was one of the originators of the American Jewish Committee, and its first President. To his energetic intervention was due the re-organization of the Jewish Theological Seminary of America, and it was he that gave the initiative to the organization of Dropsie College and Gratz College.[23]

Sulzberger was also one of the American trustees of the Baron de Hirsch Fund, set up by a German Jewish philanthropist to aid the victims of Czarist persecution.

In 1901, when the Jewish Theological Seminary was on the point of failing, Sulzberger convinced the millionaire New York banker Jacob Schiff that, although Eastern European Jews were assimilating rapidly, they were bound to the concepts and rituals of traditional Judaism and would never accept Reform. Schiff, convinced that Conservatism provided an "American" way to maintain a quasi-orthodoxy that was not "foreign," poured millions of dollars into the Seminary. Sulzberger, aided by Dr. Solomon Solis-Cohen and Cyrus Adler, persuaded the Rumanian-born Solomon Schechter to leave Cambridge University and come to New York as the revived Seminary's academic head.[24]

The spider web of connections again appears: Sulzberger's successor as the intellectual motivating force of American Jewry was Cyrus Adler whose mother was a Sulzberger. Adler's career was more national than local. His first public position was at the Smithsonian Institution. He was present at the founding of the Jewish Publication Society in 1888 and, like Sulzberger, became chairman of its Publication Committee. Adler was the imaginative energy behind the organization in 1893 of the American Jewish Historical Society. In 1899 he was the first editor of the American Jewish Year Book, a responsibility which he shouldered until 1903 when he was joined for two years by Henrietta Szold. Long involved in the affairs of the Seminary, Adler became its president in 1908 and in the same year assumed the presidency of Dropsie College. He was active in the American Jewish Committee from its founding and was himself a founder of the National Jewish Welfare Board. Cyrus Adler was the last Philadelphia-based Jew to exert a major influence on national Jewish affairs.[25]

In Philadelphia Adler was an *eminence gris,* more a respected statesman than a participant in the day-to-day activities of the city's philanthropies. It is significant that except for a mention of his presidency of the almost invisible Philadelphia Kehillah from 1911 to 1915, all that his biographer, Abraham A. Neuman, could say about Adler's participation in Philadelphia communal affairs was of a general nature:

> His counsel was sought in every important communal endeavor, and it was almost inconceivable for the community to undertake any important project without his approval.[26]

He did exert a major influence over individuals, notably Horace Stern, who followed Sulzberger as the leading Philadelphia Jewish jurist.

While Sulzberger was vice-president of the Jewish Hospital, William B. Hackenburg was president. Hackenburg was born in Philadelphia, but his father had come from Coblenz. The younger Hackenburg conducted a highly successful business in silk. As his financial ability matched his community involvement, he assumed leadership roles. He was so active in the Hebrew Charity Ball that he was made an honorary member. He succeeded Abraham S. Wolf as president of the Jewish Hospital in 1878 and held that office for four decades. With the enthusiastic support of Sulzberger, Hackenburg pushed for the building expansion that resulted in the complex of medical facilities at Broad and Tabor. So prominent was his civic position that when the Town Meeting was held at the Academy of Music in March 1882 to protest Russian persecution of the Jews, Hackenburg was secretary. When the suggestion of federation was put forth in 1900, as the head of the largest Jewish institution in town with the best record for fund-raising, he wanted to be shown that joint fund-raising would help, not hurt, the hospital.[27]

Unlike many of the early nineteenth-century immigrants whose names had a Germanic sound, Alfred T. Jones was born in Boston of a Hollander father. He went first to New York, but came to Philadelphia in 1842 and, after several other ventures, in 1859 went into the printing business. He became the first president of the Jewish Hospital and a director until 1884, and vice-president of the Hebrew Education Society from 1861 to 1867.[28] More importantly, he was the editor of the *Philadelphia Jewish Record* in which, before the *Illinois* landed, he published accounts of the Russian atrocities and, as early as September 1881, the news that hundreds had assembled at Lemberg and were on their way via England to Philadelphia. Jones urged that help for them be organized.[29]

Early in October 1881, Jones and other officers of the Philadelphia branch of the Alliance Israelite Universelle and of the United Hebrew Charities met to raise funds, seek employment and find housing for the small flow of immigrants. Helping Jones was Arnold Kohn who took on responsibility for the employment committee. Kohn came to this country from Württemberg in 1850 and worked his way up from pedlar to partner in a thriving wholesale clothing business. He was on the board of the United Hebrew Charities. His intense concern at this early period for the welfare of the Eastern European Jewish immigrants was not shared by many.[30]

By the middle 1870s, a number of Jews from Poland and Lithuania had settled "with all the customs, observances and habits of the mother country" in the Port Richmond area.[31] In spite of a certain amount of resistance, the Hebrew Education Society at the end of 1879 opened a school to provide for "the educational and moral wants" of the Jews there. Subsequently three adjoining houses were bought and classes were held in manual training. As the demand for training in trades ballooned, another school was started on nearby Lark Street.[32] The directors were particularly proud of their cigar-making classes; in 1886, 30 boys received instruction in the cigar factory and 25 found jobs at satisfactory wages.[33]

There was far from a unanimous feeling of sympathy for the immigrants within the Philadelphia Jewish community, but the flood of refugees poured in and, like it or not, the situation had to be faced. At the annual meeting of the Hebrew Education Society, in March 1890, Moses Dropsie noted that there were between 26,000 and 28,000 Jews in Philadelphia:

> Of this number about 10,000 were born in Slavic and in Hungarian countries. This large population has settled in our midst within the last twelve years, their necessities have made great and increased demands on the Jewish charitable and educational institutions, and though many of that population have succeeded in becoming self-supporting, yet but very few of them are able to contribute or do contribute in relieving the necessities and caring for the well-being of their countrymen. It is a matter of gratulation that our Jewish community, faithful to the principles of Judaism are practically applying them in the relief of the wants, the amelioration of the condition, and the mental and physical education of these immigrants.[34]

Dropsie estimated the New York Jewish population at the time to be 80,000, but observed that the "patriotic pride of our New York co-religionists claims even a greater population than the number here given." It is of interest that by 1905 Charles S. Bernheimer put the number of Jews in Philadelphia at 100,000, 70 percent of whom were Eastern European immigrants and their children. New York at that same time counted 600,000 Jews.[35]

In the winter of 1885, seeking a way to ease immigrant women into American life, Isidore Binswanger's daughter, Fanny, with the help of 30 unmarried friends from the Women's Auxiliary of the Hebrew Education Society opened a kindergarten for the children of the "downtown" Jews, as the Eastern European immigrants who settled in Southwark were known to differentiate them from the "uptown" German Jews who lived in North Philadelphia.[36] The school was opened at 238 Pine Street with high purpose, since "It was felt that to make of the children good American citizens, to imbue them with the best American ideals, would be work that would ultimately give the best results."[37] The informal group became the Young Women's Union, and in 1918, the Neighborhood Center.

The Union provides an example of the connection between one generation of German Jews and the next as well as the emergence into leadership roles of their successors who, in the tightly knit community, married friends and philanthropic associates. Among the first donors to the Young Women's Union were Mrs. Abraham Simon Wolf and two Misses Phillips, women of the pre-Civil War era. Fanny Binswanger was Mrs. Wolf's niece. The first corresponding secretary was Martha Goldstein, soon to marry Barnett Binswanger, Fanny's brother.[38]

Among the earliest volunteer workers at the kindergarten was Rosina Fels, sister of Samuel, who was destined—with the aid of Fels Naphtha Soap—to become one of Philadelphia's most generous philanthropists. She was president of the Union. In 1896 the executors of the estate of Simon Muhr, Bavarian-born jeweler and an officer of almost every Jewish organization in town, offered the Union $5,000 if that sum could be matched in 30 days. It was. Members of families who were increasingly to take on major communal responsibilities were appointed to a Building Committee, among them Louis Gerstley, Helen Fleisher, Mrs. Charles Gimbel, Samuel Fels and Albert Wolf. Early in 1900 the building at 428 Bainbridge Street was dedicated.[39]

When Touro Hall opened in 1891, it was occupied by Sunday School and weekday sewing classes conducted by the Hebrew Sunday School Society, the office of the agent of the Association of Jewish Immigrants, the Hebrew school, night classes in English, and training groups in tinsmithing, dressmaking and carpentry.[40] The building was made possible by a gift to the Hebrew Education Society of $20,000 from the estate of Judah Touro of New Orleans[41] and a $15,000 bequest of Ellen Phillips who left well over $100,000 to local Jewish agencies in 1894.[42] A long-lived representative of colonial American heritage, Miss Phillips' grandfather, Jonas Phillips, came from Hesse in Germany to Charleston in 1756, having changed his name from Feibush to Phillips.[43]

Although women carried out much of the day-to-day work of the welfare agencies by visiting prospective beneficiaries and delivering food and clothing, it was only when the flood of immigrants changed the whole

The Hebrew Education Society, Seventh Street near Wood, 1880. *Courtesy of Maxwell Whiteman.*

character of local Jewish charity that the role of women as organizers and administrators received more than polite nods of approval from their fathers, husbands and brothers. In addition to the kindergarten the women of the Union established a "household" school to teach their poor cousins from the *shtetele* of Russia the proper American way to run a kitchen and manage a house. They taught kosher cooking and housecleaning, and took the children on group picnics in the country.[44]

Even more to the forefront of helping the newly arrived Russian and Polish Jews was the major Jewish welfare agency, the United Hebrew Charities. From 1875 until 1892 the agency had as its president Solomon Gans, the most venerable of an older generation. He had been born in Natzinger, Westphalia, in 1804, and came to the United States at age 30. Beginning as a tailor, he turned his skill into Gans, Leberman & Company, a wholesale and retail clothing firm which he ran for close to 40 years before retiring in 1873 to devote himself to civic affairs. It was said of Gans when he was at an advanced age: "Day after day, he spent hours of his time at the office of that institution (the United Hebrew Charities), listening to the appeals, and satisfying the wants of the poor."[45] An estimate of the increase in need can be gained by a comparison of expenditures for a quarter of a century from 1870. In that year, $13,350 was spent helping 682 individuals; in 1894, $46,536 went to aid 7986 persons.[46] Total needs were not being met. In 1893, an auxiliary branch of younger men established an employment bureau in Touro Hall. Significantly, two men who were to play the chief role in the formation of the Federation of Jewish Charities were then officers of the auxiliary: Louis Wolf, president, and Max Herzberg, corresponding secretary.[47]

According to the Victorian standards of charity that prevailed in late nineteenth-century Philadelphia, the inability of able-bodied men to support their families was attributed to laziness or lack of desire. The unemployed who were neither sick nor disabled were deemed unworthy of help. United Hebrew Charities did, however, aid families without a breadwinner or those stricken by illness, most commonly tuberculosis. To supervise the deserving poor, a committee visited each client at least once every four weeks. Each committee was responsible for no more than eight families. Good housekeeping methods and cleanliness were emphasized and taught by the women visitors. The men's auxiliary, in addition to seeking jobs for the newcomers, bought houses into which they moved families from overcrowded quarters, charging them only $10 a month rent for the more spacious rooms.[48] In the absence of social workers and federal relief programs, what was done was done by dedicated men and women who may indeed have shown their disgust at the stench and squalor of poverty—yet they braved it.

The United Hebrew Charities alone could not care for the flood of immigrants that landed on the Delaware River docks. The inability to do what was immediately necessary was seen by Jacob Judelsohn who was born in Marionpol, Russia, and came to this country in 1879. He called for help, and the call was answered by the formation in 1884 of the Association of Jewish Immigrants. The elderly Alfred T. Jones became its first president; the generous jeweler Simon Muhr was treasurer; and Charles I. Hoffman, one of the first editors of the *Jewish Exponent* when it was founded in 1887, was secretary. The Association's chief accomplishment was its support of an agent who met all the ships arriving in Philadelphia, acted as interpreter for the immigrants, helped seek their relatives and arranged for emergency bed and board.[49] In 1890 the Hachnosas Orchim, or Wayfarer's Lodge, sponsored by the Russian Jews themselves, took over the immigrant shelter.[50] After the death of Jones in 1888, Bohemian-born Louis E. Levy became president. Scientist and inventor of a practical method of photogravure known as Levytype, he was the real driving spirit of the immigrant aid society and made it effective.[51]

Although many times the number of immigrants who settled in Philadelphia went to New York, the established German-Jewish community there, far wealthier than their Philadelphia coreligionists, was fragmented. In his biography of Cyrus Adler, Abraham Neuman remarked:

"The relative absence of social intercourse among the leading Jewish citizens of New York astonished and baffled him on more than one occasion during the years he stayed in New York in the interest of the great projects upon which he was engaged."[52] It seems strange that this was so since the members of Stephen Birmingham's *Our Crowd* were "strikingly intramural when it came to marriage," as were the Philadelphians.[53] So indeed were "The Perennial Philadelphians" in Nathaniel Burt's upper-class web:

> Since Everybody is related or at least connected (it is a safe bet that there is nobody in this circle who is not related or connected by at least two or three removes to everyone else) and since Everybody remembers just exactly how Everybody is related and connected to each other, one's in-ness or out-ness is a pretty well-established fact.[54]

In many ways the German-Jewish community of nineteenth-century Philadelphia was self-contained, kept a low public profile and was similar to, but did not pretentiously imitate, upper-class society.[55] It is noteworthy that they called themselves "Hebrews" and were so called by polite Gentiles, but the immigrants were "Jews."[56]

That there was a difference of opinion concerning the steady inflow of Russian Jews within the Philadelphia community was perhaps inevitable. When the leaders of New York's Jewish philanthropies sought to restrict immigration, the managers of the Philadelphia Association of Jewish Immigrants castigated the New Yorkers at the annual meeting of the Association in 1886:

> . . . these friends, who are now enjoying the comforts and delights of prosperity, should remember their own antecedents—their own ancestry. They should bear in mind the important facts—that no matter how deficient these Russians and Poles, who comprise the great mass of those who now emigrate, may appear in education and refinement when judged by the standard of our Western civilization and culture, that they are far better than their surrounding in the old world. Remember it is not their faults, crimes or practices that have caused them to be driven hither, but the wretched issues of national prejudice.[57]

Only a year later, Judelsohn, then removed to New York, complained of an anti-immigration letter written by the officers of the Philadelphia United Hebrew Charities to the Secretary of the Treasury.[58] Part of the problem was indeed the inadequacy of funds. The leaders of the Philadelphia Jewish community may have been well off, but they were not men of great wealth. They had not accumulated fortunes as had the New York families of Schiff, Lehman, Warburg, Loeb, Seligman, Lewisohn and Guggenheim, who had financial resources far greater and lived on a scale far grander than any Philadelphia Jews. Furthermore, no Jewish businesses in Philadelphia before or after the turn of the century were as large or as profitable as those of some of their Christian fellow citizens. No Jews were possessed of dollars comparable to those of the coal barons, the railroad, streetcar and utility magnates, the textile manufacturers, the sugar refiners or the owners of chemical companies. And virtually all the nineteenth-century German immigrants had come to this country from villages, with no financial resources, and had by hard work made their way to middle-class competence. The Russian Jews, seeing them established and well-to-do, were sure they had arrived in America with pockets filled with gold.

The hegemony of the German Jews in the community's charities was comprehensively expressed in the hardbound *Souvenir Program* of the Hebrew Charity Ball which took place at the Academy of Music on February 7, 1899. The participants did not realize that in a year or two *the* social event of the German-Jewish establishment would cease to be. It is interesting to note that there has only once since been a Jewish "social" ball, as differentiated from a money-raising event without social pretensions.

The *Program* included advertisements from non-Jewish firms: Jacob Reed's Sons, the Pennsylvania Railroad, Western Union and others, as well as those of J. S. Bache & Co., bankers and brokers; H. Muhr's Sons, jewelers; Tradesmens National Bank, of which Augustus B. Loeb was vice-president; Lit Brothers, "The Leading Millinery House of Philadelphia," showing for the first time its ownership of the whole block of stores; and many New York wholesale houses. In their advertisement, A. Wimpfheimer & Bro. of Spring Street, New York, quoted Sarah Bernhardt as saying that their velvet was "of a superior quality."[59]

The "in" group, however, was gratified by the photographs and flattering biographical sketches of the men and women who were what is now termed "the movers and shakers" of the turn-of-the-century Philadelphia Jewish community. Many of them have been noticed earlier; the photographs indicate that, except for the bearded elders, almost everyone wore a moustache almost exactly like that favored by young Jewish and non-Jewish lawyers today. Eli Kahn Selig, a partner in the Kirschbaum clothing business, described perhaps grandiosely as "the largest of its character in the United States," was president of the Hebrew Charity Ball Association. He originated the idea of a "Souvenir Journal," first issued in 1898; he also married a Kirschbaum.[60]

Benjamin F. Teller, the secretary for 20 years of the Ball Association, was the first of a succession of Philadelphia Jewish real-estate entrepreneurs. He was secretary of the Jewish Foster Home, treasurer of a fund to endow a chair at the Jewish Theological Seminary in the name of Sabato Morais, and at the same time, in 1899, president of Rodeph Shalom. He employed 60 persons in his business, which occupied the whole second floor of the Ledger Building. Morais stated that his real-estate business was "by far, the largest ever known in the history of Philadelphia, and vieing [*sic*] with the

most extensive houses of the same kind in the United States." In 1893 he had
for rental or sale 6,000 houses and did $3 million worth of business. When
the *Jewish Exponent* was organized in 1887, he was chosen its president, and
he was for over 20 years treasurer of the Mercantile Club.[61]

One of the few honorary members of the Charity Ball was Levi Mayer,
who came to the United States from the Rheinpfalz in 1845. He settled in
Philadelphia in 1855 and eventually joined his brother-in-law, Elias Wolf, in
the wholesale clothing business. There were not many Jewish civic enterprises in which he was not involved. He was president of Rodeph Shalom,
an original member of the United Hebrew Charities, a manager of the
Jewish Foster Home and chairman of its education committee, treasurer of
the Hebrew Education Society and for almost 20 years chairman of the Ball's
Committee of Arrangements.[62]

In 1899, Samuel D. Lit, just emerging as one of the Jewish community's
most generous and most influential figures, was chairman of the Ball's executive committee. His photograph appeared in the *Program*, along with
biographies of Mayer Sulzberger and William B. Hackenburg, who shared
with Mayer the honor of being honorary members. In the rest of the volume
were printed portraits and brief sketches of the presidents of the Ball's
beneficiaries: Max Herzberg was included as president of the United Hebrew Charities, Leo Loeb holding that office in the Foster Home; Arnold
Kohn was listed as head of the Orphans' Guardians; Benjamin Wolf as
president of the Hebrew Education Society, together with his predecessor,
Isaac Rosskam; Julia Gans Arnold as the chief executive of the Jewish
Maternity Home, along with Julia Friedberger of the Young Women's Union and Louis E. Levy, president of the Association of Jewish Immigrants.
These were the German-Jewish leaders of the communal organizations,
most of whom were still in office when the Federation was formed in 1901.[63]

From 1882 to 1904, the number of Jewish immigrants who landed at the
port of Philadelphia was estimated at about 60,000. In a summary of the
situation of the immigrant there, Charles S. Bernheimer wrote:

> When the immigrant first arrives here, if he needs immediate aid or advice, the
> agent of the Association of Jewish Immigrants directs him. The Sheltering
> Home, a Russian Jewish institution, may keep him for a few days. Then the
> employment bureau of the Hebrew Charities, or the Baron de Hirsch Fund is
> brought into play, and he is found work. Later, he, or his family, may require
> the services of the hospital, the orphan asylum, or the burial society. All are
> provided for. It is still true that Jews do not become public charges as the
> result of dependency.[64]

In addition to the poverty of the arrivals and their language difficulties (as
well as the need to find them initial sustenance and lodging), there were
confidence men on the docks, seeking to take advantage of the greenhorns
and, worse yet, pimps offering a golden future to young, unaccompanied
females. The sums of money spent were a pitiful testimony.[65] The Associa-

tion secured quarters in Touro Hall, the major center of Jewish activity. Eventually the agency was incorporated into the Hebrew Immigrant Aid Society, well-known today as HIAS.

The sheer weight of numbers, the tension caused by the foreign ways and Old World appearance of the newcomers—a perceived threat to the hard-won German-Jewish position in the general community—on the one hand, and scorn of the "uptowners'" seeming lack of Jewishness on the other, created problems that led to antagonisms and frustrations. There simply was never enough money to solve the economic and welfare needs of the Eastern European Jews. Philanthropy was personal—the givers of the funds were those who dispensed them. Charitable Jews regularly took in struggling newcomers for Sabbath meals. Being an object of charity caused resentment. Harry Kalodner, a federal judge, never got over his antipathy to Morris Wolf because his father, a carpenter, had been the Wolf family's Sabbath guest. The friction between German bosses and Russian workers lasted only until there were Russian bosses too, and then place of origin could no longer be blamed for the sins of the bourgeoisie or the proletariat. Threatened by hordes of new Americans, the Jews, like the larger society around them, became exclusionary. The Mercantile Club, the Philmont Country Club, and most of the charities became citadels of German-Jewish society, small social organisms where many were related, others neighbors and all acceptable through business and civic connections. However, even with their exclusive social activities, the "uptown" German Jews maintained an inherited, traditional and inescapable feeling of responsibility for the welfare of fellow Jews that the general community, with the possible exception of the Quakers, never felt for their fellows in need.

This feeling, exacerbated by the frustration of too few persons with too little money faced by needs that not only seemed—but were—overwhelming, gave birth to the idea of a single Jewish community-wide fund-raising agency. Through the turn of the century the main source of revenue for the many separate charities had been the Hebrew Charity Ball, which over the years had brought in an average of $20,000 for distribution, supplementing bequests, memberships and a bewildering variety of functions, including dances, dinners, strawberry festivals, concerts, spelling bees, bazaars and "other wiles and blandishments." Advertisements were disproportionately obtained from New York wholesalers by their Philadelphia customers. Already the Jewish communities of Boston, Chicago and Cincinnati had successfully adopted the so-called Liverpool Plan of federated fund-raising. Max Herzberg, a lawyer with interests in building and loan associations and then president of the United Hebrew Charities, came back in 1899 from the National Conference of Jewish Charities, full of enthusiasm for the idea. He gained the interest of Louis Wolf, a fellow officer in the United Hebrew Charities and a paper-box manufacturer, one of the rising American-born generation of German Jews who were to maintain influential positions for the first three decades of the twentieth century.[66]

At their instance on February 10, 1901, representatives of the Jewish Hospital, United Hebrew Charities, Jewish Foster Home, Hebrew Education Society, Orphans' Guardians, Jewish Maternity Association, Jewish Immigrant Aid Society, Young Women's Union and Hebrew Sunday School Society met at the Mercantile Club "to consider the question of a Federation of Jewish Charities of Philadelphia." A committee was appointed to consider the matter. William L. Hackenburg, the perennial president of the hospital, made a separate motion "to invite representatives of the downtown societies to the next meeting." His suggestion—which might have strengthened the new body from its beginning and avoided the alienation of a large potential constituency—was defeated.[67] The committee voted unanimously that the scheme of Federation was both feasible and practical. Herzberg and Wolf furnished the best possible proof by soliciting some of the larger prospects and obtaining pledges for Federation amounting to $60,000, a sum representing enough of an increase over the same men's aggregate gifts to the separate agencies to convince even the most skeptical. A public meeting was called for March 17. Five hundred persons attended. They resolved

> That we, the Israelites of Philadelphia, members of the several Jewish Charity Associations thereof, deem it expedient and timely to form a Federation of Charities to the end that each several Charity may eventually be released from the necessity of collecting funds and also that the contributors may be enabled to pay their contribution to a single authority.

With Judge Sulzberger in the chair, a constitution and bylaws were adopted and officers elected. No officer or member of the board of any of the constituent agencies was to be eligible. To carry out the spirit of nonpartisanship the community sought as its first president Jacob Gimbel, a leading merchant but a man who had played little or no part in organizational life up to that time. Among the other officers and directors, most of them comparatively young, were Benjamin W. Fleisher, yarn manufacturer; Morris Dannenbaum, head of the Pine Tree Silk Mill; Samuel S. Fels of Fels-Naphtha soap; Edward Stern, printer; Louis Fleisher in the clothing business; Ely K. Selig, knit-goods manufacturer; Jacob D. Lit, department store owner; Samuel Kind, jeweler; Simon Miller in the shirt business; and Edwin Wolf, banker and broker.[68]

The last Charity Ball was held in 1901 and realized about $18,500; from other sources the separate agencies raised an additional $75,500. The first Federation drive secured $122,465 from 1,782 subscribers and allocated $113,185 to its constituents. The largest sums went to the Jewish Hospital ($32,505), the United Charities ($29,195) and the Foster Home ($20,030), reflecting as much numbers of past contributing members as urgent needs.

The Mercantile Club. *Courtesy of the Library Company of Philadelphia.*

Before the end of the year the National Farm School in Doylestown, a diehard dream of turning Russian Jews into American farmers and dispersing them across the land, and the Denver Hospital for Consumptives were admitted to constituency. The application of the Jewish Sheltering Home was turned down, but a small grant was given to the United Charities to be turned over for services rendered.[69] The Home had been taken over from the Association of Jewish Immigrants in 1890 by a group of "downtowners" who continued to operate a house for the temporary shelter of immigrants waiting to find employment, relatives or friends.[70]

Although most of the clients of the old agencies were Eastern European Jews, those agencies were controlled and managed by the second generation of German Jews. Poor health, and particularly tuberculosis, that resulted from slum living was found to be a major contributing cause of dependency on charity. The Jewish Hospital expanded immensely after the turn of the century as the result of large benefactions with the building of the Lucien Moss Home for Incurables (now Moss Rehabilitation Center), the Henry S. Frank Memorial Synagogue, the Meyer Guggenheim Private Hospital, and the Loeb Operating Building.[71] The Federation began its existence as an expression of the nineteenth century, but was faced with twentieth century problems. Buildings which had been adequate some years before were too small and too old. The community was not only supporting the operations of its charities; it was providing money at the same time for physical growth and improvement. As far as annual subscriptions to the Federation were concerned, the early years were ones of consolidation rather than increase.

The new century saw the emergence of new leaders, most of them the native-born sons and daughters of the earlier German-Jewish immigrants. For over half a century the Wolf and Gerstley families continued to be active in the Federation. Louis Wolf and his son Elias, and Morris Wolf and his son Edwin were all presidents of Federation, a span of three generations. The Gerstley-by-marriage presidents were Arthur Loeb, whose mother was a Wolf, Leon Sunstein and his son-in-law, Abraham L. Freedman. The Lits, Snellenburgs and Gimbels became major figures in the city and the community. The Fleishers flourished. By the early 1920s, Jules E. Mastbaum was the most prominent, most influential and most generous Jew in Philadelphia. As time went on, more successful Russian Jews took over the reins and complained bitterly that German Jews lacked generosity, little realizing that their own active participation in communal affairs and major financial support would, in most instances, not be continued by their children. Today there is nothing so fleeting as the memory of last year's "Man of the Year."

It is, perhaps, interesting after 80 years to record the thoughts of Henrietta Szold, the founder of Hadassah. In her summation of the year 1900–01 she wrote:

> The field of charitable work cannot be left without giving a word to a development, distinctly marked, that has been going on for some years, and has now culminated in many of the larger cities. In Boston, in New York, in Baltimore, in Chicago, in Philadelphia, institutions have been or are about to be created that duplicate the hospitals, the orphan asylums, the homes for the aged, established a generation ago. What impels this parallel movement among Russian Jews is dubious—whether the older asylums are not conducted with due regard to religious feeling; whether the social division line between the two classes is as sharp as some maintain; or whether the desire to prove their mettle exists on the part of those currently regarded as beneficiaries *par excellence*. The movement may be ill-advised—though there may be two views on the subject—it certainly is not discreditable.[72]

Henrietta Szold was the daughter of a German-born rabbi.

"Making Do": Jewish Women and Philanthropy

Evelyn Bodek

"At a period like the present, when all classes of the community are experiencing that the times are hard, that money is scarce, and the means of living costly, it behooves societies and individuals to investigate in what manner they may meet the difficulty with the least sacrifice of duty and convenience . . . Daughters of Israel! let us reduce our own personal wants, that we may not be obliged to economize in our charities; let us look among our superfluities for something to spare, over and above our usual contributions: for many applicants will be added to our pensioners' lists."[1] Thus wrote Rebecca Gratz, secretary of the Philadelphia Female Hebrew Benevolent Society, in 1857 in the midst of a severe economic depression. Her plea did not go unanswered, for Philadelphia Jewish women, like Jewish and non-Jewish women everywhere, were accustomed to catering to the needs of the poor, the sick and the indigent. In fact, in nineteenth-century America, charity was woman's work, the only work outside the home—with the possible exception of the teaching of young children—into which educated, affluent women were welcomed. Barred from businesses and professions by male prejudice and societal strictures, and from factory, mill, and shop by class and inclination, middle- and upper-middle-class women rushed to fill their leisure with volunteering. Their efforts were so successful that by mid-century women were operating a whole welfare system in towns and cities across the country; every major American city had its female societies for widows, orphans, the homeless, and the destitute.[2] Moreover, these thousands of anonymous women, in their response to local suffering, provided needed social services long before political leadership admitted the need for public intervention.[3]

By and large, historians have neglected these early efforts of women's benevolence. This is unfortunate because even a brief survey of women's charitable activities in the nineteenth century yields some valuable insights. Women were deeply committed to their community work, and their commitment benefited both themselves and their communities. The leadership roles of a handful of Philadelphia "German-Jewish" women who, from 1840 to 1900, dedicated themselves to local charity, illuminates this deep commitment. It also illuminates a hitherto unexamined aspect of female participation in volunteer work. For though the major thrust of their volunteering benefited the poor, the homeless, the sick and the destitute, it also benefited the women themselves. Community involvement provided women an opportunity to socialize. It afforded them an education in politics, economics, business administration and management impossible to obtain elsewhere. Also it enabled them to use their acquired skills, intelligence and native abilities outside of the home. This movement into the community gave women status and prestige, enhancing their self-image and assuring them a respected place among their peers.

By examining a small local segment of female volunteers we can pinpoint those factors responsible for the ebb and flow of women's participation in community charity, and, by extension, their contribution to certain aspects of our national life. Philadelphia's Jewish "Lady Bountifuls" began their activities in small female circles, usually attached to religious interests stemming from synagogue work. As local needs grew, women's groups expanded to meet them. By the turn of the century Philadelphia Jewish women had entered into almost every area of community work and had created institutions that would outlast the predominance and leadership of the female volunteer.

According to Digby Baltzell, the major prerequisite for leadership in charity work was the right background and upbringing. The woman who plunged into community work came from the "Jewish elite." This meant that she was born in the United States or that she or her parents hailed from western or central Europe. The appellation "German-Jewess" was used to distinguish her from the Eastern European immigrant who arrived after 1880. By the 1840s she and her family would have migrated to the area around Franklin Square. Probably she and her family would belong to the Sephardic synagogue, Mikveh Israel. By the 1880s, as the Eastern European immigrant population swelled Jewish ranks, families moved north and spread their synagogue affiliations. Wherever she lived, however, and whatever her synagogue affiliation, the German-Jewess's inclusion in the social and economic elite assured her the leisure to engage in philanthropic activity.[4]

Our knowledge of the education of these women is limited. Judging from their letters, cultural and social activities, and volunteer efforts they were fairly well-educated and at least well-read. An important part of their education was in philanthropy. Again, according to Baltzell, one's social position within the Jewish community was more dependent upon his charitable contributions than is the case in the Gentile community. Consequently the members of the Jewish upper class in Philadelphia took the lead in founding various charitable organizations.[6]

Male leadership roles in Philadelphia charitable institutions have been well documented and can be followed by a study of family names on subscription lists. It is obviously more difficult to untangle the web of female relationships responsible for the founding and continuance of women's societies. Nevertheless, a glance at the charitable subscription list suggests that the tradition of communal service was handed down by the distaff side of the family, as well as the male, with nieces, daughters, and even daughters-in-law following aunts, mothers, and mothers-in-law into community service.

In this respect, as in so many others, Rebecca Gratz (1781–1869) serves as the paradigm of the nineteenth-century Jewish volunteer. Gratz participated with her mother, the former Miriam Simon of Lancaster, and two of her sisters on the first Board of the nonsectarian Female Association for the Relief of Women and Children in Reduced Circumstances, founded in 1801.[7] She, in turn, was responsible for the participation of her nieces, sisters, and sisters-in-law in succeeding charitable activities.[8] Like her parents Rebecca was deeply religious and involved in her synagogue, Mikveh Israel. The latter and its rabbi, Isaac Leeser, were sources of inspiration, as well as financial and ideological support for many of her projects. Her religiosity and her long unmarried life were two decisive influences on her subsequent activities.

Religious obligation probably prompted Gratz and a few women from Mikveh Israel to found, in 1819, the first non-synagogal Jewish charitable organization in the United States, the Female Hebrew Benevolent Society. The women's original goal was to aid a handful of poor Jewish families, especially "their indigent sisters from the House of Israel."[9] For this purpose, Gratz and her friends organized themselves according to the prototype established by the earlier Association for the Relief of Women and Children in Reduced Circumstances. Characteristically, they "divided the city into districts, themselves into committees to cover each district, and set out to investigate the situation of applicants and administer to their relief."[10]

The Society was governed by a board of 12 or 13 managers and depended for its existence on annual dues and on free will offerings of goods and money. From time to time Mikveh Israel gave some financial support, and in 1843 when the Hebrew Charity Ball Association was founded to raise funds for various organizations, the Female Hebrew Benevolent Society became one of the recipients.[11] Each succeeding female society tended to

Portrait of Rebecca Gratz (about 1830) by Thomas Sully.
Courtesy of the Hebrew Sunday School Society.

adopt an organizational pattern that depended on these same voluntary contributions of time and money and on concepts of personal and often individualized service.

One characteristic of this early benevolence which was to surface again and again was the partiality shown to women's needs. Some historians claim this partiality cloaked a desire for autonomy; others maintain it indicated a mounting female radicalism.[12] It may, however, have been an empathy and a recognition that women's needs were not being met by the larger society. At any rate, the minute books, annual reports, and personal appeals of the Female Hebrew Benevolent Society do list scores of disabled, poor, destitute and deserted women. The Society supplied many with food, clothing, fuel, rent money, and other necessities, and often complied with unusual requests. For example, in 1848, a young girl who came to the United States looking for her brother found he had died. She asked the Society to aid her in returning home to Germany. The Society found an elderly gentleman to accompany her back home.[13]

As the numbers of less fortunate Jews increased, however, the women realized that personal relief would no longer suffice. Thus they began to provide various services, such as visiting nurses, doctors, a traveler's aid society, and an employment bureau for women and children. They also envisioned educating the children of these "indigent Israelites."[14] This flexibility in meeting expanding community necessities was a characteristic of women's benevolence that repeated itself throughout the century.

An awareness of the expanding needs of the poor coupled with a fervent religiosity led Rebecca Gratz and the women of Mikveh Israel to found the first Hebrew Sunday School in America. Beginning in the late eighteenth century, a formal Christian Sunday School movement had originated in Philadelphia and by the 1840s had formed the American Sunday School Union, but until that time there was no comparable Jewish institution. Jewish children whose parents desired they have a religious education had to set up meetings with private tutors or small classes in people's homes. That these options were not available to poor children, and that the public schools included Christian religious content necessitated an institution that would teach at least the rudiments of Judaism. Noting that "We have never yet had a Sunday School of our own," Rebecca Gratz called on her friends from the Female Hebrew Benevolent Society, and by 1838, the Hebrew Sunday School was born.[15]

In founding the Hebrew Sunday School, Rebecca Gratz was influenced by the Christian Sunday Schools, certain congregational attempts to found religious schools, and especially by her friend, Isaac Leeser, but still the Hebrew Sunday School was uniquely hers.[16] it was a community school unattached to any congregation. It was free and open to all, especially girls.[17] This was the first time girls were welcomed on an equal basis with boys in any school in Philadelphia.

The school, of course, was more than just a school. Its purpose was to serve and "save" the children of the community. As Gratz wrote to her sister-in-law, Maria Gist Gratz, the school would improve "a large class of children in religious knowledge" and gain "consideration in the minds of their parents." Hopefully it would also revive the "degenerate portion of a once great people . . . and induce wiser and better Jews to take the work in hand."[18]

Those parents who might be suspicious of, or opposed to, a school that sent teachers on personal visits to children's homes to inculcate the virtues of punctuality, respectful deportment, affectionate behavior to companions and a reverence for truth and industry[19] were admonished by Gratz to understand that nothing was expected of parents other than to "send them [children] decently attired and ready to receive instruction."[20] Those parents who could not provide clothing were aided by the Female Hebrew Sewing Society, an adjunct of the Female Hebrew Benevolent Society, and one of the many sewing societies of the day.

Besides ministering to the children of the Jewish community, the school provided single women, of whom there were many during this period, with employment and an outlet for their considerable talents. The four "founding mothers," Gratz, Louisa B. Hart, Ellen Phillips, and Sim'ha Peixotto, as well as many other volunteers, were unmarried. The four "mothers" served as teachers, superintendents, and managers of the school.[21] Peixotto, well-versed in Hebrew and Bible history, published a series of Bible questions for the school in 1839; her sister, Rachel, Mrs. Eleazer Pyke, contributed a rhymed catechism for young children in 1840. The story is often told of how Gratz, having no text, pasted little bits of paper over objectional passages of a Bible history written many years before by the Christian Sunday Schools.[22]

The school which required long hours of service from its volunteers became a labor of love for all who taught, planned its curriculum, and managed its affairs. Gratz, who taught every Sunday and was its President and Superintendent almost until her death, referred to her work there as "the crowning happiness of my days."[23] Peixotto became so attached that when asked to resign from the Board in 1885 at the age of 78, she refused: "I must state that I find myself so identified with said society in which I have ardently and lovingly labored . . . that I cannot voluntarily yield my position among you, and though no longer capable of active duty, . . . I am not a dead head, and can [still] serve in the holy cause."[24]

One of the reasons it was so difficult to leave was that the Sunday School, like other women's activities, was a focus of social life. Louisa B. Hart's home was often the center for after hours socializing[25] and Gratz was in the habit of calling pupils and teachers together for dinners and social gatherings to plan and discuss school functions.[26]

Though the Hebrew Sunday School fulfilled the needs of many of the community's women and children, by mid-century there were a number of poor, destitute, homeless children who needed more than a religious education; they needed a home. Gratz, whose earliest work had been with the Philadelphia Orphan Asylum, recognized this need. She had often pleaded with her sisters of the Female Hebrew Benevolent Society "to provide a home for destitute children and to obtain for them such a degree of early education as would tend to establish industrious habits and high moral and religious principles."[27] Isaac Leeser became an ally in Gratz's cause and promoted her ideas in his journal, *The Occident.*[28]

Leeser's backing plus that of other prominent men and women of the community, and the enthusiasm of the women of the Female Hebrew Benevolent Society finally resulted in the opening of the Jewish Foster Home at 799 North Eleventh Street in March 1855, with five children.[29] Like its sister organizations, the Home was governed by a female Board of Managers, required modest dues and depended on free-will offerings and gifts for sustenance. The appearance of a Board of Council of six gentlemen "for consultation and advice," however, indicated a change in the women's thinking. Money had always been a problem for women's societies; the Board of Council's main task was to raise money and conduct financial transactions. In this way the bulk of the managerial and administrative duties was left to the women.[30] While this step was viewed as both necessary and positive, it emphasized and gave recognition to the accepted spheres of male and female labor.

While the men raised the money, the women concentrated on rescuing children from the evils of ignorance and vice and instructing them in moral and religious duties so that they could become respected members of society. Morais complained of the paternalism that dominated women's early efforts,[31] but women's work in the Foster Home bespoke of a frustrated *maternalism*, a maternalism which would be extended at a later date to help "save" the community. In a religion in which family was so vital, motherhood bestowed status and occupation. Volunteering allowed childless women to create their own "families," thereby enhancing their own self-images while at the same time aiding the community. What Sarah Ann Hayes wrote about Rebecca Gratz might represent all of the single women: "My aunt . . . was an old maid, at least in the common acceptance of the term. True, she never married, but she was a mother to the orphan and the destitute, to the friendless and oppressed, to those in poverty and want, and to the sinner and contrite."[32]

These surrogate mothers provided for the education, feeding, clothing, and spiritual welfare of their charges. Although they hired teachers and a matron to oversee the total running of the Home, the "mothers" drew up a lengthy and detailed set of rules specifying the domestic care required for the children. Their linens, aprons and pocket handkerchiefs were to be changed twice a week, "their heads combed every day, and their whole persons bathed every day in summer in cold water, and twice a week in winter in tepid water."[33]

As the children's needs grew, or as the women perceived they did, new services and classes were added. In addition to an elementary education, children were given Hebrew and religious instruction. From 1863 to 1878 Peixotto taught Hebrew for the *Bar-Mitzvah*.[34] Music and gymnastics were added in the eighties, and an employment bureau in the late sixties.[35]

The Jewish Foster Home continued to grow throughout the century, moving its quarters to accommodate a larger population. Its establishment marked the culmination and signaled the end of the efforts of the earliest generation of women volunteers. It was the last institution connected with the Female Hebrew Benevolent Society, the last to be influenced by Rebecca Gratz and, with one exception, the last *major*, independent effort of

Rebecca Gratz in old age, about 1860. *Courtesy of the Hebrew Sunday School Society.*

Philadelphia German Jewish women. Shifting priorities, new stresses and strains and the dying off of the founding "mothers" gradually altered the nature of Jewish charity and women's participation in its management.

The Civil War imposed severe strains on Philadelphia Jewish Charities. Synagogues, welfare societies and individuals rose to meet the emergency. Mikveh Israel on Cherry Street was used as a hospital, women's sewing societies were used to provide clothing for the soldiers, and the Female Hebrew Benevolent Society extended itself to meet the needs of women displaced by the war.[36] On April 19, 1863, at the annual exercises of the Hebrew Sunday School Society, women were called upon for an even greater effort. At that meeting, as a result of the correspondence between Mrs. Mary Rose Smith, head of the Visiting Committee of the Women's Branch of the United States Sanitary Commission, and the Rev. Sabato Morais of Mikveh Israel, a letter was read asking for the "co-operation of the Jewish Ladies in the great work they have undertaken, and that a Jewish lady may be appointed to represent the congregation and report its action."[37]

Responding immediately, the Jewish Ladies held a meeting and elected

Matilda Cohen as their delegate to the United States Sanitary Commission. In addition, a week after their initial meeting on May 4, these women formed the Ladies Hebrew Relief Association for the Sick and Wounded Soldiers, and elected Celia Meyers as president.[38] According to the *Philadelphia Public Ledger,* the Association's objective was "to provide sick and wounded soldiers, irrespective of religious creed . . . with delicacies and clothing while they lie in army hospitals."[39]

Within a month the women's efforts added 250 members to the Society. By May 1865, Rebecca Moss, secretary, reported that ten crates of supplies had been sent to the Commission.[40] Jewish women also contributed to the Sanitary Fair held in Philadelphia, June 1864. Nine young women organized a club called "Alert" to prepare embroidery and needle work.[41] Among the list of Jewish women on the many committees of the fair were Mrs. Henry Cohen, Mrs. Marian J. Moss, Mrs. Morris S. Stroud, Louisa Gratz, Rachel Morris, and Rebecca Moss.[42]

In many ways the Civil War was a turning point and a transition for Jewish charitable endeavors and women's leadership in charitable activities. Less than six months after the war, and probably prompted by their experience with the sick and wounded, a group of prominent men formed the Jewish Hospital Association to establish a Jewish hospital in the city.[43] In 1869 a similar group merged several of the small competing relief agencies in the city into the United Hebrew Charities.[44] Women played auxiliary roles in both organizations. Although the men of the Hospital Association thanked the "daughters of Israel . . . enlisted in the cause,"[45] and invited a number of ladies on its board, the officers, a majority of the Board, and the policymakers were men. The latter asked women to visit wards, serve on sewing circles, and solicit membership.

Similarly the United Hebrew Charities excluded women from "the general executive duties and the charge of the financial department" which were under the sole direction of the male Board. The Board assigned women the "noble self-sacrificing labors of visiting the poor, comforting the afflicted, attending the wants of the sick." It also gave them "the entire control of the clothing department."[46]

The Ladies Hebrew Sewing Society and the German Ladies Hebrew Benevolent Society (founded in 1843) were the only two women's organizations to join the United Hebrew Charities. The Female Hebrew Benevolent Society, though willing to contribute "to the extent of its limited income" by paying rents, supplying nurses and joining as efficient members of the district visiting committees, refused membership. The men accused them of "pride of age," but they probably preferred remaining small and independent and able to control all aspects of their organization to being consigned to a narrower sphere of action.[47]

Although the women of the Jewish Foster Home retained their independence, it was not long before financial difficulties, which plagued the

Sewing class in "Jewtown" (Port Richmond), 1880. *Courtesy of Maxwell Whiteman.*

institution from its inception, altered this state of affairs. In 1875 the Home became the Jewish Foster Home and Orphan Asylum and changed its by-laws and constitution, placing governance in an all male Board. Because it was considered important "to have men in the direction of the Home with particular reference to obtaining financial assistance and to perform executive duties,"[48] women were reduced to forming a Ladies Associate Board; Matilda Cohen was its first president, and Evelyn Bomeisler was its secretary. Under the new plan women *assisted* the Board of Managers in the internal affairs of the Home and supervised the children. A male superintendent replaced the matron in general charge of the Home, the latter remaining responsible for domestic arrangements and child care.[49]

The gradual drift toward consolidation and reorganization which gathered momentum as the century progressed continued to consign women to a special sphere, depriving them of executive and financial responsibilities. This trend, though powerful, was only one of several which dominated women's volunteer activities after the war. In certain cases women expanded existing agencies to meet new situations, in others they created new societies to meet new needs.

An example of the expansion of existing agencies is the response of the Hebrew Sunday School Society to the growing Eastern European population in the Southern area of the city. Although it is generally acknowledged that the eighties witnessed the phenomenon of a burgeoning immigrant population from Eastern Europe which doubled the number of Jews in the city in a decade,[50] there is evidence that pressures were felt before this. In

The Jewish Foster Home, about 1915. *Courtesy of the Philadelphia Jewish Archives Center.*

1872 the School, under the superintendency of Ellen Phillips, divided into two branches. The Northern School served the established German Jewish population firmly entrenched in the area between Race Street and Columbia Avenue, and between Third and Ninth Streets. The Southern School attempted to serve the Eastern European immigrants who settled south of Spruce Street and East of Broad.[51]

In addition to responding to the population pressures, the Hebrew Sunday School proved its flexibility by meeting another challenge. In 1876 Laura Mordecai discovered on one of her visits to her pupils' homes that their faith was being undermined by Christian missionaries who competed for the allegiance of immigrants settling in the Port Richmond and South Philadelphia area. Children attending Hebrew school in the morning dropped into Christian sewing schools in the afternoon. They were lured there by pictures, books, and tickets for free classes.[52] Mordecai lost no time reporting her findings. She suggested the founding of a Hebrew Sewing School to counteract the sinister motives of missionaries, who on the plea of teaching our daughters to make their own garments, would rob them of the most precious ornament—their belief in the unity of God.[53]

In response the Hebrew Sunday School Society opened three schools.

The Rebecca Gratz Sewing School opened April 23, 1876, with 8 teachers and 53 "scholars" at Tenth and South, then the site of the Southern School.[54] This was followed by the Louisa B. Hart Sewing School located in Rodeph Shalom at Fifth and Parish, and another in the same year, 1880, in the Hebrew Education Society on Lark Street in Port Richmond.[55]

These schools moralized openly. Their goals and the goals of much of women's charitable endeavors during the period of the 1880s and 1890s are well articulated in the following appeal for funds for the Louisa B. Hart School:

> It is a mistake to imagine that simply the use of the needle is taught; in more than one sense it is a "sewing" school stitches *are* set, it is true, . . . they are drawn together to acquire neatness and thrift, to have economy and household virtues added to their attributes, but the rudiments of a broader education are also given them—their spiritual as well as temporal wants are supplied . . . their characters and aims are straightened and regulated quite as perseveringly as their stitches.[56]

During the seventies another quarter pressed its needs upon Jewish women. A Mr. Jacob Friedman, whose professional duties as mohel brought him into contact with many young mothers, apprised a group of women of the terrible condition of so many young, helpless, suffering mothers.[57] Always empathetic to the needs of their sex, a few women met at Anshe Emeth Synagogue on November 30, 1873, and formed the society *Ezrath Nashim* (Helping Women). The Society's purpose was "to aid and assist poor Jewish women during confinement." A seven-member, all-female Board of Directors managed the organization. Its first president, Mrs. Esther Amram, whose husband David was the only man among the first six subscribers, served as its head officer for 22 years. Members paid dues of 25 cents monthly or three dollars annually.[58]

For about the first 20 years of its existence the Society had no permanent home. Volunteers accompanied by nurses and doctors climbed dark narrow stairs to enter small, dark, stifling apartments, crowded with large families, to offer food, clothing, and empathy, as well as medical treatment.[59]

After the mid-eighties, this personal, ad hoc service could not hope to meet the crush of immigrants from Eastern Europe. Hence, in 1891, the Society reorganized as the Jewish Maternity Home, increased its managers from 7 to 16, maintained the stipulation that ten would always be women,[60] and purchased a building at 534 Spruce Street as its permanent home. By 1895 it had expanded from a personal ladies' visiting society to a Nurses' Training School, a Seaside Home for Invalid Women and Children, and a Nursery or temporary home for children. It also had a sewing circle which met in women's homes and contributed goods to the association.[61]

The men added to the Board never controlled the Society. In her last

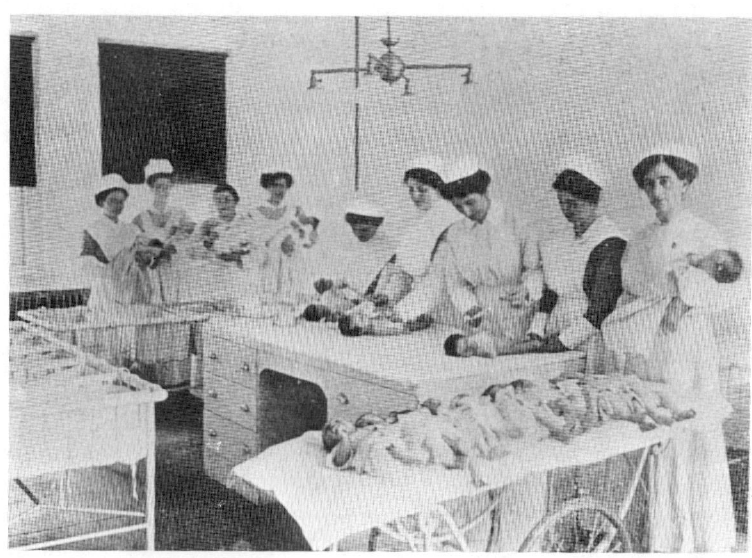

Nursery of the Jewish Maternity Home, 534 Spruce Street, in 1914. *Courtesy of Temple University Urban Archives.*

Annual Report, Esther Amram maintained that the Society was "essentially a women's Society—its purpose, its foundation and its management have stamped it as such."[62] Women continued to serve as officers and staff the committees of the Society. It is interesting to note, however, that the sole members of the Finance and Building and Property Committees were men.

Like earlier societies the Maternity Home had a dual agenda. It still relied on its Ladies Visiting Committee to assure that "only the deserving and needy receive assistance." Once the applicant was found worthy, the doors of the Home were opened wide. The needy woman was "brought into an atmosphere of cleanliness, of refinement, of quiet, calm and peace, such as her life [had] never known before." It was hoped that after a stay in the Home, she would return to her home with the "lessons of cheerfulness and cleanliness and of order impressed in her mind," and that these lessons would manifest themselves in the future conduct of her household.[63]

These efforts to influence the character and values of their less fortunate co-religionists intensified as the immigrant population increased during the last two decades of the century.[64] The community called upon its women to take their manners, their morality and their empathy into immigrants' homes and introduce them to civilized ways. Even Alfred T. Jones, editor of the *Jewish Record* and generally sympathetic to the immigrants, wanted women, through missionary work and education of children, to end the ghetto.[65] Communal philanthropy utilized the "Ladies" as an auxilliary force, almost an "army," to socialize and acculturate the poor, the ignorant, the destitute with their superior "weapons" of domesticity, piety, and moral motherhood.

Thus when the Philadelphia branch of the Alliance Israelite Universelle received word that the steamship *Illinois* had left Liverpool on February 11, with hundreds of Russian immigrants on board, it immediately created a Ladies Auxiliary to deal with families, and placed representative "ladies" on each of its committees.[66] The United Hebrew Charities reorganized its ladies auxiliary to handle the influx of families besieging the office on Friday mornings. The women were organized into committees of two or three; each committee was assigned five or six families and visited each of these in their homes bringing envelopes containing sums apportioned. On March 9, 1892, the United Hebrew Charities further refined personal visiting by establishing a Personal Interest Society, with Esther Baum as its first president. The object of the Society was for "each person or persons to take care of a family who are in destitute circumstances, . . . see that they are properly employed and . . . look to their general interest."[67]

Increased personal visitation, however, could no longer adequately meet the pressing needs of the immigrants who, in addition to food, clothing, and shelter, required language and work skills, medical attention, schooling, and day care facilities. It was primarily in response to the latter that Fanny Binswanger invited 30 unmarried women to meet on February 5, 1885, at the Young Men's Hebrew Association to organize a kindergarten to teach English to children of Russian immigrants. The women, under the auspices of the Hebrew Education Society, formed the Young Women's Union, and opened, on March 1, 1885, a kindergarten with 15 children at 238 Pine Street. The young women who taught at the school also provided the children with food, clothing and medical care, and visited homes to keep in close contact with the families of the children.[68]

Within a year the community's growth necessitated a larger kindergarten and a multiplicity of services. In response the Union moved several times, finally settling in February 1900, at 422–28 Bainbridge Street in South Philadelphia. In 1886 the women established a Household School for girls ten to thirteen, with Amelia J. Allen at its head. The school gave instruction in household management, domestic duties, sewing, cutting garments, millinary and mantua making, and typing. Working girls were encouraged to attend on Sundays so that they could come "under the critical observation and direct supervision of the managers of the society." In 1888 Mary Cohen taught working girls English, reading and arithmetic in the evenings. In the same year, in conjunction with the non-sectarian Country Week Association, the Union sent 42 children to the country for two weeks. By 1909, 1,127 children were able to enjoy a country vacation.[69] In 1893 the Union met the needs of working mothers and those who because of illness could not properly care for their children. They established a day nursery and shelter. Every child admitted to the shelter was thoroughly examined and vaccinated.[70]

Venturing well beyond its original purpose, the Young Women's Union created a Penny Savings Bank in 1895 to encourage thrift. In the same year, the nucleus of what was to become the Graphic Sketch Club emerged in art classes given by Samuel Fleisher.[71] The next year Henrietta Szold taught an evening course in American literature.[72] In 1898 the Union continued its efforts to reach working girls and organized a Working Girl's Club that would bring cheer and entertainment and foster fellowship among working women.[73]

In its activities the Young Women's Union, founded four years before the first settlement house in the United States, was taking on the trappings of a settlement house. It also provided education for young single women, outlets for their energies, talents, and social conscience, and made special provisions for their membership in the Union. Although previous societies included large numbers of single women, no special provisions had been made for them. In the early years of the Union, membership was limited to only unmarried women; once married a woman became an associate or contributing member, but was not allowed to sit on its Board.[74] By 1906 the specification of unmarried was dropped from the constitution, but "any unmarried Jewess (still) paying $1.00 a year" could be a member. Dues for all "other Israelites" were $3.00.[75]

At this point one must ask why the Union singled out unmarried women when previously they simply worked alongside their married sisters. A partial explanation can be found by looking at certain changes in American society after the Civil War, changes which affected the status of women, thereby causing a certain ferment in the Jewish community.

After 1865 American women were presented with many more opportunities to pursue their professional, educational and career objectives. By the late 1870s and 1880s, coeducational and women's colleges proliferated, a domestic revolution enabled women to leave the drudgery of housework behind and an increased pool of unskilled immigrant women offered household help to those who could afford it. Thus upper- and middle-class Jewish women could now work to enhance their own self-esteem directly instead of working for and through others. But Jewish women, like their non-Jewish sisters, were under serious disadvantages: in the late nineteenth century opportunities for women to educate themselves and to work in the business and professional worlds were severely limited; then too, the public at large still advised women to remain at home in their appointed sphere. Jewish women's time-hallowed place in the family put an added burden on those women who wished to be out in the world yet also wanted to remain faithful to Judaism and its traditions.

This tension is reflected in the Jewish press. Though there were a few references earlier in the century to "Woman's Place," the last three decades witnessed a growing debate on the subject in the *Jewish Record* and the *Jewish Exponent*. Both papers recognized that women were making advances, but doubted that they would or should ever achieve equality with men. The laws of nature had assigned woman to the home; that was her sphere. From the home her duty was to "promote purity, piety, and virtue in society."[76] When she stepped out of her sphere, the whole world suffered. A noted New York rabbi blamed all of the world's ills on women who have forgotten their "only noble, true sphere of action."[77]

As scholars searched the Talmud and antiquity to find models of subordinate women, and women's columns elevated homemaking to a science to satisfy women's new thirst for learning, a few women protested that "all women were not born simply to adorn the household fireside."[78] In 1886 Mary Cohen, Matilda Cohen's daughter, read a paper to the Philadelphia Social Science Association which insisted on the intellectual equality between the sexes.[79] Nina Morais, daughter of Rabbi Sabato Morais, championed women's suffrage in a variety of journals, and Judith Solis-Cohen, under the pen name Guidetta, edited a column in the *Jewish Exponent* in which she expressed advanced views on women's education and suffrage.[80]

It is noteworthy that these young women and others were active in benevolent activities and came from families in which the traditions of communal service and philanthropy were emphasized. Nevertheless, as late as 1897, the *Exponent* carried an article stating that "the tendency of the Jewish woman to emancipate herself is certainly to be regretted."[81] Another article asked "Does college make the Jewish girl irreligious?"[82] "The School of the Jewess is at home!"[83] Nina Morais was an acceptable intellectual only because she was thought of as an unassuming girl with a practical knowledge of the "woman's sphere." She was considered a model housekeeper for her widowed father, and took excellent care of half a dozen younger sisters.

Obviously the changing opportunities for women were accompanied by fear of change in the Jewish community. The story is told about Fanny Binswanger, who wanted to go to college, but whose father was against the idea.[84] She created an alternative, an organization within which young single women could work without overstepping the bounds of propriety. Seen in this light, the stipulation of the Union about single women made a great deal of sense. It continued the tradition of Rebecca Gratz's generation, whereby unmarried women served the community while at the same time carving a place for themselves within the established religious conceptions of womanhood.

Toward the end of the century the parochialism exhibited by local agencies was challenged by a new organization, the National Council of Jewish Women. This was the first such national organization in the United States and the last to be dominated by German-Jewish women. Founded in Chicago in 1893, its aims were to promote religion, philanthropy, education

Nursing students at Jewish Hospital, about 1910. *Courtesy of the Balch Institute for Ethnic Studies.*

social reform and, in the words of its first president, Hannah Solomon, "practical good works."[85] Basically the organization was designed primarily to educate women in Judaism through various projects such as educating Jewish immigrants, sponsoring work rooms and visiting women in jail. However, though it professed to speak for and to all Jewish women, the organization was elitist. This elitism was reflected in the tendency to give some speeches in German, to hold meetings in the afternoons when working women could not attend, and to deliver papers that addressed such topics as the "Attitude of Women of Leisure to their Wage Earning Sisters."[86]

On May 14, 1894, Philadelphia Jewish women organized a branch of the National Council of Jewish Women. Laura Mordecai, Rebecca Gratz's niece, served as its first president. The Council contributed little to local philanthropy. Instead, in conjunction with the Hebrew Education Society, it established a sewing school and was active in combatting missionary activity in the city. It is also believed to have formed a contingent of women to meet female immigrants at the docks to save them from the perils of the "White Slave Traffic."[87] In 1896 the branch contemplated "mothers' meetings among Russian Jews." In the words of Mordecai, however, Philadelphia was "handicapped by many existing charity organizations."[88] Thus the Philadelphia section devoted itself to education.

The almost 200 women of the Philadelphia Section met twice monthly in one another's homes to read papers, ask questions and discuss the Bible, Jewish history and topics of contemporary interest. Mrs. Charles Hoffman, the former Fanny Binswanger, held the first study circle in her home at 1517 Centennial Avenue. These meetings, held in the afternoons at the homes of prominent married women,[89] covered such topics as, "What Was and Is the Messianic Idea among the Jews?" "The Mental, Moral and Physical Training of Children," and "Our Sabbath Schools—What They Are and What They Should Be."[90]

Jewish women were beginning to interest themselves in "higher education." It has been suggested that Jewish women were slow to avail themselves of formal higher education after the Civil War.[91] If this was the case, then it is a sign of tremendous ingenuity and creativity that these women who, because of family prejudice, traditional religious beliefs or personal inclination, were reluctant to rush into formal institutionalized educational establishments, created their own community of learning within their special province of benevolence. In many ways they can be likened to the English Bluestockings or French *Salonniers* who a century earlier had utilized their traditional hostessing roles to create situations within which they could learn.[92]

The tendency for Jewish women to begin to concentrate on study and self-enrichment was not limited to married women, nor was it a special manifestation of the National Council. In the seventies and eighties the synagogues, local clubs, and Young Women's Union offered women classes in literature, language, Bible study and other subjects. The popularity and appeal these classes had for women is evident in women's activities in the YMHA. In 1878, when women were admitted to "contributing" membership, they devoted themselves wholeheartedly to establishing classes in French, German, literature, dramatics, art and gymnastics. Many prominent, "charitably oriented" women such as Mary Cohen, Judith Solis-Cohen and Esther Amram took the lead in organizing the educational activities of the "Y." Their efforts and the efforts of many other female teachers, students and volunteers helped women straddle the transitional period during which college was not yet acceptable for the "cultured Jewess."[93]

The National Council of Jewish Women helped Jewish women bridge another gap, that of political participation in the larger community. The view is still common that social reform in America was largely the work of Protestants, that few Jewish women were involved in any of the larger moral crusades of the century. Their names do not appear on the lists of those women actively opposing slavery. They were not a part of the network of rural women's associations that formed the backbone of the Temperance and Suffrage movements.

One of the factors which may have kept Jewish women out of the suffrage movement until its later stages was the small Jewish population; by 1880 American Jews, mainly of German origin, numbered about 250,000. An additional factor may have been antisemitism. By the eighties, the Woman's Movement had an anti-immigrant character. Jewish women who were aiding their co-religionists could not help but be alienated from it.

Nevertheless Jewish women's involvement in the National Council, plus their admission to the world of "women's clubs" which concentrated on broad cultural, ethical, historical, and political interests, broadened *their* interests to include social issues. Besides, the National Council emphasized women's rights in a Jewish context. There were continuing debates about the place of woman in society, her right to an education, her dependence on man[94] and a rather protracted discussion on the necessity of an official Council journal which would be run by women.[95] Specifically, the Philadelphia Section supported two political issues in 1896. It petitioned the legislature to raise the age at which children could be employed in factories from twelve to thirteen, and it participated in a survey of religious schools and school boards to determine whether women were adequately represented. Through its efforts in the latter cause two more women were placed on boards of city Sunday Schools.[96]

Ironically, in opening up a new vista for Jewish women, the Council and the club movement introduced the Jewish woman to a wider world and consequently weakened her role in charitable activities. The small benevolent circle to which the nineteenth-century "Jewess" belonged and in which she utilized her talents and energies for the community, was becoming only one of many institutions for women who wanted to fulfill themselves beyond marriage and family. Industrialization and urbanization, with the breakdown of strong family ties and the loosening of traditional values, encouraged the twentieth-century Jewish woman to seek self-fulfillment and professional advancement outside the community.

By the late 1800s, the women's societies, born in an antebellum period when the privileged Jewish community was small and more or less cohesive, was dominated by unified religious and family values. They were simply not equipped to cope financially, organizationally or ideologically with the multiplicity and complexity of problems unleashed by the increased numbers. Lack of funding for the increased population and the rise in juvenile deliquency, crime, transiency, family desertion, serious illness and prostitution were overwhelming. In addition, the Russian immigrants, perhaps resenting the attitudes of women who wanted to provide them with "moral uplift," formed their own self-help societies, and were often hostile to interference with their way of life.[97]

The general inadequacy of volunteering led to the professionalization of social work at the end of the century. Professionalization demanded schooling, licensing, and status and signaled the end of leadership positions for women in local agencies. Women who had learned on the job, who had years of experience and expertise would be passed over by the professional who, in the early years, would almost certainly be male. The situation of the woman volunteer was akin to the midwife in early modern Europe who, barred from male-dominated universities and medical schools, was dissuaded from practicing her profession and gradually replaced by the male obstetrician. Without belaboring the analogy—professionalization meant male institutions which in turn meant limiting the social service career aspirations of women.

Along with professionalization, coordination, rather than proliferation, of agencies became the trend in the twentieth century, encouraging consolidation rather than competition for funds and personnel. In 1901 the movement to consolidate Philadelphia's Jewish charities culminated in the founding of the Federation of Jewish Charities, an entity designed to coordinate fund raising and planning for the Jewish community.[98] The executive leadership of the Hebrew Sunday School Society, the Jewish Maternity Home and the Young Women's Union participated in the discussions leading to the formation of the Federation. They joined the Federation immediately. Characteristically, the Female Hebrew Benevolent Society declined an invitation to join, but did eventually accept membership.

The founding of the Federation was another watershed for female leadership in Jewish charity. Though women retained leadership roles in their own agencies, none became officers or members of major committees of the new organization. Moreover, the twentieth century witnessed the decline or disappearance of those few agencies in which women had executive positions. The Female Hebrew Benevolent Society, the Hebrew Sunday School Society and the Philadelphia Section of the National Council of Jewish Women maintained relatively few members, and today have remained at the periphery of charitable activities in Philadelphia.[99]

The story of the role of women in the new Federation and in twentieth-century benevolence and charitable activities belongs to another chapter. Jewish women's role in the nineteenth century was certainly a unique one. For about 100 years Jewish women, like their Christian sisters, took control of what had been the responsibility of the town fathers in Europe, and of what would become the responsibility of the new "welfare state" and local and national charitable organizations in the United States and Europe. Because of a combination of circumstances—pressing local needs, a fluid and constantly shifting social structure, women's intense needs to fill their leisure with productive and satisfying work—women filled leadership roles in local community charity. By so doing they contributed to the origin and growth of many benevolent institutions, learning new skills along the way. The fact that women lost their primacy in local charity is reflective of changes in the nature of charity itself, the social structure, and most importantly, the constantly changing image and position of women in our society.

"The Philadelphia Group"

Maxwell Whiteman

In the crucial period of the great immigration of Jews from Eastern Europe, Philadelphia Jewry assumed a leadership of importance and sophistication in American society that has been blurred and neglected.

Today some of these Philadelphians are little known. The activities of some are forgotten; the involvement of others in American Jewish institutional life has faded and their national influence considerably diluted.

Who were these Philadelphians? What institutions did they found or influence? And what was their connection with such prominent New Yorkers as Schiff, Marshall, Kohler, the Strauses, the Seligmans and a long list of others scattered throughout the nation?

The institutions in which they were cast in principal roles, the Hebrew Immigrant Aid Society, the Jewish Theological Seminary, the Baron de Hirsch Fund, the American Jewish Committee, the Jewish Publication Society and many others, emerged in the three decades between 1880 and 1910. They were the product of the changing face of American society, the result of the greatest Jewish immigration in world history up to that time and the willingness and ability of Jews of German background to confront this vast transformation in Jewish life. Philadelphians reacted swiftly to these shifting conditions.

The complex problems of immigration made demands upon the most talented men whose course in life had determined for them other careers. Had this immigration not taken place it is likely that Louis Edward Levy, instead of devoting 35 years of his life to the problems of immigrants, would have worked exclusively in his laboratory as a chemist, inventor and a pioneer in the development of modern photography.[1] Sabato Morais, minister of Congregation Mikveh Israel, would have furthered his studies of Italian Hebrew literature rather than struggle to build the new Jewish Theological Seminary in New York City.[2] Judge Mayer Sulzberger would have continued to devote more time to his bibliophilia, the pursuit of the law and his numerous civic and social obligations as one of the first proper Jewish Philadelphians in post-bellum Philadelphia rather than immerse himself in the future of New York Seminary, the Dropsie College, the active presidency of the American Jewish Committee and other institutions of national as well as local interest.[3]

Sulzberger's cousin and silent worshipper, Cyrus Adler, may not have surrendered his post of librarian at the Smithsonian Institution to also involve himself in the success of the Seminary, the Jewish Publication Society and the American Jewish Committee. During his unusual career checkered by a domineering personality, Adler could boast concomitantly, the presidency of five major Jewish organizations. His work with the Jewish Publication Society brought him into intimate contact with Rabbi Joseph Krauskopf and Dr. Solomon Solis-Cohen.[4] Solis-Cohen might never have probed the causes and treatment of tuberculosis without the immigrant as a clinical resource. He was the first American born champion of Zionism in Philadelphia prior to 1900. But his true claim to fame came as the founder of the present Jewish Publication Society—a claim which Krauskopf sought to preempt for himself and one which history has not yet reconciled.[5] Krauskopf however is not to be lightly brushed aside because of this; his 33 volumes of Sunday Sermons brought him national fame and molded the cause of social justice as advocated by the reform rabbinate.[6]

A far more complex figure and an associate of the Philadelphians under discussion was Moses Aaron Dropsie whose image has been distorted by the presidents of the institution he made possible. Dropsie's passionate contempt for the preachings of the reform movement in Judaism and his disappointment in the location of the Seminary in New York were responsible for the provisions of his estate that made possible a specialized institution for higher Jewish learning. That it was to be completely nonsectarian was an expression of affection for his Dutch Calvinist mother who urged upon him the perpetuation of Judaism. In its early years the Dropsie College attracted an array of scholars choosing a faculty eminent in each field of Jewish studies.[7]

It is important to note that the Philadelphians lacked the real wealth of the New Yorkers who were immersed in the world of business and finance. But Philadelphians had attained respectability and prestige in the social and cultural circles of a highly conservative city when such status was presumed only for well-to-do New Yorkers. Blending into the elite criteria established by descendants of the city's older non-Jewish families, Philadelphia's Jewish leadership could be found in the art, literary, scientific and social milieu without impugning their Jewish commitments.[8]

Against a social background that brought Jews into the city's exclusive clubs while many New Yorkers were denied admittance to the clubs of their city—Morais and Sulzberger were members of The Union League with some forty others prior to 1900,[9] it is well to examine the individual chronology of their activities beyond the nutshell biographies that exist for most of them, including the restrained miniatures in the standard *Dictionary of American Biography.*

Others who attained considerable prominence in civic and social affairs like Isidore Binswanger, Abraham S. Wolf, Isaac Solis, Henry Cohen, Jacob Lit and Jacob Gimbel remained local figures. Binswanger, Cohen and Solis were League members, involved in the philanthropic leadership of the city and in its cultural life. Men like A. S. W. Rosenbach and Ellis Gimbel belong to a subsequent period.

Of the participation of women little can be said, with the exception of the daughters of Henry Cohen, Mary M. and Katherine, who were involved in local art and literary societies and prominent in the New Century Club and the Browning society and who had also entered into the proper Protestant world of middle class women while proudly maintaining their Jewish interests and commitments.[10] As for the Gratzes they had vanished from the tiny Jewish stage where they had been prominent actors in antebellum days.

The rapid ascension of East European immigrants was more incredible than we have been led to believe. Its incredibility was indeed relative to the progress of the old Jewish residents. If Dr. Solomon Solis-Cohen had the diagnostic instinct to recognize the curability of tuberculosis, it was Dr. Charles Spivak, an immigrant physician, who determined the institutional means for providing care at the Jewish Consumptives' Relief Society in Denver, Colorado. Its pattern was duplicated on a smaller scale by the Brith Sholom in establishing the Philadelphia Jewish Sanatorium for the treatment of tuberculosis at nearby Eagleville.[11]

The rich complement of East Europeans to come to America by way of Philadelphia included Yiddish literary notables of the stature of Abraham Cahan and Leon Kobrin. Hebrew scholars and memoirists of the caliber of Phineas Mordell, Moses Weinberger and Hillel Malachovsky have fallen into obscurity. Only one person of the Eastern European milieu remains central to this aspect of national influence—Rabbi Bernard Levinthal—who molded the direction of the Isaac Elchanan Yeshiva.[12]

It was to provide for the immediate needs of the vast mass of immigrants, neither scribes nor scholars, that immigrant aid societies were organized in the early 1880's. In New York City the first of these attempts were dismal failures. Overwhelmed by sheer numbers the older generation retreated in defeat. A successful organization was not formally established until 1902 as an outgrowth of the Voliner Zhitomer *landsmanshaft.*[13] But in 1884, Philadelphia's Association for the Protection of Jewish Immigrants was founded through the efforts of Louis Edward Levy and Moses Aaron Dropsie. Levy was the prime mover. New York City may have supplied the name, later known by the acronym HIAS, but under Levy's leadership the organization established a pattern that was nationally emulated.[14]

Levy's activity embraced all national immigration affairs. One of the founders of the Jewish Alliance of America, in which he was joined by Charles Spivak, and a few years later a cofounder of the more successful National Liberal Immigration League he became an active contributor to its publications and influential in shaping its policies. He was an ardent opponent of the illiteracy test which hurt more non-Jews than Jews and in its opposition Judge Sulzberger was a vocal opponent. Levy's extensive correspondence with the Jewish Colonization Association in St. Petersburg, the French Alliance in Paris and the *Deutsches Zentral Komitee für Russische Juden* gave his work an international stamp. Throughout the nation he was called upon for counsel on the many aspects of immigration problems to which he responded faithfully.

Bohemian–born Levy maintained a professional career that made his name known wherever the new developments in photography were in use— from microscopic photography to the half tone process which he helped develop for use in newspapers. And for 34 years he wrote the annual reports of the Association, conducted the major affairs of the organization and was responsible for a statistical account of immigration to Philadelphia which is as fresh and useful today as the time when it was compiled. He died in 1919 while writing the annual report for that year.

When Levy moved to Philadelphia in 1875 he immediately associated himself with Sabato Morais, the minister-hazan of Congregation Mikveh Israel. Morais' concern for immigrants dated to the eve of the Civil War when he singlehandedly organized a work program for impoverished Jews from Germany. His pattern of visiting the needy was later adopted by the United Hebrew Charities and extended to the needs of immigrants from Czarist Russia. His concept of social justice preceded that of Rabbi Krauskopf and brought him into the field of battle, unlike the pulpit theorizing of his Reform colleagues. Morais acted unusually in settling the disastrous cloak makers strike in 1890 to the chagrin of the local leaders of the community who were the clothing manufacturers.[15] His utter disillusionment with the program of Isaac Mayer Wise went beyond the much talked about *trefe* banquet held for the Hebrew Union College. He was firmly convinced that a major rabbinical institution, promoting western concepts of traditional Judaism, was necessary where the greatest number of Jews were making their residence. The result was the Jewish Theological Seminary in New York City.[16] In this challenging undertaking he sought and received the support of most Philadelphians and inspired a cadre of leadership under Sulzberger and Solis-Cohen.

When he was made an honorary member of The Union League in 1887—a year after the Seminary was founded—for his sermons upholding the programs of Lincoln, condemning slavery and for his opposition to the Oriental Exclusion Act in 1882, his reputation was established. Proper Philadelphia had invited him to the social privacy of its court. No other orthodox rabbi could make such a claim at a time when the League was still

Louis Edward Levy. *Courtesy of Maxwell Whiteman.*

glorying in the laurels of national recognition. Morais died in 1897, his work incomplete but with a following that made possible the reorganization of the Seminary and at this juncture Mayer Sulzberger quietly entered the scene.[17]

Beyond question Sulzberger was the leading Jewish layman in Philadelphia of his generation. At the time of Morais' death his devotion to Jewish causes was common knowledge at home and abroad. His public debut was not made as a member of the bar in 1865, but as the editor for one year of Isaac Leeser's *Occident.* Here he showed his knowledge of Hebrew and biblical literature. Early in his long career he became a collector of Hebraica, Judaica and books on the history of the law.[18] He was a strong proponent of a reorganized Jewish Publication Society and its first chairman, a trustee of the Baron de Hirsch Fund and active in all of the educational and philanthropic societies including the former Jewish Hospital in which his father played the leading role. His legal position involved him deeply in the Gratz and Dropsie Colleges, and from the day of its reorganization in 1897 he was an influential director of the Jewish Theological Seminary. About the time that the Seligman imbroglio on the admission of Jews to the New York

Union League, he was proposed and admitted with ease in the Philadelphia club.[19]

His literary taste, like his knowledge of the books he collected, had an avant garde character. He was responsible for making Israel Zangwill the bright star of the Anglo-American literary scene. But Sulzberger did not share the same success with Abraham Cahan whose English novels he sought for the Jewish Publication Society. These two men with opposing views of society were able to meet on a common literary ground, but Cahan, who could come to terms with Sulzberger, could not agree with the "patricians" of the Jewish Publication Society. William Dean Howells was successful in getting Cahan to write of immigrant life where Sulzberger had failed.[20]

Privately, in his Girard Avenue library, Sulzberger was the maecenas for a grand number of Hebrew and Yiddish authors and those who dreamed of being authors. The most famous was the wandering poet-mystic and author of *Hatikvah*, Naftali Herz Imber. Scores of books of Hebrew verse, prose, philosophy and mere trash found their way into print through Sulzberger's charitable purse. Many of the Yiddish writers including Sholem Asch and Shalom Aleichem hoped to see their books issued by the Publication Society and in spite of Sulzberger's powerful arguments such early prizes found their way into print elsewhere. Authors from abroad constantly appealed to him for financial aid to publish works of rabbinic literature or those eager to translate the literature of the West into Hebrew.[21]

That unique Hebrew bibliophile, Ephraim Deinard, kept him informed of the first printings of ancient Hebrew works, plied him with choice incunabula, the best of bibliographies and the rarest of manuscripts. By 1896, Deinard had compiled and published the first major collection of Sulzberger treasures which were soon to go to the Jewish Theological Seminary. Two governors of Pennsylvania, Edwin Stuart, a bookseller, and Samuel W. Pennypacker, a zealous collector, kept him advised of all Hebraica that came their way.[22] In his lifetime, Sulzberger became the major American collector of Hebrew books and manuscripts. After he inherited the mantle of the Seminary from Morais, he furnished the Seminary library with his choice rarities. His greatest contribution was the collection of manuscripts and printed Hebraica which Sulzberger acquired after he assumed his Seminary post.

It was in the pursuit of his bibliophilic interests that Sulzberger, eager to obtain examples of the recently discovered genizah fragments, became acquainted with Solomon Schechter. And through the private efforts of Solis-Cohen, Cyrus Adler and Israel Zangwill, arrangements were made to bring Schechter—the reader in rabbinics at Cambridge University—to launch the opening of Gratz College with a series of lectures in 1895. The event was interpreted as an academic feat and so great was the impression made by Schechter that in 1901, after a careful review of European institu-

Mayer Sulzberger. *Courtesy of Maxwell Whiteman.*

tions of Jewish learning and their scholars, Schechter was Sulzberger's choice for reorganizing the Seminary, bringing a new faculty and providing for a library. Altering the course of the Seminary and defining its future was exclusively the work of Philadelphians.[23]

This was possible, and even necessary, because of the interfraternal attitude of Philadelphia Jewry, making leadership a joint communal effort. New Yorkers had not reached this position. In spite of the tremendous financial support that later came from the New Yorkers, at this time they lacked a cohesive spirit and the sense of communication from which Jewish organizations traditionally spring. Many of the financiers and men of business with close family ties had placed their interests elsewhere. It was for these reasons that Jacob H. Schiff, banker, philanthropist and Jewish advocate, also turned to Mayer Sulzberger on the subject of funding the new Bible translation for English-speaking Jews.

> Will you not act as a committee of one on appeal, and at your convenience, make a draft of such an appeal? I know you understand to touch the right spot, but let me suggest that you emphasize that this is to be the Bible for American Jews, and that it ought to be their bible, and therefore its preparation should

not be paid for through a small number of wealthy men, but through contributions from the mass of the people. . . .[24]

Funding the seminary at the same time presented difficulties which were overcome through Sulzberger's adroitness. There was only one dissenting voice in the movement to reorganize the Seminary, that of Moses Aaron Dropsie. He withheld his personal support. Jewish education, especially higher Jewish education, had taken up a half century of his public activity. He was a supporter of the Jewish Sunday Schools, the Hebrew Education Society in its parochial and secular activities, and a strong voice in the Maimonides College, the first school of Jewish higher learning in the United States. With the exception of a few New Yorkers, it never received the national support it sought and after a struggle of six years Maimonides College was forced to close its doors. The failure of the college and the subsequent rise of Jewish schools in Cincinnati and New York as well as the teachings of the radical reformers within Judaism were largely responsible for Dropsie's general opposition to Jewish institutions based entirely on parochial ideologies. He was an uncompromising advocate of an institution in Philadelphia and by 1895, when he wrote his *On Deform in Judaism*, his views were clearly stated. When the Gratz Trust was activated in 1893, he became president of the Board of Trustees. Then the New Yorkers eyed Philadelphia as the future site of the Seminary but Sulzberger wisely opposed such a move.

Dropsie also was a part of proper Philadelphia. He was an early member of The Union League and belonged to the right societies. He had been an antislavery advocate before the Civil War, and at the time he became prominent in the street railway system he was a proponent for the use of public transportation by Philadelphia Negroes when other traction companies denied their facilities in the face of public controversy. His personality was as florid as the color of his skin and his staunch position on public issues brought him to the forefront of Jewish debate. His arguments over the use of the Baron de Hirsch Fund alienated him from its New York representatives who were still in a state of confusion over the vast Jewish immigration to that city.[25]

Communal action in New York City continued to be unilateral and more of an expression of individual interest and responsibility. The B'nai B'rith feared that any new organization might preempt its position while the Union of American Hebrew Congregations had taken over the moribund Board of Delegates of American Israelites and did not wish to have its new position challenged. Neither organization had as yet met the acute responsibility for the multitude of problems brought on by the great immigration or by the wanton massacre of Jews in Czarist Russia.

National concern was stirred by the violence perpetrated in Kishinev in 1903. This Christian baccanalia which left Jews wading knee deep in their

Moses A. Dropsie. *Courtesy of Maxwell Whiteman.*

own blood not only aroused Jewish fear and sentiment but reached every American through the national press. Yet the new system of Jewish federations was unable to cope with a problem of such vast terror and murder abroad and no national organization was able to cope with a problem of such magnitude.[26] Cyrus Adler pleaded with Judge Sulzberger to secure "statements in the Platforms of the various political parties in the different states of the Union, expressing sympathy with the Kishinev sufferers, and demanding that the government take steps to secure equal respect for the American passport, when borne by an American citizen without regard to race or creed. I believe that the Ohio Republicans . . . would be the first to which this proposition could be made . . ."[27] Once again individuals faced the task of raising a huge fund for the relief of the surviving victims of the deliberate Easter outrage, the Kishinev massacre of Jews.

More and more the need was recognized for an organization of national scope that would concern itself with the basic rights of Jews. The inadequacy of existing organizations, the belief that the Board of Delegates and B'nai B'rith were "no longer sufficiently adequate"[28] and also the fear that recent immigrant leaders would take matters in their own hands, brought about the organization of the American Jewish Committee. The subsequent details of its birth are well known. What is significant here is the role of Sulzberger who never sought position and who with great reluctance accepted the presidency. He preferred his bookish pursuits, his meetings of the Oriental Club of Philadelphia of which he was founder, and his duties as the President Judge of Common Pleas Court No. 2, over any national position, and as he approached the Sabbath of his years, he disdained leaving the city. At the age of 63, he accepted the presidency of the American Jewish Committee, provided he could remain in Philadelphia.

Sulzberger's extensive involvement in these and numerous other social and political affairs remain unstudied and unappreciated to this day. It comes as a surprise that the official history of the American Jewish Committee, an otherwise fine book, devotes less than two pages to his activity as the first president of this major organization. It is an additional surprise that Cyrus Adler, who worked with Sulzberger intimately, provides us with scant information of his mentor in his egocentric autobiography, for Adler was a great believer in restrained history. Other than a list of glorifying necrologies, a serious study of Sulzberger does not exist.[29]

It was possible for Sulzberger to take the presidency because Adler was competent, ambitious and carried out his every wish. Men of independent stature like Jacob H. Schiff and Oscar S. Straus, astute lawyers of the caliber of Louis Marshall, Max Kohler and Justice Julian W. Mack deferred to Sulzberger, seeking his council and frequently his approval and conferring with him before acting on an important issue. Many of the internal controversies bearing on the illiteracy test, the abrogation of the Russian treaty with the United States concerning American Jews traveling in the Czarist empire, and diverse attitudes toward East European Jews were resolved by Sulzberger.

Adler's frosty, impenetrable armor, his propriety and respectability, his public restraint and caution and his innumerable contacts placed him in a unique position to fulfill the difficult tasks envisioned by his cousin. Adler had been named president of the American Jewish Historical Society of which he was prime founder; he was deeply involved in the work of the Seminary and the Jewish Publication Society and now an unofficial liaison for Sulzberger with the American Jewish Committee on whose board he also served. Adler informed his cousin of everything of Jewish interest in Washington. While in New York on his regular visits to the Seminary he reported on the activities of the Strauses, the Schiffs and their circle. Both men arranged their schedules in such a manner that meetings of the Jewish Publication Society, the Seminary, the Gratz College, and later the Dropsie College could be packed into one day. And henceforth Adler was enabled to dominate the scene, either remotely in the American Jewish Committee, or publicly when he was named president of the Dropsie College. For the six years from 1906 to 1912, when he was president of the Committee, Sulz-

Cyrus Adler. *Courtesy of Maxwell Whiteman.*

berger recognized in his younger cousin a man of considerable talent and
saw that Adler was appointed to the Dropsie College presidency. At this
juncture in 1908, Adler resigned his post at the Smithsonian Institution and
again made his residence in Philadelphia where he eventually became the
elder statesman of American Jewry.[30]

Although Sulzberger was a confirmed advocate of quiet diplomacy and
may well fit the category of *Hofjude,* he could also storm at meetings,
speaking with scorn and sarcasm. At no time did he lose focus of the issue at
hand. Thus Sulzberger became an axis in the American Jewish leadership at
the beginning of this century.

Politically, Sulzberger was no less commanding. He was a Republican
but attracted the support of both major parties. He was the first Jew who
identified himself as a Jew to ascend the bench in Pennsylvania, succeeding
John I. C. Hare, a founder of the Union League and a distinguished jurist.
In tradition-bound Philadelphia his mark was made at the same time that his
involvement in Jewish affairs had deepened. Both Presidents Roosevelt and
Taft recognized his brilliance, but Sulzberger sought no favor from either.

When Taft as the incoming president in 1909 offered Sulzberger the appointment of Ambassador to Turkey, Sulzberger graciously turned it down. Taft
responded just as graciously: "I was very sorry that you concluded not to
accept the appointment to be Ambassador to Constantinople. . . . Still, I can
understand how a gentleman like yourself, in love with your work on the
bench, should decline to be torn up by your roots, so to speak, and sent
abroad."[31]

Oscar S. Straus, on the other hand, seized the opportunity less than
three weeks later when it was offered to him, not by Taft but by
Philander C. Knox, U.S. Attorney General and subsequently Secretary of
State. And Knox, "who is no friend" to Jews, as Sulzberger had learned
from Justice Julian Mack, found Strauss instantly willing to take up the post
he held once before under President Cleveland.[32] Straus quickly learned that
Secretary Knox was not about to join the protest against the Czarist government for the mistreatment of Jews. Nor was Knox interested in abrogating
that portion of the American-Russian Treaty which forbade American Jews
from trading or travelling through Russia. The Schiff-Straus correspondence
was referred back to Philadelphia from Constantinople for Sulzberger's
opinion. The issue concerned a meeting with President Taft and the correspondents urged that Sulzberger in his "calm and diplomatic way induce the
President to follow" a course suitable to the United States and helpful to
oppressed Russian Jewry. Schiff, Straus, Louis Marshall, Sulzberger and
Adler agreed that nothing be done "to irritate the President." One of their
ancillary concerns was the private mission of John Hays Hemmond to
Russia and what he might do to influence Taft as well as W. W. Rockhill,
ambassador to St. Petersburg.[33]

The unsettled, irritating subject of the passport question—which af-
fected not only Jews but the freedom of Americans of many different backgrounds—continued to be a matter for debate for a number of years. Under
consideration was the abrogation of the Russian treaty with the United
States. It deeply involved the American Jewish Committee, particularly
Schiff and Marshall. In summarizing his private discussions with Marshall,
Schiff wrote Sulzberger saying "I shall take this matter up at once with
Marshall, and meantime it is proper that I say to *you* that I have hardly
anything to do with the arrangements which are being made for the convention, and am myself one of the figureheads only, who are being moved by
others."[34] Before the treaty was finally terminated the probing, the
speeches, the hearings, the correspondence called forth the best as well as the
most uncertain of Jewish talents and attitudes. Justice Mack, of the Illinois
Appellate Court, at the end of a lengthy analysis of the affair succinctly
stated, "I am inclined to think that your statement to Straus and Schiff . . .
would be heeded more than anyone else's."[35]

Sulzberger's commanding position in the American Jewish Committee
also was dependent upon his rapport with the diverse temperaments of the

New Yorkers. One day it was a cooperative endeavor with Judah L. Magnes to establish joint discussions between the Committee and the Kehillah[36] and another day it was securing the involvement of the reluctant Daniel Guggenheim to chair the finance committee of the organization to which the president of the American Smelting and Refining Company responded warmly.[37] And so it continued long after the retirement of Sulzberger from the presidency and from the bench.

It is significant to note that all of Sulzberger's colleagues, with the exception of Joseph Krauskopf, who provided leadership beyond their city were, or had been, members of the old Sephardic congregation Mikveh Israel. Of these only Dr. Solomon Solis-Cohen had a proper claim to Spanish-Portuguese background. As a physician, Solis-Cohen witnessed many of the basic and major changes in American medicine and hospital practice from the last quarter of the nineteenth century to the Second World War. He had a strong and compelling personality and demanded the best among his medical associates. His record as a physician is secure.

Less known for his literary ambitions, he joined the company of such men as Owen Wister, J. Chalmers Da Costa, Ernest Lacy and S. Weir Mitchell.[38] Solis-Cohen was a prolific writer not only on medicine but on a broad variety of subjects. His Jewish activities spanned the rise of the many institutions in which he was involved to the firm positions which they hold today. Like Sulzberger he preferred not to be an officeholder. He joined his colleagues at Mikveh Israel in the many proposals to further the aims of Jewish education, support for the Jewish Theological Seminary but he was especially active in carrying forth the proposal to reestablish the defunct Jewish Publication Society. A second attempt had failed in New York and the subject again became a matter of public and private interest amid the problems of immigration. Numerous editorials and proposals were published in the press of that city. Money was privately guaranteed for the project but no further progress was made. Then Joseph Krauskopf in one of his Sunday Sermons at Congregation Keneseth Israel advocated that the congregation inaugurate its own movement. Unable to accomplish this he sought other congregations to join in establishing a Philadelphia society rather than a society with national roots. The men of Mikveh Israel favored a national society over the local one which Krauskopf preached. The two groups locked horns; Solis-Cohen was outraged and Krauskopf was outvoted by the president of his congregation.[39]

Acrimony between Krauskopf and Solis-Cohen persisted for four years. By then Sulzberger had seized the reins, acknowledged the work of Solis-Cohen who in turn recognized the contribution made by Krauskopf and Keneseth Israel. But if credit is to be given for placing the Society on its present course, Solis-Cohen warrants it.

Krauskopf's influences lay elsewhere. As an exponent of Reform Judaism and its concept of Social Justice, for which he was largely responsible, recognition came to him overnight. His Sunday sermons had as much impact on non-Jewish listeners as they did on his own congregants. With their publication he found a national audience. Emerging locally as a figure in the Model Dwellings Association, a movement to rehabilitate the southern section of the city and erase its slum life, Krauskopf was certainly a pioneer. It was a serious attempt by members of the Protestant clergy, social idealists who were attracted by the experiment of Octavia Hill, and the first crop of urban social workers. Although Krauskopf took a prominent part in this program he did not anticipate an antisemitic reaction to his participation nor the total failure of the great scheme to improve and revitalize worn out housing. The plan crumbled.[40]

As an immigrant lad from Prussian Poland he never forgot his own difficult years. His quest for education brought him to the newly founded Hebrew Union College and he was in the first class to be ordained. After holding a pulpit in Kansas City, Missouri he came to Reform Congregation Keneseth Israel where he was able to witness the arrival of Eastern European immigrants and mingle with immigrants from Germany of a previous generation. In the immediate area of the stylish Moorish Temple of Keneseth Israel, located in the lower Northern Liberties many of the immigrants were making their residence. How he could apply his principles of Social Justice in adapting immigrants to American ways was an intellectual conflict. Their work habits, their religious practices and their outlook were completely different from what was anticipated. While Sulzberger and Levy bent in the direction of the newcomers Krauskopf was bound to a different formula.

In one of the first opportunities he had to extend the new Reform teachings by helping to negotiate a bitter strike between Jewish clothing manufacturers and Jewish cloak makers, Krauskopf disappeared from the scene. Although he preached on the subject in general terms about "insufficient work and insufficient wages . . . (as) the most fertile source of poverty" it was Sabato Morais who was the final arbiter of the strike. On this issue Krauskopf's oratory did not reach beyond the pulpit. One can only speculate what his reasons were in not approaching the manufacturers who were members of his congregation.[41]

Perhaps Krauskopf benefited from his experience in the failure of the model housing program and his lack of involvement in the cloak makers' strike but his interest in Jewish immigrants from Russia did not diminish. Obsessed with this determination he made his way to Russia with the wild dream of meeting the Czar and convincing him of the necessity to settle Jews on farms. He was lucky to obtain a passport because Jewish visitors were not welcome. Through the efforts of the American ambassador he was able to see Count Leo Tolstoy at his famous farm in Yasnaya Polyana. Tolstoy convinced him of the need to bring American Jews into agriculture and deurbanize them. It was a turning point in Krauskopf's life.

A year after he returned to the United States in 1897 Krauskopf busied himself, his congregation and his friends in the organization of the National Farm School. It is difficult to say if Tolstoy was the single influence on Krauskopf's agricultural experiment. Ever since 1819 agricultural colonies for Jews had been advocated for settlement in the American midwest. Krauskopf may not have known of those plans prior to the Civil War but he was familiar with those which failed as quickly as they were launched when he lived in Kansas City. He was also familiar with the colonies in South Jersey and their innumerable difficulties and their own school in Woodbine. With the same zeal that he attacked the slums he now fulminated for a school for practical farming. The school was built, developed and today, under another name, successful. Whether it accomplished its national purpose to remove immigrants from the city's streets and embrace the mythic agrarian dream is still debatable.[42]

Of the seven men considered here, Dropsie, Solis-Cohen and Adler were American born. Dropsie and Sulzberger entered the law while Morais and Krauskopf were rabbis observing an ancient tradition and a modern trend. Levy was a chemist and inventor, Solis-Cohen a physician and poet while Adler was nurtured in the academic world. All were prolific writers on Jewish and general subjects. They shared the common mission of elevating the condition of American Jewry. Solis-Cohen described them aptly as "The Philadelphia Group," a leadership begun by Isaac Leeser and perpetuated by Morais, Sulzberger and Adler.[43]

Morais challenged the social forces about him within the context of traditional Jewish belief and offended his congregation by exposing the conditions of the sweatshop. At the same time he was able to overcome the opposition of his critics, win their hearts and obtain their financial support. Krauskopf also challenged the conditions of urban society but from the safety of the pulpit or from the rich soil of the National Farm School. Levy stepped beyond the customary convention of abiding by the rules of philanthropic respectability in creating an organization that became a national model. In his single handed battle to combat prostitution among immigrants he insisted that the factors involving prostitution be made known and he was successful in reducing the vilest practices of immigrants preying on immigrants.

Sulzberger's attitude and manner were in sharp contrast to those of his colleagues. His judicial position and the social world in which he lived did not permit radical approaches. His general restraint and sedentary preferences forced him to reject the appointment of United States Ambassador to Turkey, a post which Oscar Straus snatched at the first opportunity. The enigma of Sulzberger's position cannot be determined fully until all of his letters and addresses come to light. When they do they will complement the papers of Louis Marshall and Jacob H. Schiff and the autobiography of Oscar Straus, which up to the present time give Sulzberger the appearance of a minor and fleeting figure. The opposite is the truth.

Cyrus Adler, the quintessential figure of Philadelphia leadership who survived all of his colleagues except Dr. Solomon Solis-Cohen, lived long enough to write of Dropsie, Morais and Sulzberger for the *Dictionary of American Biography* as well as his own polite autobiography. Perhaps he had little choice in narrowing the contemporary scene and in analyzing the events in which he was a major participant. It is certain that he was aware of the tremendous influence of Sulzberger and the great respect which so many held for him. Adler's importance at home and abroad, like Sulzberger's, is yet to be estimated. The behind the scenes role of Cyrus Adler may yet come to light with the scheduled publication of his letters.

The last of the septet, Solis-Cohen, died in 1948. Unlike his early or late contemporaries he was the only declared Zionist. Even though he wavered in his views throughout his lifetime, the Jewish prestate of Palestine was a matter of deep concern to him; Krauskopf disdained political Zionism revising his views later in life; Morais concurred with the traditional orthodox view while all others were sympathetic non-Zionists and debated the subject continuously. Adler was a non-Zionist member of the Jewish Agency and his statement on the use of the Western Wall is a historic document.[44] To Sulzberger no arguments against Zionism were justified.[45]

What brought these men together in common Jewish causes? How were they able to support, influence and direct Jewish institutions whose center was in New York?

The well-spring lay in the exceptional tradition of leadership in Philadelphia which determined the conduct of Dropsie, Sulzberger, Solis-Cohen, Levy and Adler in that order. New York lacked the corresponding leadership provided by the Philadelphians in the nineteenth century. Its rapidly growing diverse immigrant population and hundreds of mushroom societies threatened and made impossible a central authority. Whereas Philadelphians had enough perception to recognize that eventually major support would come out of New York City. While the strength of New York eventually grew from year to year as an indigenous leadership emerged, at the height of Sulzberger's career, the role of Philadelphians firmly influenced the course of the great immigration of the Eastern European Jews.

National Leaders of Their Time: Philadelphia's Reform Rabbis

Malcolm H. Stern

In 1840, the Philadelphia Jewish community was divided between Sephardic-rite Mikveh Israel and German-rite Rodeph Shalom. The distinction applied more to the prayerbook used than to those who prayed from it, for from the earliest days Philadelphia was predominantly German-Polish (Ashkenazic) in origin. Mikveh Israel, like the other colonial Jewish congregations, had adopted the Spanish-Portuguese or Sephardic rite for two reasons: because their synagogue building-fund required contributions from the wealthier Sephardic communities in London, Amsterdam and the Caribbean; and because the more dignified Sephardic worship seemed appropriate to tiny Jewish communities on the North Atlantic seaboard whose Christian neighbors were viewing everything they did. So in every sense Mikveh Israel represented the American way of Jewish worship.

Rodeph Shalom, traceable to a *minyan* (quorum of ten males) of Dutch and German Jews as early as 1795, was the immigrants' congregation until 1840. As its members became Americanized and upwardly mobile, many left Rodeph Shalom to join Mikveh Israel.[1] Their places were taken by other immigrants from Germany and from Prussian-Posen, Austrian Galicia, and Russian Poland—areas that had constituted Poland in earlier centuries. In 1840, those accustomed to the Polish rite created their own congregation, Beth Israel, long known as "the Polish congregation." It was born out of Rodeph Shalom's continuing inability to find a suitable house of worship.[2]

In 1829, Mikveh Israel acquired as its *hazan* the Reverend Isaac Leeser. Although considered a champion of orthodoxy, Leeser rejected the appellation, preferring to think of himself as accepting those changes that did not violate Mosaic law. In this spirit, despite the disapproval of his congregation's leadership, he began preaching in English in 1831, thereby creating an American tradition. With Rebecca Gratz he organized the first Jewish Sunday School in 1838.[3] Three years later he began publishing his periodical *Occident and American Jewish Advocate,* which he continued until his death in 1868. This remarkable compilation of Jewish lore, news and propaganda made Leeser the dominant American Jewish voice of his generation. In his editorials he generously encouraged the creation of each of Philadelphia's new congregations. He made a point of trying to visit each of them so that he could offer first-hand comments to his national readership.

In 1846, dissension in Rodeph Shalom had two results: the former Kenild Church on Juliana Street was purchased, and a faction of Bavarian Jews under the leadership of Julius Stern created Keneseth Israel. They objected not only to the building fund, but also to the *minhag* (form of service) and the manner in which Hebrew was pronounced at Rodeph Shalom.[4] Most of the new group had been resident in America for some years and were upwardly mobile.[5] Their first meeting, held at Stern's home, took place on Purim night, March 2, 1847. Leeser noted the birth of Keneseth Israel in the July 1847 issue of the *Occident:*

> A new German congregation has been for some time in existence in our city of which we have received no official account. But we understand they have a regular organization and have fitted up a temporary synagogue besides purchasing a burying ground. They have elected a Mr. [Bernard H.] Gotthelf as their minister and their president is Mr. Julius Stern. Mr. Cohen,[6] the lately elected Hazan of the old German congregation [Rodeph Shalom] has delivered several sermons which have been well received. We regret that official duties have compelled us to be absent from the synagogue where Mr. Cohen officiated . . . or else we would have attended; to be among others edified by this new labourer among us in the cause of Israel.

Keneseth Israel's founders remained orthodox but by the early 1850s were beginning to question the liturgy and the need for a private *schochet* (ritual slaughterer) and other functionaries. In 1854 they took tentative steps in the direction of Reform which were reinforced a year later by their union with a group of young intellectuals who had formed a *Reform Gesellschaft.*[7] Leeser, who had been commenting favorably on Keneseth Israel's growth and purchase of a church, rebuked the congregation in the June 1856 *Occident:*

> The Kenesseth Israel congregation of this place has united with a number of persons, who endeavored sometime since to start a so-called temple; and we hear they are engaged in introducing the usual accompaniments of such an institution, abridged prayers, organ, and choir. If the Society prospers, it will no doubt soon look out for a preacher: indeed, we hear that this acquisition is already in the minds of the members . . . we regret to state that . . . we have to add our city to the list of those where a minority have learned to bend the knee to the modern idol. . . .

Although Keneseth Israel was to change its constitution and label itself

Rodeph Shalom, 1898. Courtesy of *Dropsie University
Library and Allen Meyers.*

thereafter "Reform Congregation Keneseth Israel,"[8] Rodeph Shalom, nominally Orthodox, was also introducing reforms. In June 1851, confirmation
services were held for six girls and two boys.[9] Two years later the sale of
mitzvot was abolished in the synagogue, a move that had Leeser's editorial
approval.[10]

In 1854, Keneseth Israel purchased a church on New Market Street
above Noble which it remodeled as a synagogue. Under the impetus of
Reform an organ was installed, the Hamburg prayerbook with German
prayers became the liturgy and the wearing of the *tallit* (prayer shawl) was
abandoned.[11]

All these events set the stage for the arrival of a new style of Jewish
functionary on the American scene, the ordained rabbi with a university
doctorate. He was accorded the title "Reverend Doctor" to distinguish him
from the *hazan* or Reader who already bore the title of "Reverend." Rodeph
Shalom was the first Philadelphia congregation to engage one of the new
breed of clergy. In 1853 they elected Bernard L. Illoway as rabbi, preacher
and superintendent of the religious school, to work in association with Rev.
Jacob Frankel, the Reader who had arrived four years earlier. To differentiate responsibilities, the board had each of the officiants sign a statement

of duties. A year later, Illoway was put on trial for laxity in his ritual observances. He successfully defended himself, but his reelection was questioned and he departed.[12]

Keneseth Israel did not secure a preacher-rabbi until 1857, when it defrayed the travel expenses from Germany of Rev. Dr. Solomon Deutsch. Known as a reformer, Deutsch soon abolished the separation of men and women at worship as well as the second day of all holidays except Rosh Hashana. A personality conflict between Deutsch and the incumbent Reader, Rev. L. Naumburg, led to the dismissal of both. Keneseth Israel remained without ongoing leadership for several years. However, in 1860 it adopted the radical Reform prayerbook that Rabbi David Einhorn of Baltimore had published under the title *Olath Tamid (A Perpetual Offering)*.[13]

Einhorn was an outspoken abolitionist, and when the Civil War broke out, Confederate sympathizers in Baltimore threatened him and his family. His congregation, Har Sinai, reluctantly urged him to take refuge in Philadelphia. Within a month they invited him to return, stipulating that he avoid talking from the pulpit on "the explosive questions of the day." Einhorn promptly resigned, and shortly thereafter—within hours—received an invitation to become rabbi-preacher at Keneseth Israel.[14] Certainly one of his stipulations must have been complete freedom of the pulpit. With Einhorn's arrival Keneseth Israel's era of leadership in the national Reform movement began.

Soon after the beginning of his American career in 1855, Einhorn published a monthly periodical, *Sinai*, as a Reform rival to Leeser's far more conservative *Occident*. The *Sinai* did not hesitate to challenge any opponent. When Rabbi Morris J. Raphall of New York's Congregation B'nai Jeshurun preached a widely quoted sermon on the Bible's support for the institution of slavery, Einhorn was most vociferous in rebutting in print. He insisted, again and again, that the Talmud was a misinterpretation of the Bible's intent, and therefore, had no validity for modern times. When Leeser tried to organize the Philadelphia congregations into a synod, Einhorn denounced the move as an attempt to restrict religious freedom. He lost patience with Isaac M. Wise, whose two publications, *The Israelite* and *Die Deborah*, pragmatically counseled a slower move away from orthodoxy.

By January 1863, Einhorn's diatribes had so alienated half his subscribers that he was forced to cease publishing for lack of funds.[15] He blamed the alienation on his antislavery stand, even though it earned him commendation from the Union League Club. His prayerbook, *Olath Tamid*, at first won acceptance only in a few radically Reform congregations. However, a generation later, when the Central Conference of American Rabbis determined on publishing a Union Prayer Book for the entire Reform movement, it was Einhorn's well thought through Reform ideology that caused the movement to adopt an English translation of his prayerbook practically *in toto*. Even though Isaac M. Wise was the founder of the Central Conference and the majority of its members his disciples, they ignored his prayerbook, *Minhag America*, and Wise, himself, applauded their choice of Einhorn's liturgy.[16]

The year 1866 was significant in Philadelphia's rabbinical history. Einhorn accepted a call to a larger New York congregation, and both Rodeph Shalom and Keneseth Israel brought outstanding rabbi-preachers from Germany.

Rodeph Shalom imported the scholarly Morris Jastrow, who had established a reputation in Warsaw for his active partisanship in the Polish uprising against the Russian-dominated Polish government. Jastrow had been imprisoned and subsequently exiled for his revolutionary activities. Organizationally progressive, however, he remained a religious conservative.[17] Soon after his arrival in Philadelphia, he joined with Leeser (by then rabbi of Beth El Emeth Congregation), Sabato Morais (Leeser's successor at Mikveh Israel) and others in forming a short-lived rabbinical seminary, Maimonides College of Philadelphia. Jastrow taught Talmud, philosophy, Jewish history, and later, biblical exegesis. When Leeser died, Jastrow succeeded him as provost.[18]

Jastrow's most lasting contributions were in the realm of scholarship. His Aramaic-English *Dictionary of the Targumim, the Talmud Babli and Yerushalmi, and the Midrashic Literature*, became a classic. At the time of his death in 1904 he was serving as editor-in-chief of the Jewish Publication Society's important Bible translation, *The Holy Scriptures*. His scholarly sermons at Rodeph Shalom attracted an ever-wider membership so that by 1869 the congregation was compelled to erect its first building, a handsome Moorish edifice, at Broad and Mount Vernon Streets. Jastrow, himself, recommended the installation of an organ and the employment of a mixed choir, both gestures toward Reform, as were his abolition of the sale of *mitzvot* and the women's gallery, even though he maintained separate seating on the floor of the sanctuary.[19]

The Civil War, understandably, had a strong assimilative effect on the Jewish immigrants from Germany, further propelling the reforms within the synagogue. Jastrow's ability to preach in English defeated his own attempts to hold back the tide. As he grew more conservative, his congregants demanded more change, with the result that they forced him to retire in 1892. Angered by this and by his frustration with Reform, he preached a bitter farewell sermon rebuking the congregation for its laxity in Jewish observance.

Despite his sense of failure, however, Jastrow had been very successful on the larger scene. Within three years of his arrival in America he had been invited to Washington to open the House of Representatives with prayer. That same year, 1869, he hosted the Rodeph Shalom meeting at which Philadelphia's Jewish charities were welded into the United Hebrew Charities, forerunner of the present-day Federation. He encouraged the work of the Jewish Foster Home and the development of the Young Men's Hebrew Association. The plight of Russian Jewry moved him to work for the immigrants, even to the extent of writing to the czar, pleading for the abolition of Siberian exile.[20]

Jastrow's 1866 arrival at Rodeph Shalom coincided with the coming to Keneseth Israel of Rev. Dr. Samuel Hirsch. In Germany Hirsch was a recognized spokesman of Reform, having published a number of philosophical essays on the subject. Twenty years later, he left his position as Grand Rabbi of the Duchy of Luxembourg to accept Keneseth Israel's invitation. His first act in his new post was to abolish head covering.

Within three years, in 1869, Dr. Hirsch was hosting America's first Reform rabbinical conference. Thirteen rabbis of liberal persuasion came to Philadelphia in response to an invitation issued by Einhorn and his fellow New Yorker, Rabbi Samuel Adler of Temple Emanu-el. Hirsch presided. Considering themselves the American continuation of the German conferences, the Philadelphia rabbis enunciated the following principles for American Reform:

1. The Messiah will appear as an *era* of enlightenment, not a person.
2. The destruction of the Hebrew commonwealth in 70 C.E. was part of God's plan to send the Jew abroad to teach the world about God.
3. Prayer replaces the sacrificial cult.
4. The distinctions among Jews of priests, Levites, and Israelites, are no longer valid in our ritual.
5. "Chosen people" means chosen by God to teach the world about God.
6. The belief in immortality of the soul replaces belief in the resurrection of the body.
7. While knowledge of Hebrew is a sacred obligation, intelligible language in prayer is essential.

Regarding marriage and divorce, the Philadelphia Conference made these pronouncements:

1. Bride and groom are equal, and both should exchange vows.
2. The ritual should be altered to emphasize holiness and purity in the marital relationship.
3. Civil law will apply to divorce in place of the traditional Jewish *get*.[21]

The conferees intended that their Philadelphia meeting be the first of regular annual sessions, but growing dissension among the participants frustrated the plan and the effectiveness of the pronouncements. Reform was still evolving in America, and each rabbi interpreted for his congregation— or was led by his congregants—to adopt or reject whatever suited the need of the moment.[22]

By 1880, Keneseth Israel's membership was predominantly English-speaking and they wanted sermons in English which Hirsch was incapable of providing. He opposed the idea of an English-speaking assistant rabbi and proposed instead a series of Sunday services with visiting lecturers. This was attempted, but the lack of available rabbis and the fact that these guests had no connection with Keneseth Israel doomed the project. By 1886 Hirsch had passed his 70th birthday and he requested permission to retire. Appropriate arrangements were made and he spent the remaining three years of his life at the home of his brilliant son, Rabbi Emil G. Hirsch of Chicago's Temple Sinai.[23]

Challenged by Jastrow's monthly sermons in English at Rodeph Shalom, Keneseth Israel determined to find an outstanding preacher in the vernacular. Their choice fell on a young graduate of the first class of Hebrew Union College. Joseph Krauskopf was by then in his fourth year of service to Congregation B'nai Jehudah of Kansas City, and he agreed to accept Keneseth Israel's invitation if he could obtain a release from his contract. B'nai Jehudah granted the release, then had second thoughts, but by that time Krauskopf had committed himself to Keneseth Israel and the latter's leadership insisted that he be their rabbi. Tall and handsome, a compelling speaker and a man of great intellect and energy, Krauskopf was to build on the foundation laid by his predecessors and to make Keneseth Israel one of the most prestigious American congregations of his day.

In 1885, two years before his arrival in Philadelphia, Krauskopf had proposed to the then intellectual leader of Reform Judaism, Rabbi Kaufmann Kohler of New York, that the time had come for the Reform movement to declare its independence of orthodoxy. The result was the Pittsburgh Conference of 1885, attended by 15 rabbis. The venerable Isaac M. Wise presided; his 27-year-old disciple, Joseph Krauskopf, was elected vice-president. This conference issued the so-called Pittsburgh Platform, which so captured the thinking of most of America's German Jews that it remained the definitive statement of Reform Judaism until 1937, and influenced many Reform Jews for more than a generation after that. Briefly stated the platform proclaimed:

1. Judaism's God is universal; we Jews preserve Him for humanity.
2. The Bible consecrated us to teach the world about God, but we also accept the teachings of science.
3. Of the Mosaic law we observe only the moral teachings and those ceremonies that elevate and sanctify.
4. The laws regulating diet, the priesthood and special garments are meaningless today.
5. We seek a Messianic era, not a person; we are a religion, not a nation, and deny the need for a Jewish state in Palestine or anywhere.

6. Our faith is governed by reason and we welcome all faiths that teach service to the one God.
7. We teach the immortality of the soul, deny heaven or hell.
8. We affirm social justice and social action.[24]

In essence this platform was a call to total identification of the Reform Jew with America. It reflected the thinking that was to dominate America until World War II; namely the Americanization of the immigrant as rapidly as possible. The Jews of that era who rejected the platform created the Conservative movement. The platform itself made Reform Judaism a bastion for German Jews and their descendants for more than two generations and separated them from the growing population of East European immigrants, the so-called Russian Jews. Most significantly, the platform identified most Reform Jews with antizionism until Hitler, the Holocaust and the birth of Israel.

In October 1887, Krauskopf made a triumphal entry into Philadelphia.[25] One of his first acts was to establish formally the weekly Sunday service with lectures on topics of the day. Philadelphia's newly established *Jewish Exponent* was quick to publish major excerpts from his Sunday lectures, but it soon became apparent that Editor Felix Gerson and Krauskopf were in different Jewish ideological camps. The *Exponent* excerpts became briefer. However, Krauskopf had already arranged with his temple's sexton, Herman Klonower, a printer, to publish the full text of the Sunday lectures. The individual pamphlets, later issued as bound annual volumes, were sold by subscription to readers all over the country.

Krauskopf lost no time in instituting innovations within the congregation; a mixed choral society performed at services, departmentalized religious school classes and classes in Bible ethics for adults were taught in both English and German. For young adults he created "The Society of Knowledge Seekers," whom he inspired with the idea of revitalizing a Jewish Publication Society, since two prior attempts had failed. Funds were raised and other organizations involved. A brochure issued in May 1888 by Krauskopf and Dr. Solomon Solis-Cohen, prominent lay leader of Mikveh Israel, launched the Publication Society nationally.[26]

Since Einhorn's incumbency Keneseth Israel had been worshipping in a temple it had erected at Sixth and Brown Streets. The popularity of Krauskopf's lectures forced the congregation to enlarge the seating capacity. By 1890, a lot on Broad Street above Columbia was purchased and within two years a new temple was dedicated.[27] Testifying to his belief in the universality of religion, Krauskopf demanded the inclusion of two architectural features: a campanile copied from St. Marks' Square in Venice and a dome copied from the Mosque of Omar in Jerusalem. These symbolized Judaism's daughter faiths, Christianity and Islam.[28]

The new facility gave the rabbi's creative energies wider scope. He

Keneseth Israel, 1909. Courtesy of *Dropsie University Library and Allen Meyers.*

inspired the Knowledge Seekers to establish a free circulating library to serve both congregation and neighborhood, and he encouraged the women of the congregation to create a Sewing Circle to aid charitable causes.[29] In his opening Sunday lecture for 1893, Krauskopf attacked community interests for failing to provide proper housing for the poor, especially the growing tide of immigrants. He recommended a profit motive that might interest investors and urged that a model be tried as a pilot project. He was persuaded by a young Christian clergyman, Walter Vrooman, to ally his association with the Conference of Moral Workers, aimed at slum clearance. Even though Krauskopf with others raised $70,000 toward the model, it was insufficient for ongoing maintenance and the project died. But sufficient public concern had been aroused to prod the city into committing itself to improve sanitation in slum areas and to provide some urban renewal.[30]

Another of Krauskopf's idealistic schemes was his Personal Interest Society, begun in 1890. He tried to prevail on economically established Jews to develop a one-to-one relationship with poor families. As might have been expected, the response was not enthusiastic, but he may have raised consciousness of the poor in some minds.[31]

Krauskopf is best remembered for his most lasting creation, the National Farm School near Doylestown, Pennsylvania—now the Delaware Valley College of Science and Agriculture. The idea for the school emerged out of Krauskopf's 1894 visit to czarist Russia whose government initially refused a visa on the ground that Jews were not permitted to travel in Russia. In a Memorial Day address to the veterans of the Grand Army of the Republic, Krauskopf made the issue public, asserting his right to travel as an American under the Russo-American trade treaty. The story was circulated by the press and a bill was introduced in the House of Representatives to abrogate the treaty if any American were denied admission to Russia. Krauskopf was fearful that this might have an adverse effect on his mission, but his fears proved groundless. Through the American Ambassador at St. Petersburg, Krauskopf and the Reverend Russell Conwell, his travelling companion, were extended every courtesy and traveled freely. Krauskopf even secured letters of introduction to the czar's chief ministers, Witte and Pobedonostev. He later wrote to Witte, pleading that Jews be given arable land to cultivate in some less inhabited parts of Russia, hoping to turn the flow of immigrants away from America. He also met philosopher-author Leo Tolstoy who told him that the Jews had no future in Russia and urged the establishment of agricultural colonies for Jews in America.

Krauskopf was shown a model Jewish farm at Odessa. His experiences inspired him on his return to purchase at his own expense the farm near Doylestown on which he established a school to train youth from the slums in all aspects of agriculture. To raise the necessary funds for buildings, library and equipment, Krauskopf wandered the country, giving lectures for fees and tapping wealthy individuals. By fall 1897 Krauskopf's school had been dedicated and ten boys were enrolled. Thanks to his energetic efforts, the school grew in physical facilities and in educational scope. In the early years, Krauskopf made two trips per week to the campus, having persuaded the Philadelphia and Reading Railroad to put a station where its Doylestown branch line ran through the campus. He served on the faculty until the school grew to the point where he had to limit his visits to giving lectures to "the boys" on those Sunday afternoons when he was free of congregational responsibilities.[32]

Fortunately, as early as 1892, Keneseth Israel had recognized that the growth of activities engendered by Krauskopf called for staff, and they engaged the first of many young rabbis who were to move from Keneseth Israel to positions of prominence in the American rabbinate.[33] The Rev. Dr. J. Leonard Levy left his mark on Philadelphia by creating a community center, "The Home of Delight," at 426 Pine Street to serve the cultural and social needs of the residents of the area.

Long before "ecumenical" entered the common vocabulary, Krauskopf brought the clergy of Philadelphia together to organize the Liberal Ministers Conference out of which grew the National Federation of Religious Liber-

Interior of Keneseth Israel, 1894. *Courtesy of Dropsie University Library and Allen Meyers.*

als. His organizing energy also extended to the rabbis when, in 1901, he put together the Board of Jewish Ministers of Philadelphia.

The year 1903 was one of major recognition for Krauskopf—the Alumni Association of Hebrew Union College asked him to become Director General of the Isaac M. Wise Memorial Fund for the support of the College and his colleagues elected him the third President of the Central Conference of American Rabbis. Both positions were exceedingly time-consuming, but his temple's leadership recognized the honor involved and gave him the time needed to travel the country. For the College he raised the immense sum of $325,000.[34] For the Central Conference he advocated the appointment of a permanent clerk, later called Executive Secretary, and encouraged the creation of Reform-style synagogues in immigrant neighborhoods. Krauskopf wanted to involve laypersons in the decisions of the Central Conference, but his colleagues vetoed the idea. A number of his far-seeing suggestions were referred to other bodies.[35]

Despite Krauskopf's many activities, his congregation never complained of being neglected. In addition to Sabbath sermons and his carefully edited and printed Sunday lectures, he created a *Service Manual* of Sabbath and holiday prayers. Consistent with his thinking, most of the prayers were in English with only an occasional line of Hebrew. Published first in 1892, this prayerbook went to three editions and was adopted by a number of other congregations that shared Krauskopf's views of Reform Judaism. For his Sunday services he wrote and published *Service Ritual* and *Service Hymnal*. The annual congregational yearbooks, published at his instigation, record his many activities in the larger community where he was frequently a spokesman for important causes, as well as being a member or leader of boards and committees.[36]

Three times during his career, Krauskopf lectured to his congregation on the subject of Zionism. The announcement of the first Zionist Conference in 1898 evoked from him "Noble Impulses are Speechless Prophets," in which he applauded the agricultural efforts of the Zionist pioneers in Palestine and recognized the validity of Herzl's goal of a land of refuge, but still he questioned the concept of a "national" home. While affirming his admiration for Herzl, Krauskopf was vociferous in proclaiming that the cure for antisemitism was not to run away to any land, either Palestine or, as author Israel Zangwill was proposing, Uganda, but to fight antisemitism with knowledge of the Jew at his best.

In 1916, Krauskopf made a trip to Palestine where he toured extensively. He reported his findings in a series of eleven Sunday lectures, ending with "The Dream of the Zionist." Krauskopf came back impressed with what had been accomplished by the pioneers, some 15,000 of them already in the land. While reaffirming his own belief in Judaism as a religion and not a nation, Krauskopf came to disdain those who said that Palestine could not support all those who were willing to go. Nor did he share the fears of dual loyalty expressed by some antizionists. Krauskopf recognized the problems facing the Zionist dream, but he admired the dream.[37]

As a result of his trip, Krauskopf became a strong defender of Zionism against the antizionists. His daughter, Madeleine, who had shared his trip, told of his having been especially moved by the arrival at the Jordan of four tired men, their feet bound in rags, who bent down and washed themselves and then kissed the ground. They had walked from Russia to the Holy Land![38]

Under the burden of his many activities, Krauskopf collapsed. The immediate cause was a fire that destroyed one of the buildings at the Farm School. Despite warnings from his physician, he persisted in his labors until he was forced to rest at his daughter's home in Atlantic City, where he died June 12, 1923. His eventful career was reported in two-column spreads in the Philadelphia papers.[39] It is understandable that this remarkable man, who had come as an immigrant from Prussian-Posen at age 14 and achieved national recognition at barely twice that age, should have developed a strong ego. He encouraged the cult of personality by presenting each of his confirmands with an autographed photo of himself. He expected adulation and was not above saying to his second wife in the presence of a leading shirt manufacturer, "Sybil, what size shirts do I wear?"

Joseph Krauskopf with daughter Madeleine and wife Sybil.
Courtesy of Malcolm H. Stern.

But Krauskopf's dynamism and magnetic personality left a profound imprint on people who came under his influence. Many reared on his principles found it difficult to adjust to the post-World War II changes in Reform Judaism. His name and his mystique still permeate those Keneseth Israel families whose forebears were his congregants. His most lasting monument is the farm school he founded. He recognized this when he left testamentary instructions that a replica of his home library be built there and that his cremated ashes be placed in a niche in that library.

It was Krauskopf who brought Henry Berkowitz to Rodeph Shalom. The two had met in 1875 as entering students at Hebrew Union College in Cincinnati. Their friendship was immediate and they roomed together. As students they collaborated on several literary ventures. Six months after their joint ordination in 1883 they were married in a double wedding by Isaac M. Wise at Berkowitz's home. Krauskopf married Berkowitz' sister, Rose, and Berkowitz married an orphan cousin, Flora Brunn, who had grown up in his home. Berkowitz began his career in Mobile, Alabama, then followed Krauskopf in Kansas City. At the 1892 dedication of Keneseth

Israel's new building Berkowitz was the featured speaker. Krauskopf had arranged for two leaders of Rodeph Shalom to be present to hear Berkowitz, and they promptly invited him to become Jastrow's successor. He arrived at Rodeph Shalom that December.[40] Great enthusiasm greeted Philadelphia's first American-born rabbi.[41]

Following Krauskopf's lead Berkowitz began publishing his sermons, created a public library and issued an annual yearbook for the congregation. He reorganized the religious school, making German study optional and hence soon abandoned. He replaced weekly sessions with daily ones and involved the children actively in festival services. Congregational singing and a children's choir became regular features at worship services. By 1894, he had persuaded the congregation to replace Jastrow's prayerbook with the newly published *Union Prayer Book.* Each of these innovations met with opposition from the traditionalists in the congregation, but by the end of five years Berkowitz's warm, outgoing personality and his obvious sincerity and good humor made his leadership of the congregation secure.[42]

From the outset of his career Berkowitz had been disturbed by the ignorance of Judaism so evident among the laity, especially among the rising American-born generation. He was also unhappy with teaching methods imported from the European ghetto that turned off American children. He saw the need for teachers to be trained in modern pedagogy. Impressed by the Methodist programs of adult education generated at Lake Chautauqua and in local study circles around the country, Berkowitz determined to establish a Jewish Chautauqua Society. He discussed his dream with Rabbi Gustave Gottheil of New York's Temple Emanu-el who had been a speaker at Lake Chautauqua. Gottheil applauded the idea and recommended that his son, Professor Richard Gottheil of Columbia University, be enlisted to prepare a syllabus on Jewish history. After paying for the syllabus from his own pocket, Berkowitz proceeded to announce the project at a Friday evening service at Rodeph Shalom. The congregation's young adult group, the Jewish Culture Society, enthusiastically supported the idea. In April 1893 they convoked a mass meeting at Keneseth Israel at which the Jewish Chautauqua Society was born.

In the course of its history, the Jewish Chautauqua Society has changed its focus: from general Jewish adult education it moved into summer sessions for religious school teachers. A successful series of lectures in 1910 on the campus of the University of Tennessee moved the Society in the direction of having rabbis educate Gentiles about Judaism, a program it still carries on. Shelves of Judaica for college libraries are also provided. In 1939, Dr. Maurice Jacobs recommended that the Society become the national project of the National Federation of Temple Brotherhoods. They have continued its work on college campuses and added telecasts on Jewish life and lore. The Society continues to recognize its indebtedness to Henry Berkowitz as its founder and lifelong chancellor.[43]

The close relationship between Krauskopf and Berkowitz was reflected in many joint activities of Keneseth Israel and Rodeph Shalom. Both listed the other's confirmands on their confirmation programs. Joint services were held on special occasions and during the summers, the latter tradition prevailing until 1947. Both rabbis merged their young adult groups to form the Lyceum Institute.

Berkowitz maintained a deep and ongoing social concern. His youthful lecture, *Judaism and the Social Question,* was published while he was still in Mobile. Philadelphia's proliferating social agencies led him to call for a united endeavor. In 1901, at his instigation, the Federation of Jewish Charities was born. He was an early executive member of the Playgrounds Association that serviced children in underprivileged neighborhoods. The rise of prostitution among Russian-Jewish immigrant girls led to his appointment on Mayor Rudolph Blankenburg's Vice Commission. As an honorary vice-president of the Playgrounds Association, Berkowitz challenged the next mayor's patronage appointment of a superintendent of playgrounds. The mayor promptly dismissed Berkowitz from office, which led to protests in the press and from the Association. Berkowitz resigned from his honorary vice-presidency, but three years later, when illness had forced his retirement from Rodeph Shalom, the Society voted to reinstate his honorary title.

Within the congregation Berkowitz instituted a Junior Congregation with its own holiday services, choir and committees, a project that was widely imitated. He also created a popular volume for Sabbath home observance, *Kiddush, or Sabbath Sentiment,* that went to three editions. Its rituals were incorporated in both *Union Haggadah* and *Union Prayer Book.* Berkowitz was long a member of the Conference's Committee on Liturgy, and was its chairman when *Prayers for Private Devotion* was published.[44]

At a convention of the Central Conference in 1899 Berkowitz was one of several speakers in a somewhat one-sided debate on Zionism. He summarized his statement entitled "Why I am not a Zionist" as follows:

1. Because I do not believe that the misery of my people is hopeless. I have not lost faith in the triumph of justice in the world.
2. Because . . . modern organizations working out the problems of the day are practical, feasible, and sensible, while Zionism is sentimental and chimerical . . .
3. Because Zionism makes race and nationality, rather than religion, ultimate and essential for Jews. Jews have no lasting claims for a separate existence excepting their religious mission. To be faithful to this they must wilfully assume the martyrdom and the struggle and not weakly evade it. . . .[45]

The Pittsburgh Platform remained Berkowitz's creed throughout his ministry and rare was the Reform colleague who differed with this view.

During World War I Berkowitz worked actively raising funds and speaking for Jewish war relief. Under the joint sponsorship of the Jewish Welfare Board and the Jewish Chautauqua Society he toured army camps lecturing to service men. In October 1917, he was invited to Cincinnati to lecture the Hebrew Union College students on *Intimate Glimpses of the Rabbi's Career,* as the published version was called. The book became a classic in its genre.

Worn down by the numerous funerals in the influenza epidemic of 1919, Berkowitz secured a vacation and traveled west, stopping to visit family in Kansas City. Some of them were also stricken and he buried several. Shortly after his return to Philadelphia he suffered a severe coronary attack that compelled him to retire to Atlantic City. As his health permitted he returned to Philadelphia for special occasions, most notably his own thirtieth anniversary at Rodeph Shalom, which evoked an outpouring of affection for the rabbi who has gone down in Reform Jewish history as "The Beloved Rabbi."[46] Krauskopf and Berkowitz were total opposites in personality. Where Krauskopf was extravagantly admired, Berkowitz was genuinely loved. Krauskopf's wit could be sardonic, Berkowitz's was gentle. He loved puns. Hard of hearing in his later years, he wore a hearing aid with a receiving mechanism hung on his chest. He would delight young children by making the aid chirp in a birdlike sound. Both rabbis were blessed with helpmates that complemented their personalities and devoted their energies to their husbands' careers.

The death of Krauskopf in 1923 and of Berkowitz the following year left a void in both congregations that each found difficult to fill. Keneseth Israel continued with their incumbent associate rabbi, Abraham J. Feldman, as interim. Rodeph Shalom had already elected Harry W. Ettelson as Berkowitz's successor, and subsequently gave him an assistant in the person of Ferdinand M. Isserman, a young firebrand who engendered much excitement with his radical views. All three of these rabbis moved on to significant pulpits.[47]

Keneseth Israel's choice of an appropriate successor to Krauskopf was Rabbi William H. Fineshriber of Memphis, noted for the intellectual caliber of his preaching delivered in an engaging conversational manner. He arrived at Keneseth Israel for the Holy days of 1924. Although as radically Reform as Krauskopf, Fineshriber restored the reading of Torah, which Krauskopf had eliminated. For Sabbath services he replaced *Service Manual* with *Union Prayer Book,* but retained Krauskopf's *Hymnal* and *Service Ritual* at Sunday services. So popular was his religious school that it overflowed the temple and the adjacent Alumni Building, which Krauskopf had erected in 1914. Some thought was given to joining the flight to the suburbs, but this idea was abandoned in favor of two projects: the creation of a suburban religious school in Oak Lane and the redesigning of the facilities at Broad Street above Columbia. Although the suburban school was discontinued when the remodeling was completed, it was later revived and became the nucleus around which Temple Judea was opened in 1933 to become Philadelphia's third Reform congregation.[48]

Keneseth Israel also reached out to Philadelphia's two leading universities, Temple and the University of Pennsylvania. Fineshriber taught a course in Judaism at Temple and also raised funds for the University. In 1927, Temple gratefully awarded him an honorary Doctor of Divinity. To fill a need of Jewish students at the University of Pennsylvania, Fineshriber and his assistant, Rabbi Julian Feibelman, conducted lectures and programs financed by the congregation. These activities were later taken over by the Jewish Student House, now the Hillel Foundation.

The stock market crash of 1929 and the subsequent Great Depression led Fineshriber to create an Emergency Fund from donations received during services. This fund was used to assist needy individuals both in the congregation and in the larger community. An investigative case worker was engaged until the need subsided and public agencies again took over.

In 1931, Fineshriber restored Bar Mitzvah at Keneseth Israel, thereby opening membership to many who would otherwise not have joined the congregation. The departure of Russell King Miller, the long-time organist, who had composed and compiled Krauskopf's *Service Hymnal,* brought to Keneseth Israel Isadore Freed, one of America's leading Jewish composers. He served as organist, choir director and composer-in-residence, and created a number of musical Sabbath services that are still widely used around the country.

Fineshriber had a dream that he was unable to bring to reality: a central Reform temple with a group of satellites in the suburbs served by a corps of rabbis, thereby allowing for a variety of pulpit speakers and an exchange of programs. He even proposed abandoning the facilities at Broad and Columbia in favor of using Rodeph Shalom's more central location as the headquarters building, but neither congregation agreed.

In 1925, one year after Fineshriber's arrival at Keneseth Israel, Louis Wolsey came to Rodeph Shalom from the Euclid Avenue Temple (now Fairmount Temple) in Cleveland. Under his leadership that congregation had grown from 150 to 1450 families, and he was known nationally for his pulpit oratory. He was persuaded to leave his life contract in Cleveland for one in Philadelphia.

For most of its history Rodeph Shalom had been holding its religious school in a building remote from the sanctuary. One of Wolsey's first acts was to persuade the board to abandon the Benjamin F. Teller Memorial School Building at Broad and Jefferson in favor of a new and enlarged facility at Broad and Mount Vernon. Several alternate plans were abandoned before the dream became a reality, but the Broad Street subway, then under construction, convinced the leadership of the convenience of remaining at Broad and Mount Vernon.

Soon after his arrival at Rodeph Shalom, Wolsey was elected president

Rodeph Shalom, new building erected 1927. *Photograph by Michael Gillikin.*

of the Central Conference of American Rabbis and persuaded the Conference to give active support to the World Union for Progressive Judaism founded in England by Miss Lily Montagu with Wolsey as one of its founding vice-presidents. Subsequently he became chairman of the Central Conference's Committee on Synagogue Music and was responsible for the 1932 publication of the red (third edition) *Union Hymnal.* Because of the Great Depression, the committee decided to include worship services and music for all the Jewish year so that impoverished congregations could worship with one volume. The book pioneered by soliciting hymns from every competent Jewish composer of the day.[49]

As the economic depression continued, Wolsey, with his assistant, Eugene J. Sack, established Mt. Vernon Center, utilizing Rodeph Shalom's facilities as a community center for underprivileged youth in the neighborhood, with a Well Baby Clinic offering young mothers preventive medical care and classes in homemaking.[50] Wolsey was appointed by the mayor in 1937 to be chairman of the Vice and Crime Commission. In this position, he made major recommendations that were to affect Pennsylvania's parole system.[51]

Tall, portly and imposing in appearance, Wolsey was a forceful speaker and an intimidating adversary. He never hesitated to challenge what he considered wrong or unjust. He and Fineshriber, like most of their predecessors and the majority of their congregants, were vocal opponents of political Zionism. In 1937, the Central Conference of American Rabbis, meeting in Columbus, Ohio, attempted to replace the 1885 Pittsburgh Platform with "Guiding Principles of Reform Judaism." These principles included the theme of Jewish peoplehood and stated that Zionism and Reform Judaism are not incompatible. A heated debate led to a tie vote and the principles were approved only by having the president cast the deciding ballot.

Recognizing the divisiveness of the Zionist issue, the Conference factions agreed to a truce in which matters relating to a Jewish state were to be ruled out of order. At the 1942 Conference, Wolsey and others felt that this truce had been violated when a resolution in support of a Jewish army under the British was brought to the floor and approved at a time when many of the rabbis were absent. Upon his return to Philadelphia after the Conference, Wolsey issued an invitation to like-minded rabbis to join him in an Antizionist Manifesto and to meeting in Atlantic City. Ninety-three rabbis signed the manifesto. Subsequently, leading laymen were enlisted and the American Council for Judaism was formed. When the full horror of the Holocaust was revealed and the State of Israel born, Wolsey and many of the other rabbis involved repudiated the American Council. Fineshriber, however, along with many of the lay leaders, remained a member, and he was an honorary vice-president for the rest of his life.

It is regrettable that the Zionist issue, that split American Jewry for the first half of this century, has allowed the memory of these Reform leaders to be belittled. As we have attempted to show, they were among the ablest spokesmen of their generations, often placing Philadelphia far ahead of New York in influencing national Jewish issues. They not only built their congregations to positions of eminence in the nation, they helped their congregants reach a balance between assimilation and faith at a time when America's assimilative pull was at its strongest. In the process they became role models in service to the larger community, establishing bridges of interfaith understanding and building for community betterment. Their names were far better known nationally than even the capable rabbis who succeeded them. They lived in an age when the rabbi was among the few Jews with a postgraduate education or degree. They also lived at a time of blatant antisemitism, when Jews were excluded from many fields of endeavor, from resorts and from corporate executive posts. As a consequence, they received greater support—and even adulation—from the Jewish community than do present-day rabbis, because theirs was the voice that defended the Jew, interpreting him to the Gentile. The rabbis of Philadelphia achieved greatness, and today's Philadelphia Jewish community owes much to their pioneering endeavors.

German Jews vs. Russian Jews in Philadelphia Philanthropy

Philip Rosen

"Mr. Hackenburg then moved that the representatives of the downtown societies should be asked to the next meeting. After argument the motion was lost." Thus read the minutes of the first meeting of the Federation of Jewish Charities, March 12, 1901.[1] The results of that decision and the style of the leaders were to imprint the nature of leadership within Federation for five decades.

"We, here in Philadelphia are too prone to expect a few people—the village work horses to do the work and confine our efforts to a limited circle," complained Jacob Gimbel, president in 1905.[2] The FJC was dominated by an interlocking directorate of German Jews, an elite group who devoted themselves to charities supported by their wealthy and not-so-wealthy friends.

From the beginning, the German Jews who lived north of Market Street and in between Broad and Fourth, the "uptowners" as they were called, did *for* the vast majority of Jews of Philadelphia, East European in origin, not *with*. They held their Federation meetings and made their decisions at their select social club, The Mercantile. They survived exclusively for at least two decades by the donations of time and money of the uptown "big givers." The "downtowners" or "Russian Jews," as the masses of Balkan, Russian and Austro-Hungarian immigrants were called, sat on their hands at donation time. When the United Hebrew Charities, a Federation constituent, was pushing for the building of Eagleville Sanitarium for consumptives, department store owner Samuel Lit is said to have told a well-to-do Russian Jew that newcomers who prosper should contribute. "You're right," said the other, "so I'll tell you—You German Jews contribute the money, and we Russian Jews will contribute the tuberculosis."[3]

At the annual meeting of the Federation in May 1910, Dr Cyrus Adler, *eminence gris*, president of Dropsie College in Philadelphia, moved that a committee be formed to make recommendations "whereby the scope of the Federation may be so increased as to affiliate with itself such organizations as did not participate in the original foundation."[4] The "such organizations" that Adler suggested were the myriad of institutions set up by the East European Jews to serve themselves in charitable, fraternal, religious, educational and cultural pursuits. They were the synagogues the orthodox Jews established with free loan societies *(Gemulat Hasadim)*, free or inexpensive burial plots *(Hevra Kadisha)*, visiting the sick committees *(Bikur Holim)* and other devices for charitable giving. They were the fraternal organizations that offered low-cost sickness and death insurance plans as well as the low-cost verein (organization) doctors and they were the trade union, socialist and zionist organizations that established an immigrant sheltering home, old home, orphan's home and two day nurseries.[5]

In establishing these institutions, the Russian Jews like the German Jews before them operated from a tradition of *Tzedakah*, charitable righteousness, organizing the community to care for its own. This concept found its root in Biblical law, the *mitzvah* of giving to the poor.

Torah study was another foundation of organized Jewish life. The East European downtown Jews established their own. Some were modeled like the European *Heder*, which involved individualized, intensive Hebrew langauge lessons centered around the sacred texts of the Bible and Talmud. The first religious afternoon community school, Talmud Torah, was founded in 1892. By 1918, fifteen separate schools with 3000 students formed the Associated Talmud Torahs, an umbrella organization that merged finances and set standards for teachers, methods and curricula.

Two organizations created before this century, then part of the original Federation in 1901, changed greatly as Russian Jews impacted on Philadelphia. The first was the Hebrew Education Society which started as an all-day Jewish parochial school designed to arrest assimilation among German Jews. By 1901, the all-day school disappeared, but its Hebrew schools and a large building called Touro Hall at Tenth and Carpenter Streets hummed. Its classes instructed downtowners in Hebrew, corrected their English, gave intellectuals university extension programs and book lovers a chance to read thousands of books of Jewish interest. Women learned millinery and dress-making and men learned cigar-making and garment-cutting.[6]

However, by 1905, attendance at the Hebrew schools was slipping. Charles Bernheimer, a scholarly writer and social worker in Philadelphia wrote:

> Schools established by the Hebrew Sunday School Society and the Hebrew Education Society, although largely patronized by children of Russian Jews, were not considered sufficient by parents because Hebrew was not regarded as

prime importance in the curriculum, or because modern methods employed in the schools were looked upon with suspicion.[7]

Bernheimer went on to relate how the downtowners set up their own religious educational system.

The industrial classes did not do too well as the century turned. Even the HES *50-Year Commemorative Book* related that interest in and attendance in industrial classes were eroding. Young Russian Jews had no desire to stay in factories. By 1918, no religious or vocational classes took place at Touro Hall. The building became a settlement house focusing on recreational and social activities.[8]

By 1926, the rapid rise of Russian Jews into white-collar and business occupations put the Society out of business altogether. Its settlement work was taken over by the YM and YWHAs and Neighborhood Center, Gratz College and the religious teachers training institute.[9]

The Young Women's Union was another organization that underwent great change. It started as a kindergarten for Russian Jewish children. The unmarried women of the Union were moved by the conditions of improperly supervised children while their mothers slaved away at work to make ends meet. The Union created a "first" by its kindergarten, added another Philadelphia "first" with its nursery school, and yet another with its day care center. The YWU activities were models for similar Gentile and secular philanthropy on behalf of children.[10]

When the Federation of Jewish Charities began in 1901, the Union was one of the original nine constituent agencies. Like the Hebrew Education Society, it sought to help recent arrivals adjust to an American milieu. The Union's new building constructed at 428 Bainbridge Street concentrated on settlement work. This meant athletic clubs, dramatic clubs, arts and crafts clubs and music clubs. The kindergarten was turned over to the Philadelphia Board of Education, a move that indicated the assimilationist/secularist thinking of the officers.[11]

The Young Women's Union pioneered in other plans to aid their poor cousins. In 1901, an offshoot, the Juvenile Aid Committee, assumed probationary responsibility for young Jews released to it by the Juvenile Court. This move was a result of the efforts of Mrs. Sol Selig (*née* Bella Loeb) a Union founder who pushed for an enlightened, treatment-oriented Juvenile Court and the wide use of probation as a form of rehabilitation. The Juvenile Aid Committee also found foster homes for its charges from the court. The Committee became completely secularized, breaking off from the YWU to form the Juvenile Aid Society.[12]

In 1918, the YWU was reincorporated within the Federation as the Neighborhood Center. For the first time men were admitted. By 1923, Charles Edwin Fox, noted Philadelphia lawyer and founder of the Big Brothers Association, became president of the Center. Other centers were added, the focus of which was settlement work, indistinguishable from Christian or secular settlements.[13] Julian Greifer, past head of the Neighborhood Centers reminisced:

> Kurt Peiser, executive director of the Federation wanted to replace the head worker who was a Christian Scientist, with someone with a strong Jewish background. The Neighborhood Center was exclusively a settlement of Americanization for Russian Jews. Now Peiser and the National Jewish Welfare Board wanted to change focus and make the Center more Jewish.[14]

The Center's board, made up entirely of daughters of upper-class German Jews, had mixed feelings on this Jewish identity direction in 1942. Three board members resigned, claiming that the role of the settlement house *was* assimilation. The rest of the board went on to aid the new director.[15]

In their zeal to "Americanize" the Russian immigrant and his children, the uptowners caused resentment among the downtowners who were either religious or had moved from religious identity to ethnic identity. While the "founding fathers" of charities among German Jews—the Adler, Sulzberger and Solis-Cohen families—were strongly oriented toward Jewish tradition and concerned with the too rapid assimilation of both German and Russian young people, the second and third generation uptowners had much less Jewish orientation. The secularization of Federation agencies increased alienization among Russian Jews, and was a contributing factor in the lack of mass support until the fifth decade of FJC's existence.

The existence of two separate communities, two separate agencies of charities and parallel organizations caused concern in leadership circles. There was an attempt to unite all the Jews of Philadelphia, both Russian and German, into one large organization. In June 1911, a formal organization, the Jewish Community of Philadelphia, or Kehilla, was created. Its model, the Jewish Community of New York, had been organized three years earlier. Like the one 90 miles away, the Philadelphia version was originated by, and was part and parcel of the American Jewish Committee.

The Jewish Community of Philadelphia grew out of the efforts of Judge Mayer Sulzberger, Dr. Cyrus Adler, and Dr. Solomon Solis-Cohen, all most active in creating Jewish cultural, educational and philanthropic organizations and prominent in the Federation of Jewish Charities. Both Mayer Sulzberger and Cyrus Adler split their time between New York and Philadelphia. Indeed, the two men, officers of both the New York Kehilla and the American Jewish Committee on a national level, brought New York's experiences back to the City of Brotherly Love.[16]

For months prior to its formation, Sulzberger, Adler and Solis-Cohen visited synagogues, lodges, charitable and other Jewish groups in the city urging them to become part of the new umbrella organization, a kind of local League of Nations. The result was that by November 1911 the Kehilla

Solomon Solis-Cohen. *Courtesy of Maxwell Whiteman.*

constituted 117 organizations represented by 197 delegates. The delegates themselves, however, had very little power. They elected six representatives to the American Jewish Committee and acted merely as an advisory board to Committee. Since the latter was firmly in the hands of German Jews, the uptowners were again inviting support but not sharing power or meaningful participation with Russian Jews.[17]

The New York organized community had been triggered by an anti-semitic article in the *North American Review*. New York Police Commissioner Theodore Bingham charged in that article that New York Jews, while constituting 25 percent of the city's population, committed 50 percent of the crime. The Kehilla of New York was to act as one united Jewish body against such false attacks, and to protect the civil and religious rights in the city. The stated purposes of the Philadelphia Kehilla were similar.[18]

The urge to unify Philadelphia's Jews loomed large in the formation of the Kehilla. On May 12, 1911, the *Exponent* editorial noted that there were "at least as many downtown Jewish charities *out* of Federation as there were inside it." It went on to urge Kehilla to "end waste and duplication and distinctions between various elements of the community."

The same people who controlled the Federation of Jewish Charities controlled the Kehilla. They included Louis Edward Levy, printer and publisher and Kehilla president after Adler, Louis Gerstley, liquor magnate, and Keneseth Israel's ulta-Reform rabbi Joseph Krauskopf. The two Russian Jewish leaders were Conservative rabbi Max Klein, spiritual head of Adath Jeshurun, and Orthodox rabbi of downtown B'nai Abraham, Bernard Levinthal.[19]

In 1911, Philadelphia's leaders were very concerned about Jewish identity. In the fall of that year Kehilla undertook a census of the Philadelphia Jewish population. It discovered the greater number of some 180,000 Jews unaffiliated with synagogues and children receiving no religious education. Of 41,000 Jewish children aged 6 to 16, only 25 percent, or 10,189, were attending some Jewish religious school. Shocked, the Committee of Rabbis, the Council of Jewish Women and the YMHA sent visitors to thousands of unaffiliated families to urge them to join some Jewish organization and send their children to religious school.[20]

By 1916, one would find news of the Philadelphia Kehilla hard to find in the *Exponent*. The American Jewish Yearbooks of 1912 through 1920 gave reports of the Philadelphia Jewish Community, but in 1921, no mention of either the New York or the Philadelphia Kehilla was made. No explanation was given. Moses Freeman's book in Yiddish, *Fifty Years of Philadelphia Jewish Life,* published in 1934, fails to mention the Kehilla. Just what impact did it have and why did it die so fast?

One of its major concerns, control over Kashruth, failed miserably. Less than four years after operation began the Board of Kashruth was allowed to die for lack of funds. As in New York, various rabbis, with vested interests such as supervisor of kosher slaughterhouses and wholesale and retail butchers, had their "deals" and "interpretations" regarding Kashruth. They wanted no central supervision that would interfere with business.[21]

After World War I a wave of extreme nationalism overcame the country that spilled into antisemitism. Henry Ford reprinted the notorious forgery *The Protocols of the Elders of Zion.* Jews were blamed for Bolshevism both in Europe and America. According to Joseph Kun, who served as president of the Kehilla in its last days, this mood led to the Kehilla's demise:

> It was considered by the leaders of the Community here and in New York, ill advised under the circumstances to continue the Kehilla form of Jewish community activities . . . (actually referred to by professional anti-Semites at the time as a "Jewish government" in our own country). Accordingly, the Kehilla idea was allowed to simmer out.[22]

Scholars found more basic reasons for the demise of the New York Kehilla—resistance by Eastern European Jews to perceived manipulation by a German Jewish elite, too ambitious a superstructure, rivalry by a pro-Zionist American Jewish Congress that appealed more to the masses, lack of financial support, and the personality and political views of New York's president, Judah Magnes.[23]

The above factors attributed to New York's Kehilla hold in some measure for Philadelphia. The immigrants from Eastern Europe breathed free in America. There was no need to organize and speak "in one voice" against an oppressive government. Jewish diversity, private arrangements and the desire for laissez faire prevailed. The Jewish labor movement with its own organizations viewed German leadership with suspicion for they saw them as exploiting employers. The burden of making a living was also so great in the first two decades of the century that it diverted masses of Jews from large organizational concerns. While the Kehilla lasted a decade, the majority of Jews were alienated from it, and, by 1916, the founders and their once enthusiastic supporters lost interest.[24]

It took 18 years for the board of Federation to accept what Jacob Gimbel and Cyrus Adler had urged—to invite all charities into the Federation of Jewish Charities. In the spring of 1919, Federation expanded its constituency to include 39 instead of 14 agencies, for which it allocated $436,206. It amended its bylaws to permit directors and officers of agencies to serve on the board, which expanded from 12 to 40. This expansion brought in some organizations founded by Russian Jews. Most important of these Russian Jewish organizations were the Talmud Torah Association, Mount Sinai Hospital, the Hebrew Sheltering Home and Old Age Home.[25]

The expanded Federation brought in a dynamic social worker born in Eastern Europe as executive director, Jacob Billikopf, quite an innovation considering that for 18 years the board and its agencies operated by volunteer efforts of dedicated lay people who contributed the lion's share of their time and a great deal of their money to the philanthropic work. Jacob Gutman, one of the few Russian-born Jews to penetrate into high FJC circles commented on the first hired director:

> Jacob Billikoff was a brilliant man who knew how to unite communities around federated organizations. He was one of first to hire trained social workers, for example, and press the concept of doing our own planning and budgeting. He also had a strong Lithuanian accent.[26]

The incorporation of some downtown agencies brought a rise of subscribers to Federation. *The Annual Report of 1920* recorded about 7000, up from 2800 in 1918. This number held until the World War II period. A look through this booklet and the minutes of 1919, 1920–24 reveals that the uptowners were still firmly in charge both of the constituencies of Federation and its board. Horace Stern, president of FJC from 1924–1927, speaking at the twenty-fifth anniversary of the organization complained:

> Are our boards now selected by the Jewish people? They certainly are not. A

Louis Levinthal. *Courtesy of the Federation of Jewish Agencies of Greater Philadelphia.*

vacancy occurs by death or resignation. How is it filled? By the remaining members of the board. Whom do they select? Naturally their friends, persons whom they know and in whom they have confidence. . . . What is the result? The result is that with few exceptions each board is made up of a socially homogenous element.[27]

One Russian Jew, Orthodox Rabbi Bernard Levinthal penetrated into Philadelphia's charitable establishment. Born in Kovno, Lithuania, he came to Philadelphia in 1891, according to his son, "to stem the tide of assimilation." Rabbi Levinthal held his pulpit at B'nai Abraham (5th and Lombard) until his death in 1952.[28]

A year after stepping into Philadelphia, Levinthal succeeded in establishing the first Talmud Torah, Communal Hebrew School. He also created a Hebrew High School where he served as principal. In 1902, he organized a Jewish Academy, *Mishkan Yisroel*, where he taught Talmud. He succeeded in bringing together 18 synagogues to supervise Kashruth. In 1894, he called into being the important Russian Jewish Hevra Kaddisha, the Free Burial Society.[29]

Rabbi Levinthal believed that he must cooperate with all Jewish groups, Orthodox or not. He was chosen by Judge Mayer Sulzberger to be a member of the American Jewish Committee, one of five from Philadelphia. He founded the Council of Jewish Clubs in the city and organized the first Philadelphia Brith Sholom lodge.[30]

He spoke whenever and wherever called. He told immigrants at Touro Hall that Judaism and Americanism were compatible. He walked to the socialist-leaning Hebrew Literature Society on Friday evenings to tell the radicals how the Bible and Talmud preached social justice.[31] When the Kehilla was started in Philadelphia, Levinthal was part of it, taking particular interest in Kashruth and Jewish education. He helped bring the Associated Talmud Torahs into Federation in 1919.[32]

Rabbi Levinthal's efforts, like those of his learned friends, Judge Mayer Sulzberger and Dr. Cyrus Adler, were not confined to the local level. Rabbi Levinthal also founded some national organizations. Together with Theodor Herzl, Max Nordau, Israel Zangwill and Menachem Ussishkin, he helped to start the Zionist movement. He was one of the founders of Mizracachi, the religious Zionist organization. He was a close friend of Reform Rabbi Stephen Wise, working with him in the United Palestine Appeal. This versatile and many faceted man became the vice president of the Federation of American Zionists.[33]

Bernard Levinthal's example of cooperation with German Jews in constructive endeavors was followed by a number of wealthy Russian Jews. The period of the 1920s was one of expansion in buildings and budgets as the Federation became more and more professionalized. The FJC Annual Reports showed a number of Russian Jewish big givers. They included such names as Bayuk (cigars), Grabowsky (cigars), Paley (cigars and radio), Publicker (whiskey and alcohol), and Schorr (law). Moreover, two prosperous real estate men, Albert Greenfield and Albert Lieberman, were very active. Involved also was a jurist, Louis Levinthal, and two in the clothing industry, Samuel and Joseph Daroff. Jacob Gutman, who made his fortune in textiles, was also accepted by the established Jewish leadership who respected philanthropy as a means of admission to society.[34]

One of the first Russian Jews to enter into Jewish philanthrophy was a man who made his fortune in real estate following the tradition of Benjamin Teller, Felix Isman, and Jules Mastbaum. In the world of Jewish charities Albert Greenfield's name crops up as a minor subscriber to the Mount Sinai campaign in 1906. By the early 1920's, Greenfield was a major figure in Federation money raising campaigns. FJC Board Minutes of 1922 note that Albert Greenfield presided over a high level campaign meeting at the exclusive Mercantile Club, the frequent site of parleys on Federation business. Membership in this uptown club was a sign of acceptance.[35]

Later known as "Mr. Philadelphia," Greenfield became a member of both the campaign building and finance committees of FJC. Mr. Philadelphia was so preoccupied with his vast business interests, civic and political activities as well as Catholic charities, that he didn't have time to concentrate on the Federation of Jewish Charities.[36]

Another Albert, Albert Lieberman, came into Federation leadership circles. Like Greenfield, he was born in Russia in the late 1800s and made his fortune in the real estate business.

Again like Greenfield, Lieberman's first Federation activities dealt with money raising and financial matters. Under the presidency of his friend, Horace Stern (1924–1927), Lieberman rose to importance on the Federation board, and was chosen president of its core agency, the Jewish Welfare Society (the expanded old United Hebrew Charities). He was to guide this organization from 1925, in the Depression, through World War II.[37]

In addition to the Welfare Society, Lieberman supported the cause of the Beth Jacob Schools (Orthodox all-day schools) within Federation. In the thirties, as a member of the Joint Distribution Committee, his heart went out to Jewish refugees fleeing Hitler's barbarism. He helped found a national coordinating committee to aid refugees and created its local branch out of the Welfare Society in Philadelphia. Most of the refugees arrived at the port of New York. Lieberman arranged to have a number of them sent to Philadelphia.[38]

In the depths of the Depression in 1931, because of the great difficulty of raising money for all of the needy due to impoverishment, the FJC was forced to become part of a city-wide, united effort campaign for charity which included secular and other non-Jewish charities. In 1937, seeing the need for a particularly *Jewish* agency (allotments to Jewish charities from the United Community Campaign were seen as "secular" relief to the whole Philadelphia community) to aid overseas Jewry, to bolster Palestine as a haven and to fight antisemitism,[39] Lieberman helped to found a new federation—Allied Jewish Appeal. He had a number of fellow Russian Jews to work with him; outstanding was Louis Levinthal.[40]

Louis Levinthal was born into rabbinic nobility. Both his father and grandfather were rabbis. His father, Bernard, was considered the ecumenical person in the Russian Jewish Orthodox community who worked with the German Jewish leadership in Federation, its constituencies, with the Kehilla, and in the American Jewish Committee. Throughout his life, Louis tried to follow his father's example. Born in Philadelphia in 1892, he studied in *Yeshivot* (religious academies). His interest in Talmudic law prompted his interest in secular law. He graduated from the University of Pennsylvania as a lawyer in 1916. Louis practiced until 1937 until he became a judge in Philadelphia's Common Pleas Court,[41] taking the "Jewish spot" once held by Sulzberger.

It was Judge Mayer Sulzberger and Jacob Billikoff who introduced him to the Federation of Jewish Charities in 1921. He became a director of the Talmud Torah Association, then its president (1929–34). With his father he insisted that Mount Sinai Hospital be strictly Kosher according to Jewish law with a *Mashgiah* (Kosher supervisor) present. This was not achieved, however, until 1930.

Attorney Levinthal was intensely interested in Zionist causes. He became president of the Philadelphia chapter of the Zionist Organization of America (1924–1929), and was one of the founders of the Jewish National Fund, a worldwide agency devoted to buying and reclaiming land in Palestine. Levinthal also organized the American Palestine Appeal in Philadelphia.[42] These organizations were looked down upon by the non-Zionist or anti-Zionist uptowners who believed Palestine was not the place for most Jews; the Jewish homeland was the countries where Jews resided. These Palestine-related agencies were not part of Federation.[43]

Levinthal was active on the FJC board and the board of the Jewish Welfare Society. However, his attention turned most decidedly overseas to his brethren faced with Nazi terror. A Zionist, he saw vindicated the fears of those who objected to British control over the land of Israel. The British were slowing immigration to the one place international law had set aside for Jewish refuge.[44]

The Federation was by this time part of a city-wide fund raising campaign known by various names—Community Fund, Community Chest, United Community Campaign, and now the United Fund. The idea of one large fund raising drive was borrowed by the general Philadelphia community from Federation of Jewish Charities. However, FJC could only stay within local charitable relief.[45] Levinthal with others wanted money for the Joint Distribution Committee and projects to enlarge the *Yisnuv,* or Jewish settlement in Palestine. The judge remembered his struggle for a new federation:

> Hebrew education couldn't penetrate the Federation of Jewish Charities. The Hebrew University couldn't get into Federation. We organized the Allied Jewish Appeal out of the American Palestine Appeal.[46]

Judge Levinthal became president of the Zionist Organization of America in 1941. By 1942, with the Holocaust in full swing, and Britain in the middle of war, enforcing its White Paper of 1939 that virtually closed the gates of Palestine to Jews, many Jews who had their doubts about political sovereignty in Palestine moved toward the position stated by President Levinthal in the fall: "We see no political arrangement which could be workable other than the establishment of all Palestine in its historic boundaries as the Jewish Commonwealth."[47]

Louis Levinthal, like his friends Mayer Sulzberger and Cyrus Adler and his father, Rabbi Bernard Levinthal, helped to create national organizations. The Judge went on to become national co-chairman of the United Jewish Appeal, the national arm of Allied created one year after the local organiza-

Leon Sunstein. *Courtesy of the Federation of Jewish Agencies of Greater Philadelphia.*

tion. In his efforts Louis Levinthal received strong support from his colleagues, Sam and Joseph Daroff.[48]

The Daroffs, born at the end of the last century, were sons of an immigrant tailor. Their father, like many Russian Jews, soon found a way to increase his income by turning to the manufacturing of clothing. The elder Daroff, like the German Jewish first families, established a tradition of service in the local synagogue and charities. Daroff senior became the president of the Neziner Synagogue at 771 South Second Street. He set an example of philanthropy by opening his home to newly arrived immigrants.[49]

The boys spoke Yiddish in their home and played with Albert Greenfield, who also lived on Tasker Street.[50] The brothers entered the men's clothing business and became a huge success. Botany 500 became a national trademark.

The Daroff's first interest in charity was bringing baskets of ritual foods and materials for the needy through the Passover League. Joseph Daroff remembers getting married in his twenties at the Mercantile Club. Evidently, this elite German Jewish organization was ready to accept newcomers. Arthur Loeb, the builder and very active member of the Federation, introduced the Daroffs to FJC and placed them on the board. Sam became obsessed with service. According to Joseph Daroff, who recalled his brother's philanthropic efforts in a taped interview, "Sam spent only 20% of the time in the business and 80% in Jewish charities. He admits that he never could have done this without the approval of his four brothers and their support, for we attended the affairs of the business."[51]

Sam Daroff served on the board of four constituent agencies of Federation—the Mount Sinai Hospital Association, the Psychiatric Hospital Association, the Willow Crest Convalescent Home and the Jewish Employment Bureau. In the thirties, Hitler's barbarism fell upon Jews and Sam's attention fell upon Palestine as a place of refuge. He joined the national board of the Joint Distribution Committee, the Palestine Economic Corporation, the Jewish National Fund and Technion (an engineering college). In 1938, the two brothers joined with others to form the Allied Jewish Appeal.[52] Allied was formed by Jewish leaders who were concerned with the growth of antisemitism and particularly the plight of Jews living in countries infected by the Nazi virus. The tide of refugees was turning into a flood. Much more money was needed for the Joint Distribution Committee, the National Refugee Service and the United Palestine Appeal.[53]

Although it was the vehicle with which Russian Jews most closely identified, key elements in the old leadership played major roles in bringing it into existence, including Morris Wolf, Horace Stern and Leon Sunstein. An investment banker who was active in a variety of Jewish and civic causes, Sunstein recalled in a speech in 1948:

> In the AJA and in the presence of the overpowering tragedy of our people in Europe, the lines between the German and Russian, Polish and Rumanian Jews, between first families and newcomers, began to melt away. Groups who never before participated in organized community activity came into action side by side with those who had long traditions of public service. Very quickly, new and dynamic workers and leaders came to the fore. New resources, not only in money, but ability and devotion, were brought into play in the common cause. The number of contributors increased from 7000 to 90,000—in other words to include almost every Jewish family in the city . . . The 'old' and the 'new' came to know and respect each other both as community workers and as individuals. Again, it must be admitted the process is not complete.[54]

Within the new parallel federation, Sam Daroff assumed so many duties and was so generous that he became known as "Mr. Allied." In 1945, he was chosen president of the Allied Jewish Appeal, succeeding Leon C. Sunstein, president from 1939 to 1945, who was of Polish Jewish extraction.[55] Thus in Allied, the German Jewish hegemony over charities was broken. Four years after Daroff assumed his office, another Russian Jew—Jacob Gutman—become president of the Federation of Jewish Charities itself.

Jacob Gutman. *Courtesy of the Federation of Jewish Agencies of Greater Philadelphia.*

Gutman started his philanthropic career in 1907 at age 17, serving milk and eggs to patients at the Jewish Consumptive Society (later absorbed by Eagleville). He married soon afterwards and was accepted as a partner in his father-in-law's budding textile firm. Gutman's business fortunes rose and in 1919, he was invited by prominent philanthropist Irving Kohn to work on fund-raising for the expanded Federation. Jacob accepted, later became president of that agency and served on the board to his death.[56]

The textile manufacturer revealed in an interview how uptowners and downtowners got together in the 1920s and 1930s:

Contacts were made first on a business basis. Albert Lieberman did business with Morris Wolf. A. Gerstley [son of Louis] sought me out for securities. They discovered that we were dignified and generous; they sought our help in Federation. We Russian Jews were generous, so generous at times that we shamed the German Jews. Once we gave money, the pay off was to make us members of boards of directors.[57]

Jacob Gutman was one of seven officers of FJC who constituted a committee to aid in the forming of the United Jewish Appeal, national arm of overseas fund raising. With him were "old stock" Arthur Fleisher, Howard Loeb, Howard Wolf and Morris Wolf, and "new stock" Albert Lieberman and Louis Levinthal.[58] In 1949, Jacob Gutman was the first Russian Jew to became president of the Federation of Jewish Charities.[59]

The final integration of the German-Jewish and Russian-Jewish leaderships came with the merging of the Allied Jewish Appeal with the Federation of Jewish Charities in 1956. While this statement by Gutman may be exaggerated, it does contain a kernel of truth:

> We had, don't forget, two competing organizations by 1940, two different philosophies—the Federation of Jewish Charities, which supposedly represented the old German influence, and the Allied Jewish Appeal, founded in 1938 by the Eastern European influence to aid Jewish communities in Palestine and those threatened by the Nazis. It took a Holocaust and the successful establishment of the Jewish state to cause some sanity among the second generation, enough so that the two organizations could finally unite as the Federation of Jewish Agencies.[60]

By 1956 it could be said that one organization—the Federation of Jewish Agencies—was the instrument for almost all Jewish philanthropic enterprises in Philadelphia. The new name was a de facto victory for the "uptown" element. However, the fund-raising arm of the new federation was called the Allied Jewish Appeal and that was a symbolic victory for the "downtowners."

(12)

The Rise of
Albert M. Greenfield

Dan Rottenberg

The story of the Jews of Philadelphia in the first half of this century is in
large degree the story of Eastern European immigrants struggling for prosperity and social acceptance in the face of resistance from both the city's
Gentile business elite and the local German Jewish establishment. The most
dramatic of these success stories was that of Albert M. Greenfield, a Russian
immigrant who rose from office boy to ruler of an immense business empire
encompassing real estate, retail stores, banks, hotels, and transportation
companies. In the course of his career, which stretched from 1904 to his
death in 1967, Greenfield's influence extended into so many aspects of the
city's life that he was assured a place as one of the most powerful figures—
Jew or Gentile—in the history of Philadelphia.

Hundreds of thousands of Philadelphians lived, worked, or did business in buildings he owned, managed, leased, bought or sold. He controlled
a chain of department stores with 112 units in 19 states, a mortgage banking

Except where otherwise noted, the material contained here comes from personal
interviews and from a few definitive newspaper articles: Greenfield's obituary in the
New York Times, January 6, 1967, and in the *Philadelphia Bulletin*, January 5, 1967,
and an article entitled "The Greenfield Story: A Titan Looks Back Over Half a
Century," from the *Philadelphia Bulletin*, May 15, 1955. Material gathered in per-
sonal interviews has not been annotated because all interviews were conducted with
the understanding that no information would be attributed. The following, however,
is a partial list of subjects interviewed in connection with this research: Gustave
Amsterdam, E. Digby Baltzell, Boyd Barnard, Alfred Blasband, Clifford Brenner,
John Bunting, Chester Cincotta, Bruce Greenfield, William Greenfield, W. Carlton
Harris, Thomas LaBrum, D. Herbert Lipson, John O'Shea, Elizabeth Petrie, Irwin
Solomon, Malcolm Stern, Emily Sunstein, and Elizabeth Zeidman. Much of the
research was done in connection with an article that appeared in *Philadelphia*
magazine in May 1976.

company, the nation's largest real estate concern, Philadelphia's Yellow Cab Company, the Loft Candy Corporation and six major downtown hotels. At their peak, his holdings had a gross annual volume of $850 million.[1] Presidents, governors and mayors paid court to him. And far beyond exercising mere control over the city, Greenfield actively *changed* the face of the city: Society Hill, the Hopkinson House, the Ben Franklin Hotel, the Greenfield Building, the conversion of the old Ritz-Carlton Hotel into an office building, the Bankers Securities Building, the first modernization of the Bellevue-Stratford Hotel, the Sylvania Hotel, Bonwit Teller and the whole movement of finer stores from the east side of Broad Street to the west were all projects controlled or substantially influenced by Greenfield.

Greenfield was the prototypical immigrant outsider challenging the business elite—Jewish as well as Gentile. His rise to power worried some of Philadelphia's establishment leaders and alarmed others. They were cautious and proper; he was a flamboyant wheeler-dealer fond of aphorisms like "I would rather fall off the top rung than never climb the ladder."[2] As *Fortune* magazine observed in 1936, "He doesn't operate according to tradition, doesn't look back longingly to the Golden Age of Franklin or even the Steel Age of McKinley. He is therefore incalculable."[3]

The confrontation between Greenfield and Philadelphia's WASP establishment was epitomized by a single episode—a series of frantic meetings that took place among the city's leading bankers over the weekend of December 19–21, 1930. The problem was the Bankers Trust Company, whose primary stockholder was Greenfield. Bankers Trust was the tenth largest bank in Philadelphia, with $50 million in deposits, but a run on the bank had started in September, and by Friday, December 19, over $17 million had been withdrawn, more than exhausting the bank's supply of available cash. The heads of Philadelphia's leading banks, all Anglo-Saxon Protestants, knew that if Bankers Trust were forced to close its doors, the resulting loss of public confidence could lead to withdrawal stampedes at all of the city's 128 banks.[4] Indeed, to avert just such a closing, these bankers had already lent $7 million to Bankers Trust. But the end of the run on Bankers Trust was nowhere in sight: tens of millions of dollars more might be needed, and who could be sure that, even with that infusion, Bankers Trust might not fold anyway?

Greenfield had assured the major bankers that his bank was sound. He had agreed to their demands that he personally put up funds and collateral to guarantee any future loans to Bankers Trust. That had satisfied the members of the banking coalition a few days earlier, but by the 19th they were having second thoughts.

The bankers who gathered to pass judgment on Greenfield's fate reflected every popular stereotype of the tradition-encrusted Philadelphia WASP establishment, just as Greenfield epitomized the "Jew-on-the-make." The bankers' group included William Purves Gest, the calm, aristocratic, bushy-whiskered chairman of the Fidelity-Philadelphia Trust Company; Edward Hopkinson Jr., most active partner in Drexel & Company, the city's most influential banking concern—a man whose great-great-great-grandfather was a close friend of Benjamin Franklin, whose great-great-grandfather signed the Declaration of Independence and whose great-grandfather wrote "Hail Columbia"; also E. T. Stotesbury, senior among the Philadelphia Drexel partners, aging but dapper, who had been a drummer boy in the Civil War; Joseph Wayne Jr., former baseball and cricket player, president of the Philadelphia National Bank, largest in the city with $400 million in deposits; C. Stevenson Newhall, soft-spoken and beaverlike, president of the Pennsylvania Company (later First Pennsylvania Bank); Stacy B. Lloyd, tall and Quakerlike, president of the Philadelphia Saving Fund Society, oldest mutual savings bank in the U.S. and repository of $328 million in deposits.[5]

None of the participants is alive today, and the two best accounts of those meetings conflict in some details. *Fortune*, in June 1936, said the climactic meeting took place on the night of Sunday, December 21, at Gest's home in Merion, and that neither Greenfield nor his representatives were present. The 1933 memoirs of film magnate William Fox, a friend and fellow stockholder of Greenfield, describe a meeting the same night in the downtown boardroom of Drexel & Company, at which Fox personally made an impassioned plea on his friend's behalf. Most likely both meetings took place over that weekend, although not on the same night.

In subdued tones that masked the tension of that final night, the bankers discussed the value of Greenfield's properties, his operations, his companies, his collateral and his supposed wealth, just as they had been doing all week. Greenfield appeared to have money and property, and he was so persuasive that it was impossible to argue with his contention that his bank was sound. But now, finally, the bankers set aside those considerations to get at the underlying issue that troubled them: When all was said and done, they simply did not trust Greenfield, did not like him, were not comfortable dealing with him. The guiding principle of finance had been set down 18 years earlier by J. P. Morgan Sr., himself the dominant partner of Drexel & Company: "A man I do not trust could not get money from me on all the bonds in Christendom." Under that rule, and according to the judgment of Philadelphia's leading bankers, Greenfield failed to qualify for further assistance.

The sense of the Bankers Trust crisis as a clash of Gentile insiders against Jewish outsiders is conveyed in one vignette from the memoirs of Fox, who pleaded with the bankers for additional loans—in support of which, Fox dramatically told them, Greenfield would pledge $1.5 million of his own funds as collateral, and Fox would pledge an additional $1 million.

"While I was making this address, which I thought most eloquent," Fox later wrote, "I noticed the president of the second largest bank in

Philadelphia [presumably Joseph Wayne of Philadelphia National] take his handkerchief out of his pocket, presumably wiping his face, and place it at the right side of his mouth, and then grin and laugh and smile at the head of the largest bank, the Drexel Bank [presumably Hopkinson or Stotesbury]."[6]

Thus the bankers refused to commit any more funds to the rescue of Bankers Trust. On the morning of Monday, December 22, Bankers Trust failed to open its doors, and they never opened again. At 43, Albert Greenfield appeared to have been ruined. Yet within a few years he had recovered to such an extent that some of the bankers who had rejected him found themselves turning to him for financial help—help he magnanimously granted, no doubt relishing the irony of the situation. In the process of climbing Philadelphia's social ladder, Greenfield and other Jews of his generation did more than adapt to the city's way of doing things; they changed the city so that, in many ways, the old rules no longer applied. For better or worse, the outsiders became the insiders, and vice versa.

At bottom the Greenfield story is a tale of skillful use of human connections over a long period of time. For Serody the storekeeper in the Ukrainian village of Lozovata the connection was 30 viersts away in the small Jewish settlement of Nemerov.[7] Serody had opened a general store in his straw-roofed log cabin, and to stock the store once or twice each month Serody made the two-hour wagon drive to Nemerov. Since Serody's clan was one of only two Jewish families in Lozovata, it was logical that he came to Nemerov not merely for merchandise, but also to find a husband for his daughter, Esther. Grunfeld the trader, with whom Serody did much of his business in Nemerov, had a son, Jacob, who pleased Serody. So when Serody returned from one of his trips to Nemerov, about 1880, Jacob Grunfeld came with him. Jacob and Esther were married shortly after and moved into the Serody house, where Jacob made a living buying excess grain and livestock from peasants around Lozovata and shipping it to Kiev or Odessa. Jacob and Esther's first son, William, was born in 1882; a daughter followed three years later, and on August 4, 1887, their third child, Avrum Moishe Grunfeld, was born.

By that time anti-Jewish pogroms had been sweeping the northern Ukraine for five years, but in the south, where the Grunfelds lived, all was quiet. Still Russian Jews were prohibited from living in cities, and it was only in the cities that one could find a good job. In 1892, Jacob Grunfeld left for New York, where he went to work in a factory; four years later the family followed him. They lived in New York for six months until, one Friday in the fall of 1896, Jacob Grunfeld got a letter from one of his old friends from the factory. The friend had moved to Philadelphia, where he had found a better factory job and where, he added, there was a good job waiting for Jacob. Jacob wouldn't travel on Saturday, but on Sunday he entrained for Philadelphia to investigate. Two weeks later he wrote to Esther, telling her to sell whatever possessions she could and ship the rest to Philadelphia, their new home. Avrum—his name Anglicized to Albert Monroe Greenfield—was nine years old.

The family settled in South Philadelphia, and Jacob soon opened a neighborhood grocery and furniture store in his home, near Sixth and Spruce Streets. Albert attended Horace Binney Public School nearby and later Central High, but he quit school when he was 15 to take a job as a clerk and errand boy in the law office of John J. McDevitt Jr., who later became a judge, and J. Quincy Hunsicker, a leading real estate lawyer. It was here that Albert first saw the possibilities of real estate and made his first contacts in the field. Two of McDevitt's clients—Finberg, a Russian Jew, and D. E. Simon, a German Jew—were the biggest Jewish realtors in Philadelphia, and both took a liking to the bright young lad and the industrious way he wrote out deeds and mortgages in long-hand.

It was through them that Albert met Louis H. Cahan, and it was in Cahan's building at 218 South Fourth Street that Albert Greenfield first opened his real estate business, probably in May 1904. Thus from the very beginning of his business career in McDevitt's law office, Greenfield was involved with Jews and Gentiles simultaneously. This dual involvement would open up opportunities that were not available to Jews who restricted their business dealing to the Jewish community—the usual custom among Jews who were newly arrived and distrustful of the Gentile world. On the other hand, this involvement left Greenfield vulnerable to the sort of discrimination and social rejection that were not experienced as much by Jews who kept to themselves.

A secretary who worked in his office in 1908 recalls that Greenfield was then so poor that some days he had to go next door to borrow postage stamps. She also recalled that Greenfield was "so bright that he frightened me." Greenfield was 21 at the time; his secretary was 16.

Within two years of opening his business Greenfield would own the house where his parents lived; within seven years he would be making $60,000 annually; within 12 years he would be worth about $15 million; within 25 years his company would be the largest real estate concern in the country; within 50 years there would be virtually no endeavor in Philadelphia that he did not somehow influence.

His initial capital was $500 borrowed from his mother and another $500 borrowed from his older brother, William. But contacts were more important than capital. These he got from his landlord, Cahan the printer. Although he took no money from Cahan, Albert gave Cahan a partnership in his real estate company, figuring—correctly—that Cahan would thus be motivated to steer his printing customers to Albert when they had real estate business to transact. Finberg and Simon gave Albert some of their real estate business to help him get started, but he didn't need much help. Word quickly spread that young Greenfield was able to move property that other realtors could not. His success was due partly to his persuasive personality and his instinctive sense of timing in dealing with people, and partly because he knew—or gave the impression of knowing—so much that was important in Philadelphia. But his main asset was simply the fact that Albert, unlike most other Philadelphia realtors, did his homework.

Many realtors knew nothing about the properties they were given to sell, but when Greenfield was asked to sell real estate he immediately launched an investigation of the neighborhood in which the property was located. He reasoned that people buy real estate based on their expectation of what the property will be worth five years later, and the best way to determine that is to look at the condition of the stores and businesses in the neighborhood: if they are prospering, property values are likely to go up. So he would scour the neighborhood where his client's property was located, interviewing merchants and unearthing so many examples of business prosperity that no potential buyer could argue with him. If a neighborhood's businesses were failing, Greenfield studied these, too, to find out why. He did not, of course, discuss these failures with prospective buyers, but if a potential customer happened to mention them, Greenfield would be ready with an answer.

"What about Jacobson's Shoe Store?" the customer might ask. "It isn't doing well. Nobody ever goes in there."

"That's true," Greenfield would readily acknowledge. "But have you seen the shoes Jacobson is stocking? It isn't the neighborhood's fault that he's doing poorly." He had an answer for everything, and thus it was hard to turn him down.

In 1907, the Market Street Elevated opened and Greenfield—theorizing that where rapid transit goes, new development follows—began buying up lots in West Philadelphia. As agent for movie theatre interests, he bought several lots on 52nd Street between Spruce and Market; he also formed a syndicate that built several stores along that strip. When the biggest realtors in town—Felix Isman and Mastbaum Brothers & Fleisher—were ready to move into West Philadelphia, Greenfield was the logical choice to assemble a huge $2.5 million parcel for them along 52nd Street. His 2½ percent commission came to $62,500. The following year he did the same thing for Mastbaum Brothers & Fleisher along 60th Street, and over the next four years he branched out into Logan and the Northeast, selling millions of dollars of property there.

One of the first people with whom Greenfield dealt—in 1906, when he was 19—was Sol C. Kraus, a leading Jewish realtor who lived near 33rd Street and Fairmount Park and was acknowledged as the prime realtor in that neighborhood. Greenfield and Kraus had similar personalities— aggressive, competitive, overbearing, tempestuous—and thus they took an instant dislike to each other. Each liked to be in charge of whatever he did, so the two did not work well together. On the other hand, as businessmen, each recognized the benefits to be gained from working with the other.

Greenfield did not see Kraus again until seven years later; this time his eye was caught by Kraus's 19-year-old daughter, Edna, then a student at Bryn Mawr College. Kraus's opinion of Albert had not changed—he regarded the young man as an upstart—but he reluctantly consented to their marriage, perhaps mindful of the business advantages. It was through Sol Kraus that Greenfield subsequently got involved with building and loan associations and mortgage financing, which in turn led him into banking and then to his investment company, Bankers Securities Corporation. On the eve of his wedding in 1914, Greenfield was already a real estate titan in South and West Philadelphia and, through his alliance with Kraus, in North Philadelphia and the Northeast. But that was mere prologue. Now he was ready to crack Center City.

For Greenfield, as for so many others in American business, the hard-earned successes of the pre-World War I era snowballed amid the speculation of the twenties. He was now doing about $125 million a year in real estate. His activity and contributions to the Philadelphia Republican Party earned him a seat on the Philadelphia Common Council, predecessor to City Council, from 1917 to 1920, and this in turn gave him access to city business. It was in 1917, for example, that he first began handling real estate transactions for the Philadelphia Rapid Transit Company. In 1916, he had sold a string of movie theatres he owned for $2 million. In 1920, he had negotiated his first major downtown sale, that of the Metropolitan Opera House at Broad and Poplar, for $655,000.[8] In 1921, he had bought the Colonnade Hotel at 15th and Chestnut Streets and replaced it with the 20-story Greenfield Building, which still stands.[9] He was beginning to change the face of Philadelphia.

By the early twenties, with his father-in-law, Greenfield had bought control of 27 building and loan associations with total assets of $35 million, thus enhancing his value as a realtor by giving himself control over the financing of his real estate. No more could a potential customer turn down a Greenfield house or store by saying he had no money: Greenfield would *lend* him the money, through one of his loan associations. In 1924, he and Kraus formed Bankers Bond & Mortgage Company to finance mortgages and real estate; four years later, through the acquisition of two Newark mortgage companies, this concern—renamed Bankers Bond & Mortgage Company of America—had $12 million in assets and a foothold in New York. Greenfield had little trouble raising capital for these projects, and not just because of his persuasiveness. In the twenties everything seemed to make money, and Greenfield projects had a reputation for making more money than most.

The rise of all those building and loan mortgage companies was fed by

Albert M. Greenfield in the summer of 1926. *Courtesy of the Historical Society of Pennsylvania.*

the insatiable appetites of Philadelphians for homes of their own. At the time Philadelphia had more single-family homes than New York and Boston combined, and more than 50 percent of these were owner-occupied. In 1925, Philadelphians were so keen to get title that there were 3400 building and loan companies in the city (out of 4500 in the entire state) with total assets of $625 million and 1,250,000 shareholders. Inevitably some of these were mismanaged, and when 17 building and loan companies were seized by the state as insolvent in 1925, Greenfield was appointed receiver and asked to reorganize them.[10] There were inherent conflicts in Greenfield's being asked to reorganize his competitors, just as there were conflicts in a realtor's acting as a banker in the first place. But these proprieties were overshadowed by the needs of the moment: Greenfield, everyone knew, would get the job done, whereas someone with no conflicting involvements might not. Besides, Greenfield was a good Republican with close ties to the Vare machine in City Hall. And, to be sure, he *did* successfully reorganize the building and loan companies—under his control.

Buoyed by this success, Greenfield next moved to enter commercial banking in 1925 by acquiring a small West Philadelphia bank and moving it downtown to Walnut Street under the name of Bankers Trust Company. There were 128 banks in Philadelphia at the time, and Bankers Trust Company proceeded to buy up nine of them over the next five years. By the beginning of 1930, Bankers Trust had 11 offices throughout the city with 115,000 depositors and $35 million in deposits.

But the brightest jewel in Greenfield's rapidly expanding crown was Bankers Securities Corporation, an investment firm he created in 1928 by raising $12 million in capital from 1628 investors. It ultimately became the parent of virtually all of Greenfield's concerns. One half of the stock in Bankers Securities was subscribed to by Greenfield's Bankers Trust, which promptly sold the stock to the bank's own stockholders, including Greenfield.

Although many of the key figures in Bankers Securities were Jewish, it was by no means a "Jewish" company—a condition which was unusual for Philadelphia in the 1920s, but not at all unusual for Greenfield's ecumenical operating style. For example, the president of Bankers Securities—second only to Greenfield himself—was Samuel Barker, of an old established Quaker family, whose brother, Rodman Barker, had been John Wanamaker's chief financial officer.

Like most of Greenfield's enterprises, Bankers Securities did not exist for the purpose of making or doing anything, as most people think of those terms. Its sole function was to make money from money. Five months after its creation, Bankers Securities took $10.5 million—or nearly all of its initial capital—and bought control of Lit Brothers department store from the Lit family of Philadelphia; six weeks later, Bankers Securities sold Lit's to City Stores Company for $12.8 million. News of this quick $2.3 million profit— equivalent to 22 percent appreciation in just six weeks—drove the price of Bankers Securities stock up to $156 a share after having been issued seven months earlier at $60.[11] It also enabled Bankers Securities to raise an additional $19 million in a second public stock offering.

Yet in fact City Stores had never really paid Bankers Securities anything for Lit's; it had merely given Bankers Securities a three-year note for the full purchase amount. In effect, Bankers Securities had lent money it did not have to enable City Stores to purchase Lit's from Bankers Securities. The deal had all the soundness of a chain letter, but it was typical of the speculative 1920s in that nobody questioned it as long as it seemed to work. And it did seem to work: The resultant sharp rise in Bankers Securities stock greatly increased the company's total assets and provided it with the collateral—namely, its inflated stock—with which to make further investments.

To say that Philadelphia's Protestant Establishment looked upon Greenfield and his activities with alarm and apprehension is an understatement. Greenfield was more brilliant and imaginative than they were; he was also more brazen. Either way, they saw him as a threat. And because he took more risks than most, when the stock market crashed he seemed more vulnerable than most.

In July 1930, the Bank of Philadelphia & Trust Company, with $15 million in deposits and a big mortgage business, showed signs of going under. Greenfield, as had been his policy, moved in and bought the ailing bank, and on July 22, all nine of its branches opened for business under the name of Bankers Trust Company, thus bringing the deposits for Greenfield's bank up to $50 million. Greenfield later claimed that the city's leading bankers had urged him to buy the Bank of Philadelphia to save it from failure and thus avert a city-wide panic; the bankers insisted the idea of buying up the Bank of Philadelphia had been Greenfield's alone. In any case, Greenfield did not purchase the Bank of Philadelphia until he had been assured by two leading bankers—Wayne of Philadelphia National and Newhall of the Pennsylvania Company—that they would extend loans to Greenfield's Bankers Trust "upon good and sufficient collateral." The collateral was largely real estate mortgages held by Greenfield's banks.

In the eyes of the Philadelphia establishment, Greenfield's "Jewishness" was simply one aspect of a larger problem: his refusal to operate according to traditional, predictable guidelines. His greatest assets were his personal instincts and his charisma, with the result that even as his empire grew into the hundreds of millions, he still functioned largely as a one-man operation. Correspondence between Greenfield and the president of his Bankers Securities Corporation, Samuel Barker, repeatedly indicates that Barker was unaware of much of the company's dealings and had little influence in its actions. For example, on July 10, 1931, Barker wrote to Greenfield, "I am sure we are not getting out of the organization the full value of what is in it. If not, it is my fault and yours. . . . No one man can do it; nor can different officers sitting around at their desks and not keeping in close contact with what is going on." On November 7th of the same year, regarding a matter concerning debentures of Albert M. Greenfield & Company (which was not then affiliated with Bankers Securities), Barker wrote to Greenfield urging him to appoint a special committee of the board consisting of the most independent-minded members to avoid an issue of conflict of interest. Throughout the exchanges on this subject the tone of Barker, a Quaker, was that of a supplicant pleading that Greenfield make himself more accountable to independent review and to public opinion in general; Greenfield, just as consistently, resisted any attempt to make him divulge any more information than was absolutely necessary, even to Barker.

In a letter of August 10, 1931, for example, Barker rightly expressed concern about a huge debt owed to Bankers Securities by City Stores Company. "I am profoundly concerned about the City Stores problem," he wrote. "It is ours as much as theirs. The $8 million owing us constitutes 41 percent of our assets." In a reply the next day, Greenfield wrote Barker, "It is obvious that you are not acquainted with my efforts to date in this matter. Mr. Goerke [of City Stores] has already offered to pay a minimum of at least $2,000,000 on account, instead of $1,600,000 suggested by you."[12]

Greenfield with his first wife, Edna, in 1928. *Courtesy of the Historical Society of Pennsylvania.*

As Barker feared, City Stores defaulted on the loan, and in lieu of payment the company was taken over by Bankers Securities. At the time of the above exchange with Barker, Greenfield doubtless knew that the loan would be defaulted, but he seems to have been less interested in having his loan repaid than in the opportunity to gain control of a large retailing chain like City Stores. This, of course, was not a prudent posture for a moneylender to take, which explains why Greenfield kept such thoughts to himself—and why most Philadelphia business people and even his own executives felt mystified and frustrated in their dealings with him.

Unfortunately, in buying up weak banks and thus averting the public disaster of a bank failure, Greenfield deluded not only the public, but himself as well. Real estate mortgages, which had seemed like such good collateral in the twenties, became almost worthless in the Depression as homeowners lost their jobs and house payments ceased. In the ten years after 1926, 144,000 of the half-million homes in Philadelphia were auctioned off by the sheriff, and 99 percent of these sales were against mortgages, not taxes; during this period, 1600 of the city's 3400 building and loan associations were wiped out or merged.

Nevertheless, on August 1, 1930, Bankers Trust blithely paid a bonus to all of its employees, accompanied by a statement from the bank's president, Samuel Barker: "This company, for which 322 of us are now working, does some things differently from usual practice, and I believe better. You know that on all sides many are being laid off, more are working part time, and a great number see their pay reduced. Your salaries are going along with your work."

The rude awakening was just around the corner. For once, Greenfield was unable to transfer the public's confidence in him to a property he had acquired. Instead the public's doubts about the stability of the Bank of Philadelphia were now transferred to its new owner, Greenfield's Bankers Trust.

The run on the bank began in September. True to their promise, Philadelphia National Bank and the Pennsylvania Company backed Bankers Trust to the extent of $7 million in loans, but by December 18th it became clear that the dike would not hold with this sort of patchwork. The big bankers demanded that $10 million worth of Bankers Trust assets in real estate mortgages be replaced with cash; Greenfield agreed to meet that condition, and on Friday the 19th he went off to Washington to seek aid from his friend President Hoover, whose nomination Greenfield had seconded as a delegate to the Republican National Convention in 1928. But over the weekend, while Greenfield was away, the city's leading bankers suddenly decided to let his bank go.

Thus Bankers Trust failed to open on Monday the 22nd, and some 135,000 Philadelphians who had money there awoke to their first real taste of the Great Depression. Largest among those depositors was Greenfield's Bankers Securities Corporation, which had $2 million (out of the bank's $50 million total) on deposit; Greenfield personally had $300,000 deposited at Bankers Trust. In all Greenfield and his companies had some $4 million deposited at Bankers Trust, which Greenfield claimed he left in when the bank closed. But the public didn't believe this and so, rightly or wrongly, "the old manipulator" (who was all of 43) was blamed for the failure; when his children had a Christmas party at his Germantown home a few days later, guests noticed a policeman sitting at the kitchen table as a protection against death threats that Greenfield had been receiving by phone and mail.

Within 30 days of the bank's closing, its assets paid off in full the $7 million advanced to it by Philadelphia National Bank and by the Pennsylvania Company. Over the next five years, as the bank's assets were liquidated, depositors were paid off at 59 cents on the dollar—a sound proportion which suggests the bank never should have been allowed to fold.

"It closed," Greenfield said later, "only because in 1930 a small, secret group of powerful men had the power of life and death over banks."

In the wake of the Bankers Trust failure, 50 smaller banks in the Philadelphia area toppled like dominoes until Roosevelt's bank moratorium of 1933. But Philadelphians pointed with pride to the conduct of the city's leading bankers, who saved about a dozen institutions through loans, cash deposits and mergers. Indeed, aside from Bankers Trust, only one large bank, the Franklin Trust Company, was allowed to fold. Conspiracy-minded observers noted that Franklin Trust had something else in common with Bankers Trust: it, too, had been closely connected with Greenfield. And they noted the remarkably parallel situation in New York, where that city's major bankers had also assembled a credit pool that had saved all of the city's large banks with the exception of two—both owned by Jews.[13]

One of Greenfield's associates at the time recalls that Greenfield and his colleagues all felt he had been rejected by the bankers solely because he was Jewish—but that neither Greenfield nor his associates articulated that feeling among each other. Greenfield seems to have been reluctant to raise the cry of antisemitism because doing so would simply further frustrate his ambition to assimilate into the city's business establishment.

Even before the Bankers Trust debacle, Greenfield's realty company had narrowly avoided liquidation when it defaulted on the interest due on a bond issue. The creditors could have seized the Greenfield company's assets and divided them up right then and there, but they concluded, as creditors often do in such situations, that they would be likely to get more money over the long run if they kept the company in the hands of its management rather than turn it over to a bankruptcy judge or a politically appointed trustee. Thus, because of his real estate genius, Greenfield was kept in control at Albert M. Greenfield & Company—albeit with severe restrictions and a limited salary—and so managed to avoid bankruptcy during the Depression. And the confidence of his creditors was well warranted: although it took almost 15 years, he ultimately paid off all the company's bonds at par value.

Bankers Securities Corporation also managed to stay afloat, even though it had $2 million on deposit at Bankers Trust (of which it ultimately lost more than $800,000) and even though it owned $2.75 million worth of stock in the folded bank (of which it lost everything).

Most remarkable of all, Bankers Securities remained solvent even though, on December 1, 1931, City Stores Company defaulted on $11.8 million of the nearly $13 million that it owed Bankers Securities for the purchase of Lit Brothers in 1928. Bankers Securities simply took control of City Stores and Greenfield installed himself as chairman. So, suddenly, he became a retailing magnate, with a department store chain that stretched through six states and under his leadership would ultimately expand to 19 states, including such operations as Maison Blanche in New Orleans, Bonwit Teller, Franklin Simon, W. & J. Sloane and B. Lowenstein's in Memphis. Far from slowing him down, the Depression seemed only to offer new opportunities. As companies like City Stores teetered on the brink of bankruptcy, Greenfield repeatedly appeared to snap them up at bargain prices and then pump new blood into them. As property owners defaulted on mortgages and bonds, Greenfield picked them up, too, often for five cents on the dollar. When he had acquired enough of the bonds in a particular building, he would then demand that the building's management be turned over to his real estate company. In this way Greenfield gained control of the Ben Franklin Hotel, the Bellevue Stratford, the Atlantic City Steel Pier and any number of Center City office and loft buildings.

Despite his multiplicity of conflicting roles, Greenfield liked to argue that his real estate firm was the most ethical in the country. "It has to be," he would say with what newspapers described as twinkling eyes. "It's the most closely watched."

Greenfield delighted in this sort of sophistry. In its time, however, his real estate company engaged in some blatantly unethical practices whose sole redeeming virtue was that Greenfield made no effort to conceal or disguise them.

Chief among these was his practice of selling and buying real estate for himself in addition to acting as a broker for others. It is generally assumed that a broker cannot fairly represent his client if the broker himself is the other party in a transaction, or if the broker himself is interested in buying the property his client has asked him to sell.

Before Greenfield came along, a broker's owning real estate was frowned upon by realtors. Some of them, to be sure, bought property for themselves secretly through the use of "straw men." Greenfield was the first Philadelphia realtor to engage in the practice openly. And since he *did* engage in it openly, he blunted much of his critics' thrust. After all, any client who was dissatisfied with Greenfield's representation could take his business elsewhere.

But could he really? From the 1920s onward Greenfield's influence reached into all corners of the city's business life. Through his banks and building and loan associations he had instant access to financing, whereas other realtors had to work out financing arrangements just like any other bank customer. His constant trading of Center City properties meant that anyone with Center City real estate aspirations would do well to develop a relationship with him. His political contributions—first to the Republicans, later to the Democrats—gave him powerful influence over City Council. His acquisition of Lit Brothers in the thirties, and later Snellenburg's and Bonwit Teller, made him a major downtown merchant and, as such, a major advertiser in Philadelphia newspapers; if this did not give him direct influence over the papers, it did give him the sort of access to the press that other realtors lacked. Indeed, Greenfield himself became a part-owner of the *Record* when J. David Stern bought control of the paper in 1928. And so the word got around: even if you had doubts about Al Greenfield, it was a good idea to cultivate him as an ally, for you never could tell when you might need him.

The cumulative effect of so much power concentrated in one individual inevitably led to abuses. In 1926, for example, the Quaker City Cab Company went bankrupt, and the trustee in bankruptcy asked Greenfield to find a buyer for the company. At the time Greenfield was also real estate agent for the old Philadelphia Rapid Transit Company—predecessor of the PTC and SEPTA—which was then a quasi-private company operated in partnership with the city. Philadelphia Rapid Transit was being operated by Mitten Management Inc., whose president, Thomas Mitten, was a business associate and good friend of Greenfield's.

The assets of the bankrupt Quaker City Cab Company were inventoried at $387,500, and in 1927, Greenfield, as agent for the bankruptcy trustee, sold the company for that amount to a straw man representing Greenfield's friend Mitten. Then in January 1928, Greenfield negotiated the sale of Quaker City Cab from the straw man to Philadelphia Rapid Transit for $1,360,000. In effect the PRT, managed by Mitten, bought the cab company from a straw man for Mitten in a deal that netted Mitten nearly $1 million. The ultimate victims of these manipulations were the PRT stockholders and the taxpayers of Philadelphia, for the PRT was supposed to share its profits with the city, and Greenfield's manipulations on behalf of Mitten assured that the PRT had no profits whatever.

In April 1931, Philadelphia Common Pleas Court Judge Harry McDevitt delivered an opinion calling Greenfield's role in the transaction "unconscionable" and ordered that Greenfield's commissions be returned and the sale nullified.[14] Two months later, the PRT severed its relationship with Greenfield.[15] Yet when the PRT went bankrupt in 1934, Greenfield was one of the six trustees appointed by the Federal District Court, and he subsequently sat for 26 years on the board of the PRT and its successor, the Philadelphia Transportation Company. Whatever his conflicts, public officials explained, there simply was no one else who could do the job as well.

Philadelphia was a Republican city throughout most of the first half of this century, and in his early years Greenfield was a staunch Republican, too. He was a leading supporter of the Vare machine, and by 1928, when he seconded and engineered the nomination of Herbert Hoover, he was vice-chairman of the Republican national finance committee. Greenfield's friend William Fox, himself a Jewish product of New York's lower East Side, once told Hoover, "You can blame that little bald-headed Hebrew Jew who made it possible for you to become President of the United States."[16]

But after the next Presidential election he switched to the Democrats,

Greenfield as public speaker, 1936. *Courtesy of the Historical Society of Pennsylvania.*

and indeed he was soon vice-chairman of the *Democratic* national finance committee. Greenfield attributed his switch to his disillusionment with the Hoover administration; his detractors attributed it to opportunism. Some of Greenfield's turnaround probably had something to do with his growing friendship with J. David Stern, the liberal publisher whom Greenfield bankrolled in his purchases of the Philadelphia *Record* and the *New York Post*.

But for the most part his political switch probably stemmed from nothing more than an instinctive feeling about changes in American society. He seemed to grasp, as many of his contemporaries did not, that the American system was malfunctioning and that it could not be saved without a thorough overhaul. Greenfield supported Roosevelt not out of opportunism—he was virtually ostracized for his choice—but out of both conviction and a genuine love of controversy. This combination would assert itself repeatedly throughout his career—as when the PTC, under his chairmanship, first began hiring blacks; when his hotels became the first in Philadelphia to rent

rooms to blacks; when he offered convention facilities at the Bellevue Stratford to the Urban League after all other Philadelphia hotels had turned the
League down; when he scolded his fellow trustees of Albert Einstein Medical Center for refusing to allow women on the board. At a 1956 meeting, the
all-male Einstein board was asked to add a representative of its women's
auxiliary to the board. The request was greeted with clubby jokes and
furtive smiles that were probably similar to the treatment William Fox received when he went before Philadelphia's banking elite on Greenfield's
behalf in 1930. Only Greenfield remained unsmiling. "Wait a minute," he
told his colleagues. "This is no matter for facetiousness. We are, I presume,
civilized men, too civilized, I should expect, to deal in such an offhand
manner with a request that is completely proper and legitimate . . . After all,
is there a man here at this table who has not been raised by a woman, and
who among you would argue that in his case she did a bad job?"[17]

Greenfield's willingness to irritate proper Philadelphia was a factor in
the success of the *Record*, which Stern bought from the Wanamaker estate in
1928 for $2.5 million, with the aid of a $1.2 million loan from Bankers
Securities Corporation and a $100,000 investment by Greenfield himself.
Circulation promptly rose from 100,000 to 325,000 by 1936; in 1947, when
Stern sold the *Record* to the *Bulletin*—in a deal arranged by Greenfield—the
value of the paper had risen to $12 million.[18]

Among other things, the *Record* survived a knockdown challenge from
Moses Annenberg after Annenberg purchased the *Inquirer* from the Curtis
estate in 1936. Shortly after he arrived in Philadelphia, Annenberg took
steps to monopolize newspaper distribution in the area and to intimidate
newsdealers, as he had done in Chicago. Annenberg's strategy was triple-
pronged, relying simultaneously on physical intimidation, lavish promo-
tional campaigning and published attacks on Stern's friends and supporters.

"I like you, Al," Annenberg told Greenfield one day after the two had
had a pleasant lunch together. "But you're financing Dave Stern. I've got to
destroy you to destroy Dave Stern."[19]

Within a week Annenberg's *Inquirer* proclaimed in an eight-column
headline: "GREENFIELD'S FIRM DREW $300,000 FROM BANKERS
TRUST, LAWYER SAYS." The article contended that in 1930, one of
Greenfield's companies had drawn money from the bank five days before it
closed, and implied that Greenfield had done so knowing the bank would
fold. The story failed to mention that the transaction was merely a routine
renewal of an old note.[20]

Greenfield retaliated by buying newspaper ads and radio time (he also
owned WFIL through Lit Brothers) to reply. "Moses Hitler Annenberg,"
he declared, was like "a dog who had returned to its vomit."

Although Annenberg was not at all representative of the established
German-Jewish families (he was an immigrant of poor beginnings), the feud
was perceived by some observers as reinforcement of the rivalry between

America's established German Jews who had come to America in the mid-nineteenth century, and the upstart Russian Jews who had arrived forty years later. Greenfield had already broken this ethnic barrier in the 1920s when he became one of the first two members of the downtown Mercantile Club who were not of German-Jewish origin,[21] and when he became one of the first non-German Jews admitted to the Philmont Country Club near Jenkintown.

But as late as 1938, at the height of the Annenberg feud, Greenfield was visited by the rabbis of three Reform—that is, German—congregations who asked that he end his squabble with Annenberg because it was making the Jews look bad. "Why don't you go to Mr. Annenberg?" Greenfield snapped. "I've been in this city for 40 years." Annenberg, a Jew of German descent, had arrived in Philadelphia only two years earlier, but because Greenfield was a Russian Jew the quarrel was assumed to be Greenfield's responsibility; it was assumed that no German Jew would stoop to fight with a Russian.

Both Greenfield and Annenberg ultimately sued each other for libel, but the suits were withdrawn in May 1939 with the signing of mutual public apologies; Annenberg's source conceded that his charge against Greenfield was "based on a wrong interpretation of the information that was furnished."[22] By this time the Democrat-controlled federal justice apparatus had begun investigating Annenberg, and in 1940 he pleaded guilty to income tax evasion and went to prison. "He who digs a grave for his neighbor," Greenfield recited upon learning of the conviction, "is apt to fall into it himself."[23]

In his attitudes toward Judaism and the Jewish community, Greenfield reflected an ambivalence typical of many of his generation of Russian immigrants. On the one hand, he was eager to be accepted as an "American," according to what he perceived as the prevailing definition of his time; on the other hand, he was unwilling to cut himself off from his roots.

He was not an observant Jew, and he frequently seemed to bend over backwards to ingratiate himself with Gentiles, through such manifestations as throwing Christmas parties, cultivating a close friendship with the Archbishop of Philadelphia and even hanging a photograph of the Vatican on his office wall. The most likely explanation for such behavior, though, was the encyclopedic nature of Greenfield's interest: he had nothing against Jewish culture, but his thirst for variety and human drama embraced a much larger canvas. Greenfield was in fact active in Jewish secular organizations and had no use for people who tried to erase their Jewish heritage. He once wrote to Senator Barry Goldwater, soliciting a contribution to the National Conference of Christians and Jews. Goldwater mailed a check in reply but added a note advising Greenfield that he—Goldwater—was not Jewish. Greenfield, furious, returned the check uncashed.

Although Greenfield's roots were Russian, he took to emulating wealthy German Jews—dressing fastidiously, carrying a narrow walking cane and even tossing German expressions into his conversation. A friend of one of Greenfield's children recalls a birthday party Greenfield threw for his son, Albert Jr., at which the guests, all in their early teens, dressed in evening clothes and partook of a formal dinner, complete with coffee and after-dinner cigars. Such anecdotes suggest a man desperately anxious to eradicate any memory of his humble, Eastern European origins.

The need to short-cut the assimilation process by downplaying one's "Jewishness" was tacitly acknowledged by Greenfield's older brother and early partner, William Greenfield, shortly before he died. Recalling Albert's early real estate days, William remarked, "We didn't experience any anti-semitism. The goyim liked to hear the Russian stories. We tried to set an example for them by being 'better' Jews than the Bainbridge Street–South Street second-hand storekeepers. They always said we were different Jews from any they knew." The implication appears to be that the Greenfield brothers learned not to dwell on their "Jewishness" in their relations with the Gentile world.

After World War I, the Federation of Jewish Charities—then heavily dominated by German-Jewish organizations—voted for the first time to combine with the city's Russian agencies in a single fund-raising drive. This new unity was partly a response to growing antisemitism nationally, but it was also motivated by the growing wealth of the Russian Jews. In 1925, for example, prominent Sephardic and German Jews like the Rosenbachs, Gimbels, Wolfs, Loebs, Solis-Cohens, Sterns, Rosenwalds, Fels, Fleishers and Adlers gave a combined total of $52,775 to Federation; Greenfield alone gave $31,000. (To be sure, other German Jews, such as Jules Mastbaum and the Lit and Snellenburg families gave as much as, or more than Greenfield did.)[24]

But it was his fund-raising ability, more than his money, that was Greenfield's greatest attraction to the Federation (and, indeed, to the dozens of causes with which he later became associated). He was a master of the charity tactic of inviting wealthy people to a luncheon and then forcing them publicly to pledge a contribution in such a way that each was embarrassed into giving more than he intended. "Ten thousand?" Greenfield would shout incredulously from the dais. "On the X-Y-Z deal last year alone you made 20 thousand. On that deal with me you made 50 thousand." The implications of such a harangue were twofold: first, the man could afford to give a lot more than he proposed, and second, if he wanted to continue doing business with Albert Greenfield, he had better raise his pledge to this worthwhile cause.

Greenfield's Catholic connection, too, had a business basis. Early in his career Greenfield became friendly with Dennis Cardinal Dougherty, Archbishop of Philadelphia from 1918 to 1951. The friendship blossomed to such an extent that Greenfield became exclusive real estate agent for the Archdio-

Greenfield with Cardinal Dougherty, June 1928. *Courtesy of the Historical Society of Pennsylvania.*

cese of Philadelphia—during the period of its greatest growth—as well as the Cardinal's personal financial advisor. Often, on Sundays, the Cardinal would call Greenfield and the two men would drive around the city, looking over prospective sites for schools, churches, hospitals and cemeteries. And the Cardinal was a frequent dinner guest at Greenfield's home, where his Catholic servants would invariably kneel and kiss the Cardinal's ring, to the wonder of Greenfield's five children.

Greenfield cemented this relationship by contributing heavily to Catholic charities and schools like Villanova, St. Joseph's, and St. Mary's Home for Children in Ambler; the organ at St. Charles Borromeo Seminary is a gift from Greenfield. As a result of these benefactions, Dougherty arranged for the Pope to confer upon Greenfield the title of Commander of the Order of Pius IX; he was the first American Jew to receive the honor.

Although his friendship with the Cardinal was motivated by business, Greenfield was sincere in his fondness for Catholicism. He often spoke of his high regard for Catholics, and especially for their school system. "If I weren't a Jew, I'd be a Catholic," he once remarked. Catholic visitors to his office were always impressed by a large photo of St. Peter's in Rome that hung just outside Greenfield's door. And if Jewish visitors expressed dismay at finding the picture there, Greenfield would take them by the arm with a sly wink and point out that in one obscure corner of the photo, imperceptible at first glance, could be seen the figure of a man relieving himself against a wall.

In 1940, Greenfield filed two petitions in U.S. District Court, seeking protection under the federal bankruptcy laws. He listed his personal debts at $6.4 million and debts of one of his personal companies at $4.6 million.[25] The State Banking Department, as receiver for the Bankers Trust and the Franklin Trust, had earlier sued Greenfield for $2 million and Greenfield's company for over $1 million, all of which arose from defaulted loans the banks had made—and for which Greenfield had co-signed—to Greenfield's companies or his relatives or associates prior to 1932.

Throughout the thirties, Greenfield had been trying to arrange a long-term method of repaying his debts instead of going into bankruptcy. Now he offered his creditors five cents on the dollar—or, if that did not please them, a 20-year note for the full amount. The state had repeatedly rejected such offers as outrageous, largely because the notion persisted among the general public that Greenfield had hidden assets. For more than two years after 1940, the State Banking Department threatened a full-scale investigation to find Greenfield's alleged hidden assets.

But while the state threatened, Greenfield was working behind the scenes, making individual arrangements with each of his creditors to pay off debts in full over long periods. When all of his creditors had accepted his arrangements, his bankruptcy petition was discharged. And Greenfield did, ultimately, pay off every debt from that period. But he never returned to the commercial banking business.

The thirties were a turning point in other ways. After 21 years of stormy marriage, Greenfield's wife, Edna, divorced him in 1935 to marry Charles Payne of New York (today, at 89, she lives in Bryn Mawr).[26] Like most Americans, Greenfield emerged from the Depression a sadder but wiser man, aware for perhaps the first time of his own limitations and of the uncertainties of human nature. Yet this new insight in itself made him stronger than ever. In 1937, he remarried, this time to a gracious, artistic widow named Etelka Schamberg, who provided him with quiet support and companionship until her death 12 years later. By the early 1940s, he had a solid marriage, a fashionable home in Overbrook, a truce with his creditors and the chairmanship of a company that had become a conglomerate 30 years before the term was coined.

Seated at his roll-top desk on the second floor of the Bankers Securities Building at Walnut and Juniper, under signed portraits of Herbert Hoover and Franklin D. Roosevelt, surrounded by a grandfather clock, a cuspidor, pictures of George Washington, his children and grandchildren and framed mottos (such as "Be not disturbed at being misunderstood; be disturbed at not understanding"), Greenfield loomed larger than ever over the Philadelphia horizon.

"He reaches out to the city in diverse and mysterious ways," *Fortune* tried to explain to its readers. "He has the ability to attach himself to all types and classes of people and make them do what he wants. And he can still raise cash quicker than almost anyone in the city."[27]

His crises behind him, Greenfield had arrived at a plateau from which he could not be dislodged. The next phase of his life—in which he mellowed into a civic godfather reminiscent of the very Gentiles and German Jews who had once resisted him—was still to come.

Jewish Education in Philadelphia

Diane A. King

The years between 1830 and 1870 brought a considerable influx of German Jews to Philadelphia. By 1860 there were perhaps 8000 Jews residing in the city.[1] Seventy-five years later, after an unprecedented immigration from East Europe the number of Jews in Philadelphia swelled to 293,000.[2] During these years the Jewish educational needs of the community were served by a variety of Jewish institutions: the congregational school, the private teacher and the heder, the Hebrew Sunday School Society schools, and the communal school. In addition, there were established during the period two Yeshivot under traditional Orthodox auspices, and a number of secular Yiddishist Folkshulen under the Labor Zionist Movement and Workmen's Circle schools.

The Congregational School

We find first mention of such a school in 1782 with a letter documenting Mikveh Israel's intention to build a synagogue and a schoolhouse for the use of the congregants.[3] Congregation members were interested in providing a Jewish education for their children and felt that a school would answer that need. A building, however, was not enough. Teachers were needed and they were scarce. The usual arrangement at that time was to have the hazan, the Sephardic minister, of a congregation supplement his income by means of teaching. Whatever tuition charges there were, were paid directly to the hazan. Mikveh Israel was no exception. It, too, resorted to that arrangement. This left the quality of the education received totally dependent on the abilities of the hazan. Much of the time the arrangement was not successful.

On September 13, 1846 the congregation adopted a resolution authorizing a sum not exceeding $200 per year to be used as payment for a teacher of Hebrew to be under their sole direction and control and for whom they would provide free room and lighting.[4]

The Board of Managers, acting upon this resolution, decided to establish a Hebrew school under its direction. The teacher was charged with the responsibility of "educating in the Hebrew language gratis such numbers of children, not exceeding twelve at one time, as the parnas or Adjunta may recommend."[5]

By 1892, in addition to Mikveh Israel's Hebrew School, three other synagogues had established congregational schools: Rodeph Shalom, Keneseth Israel and Beth Israel. Although in Mikveh Israel the Sephardic (Spanish) pronunciation was used and in the latter three the Ashkenazic pronunciation was used, the curricula in all of these schools were similar. They were limited for the most part to the study of Hebrew prayers, Bible, Jewish religion and preparation for Bar-Mitzvah.[6] With the exception of Beth Israel, which offered classes three days a week with an additional hour on Saturday,[7] all the other congregational schools offered classes either on Sunday only (as with Rodeph Shalom) or on Sunday and one weekday.[8]

No evidence is available from which to comment on the quality of the education offered by the congregational schools. One must assume, however, that it was quite weak. The teachers were not required to have training in order to teach. Often they were volunteers. When they did get paid, remuneration was small. One can speculate, although this would not apply in every instance, that although most of the teachers who taught in the congregational schools were probably American born or at least "Americanized," their greater understanding of American pupils was offset by their lack of sufficient knowledge of the Hebrew language and Jewish culture. Add to this the few hours allotted for Jewish education by the congregational schools, and it becomes reasonable to conclude that the achievements of the early schools were minimal.

Despite the questionable quality of education in the congregational schools, the year 1912 saw 13 of them serving 2003 pupils.[9] This type of school was destined to grow and become in the next three decades the major form of Jewish education in Philadelphia.

A survey of Jewish education in Philadelphia in 1943 reveals that as of that date there were 31 congregational schools serving 5233 pupils, including 16 that were Conservative,[10] 6 Orthodox, 3 Reform, and 6 independent.[11] A general evaluation of these schools at the time of the survey points to the same problems that the schools faced when they were first established. The school was often not large enough to permit proper classification of students. Because it functioned only two hours per day (in most cases) the school was frequently unwilling to engage full-time professional Jewish teachers and availed itself of teachers whose main work and interests were outside the field of Jewish education. Moreover, these teachers were frequently inadequately prepared for the particular task of the Jewish school.[12]

With their weaknesses, the congregational schools did have one definite advantage. Since the parents were affiliated with the synagogue, it made it possible for the involvement of the entire family in the life of the institution. The child's involvement in the institution went beyond the six hours he normally spent at the school and ideally the child's interest in the school was enhanced by the parents' involvement with the synagogue.

The Private Teacher and the Heder

In addition to relying on the hazan to teach the children, the early German arrivals, still too few to launch schools, depended on an itinerant private teacher, the *melamed*.[13] By 1860, many German families hired tutors to instruct their children in the elements of Hebrew and basic religious precepts. With the increase in East European immigration in the 1870s, the *melamed* became a familiar figure among the Russian immigrants as well. Some still traveled from house to house. The more enterprising, however, assembled enough students to conduct classes after public school hours. Such a private school was called a *heder*. Independent of the synagogue, its locale could be the teacher's apartment, a vacant store, or basement.[14]

There was little about the *hadarim* to attract an American youngster. Instruction was usually in Yiddish; the methodology was backward; incentive was the "rabbi's" strap and the "rabbi" himself was often poorly qualified. With few exceptions, the *hadarim* were unsuccessful.[15] However, since the *heder* was a private enterprise, the possibility existed that, given the improbable circumstances that the teacher was knowledgeable and instinctively knew how to interact successfully with American children, the daily program could achieve some success. In some few instances it probably did.

During the first decade of the twentieth century a very large number of *hadarim* were in operation. By 1912, 23 such *hadarim* were recorded, with a pupil population of 511 students, all but 15 of whom were males.[16]

Hadarim were still functioning in Philadelphia in the 1940s. They continued to function for the profit of an individual teacher. For the most part the curriculum was limited to the reading of prayers, to a little *Humash* and to preparation for the Bar Mitzvah ceremony. Generally speaking, the physical facilities were poor and the number of pupils too small to permit proper grading.[17]

It must be assumed that the achievements were limited and that the *heder* was not a significant model in Jewish education in Philadelphia at that time.

Isaac Leeser

It is impossible to discuss certain developments in Jewish education without making mention of Isaac Leeser, whose drive and determination made Philadelphia a center of Jewish creatvity. Isaac Leeser emigrated to Richmond from Westphalia in 1824 at the age of 18 to work in his uncle's store, training as a bookkeeper. He quickly learned English, although his love of Jewish tradition led him to spend most of his free time on Jewish studies.[18] Leeser volunteered to assist the Richmond hazan in his work, learning, in the course of his assistance, the Sephardic rite. He taught the children of the congregation as well. In 1828, when he wrote a strong, well-written response in the Richmond *Whig* to an article in the *London Quarterly Review* that attacked Jews and Judaism, Leeser emerged into prominence. In 1829, at the age of 23, he was recommended to the congregation Mikveh Israel as a candidate for the position of hazan.[19] On September 6, 1829 he was elected for two years, although he continued to serve the congregation as its hazan until 1851.[20]

During his lifetime Isaac Leeser wrote schoolbooks for children, prayer-books for his congregants, and an English translation of the Bible, which remained standard for American Jewry until the twentieth century. He wrote treatises on Judaism and worked tirelessly to promote Jewish education on all levels. From the beginning Isaac Leeser deplored the fact that poor children had to get their scanty education in the common free schools, with no opportunity to acquire a knowledge of their own religion, while wealthy Jews, on the other hand, had their children educated privately. He begged the congregation to support a school such as the one that he had established and, short of that, to start one of its own.

> I again and respectfully address you a fourth time . . . My purposes are answered if a good man, capable and true, is entrusted with the education of our youth, and if even not the smallest part of enrollment should come to my share I would be satisfied to give all the aid in my power and even attend one hour every day to teach the Hebrew . . . Should we be willing to see our religion go down because unknown to a rising generation![21]

Following the Revolutionary War, many Americans realized that separate private, secular, and religious schools would not provide the equality, unity and freedom necessary for the new democratic nation. Beginning in the early 1830s, public schools were organized to be open equally and freely to all. To preserve the religious freedom of all, no special religious instruction was permitted in these schools. Isaac Leeser foresaw a great danger to the perpetuation of Judaism in the development of this American form of secular eduction with its mandatory separation from religious studies, but he seemed a lone voice in Philadelphia at this time. He called out, but what came back for the most part was just an echo. His commitment to the idea, however, would not let him rest, and in time his efforts would be successful.

The Sunday School

While he was calling for more intensive Jewish education, Isaac Leeser had already developed, while in Richmond, the notion of conducting Jewish classes on Sunday.[22] This pattern had been adopted by church schools, mainly Protestant, which came into prominent existence after the adoption of the Massachusetts Statute of 1827, banning religious instruction from the public schools.[23] In Philadelphia, Isaac Leeser influenced Rebecca Gratz to open such a school, under the direction of the Female Hebrew Benevolent Society.[24] It was instituted at a meeting of Jewish women, held February 4, 1838 at which it was "Resolved, That a Sunday School be established under the direction of the Board (Female Hebrew Benevolent Society) and teachers appointed among the young ladies of the Congregation (Mikveh Israel)."[25]

Contrary to the congregational schools, which were intended for the young sons and daughters of seat-holders in the congregation, the Sunday school was opened to serve all Jewish boys and girls in the community. It opened with fifty children and seven teachers and was the beginning of an educational institution that was to thrive and spread and which is still in existence today as the Hebrew Sunday School Society of Philadelphia.[26]

The Sunday school curriculum concentrated on Biblical history and religion. Hebrew language was rarely taught. Rosa Mordecai, a niece of Rebecca Gratz, wrote warmly of her recollections of a Hebrew Sunday school class conducted by her aunt.

> The instruction must have been principally oral in those primitive days. Miss Gratz always began school with "Come ye children, hearken unto me, and I will teach you the fear of the Lord." This was followed by prayer of her own composition, which she read verse by verse, and the whole school repeated after her. Then she read a chapter of the Bible . . . The closing exercises were equally simple: a Hebrew hymn sung by the children, then one of Watt's simple verses, whose rhythm the smallest child could easily catch as all repeated: "Send me the voice that Samuel heard," etc., etc.[27]

In 1854 the school was housed in the lower floor building of the Hebrew Education Society. The catechism that was used was the one Leeser wrote for the school and dedicated to Rebecca Gratz. The very concept of Jewish education based on a catechism must have troubled Isaac Leeser. It was so un-Jewish. Yet, he must have reasoned, if a catechism must be used, he could devise one that would be better than the one in use. As for a Bible, the Reverend Leeser's edition replaced the old King James version. Maps of

Palestine and the Ten Commandments adorned the walls. Generally, books
were not allowed to be taken home. As a result, the attempt to teach reading
from Hebrew primers was in vain because any progress that was made one
Sunday was entirely forgotten before the next lesson.

The educational program provided in the Sunday schools was extremely
limited. Isaac Leeser was aware of its limitations. In particular he deplored
the fact that no Hebrew was taught. He considered study of the Bible in its
original form essential to its understanding.

> At the same time we should urge on the projectors and supporters of the
> Sunday School not to rest satisfied with this fragment of religious education
> . . . they must succeed to establish regular schools under proper teachers to
> instruct all in the language of the Hebrews.[28]

His hope did not materialize. The Sunday school was the only institution
that thrived and spread during the nineteenth century.

In 1908 there were eight Hebrew Sunday School Society schools.[29] This
number grew to 12 by 1912, with a student population of 4088.[30] By 1943
there were 22 schools. However, the number of pupils enrolled in these
schools numbered only 4567.[31] The growth of this type of school had
peaked. The Reform congregational school and, in many cases, the Conservative congregational school (in addition to its three-day-a-week program) were providing a one-day-a-week program with a similar
curriculum—Jewish history, religious precepts and customs, Jewish holidays and prayers. With synagogue membership on the increase, these
schools attracted a larger share of pupils at the expense of the Hebrew
Sunday School Society schools. This trend has continued until today.

The Hebrew Education Society and the Day School

While he served as hazan to Mikveh Israel, Isaac Leeser remained undaunted
in his quest for a more intensive Jewish education for children in Philadelphia. In 1843 he began to use the pages of the *The Occident and American
Jewish Advocate* to continue his cry for the establishment of Jewish day
schools and for competent Jewish teachers. In the very first volume he
wrote:

> There is, we acknowledge, an ardent devotion among most of us to the name
> of Israel; but unfortunately there is little else to designate the character which
> this feeling should establish. How can it be otherwise? Where are our teachers?
> Where are our schools? Our colleges? They have indeed been spoken of, and
> now and then projected; but they have unfortunately never been well estab-
> lished.[32]

In the May 1846 issue, Leeser again made an eloquent appeal in an editorial which he called "A Plea for Education" which he concluded with the impassioned statement that Jewish children require Jewish teachers for their secular as well as their religious learning, "to urge on and to encourage by example and conversation a conformity to the duties first implanted by the watchful father and the anxious mother."[33]

This time Isaac Leeser's pleas were heard. Interest in establishing such a school was expressed in the community. At a meeting of the Israelites of Philadelphia on March 7, 1847, a committee of seven was appointed to collect donations and annual contributions for the organization of an English and Hebrew school.[34]

On June 4, 1848, at a town meeting of Israelites, the Constitution and By-Laws of the Hebrew Education Society of Philadelphia were adopted, detailing its objectives, structure and organization. "The School" was described as a school for both male and female students in which Hebrew, according to both the Portuguese and German reading, would be taught, as well as religion and elementary branches of a secular education. The school received a state charter on April 7, 1849. Section 3 of that charter would figure prominently in the future development of Gratz College.[35]

The school's primary purpose was the education of Jewish youth by competent teachers, with adequate means of instruction in Hebrew as well as general studies.[36] At the time the constitution and by-laws were adopted, a curriculum for the school had already been drawn up by a committee. The committee was chaired by Leeser. The curriculum included English, Hebrew, spelling and reading in the first class. The more advanced pupils were to be instructed in geometry, natural history, natural philosophy, rabbinic literature, German, French, Latin, Greek, botany and chemistry. With only seven years of schooling projected, the curriculum was extremely ambitious and seemed more like that of a high school than that of an elementary school.[37]

On April 7, 1851, the Society opened its first school. It was housed in the same building as the Hebrew Sunday School, then 13 years old.[38] Twenty-two students were present, some of whom paid tuition and others who attended free. The school was supported by private donations and by the proceeds of an annual charity dinner which was first organized in 1853. In 1854 the first and largest legacy bequeathed to the society was received. On January 18, 1854, Judah Touro, a well-known philanthropist and citizen of New Orleans died in his eightieth year and left the society $20,000. That year the society purchased an old Baptist church property on the east side of Seventh Street, between Callowhill and Wood Streets, renovated it completely and moved its school there.[39]

In the report of the Chairman of the Board of School Directors tendered at a meeting held in June 1864, the curriculum, as outlined, showed some variation from the one originally projected. The Hebrew department consisted of spelling, reading, grammar, translation and a study of the catechism. The English department offered spelling, reading, definition, grammar, etymology, geography, arithmetic, American history, English history and natural philosophy. Both German and Latin were also taught. Notably absent were rabbinic literature, Greek, French, botany and chemistry.[40]

Sessions were held five days a week, except on Jewish Festivals and Holy Days, and during a part of the summer. At its high point there were nearly 170 pupils in regular attendance.[41] The advanced subjects taught in the higher classes enabled the Society to secure permission from the state to have its graduates admitted into the public boys' and girls' high schools without any previous attendance in the public schools.[42]

While the quality of education in the secular branch of the day school was sufficiently high to win its graduates entrance into the public high schools, the same cannot be said of the Jewish studies. The results in that area were poor. The curriculum was overburdened. In addition to some six to eight secular subjects which included one or two languages, the Jewish curriculum provided Hebrew reading, translation of the prayers and the Pentateuch, Biblical history and Hebrew grammar and writing. In such a diversified curriculum Hebrew language could not have occupied too prominent a place. Furthermore, there were few excellent textbooks for teaching the language. Usually the pupils moved to the study of the Pentateuch immediately after having learned to decode the language from the prayerbook in a mechanical fashion.[43] In established Jewish communities everywhere, the 1870s witnessed the passing of the day school from the Jewish scene in America. The one established by the Hebrew Education Society in Philadelphia followed the trend. It continued to exist but became in effect a supplementary school, holding sessions after public school hours.

Maimonides College

Throughout his life, Isaac Leeser continued to fight for the establishment of a Jewish-sponsored institution of higher learning in Philadelphia. Eventually, his persistence and tenacity were successful. At a meeting of the Hebrew Education Society on June 5, 1864, Isidore Binswanger, Chairman of the Board of School Directors, signaled the beginning of serious efforts in the direction of founding just such a school:

> The founders of our Society have, with much forethought, obtained a charter to enable us to establish a High School or College. The late Judah Touro endowed our Society munificently; and shall we, the members of the Hebrew Education Society, longer permit this want in our city, nay, in our whole country, to exist, of having no institution, no house of learning, where our young men can be properly educated for the elevated position of teachers and ministers? At no time in the history of our beloved country have our people

enjoyed a greater degree of material prosperity than at present. Congregations, springing up in all parts of the land, are anxious to engage capable men for their guides and instructors.[44]

By pointing out the centrality of Philadelphia and the fact that the Hebrew Education Society was controlled by no congregation but was a community institution which recognized only the cause of religious and scientific education in its broadest sense, Mr. Binswanger left no doubt that his objective was to create a seminary that would serve the needs of Jews nationally.[45]

A decision was made to establish the seminary under the joint auspices of the Hebrew Education Society and the Board of Delegates of American Israelites. Trustees were appointed. It became necessary to create a permanent endowment fund for the support of the college. Contributions were solicited. The largest contribution on record is five hundred dollars given by both Abraham Hart[46] and Isidore Binswanger. Many individuals agreed to give a certain amount annually. The college, named Maimonides College, was formally opened on Monday, October 28, 1867. As was befitting, Isaac Leeser became provost of the college and president of its faculty.

The projected course of study was very comprehensive, for the trustees hoped to ground the students thoroughly in a knowledge of Jewish law and traditions. Included in the curriculum were Greek, Latin, German, French, Hebrew and Chaldaic languages and literatures. There were *belles lettres,* homiletics and comparative theology. The Bible, Mishna, Talmud and their respective commentaries, as well as Jewish history and literature and Jewish philosophy formed an important core of the program. In addition, the curriculum provided for studies in natural sciences, history, mathematics, astronomy, moral and intellectual philosphy, constitutional history and the laws of the United States. Among a faculty of scholars, Isaac Leeser held the chair of English literature, logic, and homiletics.[47]

On February 1, 1868, at the age of 62, just three months after the college opened, Isaac Leeser died. Moses A. Dropsie, President of the Hebrew Education Society and of Maimonides College, said of Isaac Leeser in the first report to the society on the college:

> It [the college] owes its existence to the Reverend Isaac Leeser, and none know better than you, his co-laborers in Jewish education, that for the advancement of Judaism he dedicated his existence. The establishment of this college was one of the cherished objects of his life; and at length, when his incessant efforts were rewarded by its formation, death closed his labors ere he saw the fruition of his hopes. His death is an irreparable loss to the college. In honor of his memory, the Trustees have termed the first professorships of the Talmud, the Leeser Professorship.[48]

He noted that Mr. Leeser bequeathed his valuable library to the college and he made a plea for increased support and encouragement, not only from

Jews of Philadelphia but from all who felt any interest in the success of the college.

Although it had been hoped that the school would become "the most desirable institution for education of Jewish youth in the United States,"[49] the college was destined to struggle throughout its brief existence. The Philadelphia Jewish community was not able to shoulder the total burden of its support, and nationwide support did not materialize. Even if it had found some support, the future of the school would have been in doubt. Where would the pupils have come from who would have been prepared to handle the projected curriculum, or even one less comprehensive? The gap between the Jewish education offered by Maimonides College and the one already being received in Philadelphia at that time was so great that the success of the college was doomed from the beginning. Realistically, no more than a handful of students could have been expected to matriculate. In its six years of operation, despite its excellent faculty,[50] the school failed to attract a significant number of students. By the time it closed its doors in 1873, it succeeded in graduating only three students: one teacher and two ministers.[51]

The Talmud Torah

The first Talmud Torah in Philadelphia was established in June 1892. It was known as the Central Talmud Torah and was located at 622 South Ninth Street. Its orientation was traditional Orthodox and it offered daily classes. The Talmud Torah was a more "professional" school than the *heder*, with a number of classrooms and graded classes.

By 1906, three such schools were functioning in the city. They provided an elementary education, mainly for children of East European immigrants with Hebrew, for the purpose of studying Bible and Siddur, as the main subject. In addition, there was one Yeshibah Mishkan Israel which provided a course of study for grown boys. This course centered on Bible and Talmud. Statistics reveal that the four schools provided education for 985 pupils.[52] It is interesting to note that at this time, Yiddish was still the language of instruction in these schools.[53] Classes, unfortunately, were very large—so much so that they contradicted the Talmudic precept that there should be no more than 25 children under the care of one teacher.[54] Teachers were scarce and classroom space was insufficient. No doubt, lack of sufficient funds was a reason.

With the failure of Philadelphia's pioneering attempt at a Kehilla,[55] an effort was made, in 1919, to federate the Talmud Torahs. The Federation of Jewish Charities, which was at this time interested in extending its activities to include all Jewish organizations, recognized the Associated Talmud Torahs as a constituent and agreed to cover its annual deficit. The

Associated Talmud Torahs were unable to cope with rising costs of living and the teachers' salary demands. Following a teachers' strike it became evident that the Association had to undergo a complete change. Its board would have to be given complete control of the management of its constituted schools.[56]

At the same time that the effort was made to reorganize the Associated Talmud Torahs, an attempt was made to organize an Educational Group of Federation, representing all the educational agencies receiving community support (those affiliated with Federation). Dr. Cyrus Adler, its chairman, decided that the guidance of a professional executive was necessary and invited Mr. Ben Rosen[57] to give his professional services to the educational group. He was asked, however, to give his immediate attention to the Associated Talmud Torahs. This immediate attention became fixed. The more comprehensive aspect of the original plan was lost sight of and Ben Rosen, although subsequently named director of the education group, served until the early 1940s as director of the Associated Talmud Torahs.[58]

At the time of Ben Rosen's resignation, the Associated Talmud Torahs were conducting ten schools,[59] eight elementary schools and two secondary schools.[60] There were 1,375 pupils registered. The course of study in the elementary school was four years and an additional four years in the high school. The curriculum consisted of Hebrew language, prayers, Bible, history, current events and Jewish music. Classes ranged from five to seven and a half hours per week. This represented less time than had been offered in the middle 1930s with a concomitant lowering of achievement.[61]

Subsequent events proved that a decline in enrollment which started in the late 1930s and which, more or less, coincided with the lessening of the time requirement, in fact, signaled the beginning of the decline of the Talmud Torah system. It would never recover.

Nevertheless, although it offered only a four-year elementary course, the Associated Talmud Torahs maintained a high standard. Those who were graduated from its high school, entered Gratz College. This can be attributed in part to the attention it paid to hiring only the most qualified teachers[62] and offering them full-time jobs, as opposed to most of the job offers from Jewish schools in Philadelphia at that time.

Gratz College

On December 18, 1856, a deed of trust was entered into by Hyman Gratz of Philadelphia and the Pennsylvania Company for Insurance of Lives and Granting Annuities. This deed of trust provided that from and immediately after his decease the income and interest of the properties and stocks which had been set aside were to be distributed to three heirs in the manner specified, Martha Ellen Sprigg, Robert Gratz (the adopted son of Hyman

Gratz College, York Street near Broad, 1909. *Courtesy of Gratz College and Dr. Nathaniel A. Entin.*

Gratz) and Horace Moses (nephew of Hyman Gratz).[63] It further provided that:

> In case there be no such lawful issue of the said Horace Moses, or if any, none shall live to attain the age of twenty-one years, then to convey and assign all the said trust estate and premises to the PORTUGUESE HEBREW CONGREGATION "KAAL KADOSH MICKVE ISRAEL," of the City of Philadelphia, and their successors, in trust for the establishment and support of a college for the education of Jews residing in the city and county of Philadelphia for which purpose the rents and income only of the said trust estate shall be used and applied from time to time and to and for no other use, intent or purpose whatsoever.[64]

Scarcely more than one month later, on January 27, 1857, Hyman Gratz died in his eighty-first year. Martha Ellen Spriggs received monies from the estate until her death in 1870. Seven years later, Robert Gratz died, unmarried and without lawful issue, and on October 15, 1893, Horace Moses died, also ummarried and without leaving lawful issue. Upon the death of Horace Moses, the Pennsylvania Company filed its account as trustees in the indenture.

With only limited funds available,[65] it was decided to establish a college of narrower scope, with a curriculum "especially designed for teachers who will, upon successful completion of the course, be awarded a certificate."[66] The requirements of the curriculum were to include a knowledge of Jewish history, literature, religion and Hebrew language. The Gratz College opened its doors in 1897.[67]

By 1928, the college faced severe fiscal problems. This, plus pressure for change brought by Federation, motivated the Board of Trustees to seek a reorganization of the college. The financial concerns forced the congregation and the Board of Trustees to realize that the days of the college as a private enterprise were over. In order to ensure sufficient funds to operate the college and the school, Gratz would have to move to community control. Federation, with recommendations for the expansion of the program at Gratz to meet various community needs, created the framework for the reorganization.

An agreement was arranged between Gratz College and the Hebrew Education Society.[68] By combining the two institutions, it was hoped that funds for a "proper teacher's college" could be secured and courses arranged for the training of teachers for all forms of Jewish instruction. The agreement called for the establishment of a committee of 15 to be known as the Board of Overseers of the Gratz College and the Hebrew Education Society of Philadelphia. Five members were to be elected by the Board of Trustees of Gratz College, five by the Board of Officers of the Hebrew Education Society and five by the Board of Overseers from the community.

Shortly thereafter a new curriculum was worked out, more responsive to community needs. This curriculum provided for a more advanced course in Hebrew to be given in addition and parallel to the regular course in Hebrew, on a level designed to meet the needs of the graduates of the Hebrew High School and such others as may have had an equally intensive training in Hebrew. It also provided for the organization of a two-year normal course. Sessions would be held for four hours a week and were intended to train teachers for the Sunday religious schools, in which the teaching of Hebrew did not go beyond the elements or was omitted entirely.[69] Consideration was also given to the establishment of a graduate course leading to a granting of a degree but this was not acted upon until after 1945.[70]

Following some discussion it was agreed that since students in Gratz College would be trained to be teachers for religious schools with different ideologies, it was to be understood that every subject of instruction would be approached by the instructor from the historic point of view and with academic objectivity.

With the reorganization of the college, the individual links of Jewish education in Philadelphia were forged into one continuous chain. Unfortunately, for a number of reasons,[71] relatively few pupils were attracted to the school, and among those who did matriculate, the rate of attrition was high. During the first 50 years of its existence a little less than 500 men and women

Gratz College's Class of 1907. *Courtesy of Gratz College and Dr. Nathaniel A. Entin.*

were graduated from its various departments. Nevertheless, teachers with Gratz College training were found in many of the religious schools and Talmud Torahs of the city.[72]

Yeshivot

By 1943 there were two Yeshivot in Philadelphia, with an additional branch.[73] Both of them had Talmud Torahs connected with them which served as preparatory departments for the Yeshiva. The schools were open 12 months a year and provided no vacation period. The total student population was 472 pupils, 381 in the elementary schools and 91 in the Yeshivot. Eighty-five percent of the pupils were male, as would be expected in an intensive Orthodox school.[74]

The Yeshivot proper had a three- or four-year supplementary course, ranging in time in the various schools from 7½ to 17½ hours per week. Their aim was to produce the type of learned Jew in the traditional sense and to inspire all of its students to be pious, observant Jews, devoted to traditional Judaism. The emphasis was on the study of Talmud.[75]

While the Yeshivot may have met with some success in achieving their

Gratz College Faculty, 1922. *Left to right:* Dr. Joseph Medoff, Rev. Henry M. Speaker *(seated)*, Dr. Arthur Dembitz, and Dr. Julius H. Greenstone. *Courtesy of Gratz College and Dr. Nathaniel A. Entin.*

aims, the number of pupils who availed themselves of this form of education was so small, its impact on the Jewish community was minimal.

Folkshulen

Five elementary schools and one high school with a total registration of about 240 pupils made up the Folkshulen system of the 1940s.[76] The former met for five years and the latter for four years. The emphasis of these schools was on labor ideology and Zionism. The curriculum of the elementary school consisted of both the Yiddish language and the Hebrew language, as well as Jewish history, Palestine and current Jewish life. In the high school, students studied Yiddish literature, Hebrew language and Bible in Hebrew and Yiddish. Institutions with a strong tie to *Eretz Yisrael,* such as the Jewish National Fund and United Jewish Appeal, were given prominent recognition in the schools.[77]

Critics of these schools held that the attempt to include both Hebrew and Yiddish in the curriculum did not give the child a firm grounding in either language and did not prepare him adequately for life in the Diaspora. Others felt that there was not a sufficient emphasis on Hebrew. Some questioned the need for a separate school system, expressing the opinion that the Labor Zionists could achieve their aims through existing Hebrew schools, particularly those which would be willing to cope with the special needs of the Labor Zionist. The main dissatisfaction, however, seemed to center on the contention that the schools did not serve to a sufficient degree as preparation for eventual affiliation with the Labor Zionist group, that this function was better served through Labor Zionist youth groups and summer camps.[78]

Perhaps hopes for such a school system were exaggerated. Certainly, there was no unanimity within the group as to what the desired educational programs for the Labor Zionist schools ought to be. Still those connected with the school system expressed confidence that the alumni of the schools retained a warm feeling in their hearts toward Jewish life.[79] That outcome in the eyes of many did not justify a separate school system.

Workmen's Circle Schools

The Workmen's Circle was organized in 1900 for two purposes: to provide its members with mutual aid, health and death benefits, and other fraternal services, and to support the labor and socialist movements throughout the world. It was dedicated to the promotion of progressive Yiddish culture. In 1916 it entered the field of Jewish education by opening afternoon schools for children. These grew to become the largest network of Jewish secular schools in the United States.

Starting with the 1930s, a sympathetic attitude developed among members of the Workmen's Circle school toward the historic values of the Jewish people. The educational leaders of the movement became convinced that in order to make Jewish education in America meaningful a more positive Jewish content had to be included in the curriculum. They did not, however, go as far as to include Hebrew in their curriculum.

The curriculum emphasized the Yiddish language. In the elementary school Yiddish language, Jewish history and Yiddish literature were taught. These subjects continued into the high school where the addition of social problems, labor movements, current Jewish life and singing rounded out the program. Religion was not taught, but cognizance of Jewish holidays was taken through stories read to the children and by arranging holiday celebrations.[80]

By the 1940s, the Workmen's Circle organization in Philadelphia maintained 12 schools of which one was a high school. The total pupil population was 390[81] of which 328 were in the elementary grades. The elementary schools met for three hours per week and the high school for seven hours per week. The courses in each school were four years in length.[82] Yet in none of these courses did the students learn Hebrew.

The pupils attending the school often did so because their parents wanted them to know Yiddish in order that they might be able to communicate with grandparents and read the Yiddish newspapers. Some came from observant homes.

Dropsie College

A major educational institution of higher Jewish learning in Philadelphia, not part of the network of Jewish schools, was Dropsie College for Hebrew and Cognate Learning. Moses Aaron Dropsie, the founder of the school, directed in his will that upon his death there be established and maintained a college for the promotion of and instruction in the Hebrew and cognate languages and their respective literatures. He also directed that this institution be open to all regardless of color, religion or sex.[83]

In 1907, two years after Moses Dropsie's death, the college was founded as a graduate school. Dr. Cyrus Adler was named its first president. Until 1912, when its own building was dedicated, classes were held in the Gratz College building. The curriculum offered courses in Biblical literature, Rabbinical literature, history and cognate languages. Biblical philology, Talmud and Arabic were added by 1914. Both the curriculum and the faculty remained the same for the next two decades.

A few years after its establishment, Dropsie College announced that the *Jewish Quarterly Review*, which had been published in London for 20 years, would thereafter be published by the College. This publication has remained to this day a publishing forum for scholars throughout the world.

Unfortunately, the flow of historical events prevented Dropsie College from establishing itself firmly as a center of Jewish intellectual and cultural life in the United States and beyond. The world was caught up in war in 1914. The needs of the Jews of Russia and Poland were great in the postwar period, and Dr. Adler was drawn into the work of the Joint Distribution Committee. Community resources were also drawn in that direction. The Great Depression followed and again the community's resources were limited. Throughout this period the College's desperate need for wider support went unattended. The College remained a small graduate research instituion.[84] Its graduates, however, have spread over the world and made significant contributions to scholarship.

There existed in Philadelphia by 1940 a complete network of supplementary Jewish educational institutions. For the few who desired it, an intensive Jewish education was available. Most of the children studied in either Orthodox and Conservative congregational schools or the Hebrew Sunday School Society schools.[85] For Jewish education to have a lasting impact a solution would have to be found to the basic problem at that time—of educating the Jewish family that Jewish education, in order to be effective, needed to continue for a longer period. To achieve this goal, steps would have to be taken to make the school and its educational processes more appealing to the pupil. This became the agenda of Jewish education in Philadelphia in the years that followed.

Irish-Jewish Relations in Philadelphia

Dennis Clark

This chapter sets out to furnish a basic historical description of the relative settings and social positions of Philadelphia's Jewish and Irish populations during the period from 1880 to 1940. This period saw the urban encounter of the two groups and the working out of a very American pattern of interaction. Confrontation, alienation, segregation, depersonalized contacts, competition, eventual cooperation and finally some degree of understanding were all involved. This uneven juxtaposition leading to ultimate association is one of the key processes of American life. If the maintenance of ethnic identity is one of the enrichments of American society, the balancing of one group against another is one of the secrets of the social harmony and democratic vigor of our national life.

In exploring the development of the Philadelphia Irish community over the course of two centuries, one is often struck by how this group's attitude toward itself changed from one generation to the next. There were times in the nineteenth century when the misfortunes of the Irish evoked a Biblical sense of affliction among them. Thus, in a book concerning the history of Irish seaports published in 1860, a reflection upon the great mid-nineteenth-century emigration to America occasioned the following comparison:

No emigration since the creation equalled or resembled that which landlord despotism in conjunction with the famine of 1847 produced. It was properly called the Irish exodus, although it differed in some degree from that of the Israelites, whom Egyptian taskmasters persevered so obstinately to keep in 'bondage,' and who, with arms in their hands, conquered the nations whose territories were assigned to them by Providence. But the migration of the Irish people to the land of their adoption was of a peaceful character, and their taskmasters instead of detaining them when they found them no longer politically or socially profitable, forced them, by subtle legislation to leave the country and seek refuge in the United States.[1]

Such ruminations reveal the religious preoccupation and keen historical consciousness that have been such notable characteristics of both the Irish and Jewish traditions.

Of course, it was not always that Biblical subjects were approached with gravity. In periods when Irish songs for vaudeville were composed with happy aplomb by Jewish composers, it was not beyond the Irish to disport themselves in a fantasy of what would have transpired had Moses been born with an Irish brogue, with the following ballad as a result:

> On Egypt's banks contagious to the Nile
> There the Pharoah's daughter she went to bathe in style
> She took her dip and she came onto the land,
> And to dry her royal pelt, she ran across the strand.
> She came unto some bullrushes
> Whereupon she saw
> A smiling Babby lying there
> In a wad of straw.
> She picked him up and she said in accents mild,
> "Taranagers! Daughters, which of you'se owns the child?"
>
> Tittery–ow–tow–tow–tow
> Tittery–ow–tow–tow–tow
> Tittery outen tow!
>
> She picked him up and she gave a little grin
> For she and Moses were standin' in their skin.
> "B'dad," says she, "twas someone very rude
> That left a little babby by the river in the nude."
> She took him to her old Dad sitting on his throne
> "B'dad," says she "Will you give the child a home?"
> "B'Dad" say he, "I've often brought in worse,
> So go me darlin' daughter and fetch the child a nurse."
>
> (chorus)
>
> Then they sent a bell man to the market square
> To see if he could find a skivvy there.
> But the only girl that he could find
> Was the one that left the child behind
> She went up to the Pharoah, a stranger now, agrah,
> Never lettin' on that she was the babby's ma.
> So Moses got his Mommy back
> Showing that coincidence is quite a nut to crack.[2]
>
> (chorus)

In a more serious vein we should reflect upon the fact that the Irish Catholics and the Jews have notably similar legacies. Both trace their histories to pre-Christian cultures. Both share long histories of oppression, long traditions of learning and distinctive attachments to religion. Both have experienced massive immigration movements to America, and the two groups have been especially concentrated in the urban areas of the United

States. As ethnic subgroups in America, Jews and Irish have had to deal with conditions that have shaped family and cultural life among urbanites. The Irish were statistically more numerous and shared extensively several cycles of American development in which Jews took part only marginally, such as the Westward expansion, the work of early industrialization and repeated involvement in the nation's earlier wars. The differences, however, do not efface the similarities. They simply coexist as distinct social features within the two traditions.

As strongly identified religious groups, the Jews and the Irish, at different times, both had to deal with the hostility and discrimination aimed at them by mainstream Protestant America. However, the numbers, the cycles of arrival and diffusion and their respective concerns and responsibilities did not usually permit a dovetailing of group interests.

Although both the Philadelphia Jewish community and the Irish traced their presence to colonial times, bitter anti-Irish hostility did not erupt until the 1840s and 1850s, when the huge influx of Irish brought thousands to the city, while the worst antagonism toward the Jews did not emerge until their numbers had grown in the late 1800s. In their own separate times, Irish and Jews were resilient enough to construct internal structures for self-defense against discrimination, for getting jobs despite hostility and for maintaining their own social ties and mutual assistance activities.[3]

In the 1890s the interaction of Jews and Irish expanded as more and more Jewish immigrants sought opportunities in the city. One of the traditional areas of the Irish, in fact the oldest Irish residential concentration in the city, was in Southwark, a district near the Delaware River docks in the city's Third, Fourth and Fifth Wards. This was a hard area by any standards. St. Joseph's, St. Mary's and St. Philip's parishes included dockside worlds of brutality and harsh conditions, produce and peddlers' markets, garment lofts and marginal industries of all kinds. By the time large numbers of Jews arrived, the Irish had been dug into the Southwark area for four generations.[4]

Upon arrival in Philadelphia, Jews did what experience and religion taught them was essential. They formed congregations and a community. B'nai Abraham, at Fifth and Lombard Streets, and B'nai Jacob, at Fourth and Lombard, were synagogues to which they walked on the Sabbath for worship. At Fifth and Gaskill Streets was Congregation Emunath Israel-Oheb Shalom. The Hebrew Education Society conducted English and trade classes at Touro Hall at Tenth and Carpenter Streets, and a Young Women's Union held similar classes at 230 Pine Street. These places formed the focus for immigrant Jews in South Philadelphia in the 1890s. After a decade of heavy immigration there were 30,000 Jews in the six wards in the eastern part of South Philadelphia.[5]

East of Second Street, pressed against the docks where they worked, was an enclave of Irish. To the west of the Jewish concentration beyond

Sixth Street was a larger Irish population that was mingled with Italian, German and Anglo-American residents, and numerically it was about equal to the Jewish population in South Philadelphia. The Irish parish churches of St. Philip's and St. Teresa's were the east and west poles of this group's local concentration. Thus the Irish and the Jews of the 1890s were adjacent, intermingled and interactive in the oldest and least desirable area of the city.[6]

From the 1850s on there were large numbers of Irish in the city's small businesses. Tailors, shoemakers, grocers and butchers were the kinds of craftsmen who could transfer rural and village skills to American settings, and city directories for Philadelphia show that this is exactly what happened. Into South Philadelphia came thousands of Jews, bringing the same skills into an area in which the Irish had been dominant.[7] The strains of competition, displacement and succession in small businesses were very much part of a neighborhood friction that could be expected between the two groups. The most aggressive elements of each group battled one another for years in street fights and other confrontations. The surviving Magistrate Court dockets for the early part of this century list scores of Jewish-Irish conflicts. In many of these, Jews were charged as the aggressors. A Jewish community that produced prizefighters like Benny Leonard and Lew Tendler was not without pugnacious instincts. Thus, in 1909, Magistrate Frank S. Harrison in Court No. 5 had to deal with assault and battery cases involving Patrick Flynn and Louis Hagnoski, Bessie Weinberg and John Gallen, Julius Plotz and James Sullivan, John Curran and Max Rosenbaum, and Herman Kaplan and Lillian Moore—not forgetting Ada Rosenfelt and Esther Leary. Of course, these were all cases where the police became involved. There were a multitude of cases in which no police appeared. The role of the police was a sore point as well. The arresting officers listed were frequently Irish. Mollie Weiss and Ida Kersiver were taken in by Officer Sweeney for disorderly conduct. Patrick O'Brien had Annie Rosenberg and Annie Goldberg arrested for keeping a disorderly house. Special Officer Barry and Constable Broderick made constant arrests of Jews. Such situations were bound to breed misunderstanding at best and bitter antagonism at worst.[8]

Although the more responsible leaders of both communities tried to encourage tolerance, to the Irish Catholics the Jews did seem particularly exclusive, and to the Jews, surrounded by Christians, the impulse toward self-defense was second nature. *The Jewish Exponent,* parroting some of the pseudo-scientific racial jargon of the times, wrote in 1893 of the "very important matter of the preservation of racial Jewry pure and free from unwholesome admixture." Jews were susceptible along with others to the stereotypes so prevalent about the Irish at the time. In another article on the British Parliament's debates on Irish Home Rule, *The Jewish Exponent* noted that the Irish Members of Parliament had a "proverbial disposition to internal dissension and ill-timed zeal. . . ."[9]

Intermittently some positive manifestation of good will among Irishmen would turn up. A letter written by Michael Davitt, founder of the Irish Land League and a revered Irish leader, was published in the Jewish press in 1893. Davitt criticized the call of a Mr. Crowley in Belfast, who sought to exclude Jews from Ireland. "The Jews, to my knowledge," wrote Davitt, "have never done any injury to Ireland. Like our own race they have endured a persecution the records of which will forever remain a reproach to the 'Christian' nations of Europe." It was to be regretted, he continued, "that any Nationalist or Irishman of any other political conviction should . . . give expression to such reactionary 'know-nothing' views. . . ."[10]

More concrete commitment was expressed when the steamship *Indiana* was to sail for Russia in 1892 with 3,000 tons of famine relief stores for the victims of the czar's pogroms. A dockside prayer and blessing service was held with Protestant ministers, Archbishop Patrick Ryan and Rabbi Marcus Jastrow. The Friendly Sons of St. Patrick contributed to the relief drive, and Irish-born newspaperman Robert Malachi McWade was especially active in promoting it.[11] The Irish knew what famine was and could feel deeply for its victims.

As Jews moved beyond their original immigrant ghettos, a new dimension emerged in their relationship with the Irish. Undercurrents of anti-semitism and anti-Catholicism persisted, of course, but where civility and the decencies of mutual respect could function in stable neighborhoods, relations were tolerant. One such neighborhood where Jews moved was that adjacent to North Broad Street in Our Lady of Mercy parish. The large German-Jewish concentration east of this area in North Philadelphia had been notably affected by the influx of Eastern European Jews beginning in the 1880s. The German Jews, whose substantial row homes had ranged through streets around the axis of the Franklin Street market, had viewed the Eastern European influx as a regrettable invasion and in many cases recoiled from contact with the newcomers.

The area along North Broad Street that included Our Lady of Mercy parish was a heavily Irish neighborhood. The imposing granite church with its soaring twin steeples at Broad Street and Susquehanna Avenue had been dedicated in 1893 and was a symbol of Irish respectability. Monsignor Thomas Drumgoole, the pastor, had made one of the few attempts ever launched to teach Irish history in the parish schools by installing it in the curriculum for the parish children. A few houses from the ornate rectory of the parish was the home of Cyrus Adler, publisher and philanthropist. As more Jews moved into the area, the Irish and Jewish families had to accommodate one another in business and social relations. Although there were a few Jews in the neighborhood at the turn of the century, their movement into the area in greater numbers occurred in the 1920s. Many Jewish families still found the most accessible livelihood open to them in the running of small neighborhood businesses, so that names like Morris Aaron and Louis Goldstein, tailors, appear with that of Joseph Kelly, tailor, among the businesses within sight of Broad Street. By 1930, Jews shared the main business street of the neighborhood near the church with Irish shopkeepers. West of Twelfth Street and Susquehanna Avenue, James Dugan, James Moriarty and Thomas Gorman had their businesses close to Jacob Berkowitz, tailor, and Harry Ravitz, fruit store proprietor. Margaret Coyne, dressmaker, had the same customers as Max Solomon, hairdresser. On this busy shopping street O. R. Sheridan the grocer, Mary Gilligan the notary, and James Corkran the upholsterer did business beside William Glazer, optician, and Isadore Halen's hosiery shop. Residents of the area recalled that the movement of Jews into the local businesses was gradual from 1910 until 1930, and that resentments or antagonisms were rare. Residents of the area such as David Roche recalled that Jews contributed to local collections to support the Irish fight against English rule in the 1920s. Anna McGarry remembered giving little gifts to Jewish children during their *bar mitzvahs*.[12]

The interplay of Irish and Jews in the Philadelphia neighborhoods of the 1920s unfolded in an environment of changing attitudes, slowly altering the isolation of ethnic groups that had once kept apart, each in its own ghetto world. The vaudeville comedians Gallagher and Sheen were humorously contrasting Irishman and Jew, and the play "Abie's Irish Rose," whose theme was interreligious romance, was breaking records for attendance. If it was American to be tolerant, Irishman and Jew would try to be tolerant, though there were misgivings and strains in the background. Jews were still largely excluded from business clubs, from top law firms, banks and executive posts and from some upper-class neighborhoods. The Irish were still largely unwelcome in circles where old-line Philadelphia familes dominated. The mobility and social change of the 1920s was opening new pathways, however, and the Irish and the Jews were encountering one another in an increasingly generalized framework. When Owen B. Hunt wanted to locate an office on Chestnut Street for a consulate of the newly independent Irish state in 1921, he was coldly rejected by local property owners, but finally obtained an office from a Jew. Young Tommy Regan, fresh from service with the Irish Republican Army, had the same experience in locating a site for The Terence MacSwiney Club.[13]

It was during the colorful twenties that an association began between a redoubtable Catholic prelate and the city's leading Jewish real estate magnate. Dennis Cardinal Dougherty, whose career as Archbishop of Philadelphia extended from 1918 to 1951, was for most of this time on very friendly terms with Albert M. Greenfield, a prodigious assembler of land and properties. The Cardinal had in trust a great deal of church property and needed more practical advice than his canon-law-trained priests could provide. Albert Greenfield supplied that advice, and a fast friendship developed.[14]

The Presidential election of 1928 was a flashpoint of interreligious tension in Philadelphia as elsewhere. Al Smith, the Irish Governor of New York, had to face not only the defenders of Prohibition, which he had vowed to repeal, but also a virulent stream of anti-Catholic sentiment. Smith captured 40 percent of the vote in the city and broke the Republican hold on South Philadelphia. It was in this area that Jews were concentrated, and 50 percent of them voted for Smith, along with 56 percent of the Irish. In South Philadelphia the Jews, the Irish and other ethnics raised their proportion of the vote from 21.9 percent to 38.5 percent in 1928.

To many Jews, Al Smith represented opposition to Prohibition and to Republican immigration restrictions; moreover, he was an image of social and political opportunity. The 1928 election brought together the Irish and the Jews as key builders of Roosevelt's New Deal Coalition. The extent of prejudicial rancor in that election led to the formation of a Philadelphia chapter of the National Conference of Christians and Jews. Journalist Constance O'Hara and other Irish Catholics joined in this effort, one that signaled the beginning of a slow development of interreligious collaboration against defamation and prejudice.[15]

An energetic Irish-American broadcaster, Patrick Stanton, launched an Irish radio program in the 1930s, and was soon able to charter his own radio station. Whether by design or accident, the station was assigned the call letters WJMJ. The letters "J.M.J." were a familiar acronym to Catholics. Children in Catholic schools wrote the letters on their classroom papers to dedicate their efforts to Jesus, Mary and Joseph. A zealot for civil liberties, who happened to be Jewish, confronted Stanton and insisted that the call letters were an abuse of the public airways and part of a Catholic threat to freedom of information. This infuriated one Irish lawyer who was conscious of the seriousness of any such charge before the Federal Communications Commission. Goaded repeatedly by the civil libertarian, he finally quipped, "Do you know what those letters stand for? Jews and More Jews!"[16] Thus continuing problems of misunderstanding and alienation remained to be dealt with as the Irish and the Jews became more conscious of the institutional power and social postures each wielded in a complex urban setting.

The Depression years created a desperate ferment as people sought to find ideas and leadership that would lift them out of economic disaster. Father Charles Coughlin, through his radio broadcasts and his newspaper *Social Justice*, created a large audience among Irish Catholics for his views on economic reconstruction. Unfortunately, he also gave voice to some of the oldest and most discredited stereotypes about Jews, and these were bitterly resented among Jews conscious of the growth of Hitler's antisemitic crusade overseas.

There is clear evidence that the Irish were Father Coughlin's chief supporters. During the crisis of the 1930s when the nation was subjected to what Arthur Schlesinger, Jr. called "the politics of upheaval," ordinary people searched fitfully for some voice that would interpret for them the profound maladies of American society. Father Coughlin was that voice for a large portion of Irish-Americans.

Patrick Stanton. *Courtesy of the Balch Institute for Ethnic Studies.*

As Father Coughlin's radio broadcasts became more strident after 1935, his antisemitic commentaries became more blatant. People in Philadelphia listened to his Sunday broadcasts in their kitchens and on their front steps. Jews were shocked to hear the hoary fabrications about "The Protocols of Zion" that purported to counsel Jews to exploit Gentiles. Such tactics raised tempers and contributed further to the atmosphere of unease. There is little actual documentation that community incidents resulted, but Jews were conscious of increased tension. They were probably not aware of the bitter disputes within Irish families about the character and merits of Father Coughlin. Liberal Irish Catholics found him intolerable. The Irish of Philadelphia were such a very diverse group with such far-ranging political views and social positions that their reaction to Coughlin and many other issues was bound to be full of contradictions.

By 1938, Father Coughlin was losing support and finding it harder to get air time for his anti-New Deal campaign. He requested that his weekly addresses be carried by station WJMJ, which was headed by Patrick J. Stanton, whose "Irish Hour" broadcasts were an institution in the city's Irish community. Stanton refused to carry Coughlin's program. The Rev. Thomas J. Higgins, President of St. Joseph's College, wrote Stanton at one point, urging him to carry Coughlin's program in the interests of free speech. Coughlin was the focus of fierce differences among the Irish, but Stanton didn't want to make things worse. He was a good friend of many Jews and even announced in Yiddish the musical selections on a Yiddish program. He was subjected to a barrage of antisemitic mail, and his station was picketed by Coughlin zealots. Some of the mail thundered, "Boycott Jews! Buy Gentile!"[17] Stanton stood firm, but he never forgot the rancorous episode.

The reaction to Father Coughlin was similar to the distress caused by Senator Joseph McCarthy in the years after World War II. Jews with liberal opinions were offended both by a cultural style that was demagogic and by the malevolent insinuations in which both these spokesmen indulged. Irish Catholics, for their part, were agitated by the identification of many Jews with what they regarded as atheistic Communist causes and by the high sensitivity of Jews to any attempts by public authorities to aid the single biggest social and economic community investment of the Irish—the Catholic school system. The fact that liberal Jews were more conditioned by traditions of European socialist thought than by Communism and the fact that Catholics were voluntarily supporting schools that made an enormous contribution to the public welfare were considerations usually lost in the controversial crossfire.

In a key area of urban association, Irish and Jewish entrepreneurs had similar economic development patterns. The respective contributions of Irish and Jews to the economic development of cities like Philadelphia have been only cursorily studied, partly because of the general lack of analysis of ethnic history, but also because of a sensitivity about identifying groups with what came to be seen as stereotypic occupational roles. The Irishman as rough digger and construction worker and the Jew as mercantile and retail middleman have prejudicial associations that tend to restrain objective inquiry. Nevertheless, the growth of urban contractor construction and the birth of the big city department store were economic developments of major significance, and the Irish and Jews were notable achievers in both areas of enterprise.

General contracting in construction tends to be dispersed, flexible and economically eccentric. The department store, with its fixed site, large inventories and highly developed retail practices, is more stable and routinized. Neither kind of enterprise is distinctly ethnic in itself, for both general construction contracting and department stores are features of large-scale urban economies promoted by technology and the concentration of population and commerce.[18] These forms of enterprise, however, became the vehicles for ethnic aspiration and business development as successive immigrant groups sought livelihoods and fulfilment in great cities such as Philadelphia. As ethnic representatives invested their labor and talents in specific areas of activity, they drew with them, in a natural fashion, family members, associates and clients. Eventually they became identified with

Father Charles Coughlin. *(Library of Congress) Reproduced by courtesy of the Museum of American Jewish History.*

certain enterprises, reenforcing this identification with an ethnic prominence that served to augment their business and community status. The contractor-boss is one of the central figures in the history of the American city. The builder-developer with strong political ties and influence is a familiar figure. There is a considerable literature delineating the political features of the "boss," whose influence is variously interpreted as nefarious or socially beneficial, depending upon which historian or political scientist one reads.[19] The ethnic identification of these figures has begun to be reconsidered without the subjectivity that previously attached to their description.[20] The contractor as a builder and as an agent of urban expansion and development, as distinguished from the contractor as political boss, has rarely been examined in the context of businessman, particularly an ethnic business type.

An examination of the occupational statistics concerning immigrants compiled by Edward P. Hutchinson shows a notable concentration of Irishmen as builders and contractors. According to the 1870 and 1980 United States Census figures summarized by Hutchinson, the Irish led all other immigrants in this occupational category. By 1890, the Irish had twice the proportion of builders and contractors that other immigrant groups had.[21] This concentration was not accidental. Rather it was a function of the social position of the Irish in nineteenth-century America. Among the immigrant groups in the last century, the Irish were the most urban in their demographic distribution.[22] The vast influx of refugees from the catastrophe of the Irish potato famine of the 1840s coincided with a period of rapid industrialization and urban expansion in the eastern cities.[23] Because the Irish, coming from a society that was singularly rural, entered the United States largely without skills relevant to the new industrial technology, they came into the work force as unskilled labor. Such labor was in great demand for the construction of canals, railroads and cities.[24]

For many men anxious to improve themselves and move out of the unskilled labor pool an opportune route was to become a small-scale building contractor. It is not too far from the truth to say that any man with his own shovel and wheelbarrow could style himself a "contractor." Such a pursuit required little initial capital. Only aggressiveness and strong backs were important, and these the Irish had. They also had easy access to fellow countrymen who, after a preliminary adjustment to city life, had developed skills in stonecutting, bricklaying, ironwork and most of the trades associated with building. Because of ethnic and religious discrimination in public schools, the overwhelmingly Catholic Irish felt impelled to construct a whole network of churches, schools and welfare institutions in the major cities. This they did with alacrity, and the building work for these institutions provided a continuing source of construction operations for the Irish contractors. An illustration of the evolution of the Irish construction magnate can be found in the city of Philadelphia, a city whose rich Colonial past has overshadowed its interesting history during the period of industrialization and urban expansion.[25]

When the Irish first arrived in Philadelphia in great numbers in the wave of immigration following the potato famine of 1846–47, the city was in a period of extensive growth.[26] In 1854 the consolidation of the outlying areas in the County of Philadelphia expanded the locally defined city greatly.[27] What had transpired since the 1840s was an unprecedented urban development, and the Irish contractors had ridden the wave of this growth.[28] In *Victorian Cities,* Asa Briggs has pointed out the primary role that the provision of sanitation, utilities and public works construction played in such growth.[29] It was in these areas of construction that the Irish contractors made a heavy contribution. Starting in the ditches as excavators, they had gained command of a business medium that was flexible enough to meet the needs of the fast-breaking urban building segment of the economy.

The interaction of general contracting and politics suited the Irish admirably. Their early prominence in politics was consolidated so that by the late nineteenth century they held strategic positions in both the Democratic and Republican parties in Philadelphia. As the new immigration from Southern and Eastern Europe developed, they took up the role of political intermediaries, and this role has been one of the distinctive features of the political history of the Irish in the cities.[30] In contracting, also, they were intermediaries as well as principals. In hiring labor and presiding over subcontractors, architects, engineers, union bosses and clients, the Irish demonstrated the same facility for maneuver and mobilization that they displayed in politics.

An example of the interaction of business and politics can be seen in the career of James P. "Sunny Jim" McNichol, the first Irish Catholic to become a top Republican potentate in the Philadelphia firmament. McNichol, born in the tough Tenth Ward, began by forming a building firm with his brother. Between 1893 and 1895 his business forged ahead, doing $6 million worth of work.[31] In terms of urban construction, few men in the last hundred years have changed Philadelphia's physical aspect and orientation more extensively than "Sunny Jim" McNichol.

Not all of the Irish contractors ascended to such power. Many were content to make a good living and try to keep ahead in the rough contest of competitive bidding and control of costs. Such a man was David J. Duffin, who arrived in the city from County Antrim in the north of Ireland with the strong arms of a stonecutter. He began excavating with a horse and wagon, and then with his sons went into homebuilding and roadwork. After almost going broke excavating the foundations for Philadelphia's Convention Hall because of a hidden rock formation, the firm of Duffin and Sons prospered in building Catholic churches. The strong desire of the Irish Catholics for churches, schools and institutions stimulated a huge network of parish building. With his own quarry supplying stone, Duffin worked on 30 separate parish complexes, raising wells and steeples for the "lace curtain" Irish in various parts of the city.[32]

Perhaps the most attractive of all the city's contractors was John B. Kelly, born of a family with talent to spare. One of Kelly's brothers was a Pulitzer Prize playwright, one was a noted entertainer and Kelly's daughter, Grace, was a movie star. In the case of John B. Kelly's rise from bricklayer's apprentice to ownership of the largest brickwork company in America, a somewhat more glamorous tinge is added to the contractor image. One of ten children of an immigrant from County Mayo, John B. Kelly was raised in the Falls of the Schuylkill area of the city. After service in World War I, he made a spectacular record as an oarsman, winning 125 races and endearing himself to Irishmen everywhere by beating the British sculling champion in the Olympic Games of 1920.[33] John B. worked as a bricklayer, foreman and superintendant for his contractor brother, Patrick, then set up his own company. The business grew until "Kelly for Brickwork" became a byword in Philadelphia.

A keen competitor of Kelly's for contracting work was Matthew H. McCloskey, whose activities took the "contractor-politico" evolution one step further onto the national stage. McCloskey, one of eight children of a family from Dungiven, County Derry, went into business for himself when he was only eighteen. His first large job, in 1917, was construction of a wartime building at the Philadelphia Navy Yard. It was a job that typified

Albert M. Greenfield with John B. Kelly and Frank Smith. *Courtesy of the Historical Society of Pennsylvania.*

the hard-driving McCloskey style. His men completed 160,000 square feet of construction in 60 days. Reverses hit the young builder severely in 1923, however, and he barely escaped bankruptcy. He had lost money trying to complete a barracks at the U.S. Military Academy at West Point, New York. Recovering, McCloskey built more schools in the city than any other single contractor, a fact not without political significance. He built the Philadelphia Convention Hall and government buildings in Harrisburg. For six decades Matthew McCloskey pursued his business, compounding his reputation as an intense competitor and a shrewd calculator of contract costs.[34] One of his most notable successes was a $25 million project with the Pennsylvania Railroad for the Penn Center transportation facilities, keystone of the downtown renovation that ultimately transformed the center city business district of Philadelphia in the 1960s.

In 1932, McCloskey went into politics after discussions with James Farley, Franklin D. Roosevelt's able party chieftain. From 1955 to 1962 he was National Finance Chairman of the Democratic Party, a position that he handled with mastery. In this post he was in constant interaction with such men as Albert M. Greenfield, the real estate magnate who helped finance Democratic campaigns and John F. Kennedy. McCloskey's association with President Kennedy was especially warm. In June 1962, he was appointed U.S. Ambassador to Ireland, a post that accorded with his interests and affections.[35]

Perhaps the largest contractor of all in this tradition is John McShain. Son of a County Derry carpenter, McShain built an immense construction business. His ability to figure huge contracts tightly became legendary. Beginning in Philadelphia he built the Board of Education Building in 1930, then the Municipal Court Building, as well as many schools and churches. He served on the city's Board of Zoning Adjustment from 1936 until 1952, a significant position for business and governmental ties. In Philadelphia, McShain constructed the Veterans Hospital, the Naval Hospital, and worked on the Philadelphia International Airport and various college and university building programs. He also became a director of several banks and a transportation company. The scope of McShain's work, however, extended far beyond the city. His contracts included work on the $40 million Clinical Research Building of the National Institutes of Health, the General Accounting Office, the National Airport, the Jefferson Memorial, the State Department Building, and restoration of the White House, all in the nation's capital. It is calculated that his firm has completed over $1 billion in government contract work. Largest of all his projects was the Pentagon Building, an $80 million construction.[36]

McShain's political allegiances are not as clear as those of John B. Kelly or Matthew McCloskey. He has worked with administrations of both political parties. As a contractor with a national enterprise, McShain has apparently avoided close identification with either party. The scale of the McShain work on government contracts is manifest testimony to his business and political acumen. His Irish ties have remained. A keen horse fancier, he acquired an 8500-acre estate in Killarney where his racing thoroughbreds are stabled.[37]

There are numerous other examples of the Irish contractor tradition in Philadelphia, including Austin Meehan, long a power in the Republican machine that fought the reform movement of the Democrats in the post-World War II period.[38] Other examples would not add substantially to the characteristics displayed by Kelly, McCloskey and McShain. Their careers represent the penetration of an American business medium by the sons of immigrants and a latter-day enactment of the Horatio Alger cycle.

Upon analysis the contracting enterprises described above reveal a pattern that is in accord with the general business history of urban building activities. The ethnic origins and connections of the contractors did not exempt their firms from the broad trends at work in their field. The early Irish contractors such as Thomas Costigan, Edward Lafferty and Patrick

McManus were part of the Gilded Age. Their enterprises were individually led businesses depending upon strong personal contacts and leadership. Their familiarity with the Irish laboring gangs and the reliability of their work went far in drawing together the skills and resources they needed.[39]

The businesses of men like "Sunny Jim" McNichol represent a more formalized institutional stage of contracting. Technological changes in building practices, such as the use of steel frames, elevators and the advent of electrical equipment, made construction much more technical and complex. Building regulations by municipalities raised new legal and technical problems. These trends of the late nineteenth century led to new practices in planning and managing work.[40]

The businesses of John B. Kelly, Matthew McCloskey and John McShain exemplify a third stage of contracting development. These men built enterprises that became enormous in scope, ranging far beyond the local area. They became fully diversified, with holdings in real estate and a great diversity of production and service fields. The complexity of contracting and these other business operations had become so great by the mid-twentieth century that systems management skills were mandatory. What resulted were great contracting systems backed by consolidations of capital and resources that enhanced the contractors' power tremendously.[41]

A further illustration of the process of ethnic business identification with a specific urban enterprise is provided by the attachment of Jews to the institution of the department store. The great downtown retail emporium has become one of the fixtures of our urban landscape. In the panoramic range of its retail activity and the energy of its sales promotion it is something of a synthesis of the distributive techniques of capitalism. Ranged throughout the warehouses and shelves of the department stores are the products of literally thousands of businesses. Their transmission to the public is a triumph of organizational and marketing skill. Such stores, situated as they must be in high-density areas, are monuments of urban concentration, innovation and economic success.

The first extensive retail stores existed before nineteenth-century immigrants began to penetrate the business structures of the cities. They were outgrowths of the trading genius of early America, and their owners were of the early American stock that dominated urban finance and enterprise.[42] Philadelphia families could shop in the large John Wanamaker store or from the tidy shelves of the Quaker merchants, Strawbridge and Clothier. The Anglo-Saxon Protestant character of John Wanamaker's is manifest from the regulations laid down for its clerks in 1861, requiring them to attend Sunday services, contribute a set portion of their wages to a church, and refrain from drinking alcohol, smoking Spanish cigars or being shaved at a barber shop.[43]

Since the Jewish community in Philadelphia dated to Colonial times its business activities found an early place in the city.[44] It was in the wave of Jewish immigration from Germany that the city's second great cadre of merchants arrived. These men began more as peddlers than merchants. They often worked up from peddling to sidewalk stands and then to tiny stores.[45] As a textile and dry goods center Philadelphia spawned numerous wholesale and retail outlets for fabrics. The step from dry goods to more varied retailing was natural.

Samuel and Jacob Lit arrived in Philadelphia from Holland in the 1830s. They struggled through a long series of hectic jobbing and retail operations without too much success. When their sister began to run a tiny millinery shop near Eighth and Market Streets, they joined her. By 1893 they had a corner property at this intersection, and by 1896 they had a five-story building with a much admired cast-iron front. In 1900 the entire Market Street frontage on the side between Eighth and Ninth Streets was occupied by the Lit Brothers' store, a huge operation organized by departments for the sale of ready-made wares.[46]

The career of Nathan Snellenburg reveals the ethnic background of such early department store evolution. After beginning as a peddler, Snellenberg set up a small shop selling mens' and boys' wear in the Jewish ghetto market near Third and South Streets. Working with his brothers, his business prospered. The move from the ghetto with its familiar speech and associations to the cosmopolitan atmosphere of Market Street, the city's main business thoroughfare, was not to be undertaken lightly. Prejudice against Jews among old-line property owners, business competition, and the reactions of a largely Gentile clientele had to be considered. Nevertheless, the young Snellenburg brothers, led by Nathan, made the move. Their store was located on the southeast corner of Twelfth and Market Streets. By 1894 they employed 2000 persons and operated one of the city's largest stores.[47]

Another department store figure became more of a national symbol than a local one. Adam Gimbel emigrated from Bavaria, at first landing in New Orleans, then living in Indiana. He married a girl who lived in Philadelphia. The seven sons of this union went into the retailing business like their father. In 1894 they opened their large Philadelphia store at Eighth and Market Streets. Gimbel Brothers, with great stores in various cities, became part of our urban folklore. The firm's forceful advertising under Bernard Gimbel, who was made president of the company in 1927, became proverbial.[48] Although the wealthy Jewish elite of New York might refer to the Gimbels as "storekeepers," the size of the Gimbel enterprises could hardly be mocked.[49]

Certain features of the activity of these entrepreneurs are worth highlighting. Of the three examples given, all were family businesses, dependent in the beginning on the close family ties that were part of the Jewish tradition. A symbol kept on the table during meetings of the Gimbel brothers indicates this. A bunch of small sticks bound together was placed before them, with a solitary stick laid beside it to show the weakness of a lone figure. All of the businesses reflected ghetto origins in their early days,

L.J. Levy & Company dry goods store, about 1857, a forerunner of the late-nineteenth-century department store. *(Historical Society of Pennsylvania) Reproduced by courtesy of the Museum of American Jewish History.*

either in the persons of their founders or in connections with associates in related lines of activity.[50]

As urban institutions the department stores provided a solid retail base for the downtown business districts of the city. Without them the downtown areas would have lacked large-scale commercial facilities to match the other urban functions of specialty merchandising, banking government and transportation exchange. Eventually the stores moved into the phases of incorporation, chain development and diversification—all characteristic of big retailing in this century. As the suburbs began to unfold in the metropolitan hinterlands, the department stores invested in outlying shopping centers. In doing so they again played a role in providing a focus for urban growth. By investing in and often organizing such shopping centers, they conferred upon the suburbs one of the few social and economic pivots for community concentration and exchange in the sprawling new areas.

Jewish identification with merchandising has long been a subject to be treated with some discretion because of the ambiguous feelings it has aroused in the past. While the achievement was clear, the stereotype of the Jewish merchant was a rankling peril from the days of "The Merchant of Venice." When Nathaniel Weyl attempted in 1966 to detail Jewish representation in various businesses, noting a concentration in department stores among other lines, many people became uneasy.[51] Jews had suffered too much from stereotypes of ethnic "clannishness" not to be wary of documentations of concentration in this or that business field. If the Gimbel family of Philadelphia, for all its success, had to erect its own country club because of Gentile discrimination at other clubs, the misgivings of Jews of lesser stature were not unfounded. But the very sensitivity of Jews to the discrimination they experienced is a key to some of the motivation that inspired ethnic contributions to business fields. Opposition and exclusion led at least some of the ethnic minority to compete more strongly and perhaps inventively in response.

The entry of Jews into American merchandising could be seen as a natural adaptation in the light of European background and American economic development. The prohibitions against Jews owning land and pursuing many kinds of careers in nineteenth-century Germany restricted the Old World economic experience on which the immigrants could draw in the new.[52] They arrived in the American cities when landholding and many avenues of vocational advancement were preempted by those on the ground for some generations. An area of activity that was expanding coincident with their arrival in large numbers, however, was that of retailing, and the city settlement of the Jews placed them in a position to engage in it. Between 1889 and 1909, a period of heavy Jewish influx, retail trade rose in value from $1,020 million to $2,320 million, and doubled again by 1919, Ready-to-wear clothing outlet chains grew from 1 in 1895 to 73 in 1915. After 1919 the index of sales of department stores increased fivefold up until 1957.[53] The majority of immigrant Jews could be said to have arrived in the retail age of the American economy.

The development of the department store as a mass retailing outlet corresponded with the rise of mass production of ready-to-wear clothing. After 1880 the needle trades grew swiftly. So fully were Jews involved in this growth that garment manufacturing became known as a "Jewish trade," and the organization of the labor unions in the field became one of the folk dramas of immigrant life.[54] In 1890, Moses Dropsie, in a report to Philadelphia's Hebrew Education Society, urged the training of young girls in drafting and cutting garments and millinery, as well as in typing and stenography.[55] The major stock of the department stores was at first ready-made clothing, and the ties between the making and the selling of clothing were a natural extension of activity involving Jewish workers. The rising department store entrepreneurs could not have had difficulty in finding ethnic confreres as makers, wholesalers and salesmen of clothing.

Department stores represented the movement of the economy beyond capital development and basic urban facilities to the service dimension of enterprise. As the Irish had been engaged by the one phase, the Jews were engaged by the other. The Irish contractor needed unskilled labor from his group. The Jewish department store owner needed people with a knowledge of the products he would stock from his group. The Irish contractor required city permits and contracts for construction, so politics was his medium to secure them. The store owner needed a web of suppliers and brokers, and these he found in the small business culture that was the culture of his ghetto.

The department store was the democratization of distribution. The store supplied credit, free delivery, store directories and offered restaurants, music and sewing classes. In the anonymity of its shopping aisles the house-maid could shop at the same counter as the middle-class matron. The impersonality of its operations could also, to some extent, exempt the owner from the religious discrimination that waned all too slowly in the community. One historian cites nine great Jewish department store families whose names became American bywords, and mentions Lessing Rosenwald, whose mail-order sales business extended from an urban base into rural America, helping greatly to alter and improve country habits and life.[56]

Analysis of the achievements of the Irish contractors and the Jewish department store founders indicates that there were distinctive ethnic factors in the emergence of their businesses. The social and economic conditions in which the Irish and Jews found themselves in the city influenced the business prospects in each case. The ethnic ties and labor skills of both groups represented assets that could be developed in the businesses undertaken. Social and religious discrimination against Irish Catholics led them to build religious and educational facilities that were an extensive field for construction work. Similar strictures against Jews channeled them into retailing that grew to department-store scale.

The periods of mass immigration of each group coincided with phases of economic development that were propitious for the areas of enterprise chosen as examples in this discussion. As newcomers to the urban economy, the ethnic entrepreneurs brought a fresh outlook that aided them in the innovations that they introduced in their businesses. The energy with which they entered into highly competitive fields was not only a product of the drive for success of men born into groups to which full economic participation had been denied. It also resulted from their ability to make their own the economic credo of the city that had been so well championed by such effusive spokesmen as Russell Conwell. "There was never a place on earth more adapted than the city of Philadelphia today," Conwell declaimed, "and never in the history of the world did a poor man without capital have such an opportunity to get rich quickly and honestly as he has now in our city."[57]

In addition these entrepreneurs were able to go far beyond their original affiliations and to keep pace with the fast-breaking institutional changes required of their businesses in the expanding cycles of metropolitan growth. The contractors moved from basic construction to diversified building and then to both vertical and horizontal extension of their activities. The downtown department stores became managerial bases for huge integrated operations that embraced production and service franchises as well as suburban shopping center development.

While the penetration of the urban economy was proceeding along lines such as those suggested above, each of the two ethnic groups was pursuing trends of self-organization. One example is provided by the field of charities. Religious motivation and stark privation spurred both ethnic and immigrant charitable undertakings. Among the Irish the tradition in Philadelphia of Catholic charitable work was part of the community's evolution dating from Colonial missionary times. The organization of free elementary schools, parish charitable societies, hospitals, orphanages and immigrant aid societies always had strong Irish leadership. The Irish Catholic Benevolent Union, based in Philadelphia, became a huge national organization in the 1870s and 1880s. The Society of the Friendly Sons of St. Patrick for the Relief of Immigrants from Ireland, counting both Irish Catholics and Protestants as members since its foundation in 1771, continued—and continues today—an unbroken record of local philanthropy. It was in the Victorian period, however, that the Irish Catholics constructed their great educational and human service network in the city, and the force of this work for social and educational development has had an enormous impact, not only on the Irish, but on other immigrant groups as well.[58]

An examination of how this work proceeded against obstacles of poverty, discrimination, factionalism and the demands of Irish nationalist and political influences in competition for the attention of the Irish population is instructive, but is too lengthy a story to unravel here. It is sufficient to note that it was ethnic pride and ethnic affinity that provided much of the fuel for the work, even though the Catholic church deemed itself transcultural and cosmopolitan.

Similarly, but within a shorter time frame, extensive Jewish charitable undertakings proceeded on the basis of both religious commitment and social necessity. Although mutual aid characterized Jewish life in the city from the beginning of the tiny Mikveh Israel congregation in 1740, it was the crisis of mass immigration after 1880 that compelled more careful and comprehensive organization of good works. Rabbi Bertram Korn has pointed out that "from the 1880s on, diversity, fragmentation and divisiveness were once again hallmarks of Philadelphia Jewish life." It was, oddly enough, on St. Patrick's Day in 1901 that the Federation of Jewish Charities was organized formally, at the old Mercantile Hall at Broad and Master Streets. By 1919, the Federation had raised $1,250,000 for foreign relief alone. As Louis

Wolf stated, "where formerly (fund raising) was done by a handful, it is now a part of the life of our community—it is everybody's business."[59]

To the ancient concept of *zedekah* with all its implications for community responsibility, American Jews added a distinctly American optimism that money can solve problems. An entire psychology and annual cycle of events developed for Jewish fund-raising activities. A highly nationalized system was patiently developed as an organizational means to implement the emotional and religious commitment of Jews. Irish Catholics, for their part, evolved a fund-raising cycle presided over by bishops, priests and lay aides. Regular Sunday donations and charitable society dues were supplemented by special collections for seminaries, hospital construction and overseas missions. Parish membership was the key to the Catholic contribution system, which was much less nationalized in its management than the Jewish procedure (mostly because the Catholic population was so much larger than the Jewish). In both groups the expansion of a popular base of democratic contributions was a distinctively American achievement, a tribute to both the affluence of America and its enjoyment of religious liberty.

The charitable achievements of both groups represent a remarkable democratic upsurge of initiative, with benefits radiating through the entire Philadelphia community. They are testimonies not only to human compassion and religious dedication, but also to group fidelity and solidarity. The troubled history of the attempts of American government to provide social services and to deal with social problems through contemporary bureaucratic means suggests that it was those local, intimate, grassroots qualities of the ethnically based human service networks that accounted for the economic advancement of the nineteenth-century urban immigrant Irish and Jews.

Irish liberation and Zionist fulfilment were other areas of concern in which Irish and Jews exerted themselves with ardor and with romantic yet practical commitment. For the Irish the nationalist agitation in Philadelphia was a preoccupation reaching back to the eighteenth century. The tales of sacrifice, intrigue and rebel activity against English domination of the Irish homeland were a powerful and emotional portion of the Irish-American tradition. It was, however, in the early twentieth century that the Irish revolutionary underground moved toward a climactic phase that would culminate in the achievement of partial Irish independence in 1921.

One of the most significant Irish leaders in America in this period was Joseph McGarrity, born in Carrickmore, County Tyrone. As an immigrant of some affluence deriving from his real estate and liquor businesses in Philadelphia, he found time to devote his energies to the Clan na Gael (Children of the Gael), a secret society that was the pivot of Irish revolutionary activity before World War I. McGarrity aided the key leaders who would die in the bloody aftermath of the 1916 rebellion in Dublin. He financed numerous others and their guerrilla drive that gradually paralyzed

English power in Ireland. His career continued until his death in 1940 as he persisted in secret plans for armed protest against continued British domination of the six counties of Northern Ireland.[60]

Alongside McGarrity, men like Michael J. Ryan took a more moderate course. Ryan was a lawyer, a holder of various offices including that of Attorney General of Pennsylvania, and a leader of the Irish National League, an American group working for a constitutional solution to Ireland's political evolution. Men like Ryan were upstaged by the more militant wing of the Irish organizational structure as the dramatic events of Ireland's struggle for independence unfolded.[61]

Maxwell Whiteman has traced the Zionist activity in Philadelphia contemporary with that of men like McGarrity and Michael J. Ryan. Beginning with lectures about Palestine by such figures as Cyrus Adler, then organized in "Ohavei Zion" in 1897, the interest in Zionism was nurtured, especially through the founding of the Maccabean Zion Society. The socialist Zionists of "Poale" Zionism, such as Ezekiel Edelstein, represented a more radical approach. The tireless Manuel Lisan, born in Odessa and active in Philadelphia from the 1890s onward, was typical of the propagandist and organizing cadre that fostered Zionism's following. Working with the Federation of American Zionists, Lisan made a major contribution in Philadelphia and elsewhere to the movement's early growth.[62]

Manuel Lisan was to live to see his Zionist dream fulfilled, just as Joseph McGarrity would see Irish independence, but both would also see the limitations of their dreams. Israel continued to be hemmed in by hostile neighbors, and Ireland would remain sundered by partition under British auspices. The nationalist and Zionist work of the Irish and Jewish communities in Philadelphia in the twentieth century continues, however, and these ethnic political traditions demonstrate not only the freedom of American minority life, but also the continuity of ethnic attachments that reach across time and distance to sustain the histories of ancient peoples.

This brief account of the relationships between Irish and Jewish people in Philadelphia is obviously not sufficient to delineate the scale and complexity of their intergroup connections. The mutual experience of immigration, exploitive labor conditions, struggle with urban disorder, effort to build economic futures, the touchstones of charity and the dreams of peoplehood—all these have been shared by the two traditions in America. This record has brought about tolerance, esteem and amity. This amity has grown since 1936 when, in what was then a bold venture of understanding, Cornelius O'Brien of the Knights of Columbus joined in Fairmount Park with Senator Alfred M. Cohen, international president of B'nai B'rith, to dedicate a monument to religious freedom. What remains now to grow is a more explicit comprehension of the validity and social value of the ethnic minority substructure of American social life.[63] The eighteenth-century conceit that society is composed of individuals only and that it must function on an individualized, indeed atomized, basis is still powerful among us. The absolutely essential and inescapable role of group traditions and the persistence of historic cultural streams are still only grudgingly accepted. Much of the blame for this condition of an American mentality of doctrinaire simplicity falls upon our historians and teachers who not only have not examined the ethnic infrastructure of our society, but have severely undervalued it. We must now attempt to see that this failing is remedied as we proceed with the third century of our nation's life.

(15)

Jewish Politics
in Philadelphia,
1920–1940

Sandra Featherman

In the first third of the twentieth century, Philadelphia politics was dominated by the Republican party. Members of most ethnic groups, as well as native whites, voted for Republicans in city elections. Jews and blacks were among the most staunchly Republican voters in Philadelphia. Up until the 1936 presidential election, when substantial numbers of Jews defected to the Democratic side for Franklin Delano Roosevelt, both Jews and blacks gave a majority of their votes to the Republican party.[1]

In Philadelphia in the 1920s and 1930s, Jews were strongly Republican even though the local Republican party was run by the Vare machine, an organization widely perceived as corrupt, so corrupt in fact that the U.S. Senate refused to seat Bill Vare after he was elected as a Senator, claiming he had won his election through fraud.[2]

Why did Jews, considered to be progressive and reform-minded in the latter half of this century, support a corrupt political machine in Philadelphia in the 1920s and 1930s?[3] To answer this question, we must examine what influenced the city's Jewish voters to cast Republican votes, what the Republicans did to reward or insure Jewish support, and why the radical movement made so few inroads among Jewish voters here, in spite of

The author is grateful to the nearly four dozen Philadelphians who consented to be interviewed for this study. Special thanks are due to a few of the persons for their gracious willingness to share their memories, their insights and several hours each of their time. They are Leon J. Obermayer, Herbert Salus, Jr., and Allan Weinberg. Isadore Gottlieb, Kenneth Shear, and Nochem Winnet also provided important information, as did many others.

what researchers have found to be Jewish tendencies cross-culturally to support "the more left parties."[4]

As the third decade of this century began, the Jewish community in Philadelphia found antisemitism quite pervasive. As late as 1917, a Jewish teacher had been denied an appointment in a nearby Medford County, New Jersey school because the Medford School Board was against employing any Catholic or Jewish teachers. Fortunately, the School Board's action was overruled by the New Jersey State Department of Education.[5]

The editorial pages of Philadelphia's *Jewish Exponent* were full of articles deploring anti-Jewish and anti-Catholic attitudes and activities, more often those beyond the immediate community than those in Philadelphia, however. Many of the discussions on Zionism by writers to the paper evidenced concern about possible local antisemitic repercussions.

In the aftermath of the first World War, such broad political issues that concerned the Jewish community as Palestine, Zionism and antisemitism in Eastern and Western Europe, were being addressed. By the early 1920s, regular editorials were being run, deploring, for example, the "slaughter of forty Jews by the Rumanian military," or the "Nordic Nonsense" of the racial and religious superiority materials of hate groups.[6] Another concern focused on immigration restrictions. A 1925 editorial in the *Exponent* pointed out that Jews were being accepted in Mexico, "while the U.S. puts up bars."[7]

Though the *Exponent* deplored antisemitism elsewhere, it generally eschewed discussing any but the most obvious or illegal examples of it locally. On the whole, this major local Jewish newspaper treated local political issues as if they were taboo areas for discussion. Perhaps the paper was committed to the separation of church and state at the local level. Or perhaps the editors felt that others might see in the articles the suggestion of a "Jewish Vote." Such a perception may have been deemed inimical to Jewish interests.

At any rate, the *Exponent* never exhorted Jews to use the power of their aggregated votes to obtain particular political outcomes, even though the paper was aware that the Jewish community in Philadelphia was quite large.

Rational voters support candidates or parties for one or more of the following reasons: (1) they agree with the basic position of the candidate or party; (2) they expect personal benefits from the election of the candidate or party; and (3) they expect interest group benefits from the election of the candidate or party. Jewish voters in Philadelphia supported the Republican machine for all three reasons. It provided benefits to the Philadelphia Jewish community as a whole. In terms of personal benefits or cost avoidances, no other party in the city could successfully intercede with local government on behalf of the individual the way the Republicans could.

One-time Jewish Republican politicians and activists have claimed that they were Republicans at least partly because the Republican party was the party of Abraham Lincoln and Theodore Roosevelt. Jews had particularly positive responses to both of these presidents. Lawrence Fuchs, in *The Political Behavior of American Jews*, states that Jews came to love Lincoln not just because he had a number of Jewish friends, but primarily because of his profound humanitarianism and sensitivity to Jewish concerns about discrimination. For example, when Congress passed a law requiring chaplains to be Christian, Lincoln got the law changed.

Herbert Salus, an attorney and former judge, whose father and uncle were powerful political leaders, recalls his father's belief that Jews should be Republicans because Theodore Roosevelt and McKinley made statements against pogroms, and Roosevelt appointed the first Jewish Cabinet member.

During the period of the first third of this century, the Republican party so dominated the political scene in Philadelphia that it controlled one wing of the local Democratic party—the so-called "O'Donnell Democrats" as well. These were Republicans who registered as nominal Democrats in order to control the election of Democratic precinct officials, so that the Republican machine could dictate electoral outcomes. In *The People's Choice*, J. T. Salter details just what such control meant. In one precinct the election officials started filling in the official final tallies for candidates hours before the polls closed. One precinct worker explained that they did that because if they actually bothered to count votes they might be "counting . . . until five o'clock in the morning."[8]

Such dominance allowed the Republican machine, run from 1922 to 1934 by Bill Vare, to totally control patronage, and therefore to control both political rewards to individuals and local political recognition of ethnic groups.

For individuals, rewards could be quick and direct. Allan Weinberg, archivist of the City of Philadelphia, tells how his father went to Bill Vare for a job in 1926. Vare reportedly told Mr. Weinberg, "Manny, get a cot and sleep at the Sesquicentennial. I'll put you on its payroll." Weinberg asserts that there were "a thousand political jobs" in the several wards in South Philadelphia where his father was active.

In spite of support from the Republicans, Manny Weinberg switched to the Democratic party in 1932, feeling there was more opportunity there. Only in 1935 did he return to the Republican fold to become an Independent leader in South Philadelphia, for Republican S. Davis Wilson's mayoral campaign.

Wilson's opponent that year was the very popular John B. Kelly, Sr., who ran a very close race. One would expect Kelly to have done well in South Philadelphia, where two-thirds of the voters were Catholic and many of the rest were Jewish. After all, the literature on ethnic voting indicates that such an election would catalyze Catholic voters, whose support would "surge" the first time a coreligionist headed a political ticket.[9] Furthermore Jews, too, might have been expected to support Kelly. The local Jewish community had broken away from being overwhelmingly Republican by giving almost 48 percent of its votes to Al Smith in 1928. Editorials in the *Exponent* were quite pro-Irish on a number of issues during the 1920s and 1930s, indicating that Jews may have seen their well-being as interrelated to the well-being of other minority groups, particularly the Irish-Catholic.

In fact, Herbert Salus remembers his father saying that Al Smith made Democrats of more Jews here than FDR did, because the Jews related to Al Smith. Nonetheless, Catholic and partly Jewish South Philadelphia wards such as the 39th Ward, gave S. Davis Wilson a majority. Weinberg and others say it happened because (1) voters were really indebted to their local committeemen and had to return favors at the polls, and (2) many voters feared that a Catholic could not be elected, and that therefore, if the Democrats carried their area, the voters would lose future political support for their interests and themselves.

Shortly after S. Davis Wilson took office, Manny Weinberg returned to the Democratic party. Davis apparently had not rewarded Weinberg for his service, and, as Weinberg's son indicated, his father "felt there was more opportunity for young men in the Democratic party." Manny Weinberg was later to be a Democratic City Council member from 1957 to 1967.

For many voters, help with personal problems made the difference. Jewish refugees, in particular, felt a need to support committeemen with ties to the local police district. A number of persons interviewed claimed that police captains in the 1920s were like war lords. They had total control over how vice and crime were handled in their own districts. If an immigrant or any other voter, for example, had a child in trouble, or a housing violation, it was essential for them to have a local committeeman who could intercede in their behalf at the local police station. Old-timers who remember the system say "violations" were cited far more frequently and arbitrarily then than now, and intermediaries were absolutely necessary. Allan Weinberg remembers his father's house jammed every night with people seeking help:

> My father never got to eat dinner with the family. He ate early—to avoid the crowd. He looked down on pols who were in it (favor-giving) just for money. He loved it—the ego gratification and the satisfaction of doing things for people—and the power. He didn't see conflicts of interest, but "you do for me, I do for you."

Members of a group may support a candidate or political machine because such support yields "expressive benefits"; the satisfaction a voter receives from a sense of doing one's duty for one's reference group.[10] Jewish voters could gain satisfaction from voting for candidates whose political leaders were seen as being supportive of the Jewish community as a whole. In numerous ways the Vare-dominated Republican machine indicated support for Jewish and other ethnic voters in Philadelphia. As a Congressman, Vare opposed bills to limit immigration. In his speech to the Congress on

Herbert W. Salus Sr. with Mayor J. Hampton Moore *(far left)*, Marian Pyle, William Kreider and Sen. William S. Vare *(far right). Courtesy of Herbert W. Salus Jr.*

April 8, 1924, he specifically mentioned that "I have never had a man or woman of Jewish extraction come and ask for aid, regardless of what the conditions of employment have been. I cannot say that about some of the so-called native Americans."[11]

In addition to supporting causes Jews favored, the Vare organization claimed to protect Jewish religious rights. "I recall when Jewish people first moved into the first ward," Vare once stated. "The police wanted to interfere with some of their native practices—we stood between them and the police."[12]

There is a further type of support an organization can give to a group—symbolic support. Symbolic support helps to confirm the position or importance of the group within the organization. Consultations with a group's leaders indicate such importance, as do the slating of candidates or the awarding of public jobs to members of the group.

Jewish voters might be expected to support a political machine which gave the Jewish community visible expressions of support, through the appointment of Jews to local governmental positions or the endorsement of

Jews for local political elective offices. This would provide evidence that Jewish voters had "status" to the machine leaders.

Since Jews constituted ten percent of the population and were strongly Republican, one would expect ample political rewards to have been given to the Jewish community by the Republican machine. Yet John Shover, in "Ethnicity and Religion in Philadelphia Politics, 1924–40," found that county non-Civil Service jobs requiring no special skills were overwhelmingly allocated to persons with English, Scotch, and German surnames. Only five percent of those positions were held by persons with Jewish or Italian names. By 1932, according to Shover, Jews and Italians still held only eight percent of such jobs.[13]

Shover's evidence would indicate that Jews were not being rewarded for their voting support commensurate with their numbers. Why then did they remain Republican? A closer look at the reward system is helpful in answering this question.

From 1915 through 1919 there were no Jews among the mayor's cabinet or office staff, none listed in the Public Works department, only one person under the Public Safety Director and two clerks with Jewish names working under the Superintendent of Police.

On the other hand, Jewish representation from Philadelphia in the legislative branches of local, state and national government from 1920 to 1940, generally exceeded the 10 percent of the population the Jewish community comprised, sometimes being as great as 38 to 50 percent of the seats.

The four legislative chambers to which Jewish delegates from Philadelphia were elected during the period from 1920 to 1940 were the U.S. House of Representatives, the Pennsylvania Senate, the Pennsylvania House and the Philadelphia City Council. No Jews were elected to the U.S. Senate from Pennsylvania until 1980, when Philadelphian Arlen Spector won the Republican nomination and the consequent election.

The City Council charter was revised in 1919, when the Council was changed from a bicameral legislature to a single chamber with 21 members. Of these 21 members, two were Jewish (10 percent of the Council) during the 1920–1924 Council. The next Council (1924–1928) had four Jewish members out of 20 (20 percent) not including Councilman Bernard Samuels, who later became mayor.

Throughout the twenties and thirties the Jewish share of City Council members was about 14 percent, probably slightly in excess of the share of the city population Jews represented. In fact, though the Jewish population of the area grew by at least 50 percent over the 20 year period, Jews had begun to move to the western and northern suburbs even as early as the late 1930s, so it is difficult to be sure how much greater than 10 percent the Jewish share of population within the city may have been.

Jewish representation from Philadelphia in the State House ran from a low of 7 percent during the 1920s to a high generally above 20 percent in the

1930s. While this position was not regarded with great esteem, it was a stepping stone to higher office for some. One, Benjamin Golder, became Congressman, one became a member of City Council and several moved into the minor judiciary, the Magistrate's Court. One notable member, Philip Sterling, authored the state's famous Sterling Act.

In 1981, 7 of the 34 Philadelphia representatives to the State House were Jewish, 21 percent of the delegation.

The Jewish community of Philadelphia was also numerically well represented in the State upper house. During the 1920s, Jews comprised one-fourth of the Philadelphia delegation, and during the 1930s, they comprised as much as one-half, certainly far greater than the Jewish share of local population. And these were important positions. Samuel Salus and Max Aron, two Senators during the twenties and thirties, were powerful political leaders. In fact, Sam Salus was so powerful that during the last two years of Boss Vare's life, Salus was able to help frame the Republican party's tickets. Salus and Vare were understandably close. When Vare ran for the Senate in 1926, Salus' 4th Ward brought in a vote of 4547 for Vare, with a total of only 48 votes in the ward split between Vare's two formidable opponents in the race, George Wharton Pepper and Gifford Pinchot. Salus could deliver such a result because he was the "absolute master of the 4th Ward," according to J. T. Salter.[14]

Through 1936, the Jewish Senators were all Republicans. A switch came in 1937–38, when three of the four elected Jewish Senators were Democrats. Those same three Democrats continued to occupy Senate seats in the 1939–40 and 1941–42 Senate. One of those Democrats, Harry Shapiro, had been a Republican Senator from 1933 through 1936. He apparently switched parties because he felt he might be more electable in the future as a Democrat. This, in fact, turned out to be the case.

The U.S. Congressional delegation from Philadelphia during the 1920s and 1930s included one Jewish Congressman from 1925 through 1932, and one later, from 1937 through 1942. There were seven Congressmen from Philadelphia from 1923 through 1941, so the Jewish share of the representation was 14 percent during the years with Jewish Congressmen. The first of these Jewish Congressmen was Benjamin Golder, a Republican, who eventually lost his seat because Vare withdrew support from him after they had a political split.

Benjamin Golder, as the pre-eminent local Jewish politician, was able to cross class lines. Golder, a Russian Jew, married Peggy Mastbaum, the daughter of a prominent German Jew, apparently causing quite a stir in the German Jewish community. One telling story of the period is about another successful Russian Jew who was accepted into the exclusive German-Jewish Philmont Country Club in the 1930s. "This year we got the Russian Jews— next year we'll get the Japanese beetles," is a remark that was allegedly circulated at the club.

Samuel W. Salus. *Courtesy of Arthur S. Salus.*

Leon Sacks, a Democrat, became a Congressman in 1937, and from then until 1979, Philadelphia generally had one Jewish Congressman in each Congressional delegation. This delegate was to be a Democrat from 1937 on. In 1941, for instance, Leon Sacks defeated a Republican Jewish candidate, and Benjamin Golder, running again, lost to a non-Jewish Democrat. The size of the delegation dropped to six, then to five and after the 1970 Census, to four. The delegation will shrink to three after the new redistricting. At the moment, no Philadelphia Congressmen are Jewish.

Jews were underrepresented on the bench throughout the 1920s and largely confined, through the 1930s as well, to what has been called the "Jewish Court," Common Pleas Court 2.

There were five and later six Common Pleas Courts (seven by 1938), each with a President Judge and two Associate Judges. Of these 15 positions, usually only 1 was held by a Jew. The Jewish seat was apparently limited for a long while to Court 2, where Mayer Sulzberger had presided until 1916. After Sulzberger, a non-Jew became the President Judge, and in 1920, Horace Stern became an Associate Judge in Common Pleas Court 2.

Stern became its President Judge in 1926, and in 1936 went to the Supreme Court.

Harry Kalodner, another Associate Judge in the Court 2, was defeated for reelection in 1938 by coreligionist Theodore Rosen, but was appointed a Federal Judge in 1941. By 1938, the Common Pleas Court had expanded, and so had the number of Jews serving. For the first time, Jews were endorsed for and elected to other Common Pleas Court seats.

Until the end of the 1930s, however, Jews had no representatives in the Orphans Court, and only one (out of 11) in the Municipal Court. As for the lowest court, the Magistrate's Court, Jews were not only underrepresented until the late 1930s, but also concerned about the low quality of the Magistrates. In 1921, in a rare political editorial, the *Jewish Exponent* claimed, "The inefficiency and unsuitable character of most of the twenty-eight Magistrates (candidates) is a matter of general notoriety."[15] The editorial called for reform of the minor judiciary and appealed to readers to vote only for "fit" candidates.

Today, by comparison, Jews are heavily represented in the Courthouse at all levels. Four of the 19 Judges of the U.S. District Court for the Eastern District of Pennsylvania are Jewish, as are two of the seven Justices of the Pennsylvania Supreme Court. At the Common Pleas level, 23 out of 80 Judges are Jewish (29 percent), as are seven of the 18 senior Judges. In the Municipal Court, five of the 23 Judges, or 22 percent, are Jewish

No practicing Jew has ever been elected Mayor of Philadelphia. Several Jews, including Arlen Spector and Edward Rendell, have been elected District Attorney in recent years, and one Jew, Charles Edwin Fox, an appointed Assistant District Attorney, became D.A. in the 1930s when the elected D.A. died in office. Fox, however, was not supported by Vare for reelection. In general, Jews were not supported for local row office elected positions during the years between the World Wars. In the Democratic primary of 1933, for example, there was not a single Jewish name among all the 36 candidates for City Treasurer, Controller, Register of Wills, Coroner, Judgeships and Magistrate positions.

In terms of high-level appointive positions, Jews held precious few during these years. Herbert Salus was Civil Service Commissioner, and Edwin Wolf, Cyrus Adler and later Solomon Solis-Cohen were all members of the Philadelphia Board of Education. In late 1939 Nochem Winnet was appointed Assistant Director of Public Safety, a position he was to be promoted from to the Courthouse, only six weeks later.

These were virtually the only Jews who held top-level appointive positions during the 1920 to 1940 period.

Judge Winnet, one of Philadelphia's most active and well-liked Jewish leaders, relates that his initial political appointment came as a surprise to him. He had not been very active politically before 1938, and had made only modest contributions to a few judges' campaigns. In 1938, he worked to help elect Governor Arthur James, largely because of Winnet's personal friendship with Jay Cooke, who had become the political leader of the Republican party in Philadelphia. James tried to reward Winnet's support by offering him the state Assistant Secretary of Insurance position, which Winnet turned down, because "I didn't want to spend 4 days a week in Harrisburg."

Then in 1939, Winnet got involved in Robert E. Lamberton's mayoral campaign, heading the campaign speakers' bureau. When Lamberton got elected, he offered to appoint Winnet as the Assistant Director of Public Safety, a position overseeing patronage jobs and contracts available through the police and fire departments. The position had been mired in scandal in the previous administration.

Winnet told Lamberton and Cooke he had fears about taking this position, which had never previously been held by a lawyer. They told him they needed to shield the uniformed police from political pressure. Lamberton said to Winnet, "Your job is to keep your door open to every politician who wants to come in. If you feel you can do something for someone, do it; if you can't, don't."

Winnet opened his doors but began to close unneeded police buildings quickly. His name was in the paper constantly throughout the six weeks in which he served and tried to clean up the system he oversaw. According to Winnet, he had an able police assistant to give him good information, and excellent help from the Jewish group, the Shomrim, as well as from other police and firefighter religious groups.

After his first five weeks of bristling activity, Winnet was informed by Jay Cooke that Governor James had decided to fill a court opening set aside for a Jewish appointment not with Cooke's recommendations but rather with Winnet. The Governor announced the appointment that evening.

One place where Jews always had adequate representation was among the Assistant District Attorneys. In 1919, two of the DA's were Jewish, and from 1920 to 1924, three of the fourteen were. By 1941, about 25 percent of Assistants were Jewish. In that year a Jew, Samuel Rosenberg, held the important position of Secretary to Mayor Lamberton.

By 1981 the elected District Attorney, the appointed City Solicitor and the Police Commissioner were all Jewish. Throughout recent years Jews have been active—and quite visible—in local administrative positions.

Between 1924 and 1940 the Jewish vote shifted from 7 percent to 81 percent for Democratic candidates, in Presidential elections. Although to some extent, it lagged behind, this movement paralleled national changes in Jewish support for political parties.

Samuel Lubell, examining the transformation of the Republican Party from majority to minority status between 1930 and 1944 suggests that the immigrant populations of the cities became Democrats partially because

Nochem S. Winnet. *Courtesy of Nochem Winnet.*

they owed no loyalties to Appomattox and the Homestead Act, and phrases such as Hoover's "rugged individualism" evolved no nostalgia from immigrants for a frontier they hadn't known.[16] The children of the immigrants' large families swelled the voting rolls in the Roosevelt years, as did the voters coming to the cities from the farms. In both cases, these city dwellers saw their well-being, in the tenements and factories, as far more dependent on man and government than nature. As the economy became troubled, city voters turned to the Democrats. Lubell shows that even before Roosevelt, this had begun.[17]

The immigrants who came here after the turn of the century included perhaps a million and a half Jews. Most of them were poor and looked down upon. The Jews, like other ethnic minorities, may have moved toward the Democratic column because Al Smith represented for them the underdog contesting the established order.

In Philadelphia, while the Jewish vote moved toward Smith, it went far less than other Jewish communities did. In Chicago, one Jewish ward gave Smith 75 percent of its votes. A Jewish ward in Boston went to Smith by 61 percent. Jewish wards in Brooklyn and the Bronx ranged from 65 to 71 percent for Smith.[18] Philadelphia Jews cast 48 percent of their votes for the Happy Warrior, a high level of support compared to previous votes in the city, but a lower level of support than Smith gained from Jews in other areas.

Four years later, in 1932, Roosevelt was winning the Jewish vote by wide margins; 85 percent of the vote in the most Jewish districts of Chicago and Boston, and more than 92 percent in the Jewish 17th Assembly District in Manhattan.[19] By contrast, Roosevelt got just under half of Philadelphia's Jewish vote. In the 1936 election, Roosevelt won 77.3 percent of the Jewish vote in Philadelphia but gained 97.1 percent of the Jewish votes in Chicago's most populous Jewish precincts.

At the beginning of their shift to the Democratic party, most Jews were economically disadvantaged. Like other low-income groups, they moved leftward during the Depression. But unlike the other groups, Jews were to remain Democratic even as they rose in income class, throughout the 1940s and 1950s.

While Seymour Martin Lipset and other analysts have seen Jews as more leftist than other denominations,[20] Philadelphia Jews tended to be somewhat conservative, particularly in the 1920s and even well into the 1930s. For instance, Robert La Follette, the Progressive candidate for President in 1924, ran ahead of Calvin Coolidge and John W. Davis in the most Jewish districts of Manhattan, the Bronx and Brooklyn.[21] Yet Jews in Philadelphia voted overwhelmingly for the Republican, Calvin Coolidge.

Ben Halpern has suggested that Jewish liberalism is a recent tradition, that Jews traditionally saw political stability as essential to their well-being. When nationalism swept Europe, Jews downplayed their "Jewishness," manifesting instead their patriotism. The few Jews who rejected nationalism for leftism (internationalism) rarely maintained even tenuous ties with the Jewish community. Halpern maintains that Jews did not import liberalism from Europe. They developed it here. Reform Judaism, with its rational approach, put a high value on social reform activism. Furthermore the American Constitutional guarantee of the separation of Church and State, so necessary to Jewish well-being, is a liberal principle. It is not at all surprising that Jews have been so active in support of civil liberties, Halpern claims. The Bill of Rights, after all, codifies the basic set of liberties under which our laws had to treat Jews and Christians alike.

While German Jews were too small a group to play a significant political role in this country (at best, they could occasionally become prominent individually), Eastern European immigrants came in far greater numbers and concentrated their settlements in a small number of large cities. According to Halpern, the northern Russian and Polish immigrants in particular included revolutionaries among their settlements.

Philadelphia experienced the same waves of immigration as New York and other Jewish cities. It had a small radical press similar to those in other cities. With 200,000 Jews in the city, the Jewish community didn't have to fear constant persecution if it voted "differently."

Apparently, however, Philadelphia Jews were far more conservative than New York Jews, on the whole. Radicalism, including socialism, communism and anarchism, simply never took hold here. Not that there were no radicals then. Some former leftists interviewed said they remembered mass meetings in the mid-1930s, in particular. One person claimed that for the May Day Parade in 1936, then Mayor Wilson was on the podium with the Young Communist leader. Some persons felt that there was a significant radical movement here, including the Workmen's Circle, and the Young Peoples Socialist League college branches, particularly at Temple University.

Interestingly, little documentation supports this view. While even now, many former leftists in Philadelphia do not wish to be so identified, records from the 1930s show little tangible evidence of a leftist movement. In fact, very few Jews were registered as Socialists or other left-wing party members. Former committeemen interviewed recalled no Socialists, or at best an occasional one, among their constituents. Radical groups gained few votes here and no leftists were ever elected to office locally.

It is most likely that active leftist college students of the time remember radical influence as greater than it actually was, because it was important to them. Their meetings, perhaps attended by the same regulars over and over, clearly did not have an impact on local political outcomes.

Even the labor movement here was not particularly radical. Local leaders of most of the liberal-leaning unions were headed by nonradicals who often were strongly anti-Communist, even in earlier periods.

During the twenties and thirties most left-wing activity was apparently confined to holding "pay parties" to raise money for the Abraham Lincoln Spanish Brigade, listening to radical speakers on college campuses, and parading on May Day. Several Philadelphia school teachers and university professors were to be hounded from their jobs in the fifties red-baiting hunts, but none of those persons were accused of more than mere membership in, or friendship with members of the local Communist party.

Even as late as 1948, Philadelphia and Philadelphia Jews were giving less support to left-of-center candidates than was the case elsewhere. Henry Wallace garnered more than 8.3 percent of the total vote in New York State and 13.6 percent of the vote in New York City.[22] In the Jewish 7th Assembly District in the Bronx, Wallace took 27 percent of the vote. In Boston's 14 Ward, Wallace received 12 percent of the vote. By contrast, Pennsylvania gave less than 1.5 percent of its votes to Wallace, and Philadelphia supported the Progressive candidate with 2.3 percent of its votes. Certainly no wards in Philadelphia gave the Progressives even close to the level of support they gained in some Jewish wards in other cities.

While Philadelphia's Jews remained Republican longer than Jewish voters did elsewhere, the city's bastion of Republicanism, the Union League, was closed to Jews for most of the century, even though Jews were among its early members. According to Leon Obermayer, a law partner of Hugh Scott, the Senator once came by to ask for a contribution to the Republican party. Obermayer told Scott and Senator George Wharton Pepper that he was concerned that the Union League excluded Jews. "I won't give any more money to the party until the Union League takes in a number of Jewish members," he told them. Obermayer was one of the first Jews brought in when the barriers came down, but the League's relationship with Jewish Philadelphians was only one of the problems the GOP began to have with them as they shifted to the Democratic side.

The Jewish Communities of Philadelphia and Boston: A Tale of Two Cities

*E. Digby Baltzell,
Allen Glicksman and
Jacquelyn Litt*

New York's Jewry . . . generated an uncontainable dynamic of its own which helped to reshape both New York's and the nation's culture. All other Jewish communities in America absorbed the ideas of their host cities, took standards and values which they could neither recognize nor word from the alien culture.

Theodore H. White
In Search of History

Emerson once remarked that institutions were but the shadows of great men. In a similar vein, E. Digby Baltzell argues in *Puritan Boston and Quaker Philadelphia* that institutions are largely, if not entirely, the lengthened shadows of their founders:

Just as our whole post-Christian and secular world today is still living, as a kind of cultural rentier, on the spiritual and moral capital built up in the more religious periods of the Judeo-Christian tradition, so the citizens of modern Massachusetts and Pennsylvania, whether they are professing Jews, Catholics, Presbyterians, Episcopalians, or just plain agnostics or atheists, are still marked, to a greater or lesser degree, by the original ethics of Puritanism and Quakerism. There is, for instance, a great difference between the Puritan Catholicism of Boston and the much milder Quaker Catholicism of Philadelphia. If immigrants absorb some of the values of the host society, one would predict that the Irish-Catholics of Boston would be more driven to leadership and excellence than their countrymen who settled into the milder and more egalitarian culture of Philadelphia. Whereas the first Irish-Catholic mayor of

Boston took office in the 1880s, the first Irish-Catholic mayor of Philadelphia came into office in the 1960s. Philadelphia has produced no leaders of the quality of Curley, Fitzgerald, or the Kennedys, nor incidentally has it ever had an Irish-Catholic Democratic machine in the classic style of New York, Jersey City, or Chicago. It is indeed symbolic that the most famous Irish-Catholic families of the two cities should have produced in this generation a president and two senators of the United States, on the one hand, and a charming expatriate socialite and sometime actress (Grace Kelly), on the other.[1]

And it may also be symbolic that the most famous Jew in our history was the crusading Boston lawyer, Zionist and Associate Justice of the Supreme Court of the United States, Louis D. Brandeis, while one of the more famous Philadelphia Jews was the nineteenth-century beauty and philanthropist Rebecca Gratz, painted four times by Thomas Sully and, according to tradition, the original model for Rebecca in Sir Walter Scott's *Ivanhoe*. In this discussion we shall be attempting to contrast the origins, subcultural values, and leadership structures of the Boston and Philadelphia Jewish communities. And this contrast must begin with their quite different histories.

"With Jews," wrote Jacob R. Marcus in his definitive study of *The Colonial American Jew*, "what motivated settlement was nearly always, if not always, economic opportunity."[2] "That Boston, the largest city in the British provinces of North America during the first half of the eighteenth century," Marcus continued, "was not to shelter a formally organized Jewish community until about 1849 was surely an anomaly. . . ."[3] And this anomaly was largely to be explained by the intolerant and hierarchical values of the Puritan ethic. That thriving Jewish communities existed in Newport and Philadelphia, in contrast, testified to the egalitarian and tolerant Quaker ethic which dominated these two cities.

The differences between the modern Catholic and Jewish communities of Philadelphia and Boston were partly due to the fact that small colonial communities existed in the former city but not in the latter. "Although Catholics were excluded from early Massachusetts," wrote Baltzell, "they were accepted—but not welcomed—from the beginning in Pennsylvania."[4] Thus the first Catholic church in Philadelphia, St. Joseph's, was built on an inconspicuous spot on Willing's Alley in 1732. And similarly with the Jews. Early records are inadequate, but it is believed that in the 1740s a small group of Jews began holding divine services in a house on Sterling Alley. With no synagogue or formal and visible Jewish community, however, these Jews for the most part participated in the social and economic life of Philadelphia as individuals. When the exclusive Dancing Assembly, the oldest organization of its kind in America today, was formed in 1748 by 59 of the city's most prominent families, two Jews, David Franks and Samson Levy, were among the original subscribers. And Rebecca Franks was one of the most popular belles of Revolutionary society in the city.[5]

Soon after the nation's founding, the formal Jewish community in Philadelphia began with the construction of the first synagogue, Mikveh Israel, in 1782. The construction of Mikveh Israel and hence the formation of a more visible Jewish community, resulted in the first overt, if mild, antisemitism in the city. The original plans called for the synagogue to be built in Sterling Alley; the lot, however, was contiguous to the first German Reformed congregation in the city. Such vigorous protests were made by the Protestant community that the Jewish leaders finally built the synagogue on Cherry Alley (north of High Street) between Third and Fourth Streets. This location was in the Plain Quaker part of the colonial city rather than in the fashionable and Anglican neighborhood south of High Street (now Market Street).

The 1830s were a kind of watershed in Philadelphia Jewish history. Even though there was now a definite and coherent Jewish community (two synagogues, the second, Rodeph Shalom, built in 1810), the families who had made their money and consolidated their position by the 1830s participated extensively in the Gentile world. Five members of the Gratz family, for instance, were taken into the exclusive Philadelphia Club before the Civil War. Hyman Gratz, wealthy merchant and member of Mikveh Israel, was so popular in Gentile circles that he served as temporary president of the Philadelphia Club while Commodore James Biddle was fighting in the Mexican War.[6]

Henry Meyer Phillips, the first Jew to be elected to the United States Congress from Philadelphia, was an excellent example of the relative absence of antisemitic prejudices in the city before the Civil War.[7] He was an active member of Mikveh Israel (both his father and grandfather had served as President of the Congregation) and in his younger years was active in Jewish affairs, serving as president of the Society for Visitation of Sick and Mutual Assistance. His father, Zalegman Phillips, was a leader of the local bar and the first member of the Philadelphia Jewish community to graduate from the College at the University of Pennsylvania (1797). Henry Meyer Phillips was one of the city's leading lawyers when he ran and was elected to Congress as a Democrat in 1857. He was not reelected and while never returning to governmental service, was a leader in the cultural and business life of the city until his death in 1884.

At this point a very important difference between the WASP upper classes of Boston and Philadelphia should be pointed out: on the one hand, the Boston upper-class families were almost entirely British in origin, with no clear cases of Jewish (nor Catholic) ancestry. The traditional Quaker-turned-Episcopal gentry in Philadelphia, on the other hand, were quite heterogeneous in origins. The Philadelphia gentleman was, by 1850 and since, far closer to the "promiscuous breed" which J. Hector St. John Crevecoeur called the "race now called Americans," than were his homogeneously British-stock peers of Proper Boston. Thus the historian of the Philadelphia Assembly Balls could have written in the 1940s that sub-scribers then "included families of the following racial strains: English, Welsh, Irish, French, German, Dutch, Swiss, Italian, Spanish, Portuguese, Swedish, and Polish."[8] (What he meant but did not spell out was that the impeccable WASP establishment in the city was composed of families whose ancestors included Spanish, Portuguese, German and Polish Jews, Irish, French and Italian Catholics, as well as Protestants from many nations if predominately from the British Isles.)

These striking differences between the ethnic and religious composi-tions of the Boston and Philadelphia upper classes of course were reflections of the two communities as a whole. Thus although Pennsylvania was first settled by English Quakers, they were soon followed by German and Dutch Protestants; in addition there were Anglican, Baptist and Presbyterian congregations in the city by 1700. By the end of the colonial period, Penn-sylvania was the most ethnically and religiously heterogeneous of all the colonies. On the other hand, between the founding of Massachusetts Bay in 1630 and the final disestablishment of religion there in the 1830s, Boston was surely the most homogeneous and best educated community in British North America (Tocqueville thought it the best educated in world history). In contrast to the mild and tolerant Quaker oligarchy of early Philadelphia, the early generations of Boston clergymen were learned and highly moral men but, at the same time, bigoted and to the last degree intolerant.

There was, of course, a close affinity between Judaism and early Puritanism: "The Puritans of New England," wrote Edmund Wilson, "were a kind of new Judaism, a Judaism transposed into Anglo-Saxon terms. When the Puritans came to America, they identified George III with Phar-aoh and themselves with the Israelites and their search for the promised land. . . . Winthrop and Bradford were Moses and Joshua; Anne Hutchin-son was pilloried as Jezebel."[9] Hebrew was taught as a second language not only at Harvard but also in the schools.

It is indeed one of the ironies of American history that the Calvinist Puritans of New England, whose creed and communal structure were deeply rooted in the Old Testament, turned away the Jews while Philadelphia Quakers, whose inner-light doctrine of love was an extreme form of New Testament Christianity, should have accepted them from the very begin-ning. The people of the law and the book were rejected by the Old Testa-ment Puritans and accepted by those who favored, not the ancient law but the new spirit of the Gospels.

In terms of the sociological theories of ethnic relations in America, then, the histories of these two cities have been excellent examples of what has been termed the Anglo-Ideal with assimilation (Boston) on the one hand, and cultural pluralism (Philadelphia) on the other.[10] And these two contrast-ing attitudes or theories of ethnic relations have been particularly relevant to the histories of the Jewish communities in each of the two cities.

The first definitely known Jew to come to Boston was sent home; but he was treated with more humanity than the Puritans allowed their own dissenters—Roger Williams and Anne Hutchinson turned out into the winter wilderness, and the Quaker, Mary Dyer, hung by her neck on the Boston Common, in the springtime of 1660. A decade earlier in 1649, one Solomon Franco came to Boston with a cargo assigned to the Major General of the Colony. The Great and General Court disallowed his claim for a commission and assigned "said Solomon Franco, the Jew, six shillings per week out of the treasury for ten weeks for his subsistence till he could get his passage into Holland."[11] After Solomon Franco's banishment few Jews came to Boston and none of any consequence with the exception of Judah Monis, who came to America via Jamaica, finally settling in Cambridge, where he combined peddling with the writing of a Hebrew grammar. In 1720, he submitted his manuscript to Harvard College for which he received a Master of Arts degree, thus becoming the first Jew to receive a college degree in America. But the laissez-faire cultural pluralism which characterizes Harvard Yard today had no place in Colonial times and "Rabbi" Monis converted to Christianity at a ceremony in the Common Hall of Harvard before "as numerous an assembly as the place could admit." Upon his conversion, he was appointed instructor in Hebrew, a post he occupied for nearly 40 years.[12]

Between 1776 and 1815, when immigration had slowed to a virtual standstill, America went through its longest period of undisturbed cultural consolidation.[13] After the defeat of Napoleon, however, immigration increased and Jews came along with large numbers of their fellow Germans in the half century after 1830. While the Jews of the eighteenth-century were largely merchants, these German immigrants almost invariably began as poor peddlers: William Filene, father of the founder of the famous Boston department store, began as a New England peddler before settling down as a small storekeeper in Salem; Meyer Guggenheim, founder of the wealthiest Jewish dynasty in America, came here at the age of 18 in 1848 and began his way to wealth as a peddler of shoelaces on the streets of Philadelphia. Another characteristic of the German Jewish immigration was that, in contrast to the earlier more individualistic migration, they came as families, groups of families and even whole communities of Jews from the same town in the Old Country. At any rate, there were enough German Jewish families in Boston by 1844 to establish the first Jewish cemetery. The next year the first congregation, Ohabei Shalom, was chartered by the Massachusetts legislature and a synagogue built on Warrenton Street in the South End. No sooner had the first synagogue been built when dissention set in. In 1854, 25 of the more prosperous members of Ohabei Shalom, including president Moses Ehrlich formed a new congregation Adath Israel (soon changed to Temple Israel) which first met in an old wooden building on Pleasant Street. Two years later, a small group of east Europeans separated from Ohabei

Shalom and founded Temple Mishkan Israel, which became (combining with another temple) Temple Mishkan Tefila, the first synagogue in Boston to join the Conservative Movement.

As the Civil War approached, then, both Philadelphia and Boston had clearly defined Jewish communities; while Boston's was small and only beginning to take shape, Philadelphia's, more than a hundred years old, was the most intellectually and religiously vigorous in the nation, playing the leadership role for nineteenth-century American Jewry that New York eventually assumed in the twentieth. There were five pre-Civil War synagogues in Philadelphia and three in Boston. In Philadelphia, the oldest, Mikveh Israel, was Sephardic (even though many congregants were of German or central European background) in ritual and definitely the home of the majority of elite Jews from the beginning until well into the twentieth century; Rodeph Shalom, the first Ashkenazic congregation in America, was founded in 1795; the third congregation in the city, Beth Israel, known as the Polish Synagogue for many years, was formed in 1840; Keneseth Israel, the first Reform synagogue in the city was founded in 1847; and finally, Congregation Adath Jeshurun was formed in 1859. All of the three Boston synagogues mentioned above were built in the 1850s. As we shall see, it was the synagogue leadership in each city which set, and reflected, the style and tone of the Jewish communities as a whole; this was especially true of the two elite synagogues, Mikveh Israel in Philadelphia and Temple Israel (Adath Israel) in Boston; just as Isaac Leeser (1806–1868), *hazan* of Mikveh Israel between 1829 and 1850, put his conservative and orthodox stamp on Philadelphia, so did Solomon Schindler (1842–1915), Rabbi at Boston's Temple Israel between 1874 and 1894, do the same for Boston Jewry.

Mikveh Israel: 1829–1940

When Isaac Leeser was appointed *hazan* of Mikveh Israel at the age of 23 in 1829, nobody realized that he was to make Philadelphia the creative center of American Jewry by the time of his death in 1868.[14] His influence on Philadelphia and American Jewry as a whole was carried on after his death by two remarkable lawyers, Moses Aaron Dropsie (1821–1905) and Mayer Sulzberger (1843–1923); both, as was their mentor Leeser, were bachelors and hence able to devote more of their time to the welfare of their community; both were members of Mikveh Israel and strongly influenced by Leeser's teaching and example. When Maimonides College was founded in 1864 and Isaac Leeser's brilliantly creative career was coming to a close, Philadelphia was the intellectual and institutional leader of American Jewry, which was still conservatively Orthodox and German to the core. In most synagogues German was used along with Hebrew; German was spoken within the family, where listening to German music was preferred; wealthy Jews went abroad on the Hamburg-American line and relaxed at such German

Mikveh Israel, Broad and York Streets, 1909. *Courtesy of Dropsie University Library and Allen Meyers.*

watering-places as Baden, Carlesbad or Marienbad. At the Harmonie Gesellshaft in New York, the oldest and most distinguished Jewish club in America, German remained the official language and the Kaiser's portrait hung in the hall as late as the 1890s.[15]

But while the leadership of American Jewry in Philadelphia was still orthodox and conservative, changes were going on elsewhere. Isaac Mayer Wise (1819–1900), more than a decade younger than Leeser, came to America from Bohemia in 1846 where he served a congregation in Albany, New York before going to Cincinnati in 1854.[16] Almost immediately he founded a weekly, in English, the *American Israelite,* to oppose the conservative ideas of Leeser's *Occident.* The most important index of the attempt to shift the intellectual center of American Jewry, however, was Wise's founding of Hebrew Union College, in Cincinnati, in 1875.

Just as Wise was taking the lead in organizing Reform Judaism in Cincinnati, Temple Keneseth Israel, Philadelphia's fourth oldest congregation, appointed a brilliant and radical native of Germany, David Einhorn, as its rabbi in 1861. More intellectual and perhaps even more radical than Wise, Einhorn stayed in Philadelphia for only five years before going to New York. In 1869, however, Einhorn and other rabbis of radical views met at Keneseth Israel in Philadelphia under the chairmanship of Einhorn's successor, Rabbi Samuel Hirsch (1815–1889), who had come to the city from Germany only three years before. This was the first conference on Reform

Judaism in America and, after 16 years of further discussion, the finished platform of Reform Judaism was adopted at the well-known Pittsburgh Conference (1885); the Reform position can be nicely summed up in the following sentence taken from the full document: "We consider ourselves no longer a nation, but a religious community, and therefore expect neither a return to Palestine, nor sacrificial worship under the sons of Aaron, nor the restoration of any of the laws concerning the Jewish state."[17]

There was an almost immediate counterreaction to the Pittsburgh Platform and it was led by Sabato Morais (1823–1897) who followed Isaac Leeser in 1851 as Rabbi of Mikveh Israel.[18] Morais had the support of about a dozen congregations, including the three oldest in New York City and of Rodeph Shalom in Philadelphia, which was then led by a very distinguished Talmudic scholar, Marcus Jastrow (1829–1903). Jastrow had been on the faculty of Maimonides College with Morais and was himself a leading conservative force in Philadelphia. Most important was the support of Henry Pereira Mendes (1852–1937), Rabbi of New York City's fashionable Sephardic Congregation, Shearith Israel, for almost half a century. Under the leadership of Morais, the Jewish Theological Seminary Association was formed in 1885, holding its first classes at Shearith Israel two years later. Morais was president until his death in 1897 at which time the seminary was on its last legs. In the meantime, however, ever increasing numbers of devoutly Orthodox Jews were coming to America from Eastern Europe.

Morais was the last rabbi at Mikveh Israel to play a major leadership role in either the Philadelphia or national Jewish communities; but his student and younger friend, Cyrus Adler (1863–1940), was to become a key lay force in both Philadelphia and national Judaism in the first four decades of the twentieth century.[19] Adler was not only a pupil of Morais at Mikveh Israel, he was bred in the conservative atmosphere of the Sulzbergers and other leading Philadelphia Jewish families.

According to Nathan Glazer, "Adler saw that the Jewish Theological Seminary might serve to turn young East European Jews into modern, English-speaking rabbis for the East European Orthodox masses."[20] Toward this end, Adler persuaded Jacob Schiff to put up money to revive the Seminary. A Reform Jew himself, Schiff had more sympathy with the East European masses flooding our shores at the time than many of his snobbish German Jewish peers; and he persuaded a group of like-minded friends to put up half a million dollars towards rejuvenating the Seminary, which among other things allowed it to bring from England Solomon Schechter (1874–1915) as president.[21]

When Isaac Mayer Wise founded Hebrew Union College, in 1875 in Cincinnati, Reform Judaism seemed to be on the side of the future (at least until the Holocaust and then when larger and larger numbers of descendents of immigrants from Eastern Europe rose to elite status after World War II). That so few walked out when shrimp was served at the dinner celebrating

Interior of Mikveh Israel, Seventh Street above Arch, 1909. *Courtesy of Dropsie University Library and Allen Meyers.*

the graduation of the first class at the new college in 1883, was a witness to the winds of change. The first class included a brilliant young native of Prussia, Joseph Krauskopf, who was made a vice-president of the Pittsburgh Conference in 1885 and elected soon afterwards as the rabbi of Philadelphia's Keneseth Israel (1887). In the meantime, Morais, the traditionalist rabbi at Mikveh Israel, had died in 1897 and his ally at Rodeph Shalom, Marcus Jastrow, had retired in 1892. Henceforth Krauskopf and other Reform rabbis would be major spokesmen for Philadelphia Jewry.[22]

Just as within Protestantism where the upper classes moved in ever larger numbers from the church of their ancestors into the Episcopal Church (led by Phillips Brooks, first at Holy Trinity Church on Philadelphia's Rittenhouse Square and later at Boston Brahmin's Trinity Church, on Copley Square) so, figuring in the last years of the nineteenth century, elite Jews in city after city in America moved "uptown" as it were and joined Reform temples. Thus, in Philadelphia, Keneseth Israel became one of the Jewish community's leading congregations in the first two decades of the twentieth century. At the same time, Rodeph Shalom, a bastion of conservatism under Jastrow, appointed Henry Berkowitz as its rabbi in 1892 where he remained for the next three decades, gradually bringing his congregation into the Reform movement. Krauskopf had married Berkowitz's sister and the two rabbis worked closely together, eventually establishing "joint services, joint Sunday Schools and joint efforts in behalf of Reform Judaism."[23]

While such older-stock Brahmins within the Jewish community as the Binswangers, Wolfs and Rosenbachs, moved in Mikveh Israel circles with their greatly distinguished peer, Mayer Sulzberger, Philadelphians of new wealth and distinction such as the great merchants Ellis Gimbel and Lessing Rosenwald, the real estate tycoon Albert M. Greenfield, and Judge Horace Stern, the first Jewish member of the Supreme Court of Pennsylvania, were all members of Congregation Keneseth Israel during the interwar years.

Boston's Jewish Community: Temple Israel and Reform

Congregation Temple Israel, from its founding in 1854 to the present day, has been even more closely associated with the leadership of Boston's Jewish community than has Philadelphia's Mikveh Israel. William Dean Howells once spoke of the flowering of literary Boston as the "Unitarian harvest-time of the old Puritan seed time."[24] Similarly perhaps Reform Judaism was made possible by the seeds sown by the puritanical orthodoxy of Isaac Leeser's generation in Philadelphia. And Temple Israel was founded at the height of America's first literary renaissance in Unitarian Boston as well as at the same time as the founding of Reform Judaism in Cincinnati. In the same year that Henry David Thoreau published *Walden*, the great Boston Unitarian liberals Theodore Parker, James Freeman Clark, and Octavius Brooks Frothingham were passing hostile resolutions against the Kansas-Nebraska Bill, and, as we have seen, Isaac Mayer Wise went to Congregation B'nai Jeshurun, in Cincinnati, where he established the *Israelite* in which he attacked Leeser in the very first issue.[25]

For two decades after its founding Temple Israel remained Orthodox—men and women were seated separately, men with their heads covered; the ritual was in Hebrew; the vernacular in German; all prayed for the restoration of the Holy Land; there was no sermon and the Hebrew Sabbath was still sacred.

In the meantime the congregation included more and more rapidly rising shopkeepers and merchants in a Boston business community still dominated by Brahmins who symbolized the Anglo ideal in culture and education. "These merchants of Orthodox background," wrote an historian of Temple Israel, "wanted to acquire the Boston speech, the Boston dress, the Boston religion: they wanted to be like unto others. More than that, they feared that their American children would embrace Christianity if the *shul* were not Americanized. . . ."[26] And Wise's *Israelite* warned that "unless Judaism assimilates the American way, we will have no Jews left in this country in half a century."[27]

When the leaders of Temple Israel appointed Solomon Schindler (1842–1915) as their rabbi in 1874, they were getting far more than they bargained for.[28] In the 20 years of his leadership the congregation shed most of its Orthodox traditions and became the leading Reform synagogue in New England. Born in Germany, Schindler came to Boston after three miserable years as rabbi of an Orthodox synagogue in Hoboken, New Jersey. He was determined to Americanize his new congregation. From his first days in this thinking city, he seemed to be more at home with non-Jews than with Jews, especially with intellectuals, radicals and Unitarian ministers who had done to traditional Christianity what he planned to do with Traditional Judaism at Temple Israel. His first sermons, later published as *Messianic Expectations and Modern Judaism* (1885), were delivered to large audiences which his close friend and Darwinist-Christian, Minot Savage, noted were "more than half Christian." In the preface to Schindler's book of sermons, Savage hailed the popular rabbi as true to the spirit of an age in which "Christians were ceasing to be Christians and Jews ceasing to be Jews." The Channing Club rejoiced in the fact that Reform Judaism and Unitarianism had "few if any . . . theological differences." Both of course were casting out the Old Testament values of their Puritan and Orthodox ancestors.

By the middle of the 1880s, Temple Israel had tripled its membership, which included "100 of the richest and most influential Hebrews in the city." In 1885, in an attractive section of the South End, a new temple was built in the Romanesque style of H. H. Richardson's celebrated Trinity Church on Copley Square. The dedication address was delivered by the Reverend Dr. Gustav Gottheil, Rabbi of Temple Emanu-el in New York, the "Canterbury of American Judaism," who charmed his listeners with his impeccable Anglo-American diction. Minot Savage, Edward Everett Hale and Phillips Brooks himself also spoke. By now the prosperous congregation was thoroughly Americanized: the first sermons in English rather than German were delivered at Sunday services soon after moving into the new synagogue; family pews, an organ, a choir with hymns and the Reform prayer book containing no reference to a future return to Palestine had already become standard.

But Schindler was moving away from traditional roots too fast and too far for all but the most liberal of his congregants. Though they wanted to Americanize, they wanted to retain their Jewish identity, while Schindler wanted to destroy it. He had introduced the Sunday services too fast and they were soon done away with; then in the early 1890s, when he advocated intermarriage with liberal Christians his congregants were outraged; above all they failed to follow him when he preached the socialism of Edward Bellamy, which he embraced with the idea of creating a society free of class, race, and religious differences (he had befriended Bellamy and translated his classic, *Looking Backward,* into German). Though the Jews of Temple

Israel aspired to the rational religion of their liberal Christian peers, the Unitarians, they did not want to revolutionize society or convert their temple into a community church. Finally, in 1893, Schindler and his congregants agreed to part, and Charles Fleischer, assistant to Rabbi Berkowitz of Philadelphia's Rodeph Shalom, was called to Temple Israel as rabbi.

If possible, Charles Fleischer (1871–1942) was an even more ardent Americanist than his predecessor and was of course pleased when he was welcomed to Boston at the railroad station by Dr. Edward Everett Hale, the incarnation of the liberal spirit of the city, in the following words: "Now, my son, you too are one of the preachers of New England."[29]

Fleischer had been appointed rabbi of Temple Israel in order to preserve the Jewish identity of the congregation and, for at least a dozen years, he did not, *in the pulpit*, go beyond the limit of Reform Judaism or the Unitarianism upon which it had been modeled. He was a "cultural pluralist" long before the Harvard-trained philosopher, Horace Kallen, first used the term. "The strength of a community," Fleischer told a Congregationalist men's club, "is measured by the variety within it." That the Jew should maintain his traditional identity was symbolized in the architecture of the new temple erected on Commonwealth Avenue, in 1907. Instead of following the Romanesque style of the old synagogue which was modeled after Episcopalian Trinity Church, the new Commonwealth Avenue temple was a modern Moorish-style tabernacle which was referred to by the press as "Solomon's Temple." The dedication ceremonies were attended by a host of community leaders, including "the Grand Old Man of Boston," Edward Everett Hale. The main address, delivered by Rabbi Stephen S. Wise, an early Zionist, evoked a spontaneous ovation.

Charles Fleischer, German-born but educated in New York, was a hauntingly handsome bachelor during his years at Temple Israel; referred to as the "Beau Brummel of the Back Bay," he soon became a star in the intellectual and artistic circles of Boston; his portrait was done in black and white by his good friend John Singer Sargent and in addition to his many Unitarian minister friends, he was admired and was friends with other liberals like Charles W. Eliot of Harvard and Robert A. Woods of South End House. When Sunday services were reintroduced after moving to the Commonwealth Avenue Temple, he preached to audiences made up of almost as many non-Jews as Jews. He was in fact making Temple Israel into a veritable civic forum; and, spending more time with non-Jews than with Jews, he was soon a popular preacher in pulpits once occupied by Cotton Mather and Ralph Waldo Emerson. By 1908, he publicly noted that he admired Emerson more than Moses and felt it was time to leave Temple Israel. In the meantime, in 1909, President Eliot, who had been a firm believer in the melting-pot in his youth, came out squarely against assimilation and uniformity and stressed the desirability of a diversity of races and ethnic groups living side by side. He also acknowledged his kinship with Fleischer in a letter in which he too saw the need for a new religion which reverenced truth, science, the individual, and social service.

The end came in 1911, when Rabbi Emeritus, Solomon Schindler, preached a sermon at Temple Israel on "Mistakes I Have Made." My chief mistake, Schindler noted, was in "trying to make the Jew like the Gentile, . . . "the Jew will never succumb to the melting pot." Fleischer replied by preaching on "Some Mistakes Which I Have Gladly Made." He did not want to make Jews like Gentiles, but hoped to fuse all Americans into a new people. And he soon left Temple Israel forever to found the Sunday Commons, a nonsectarian religion for persons of all backgrounds, stocks and traditions; it was Boston's first community church. In 1919 he married a gifted and intellectual Vermonter of Scotch descent and Presbyterian upbringing, who shared his liberal views.

Both Schindler and Fleischer were German-born intellectuals and marginal men in America. And they served Temple Israel during the Indian Summer of Boston's intellectual leadership of the nation when local politics were following a dialectical pattern of reform and reaction: until William Dean Howells moved to New York in 1891, Boston was still the literary capital of America; in 1884, Boston Brahmins led the nation's Mugwumps and in that same year young Josiah Quincy graduated from Harvard, became a Democrat and then went on to become Mayor of Boston in 1896 (the third of his family to do so) and to make his city "the cutting edge of reform in America."[30]

At the same time, the very Brahmin class which adopted Howells and produced Quincy and the liberal Unitarian ministers who welcomed both Schindler and Fleischer to Boston, also produced the leaders of a newly rising tide of anti-immigrant and antisemitic sentiment which gradually infected much of old-stock America between 1881, when the pogroms against the Jews began in Russia, and the final closing of the gates of unrestricted immigration in America in 1924. In the early 1880s, for instance, Phillips Brooks, the barometer of the Brahmin mind, prayed for the newer Americans in our "strange meeting place of races;" in 1891, he joined the Sons of the Revolution, because he felt it was well to "go in for the assertion that our dear land at least used to be American."[31] Similarly, Henry Adams, in his 1880 novel, *Democracy,* wrote of Jews as upper-class Americans with no ethnic stigma; by the time of the Dreyfus Affair (1894), he was becoming a pretty rigid antisemite. At any rate, the Immigration Restriction League was founded in Boston in 1894 by three Brahmin graduates of the Noble's Country Day School and the class of 1889 at Harvard—Robert DeCourcy Ward, Prescott Farnsworth Hall, and Charles Warren. Ironically enough, young Warren was the son of Winslow Warren, a Brahmin Mugwump and later a Democratic ally of the reforming Josiah Quincy. Henry Cabot Lodge was a major advocate of the restriction of immigration while a supporter of the League of Nations from its beginning, as was A. Lawrence Lowell of Harvard; others like Charles W. Eliot and William James, as might be expected, were openly opposed; many, like John Murray Forbes, stood on the sidelines but privately were pleased with the League's work. It was in this climate of opinion that young Louis D. Brandeis practiced law in partnership with his closest Yankee friend Samuel D. Warren, between 1879 and 1897. We shall return to the fascinating story of how Brandeis, an assimilationist and philo-Puritan who stood socially aloof from the conservative German-Jewish community at Temple Israel, eventually became an ardent Zionist and the most famous Jew in America by the time he went on to the United States Supreme Court in 1916.

We have emphasized here the articulate, bigoted but ambivalent nature of the Boston community in the days when Schindler and Fleischer led their congregation at Temple Israel. There was no such ferment in Philadelphia. Mugwumpery was hardly a real issue among Philadelphia gentlemen who, as in most other issues, preferred to enjoy their privileges in a tolerant, live-and-let-live atmosphere. While Justice Brandeis of Boston had led a lonely life of controversy for the 30 years before he went on the Supreme Court, his counterpart in Philadelphia, Judge Mayer Sulzberger, was warmly rooted in the conservative Jewish community there; while Brandeis was always a controversial intellectual, Sulzberger was the secluded scholar at heart who avoided a controversial issue if it was at all possible.

Philadelphia and Boston Jewish Communities: Comparative Institutions

In addition to the synagogues founded before the Civil War which we have already discussed, the major secular institutions in each city are listed here. One is immediately impressed how essentially similar institutions developed in each city. Though often founded earlier in the far older community of Philadelphia, the two exceptions, centrally organized charities and hospitals in Boston, are of importance in understanding the two communities.

In addition to the synagogue, of course, the organization and leadership of charitable giving has been of central importance to all American Jewish communities. It is our thesis here, moreover, that Jews have done so well in the American Horatio Alger tradition largely because equality of opportunity, not equality of conditions, is so deeply imbedded in their own traditions; at the same time, equality of opportunity has been combined with a definitely hierarchical society, centralization of leadership, and a powerful tradition of charitable giving; by ancient religious law and long social habit, both the rights of the poor and the obligations of the rich and successful were implied in the Hebrew concept of *Tzedakah*.[32] Charity balls have

Philadelphia	Boston

Pre-Civil War Synagogues

Philadelphia	Boston
Mikveh Israel (1782)	Ohabei Shalom (1852)
Rodeph Shalom (1810)	Adath Israel (1854)
Beth Israel (1840)	Mishkan Israel (1858)
Keneseth Israel (1846)	
Adath Jeshurun (1859)	

Charitable Organizations

Philadelphia	Boston
United Hebrew Charities (1869)	United Hebrew Benevolent Association (1864)
Hebrew Charity Balls (1843)	Purim Balls (1869)
Federation of Jewish Charities (1901)	Federation of Jewish Charities (1895)

Hospitals

Philadelphia	Boston
Jewish Hospital Association (1865)	Jewish Dispensary
56th and Haverford (1865)	North End (1892)
Old York and Tabor Roads (1873)	
Mt. Sinai (1899–1905)	Mt. Sinai Hospital Association (1902)
Second and Pine	North and West End
Fifth and Wilder	South End and Roxbury
Lebanon Hospital, North Fourth (1907)	Beth Israel Hospital
Northern Liberties (1920)	Roxbury (1916)
Albert Einstein Medical Center (1951)	Brookline Avenue (1928)

Educational Institutions

Philadelphia	Boston
Hebrew Education Society (1848)	Hebrew Education Society (1868)
Maimonides College (1867–1873)	Hebrew Teachers College (1920)
Gratz College (1895)	
Dropsie College (1908)	Brandeis University (1958)

Newspapers

Philadelphia	Boston
Jewish Exponent (1887)	Jewish Advocate (1902)

Social Clubs

Philadelphia	Boston
Mercantile Club (1853)	Elysium Club (1880)
Philmont Country Club (1906)	New Century Club (1900)
Locust Club (1920)	Kernwood Country Club (1914)
	Belmont Country Club (1940)

Neighborhoods

German middle class (19th, early 20th century)

Philadelphia	Boston
Franklin Square, Green Street	South End, Brookline

East European ghetto (19th, early 20th century)

Philadelphia	Boston
Delaware River-Front to Sixth	West End-North End
Girard to Tasker	Chelsea

Middle class

Philadelphia	Boston
Strawberry Mansion-Logan	Roxbury-Dorchester
Old York Road-Wynnefield	Brookline-Newton

Upper class

Philadelphia	Boston
Rittenhouse Square (Chestnut Hill)	Back Bay (Cambridge)

always had a place in Christian society but never of first importance as were the early Hebrew Charity Balls in Philadelphia, or the Purim Balls in Boston.

While charity has always been central to the Christian religion, organized philanthropy has, from the beginning, been more characteristic of the Puritans in England and America than of the Quakers, who clung to the more Catholic idea of spontaneous charity (not necessarily to correct the abuses of inequality or the condition of poverty but to soften differences and, some would say, ease the conscience of the rich if not the bitterness of the poor). It was in these rather different climates of opinion in the Puritan "City Upon a Hill" and the Quaker "City of Brotherly Love" that the younger Jewish community in Boston organized the centralization of charitable fund-raising in the United Hebrew Benevolent Association in 1864, five years before Philadelphia Jews united their efforts in the United Hebrew Charities. Similarly, the Federation of Jewish Charities in Boston was the first of its kind in the nation and its founding in 1895 came six years before a similar consolidation in Philadelphia.

That business success and community leadership in the Jewish community is closely tied to charitable giving is nicely illustrated in both Philadelphia and Boston. In Philadelphia, for example, the Jewish community was large and stable enough in the pre-Civil War decade to produce a coherent and familistic upper class which stood at the forefront of community leadership down to 1940, as shown in the preceding pages.[33] Within a decade of the founding of Temple Israel in Boston, when the entire Jewish community only numbered about 400 families, 26 of the more prosperous businessmen gathered at the synagogue to found the United Hebrew Benevolent Association, which remained virtually the exclusive charity project of Temple Israel until 1876. When the congregation's leading member, a German immigrant, Jacob Hecht, agreed to accept the presidency on condition that he be given support in making reforms, he immediately changed the leadership structure so as to include members of the Ohabei Shalom congregation and streamlined operating procedures so that the Association became the Jewish counterpart of the Yankee-dominated Provident Association, a pioneer in the nation.

Just as solid and successful German Jews were settling into Boston's South End and Philadelphia's Green Street neighborhood, with their comfortable social life centered in their favorite congregations, their exclusive Elysium and Mercantile Clubs, and their charitable organizations, a great wave of Jewish immigrants from Eastern Europe (so-called "Russians") came to Boston's North and West Ends and Chelsea and in the neighborhoods along the Delaware riverfront in Philadelphia, beginning in 1881.

In the following decades, thousands upon thousands of desperately poor and fiercely Orthodox Jews flocked into the small "East Side" ghettos in all of America's major cities. By 1900, in Philadelphia, six Orthodox

synagogues had been built within an area of two city blocks (between
Fourth and Fifth and Pine and South Streets).[34] In Boston, the first real
ghetto was a small area in the North End, bounded by Hanover, Prince,
Endicott and Bennett Streets. With unbounded energy and thrift, these poor
immigrants to Boston's North End had saved enough under the leadership
of their Rabbi Morish Margolies to construct a brand new synagogue (two
small congregations already existed in the area) for Congregation Beth Israel
at a cost of $50,000. It soon became the center of social and religious life in
the North End.[35]

Many of America's German-Jews were shocked at the alien hordes of
"Russians" who came to their cities, causing, so they thought, a new and
unbending kind of antisemitism within the Protestant establishment. Fortunately, the wisest of the uptown Jews in America knew that, in spite of their
vast cultural differences, both the "Germans" and the "Russians" were ultimately one people, Jews in a Gentile world. At any rate, it was partly as a
response to the need for helping these new immigrants that the German Jews
of Boston founded the Federation of Jewish Charities in 1895, and Philadelphia Jews did the same six years later.

Solomon Schindler not only introduced Reform Judaism to Boston's
Temple Israel, but he also recommended Yankee techniques of philanthropy: "Participating in a study of urban poverty with native spokesmen of
social reform," wrote Barbara Miller Solomon, "Rabbi Schindler transmitted to the Hecht coterie contemporary approaches to immigrants' problems."[36] And Schindler envisioned the need for federation at least a dozen
years before he and the Hechts finally brought it about in 1895. In many
ways, the path to Federation began in 1889, when the leaders of the newly
completed synagogue of Beth Israel in the North End allowed Lina Hecht to
start a Sunday School for girls on the premises. Although Solomon Schindler
agreed to step down as rabbi at Temple Israel in 1893, his dream of a more
centralized and professional federation finally came about when he was
made the first paid superintendent of the Federation of Jewish Charities
after its founding in 1895. The lay officers included Jacob Hecht as president.

Federation came to Philadelphia Jewry in 1901, after Boston, Chicago
and Cincinnati had already followed the so-called Liverpool plan of
federated fund-raising. Unlike the Boston Federation where three big men
(each the leader of his community in his day) served for three decades
between them, the presidency of Federation in Philadelphia was less central
to the city's Jewish leadership as a whole and more of a temporary honor
and chore to be done in one's fair turn. The two Federations were also
different in that Boston hired a paid full-time executive from the beginning,
while Philadelphia's Federation was run by a small nucleus of German-
Jewish laymen who were allied by marriage and social ties; the first executive director was hired in 1918, when the Federation expanded from 14 to 39

constituent agencies, and when, for the first time, recognition was given to leaders of East European ("Russian") origins. The change in leadership was also a result of the great increase in the size of Philadelphia Jewry.

Jewish communities all over urban America are justifiably proud of their support of medicine and hospitals. In Philadelphia, the first Jewish hospital was opened soon after the Civil War, and the site of the Albert Einstein Medical Center, at Old York and Tabor Roads, was purchased in 1873.[37] In both cities hospitals were founded by the German-Jewish leadership as a response to the Orthodox immigrants who needed hospital care by people who understood and sympathized with their special dietary and other needs. Thus the Jewish Dispensary was founded in Boston's North End in 1892. Similarly the Mt. Sinai Hospital Association founded hospitals both in the ghettos of the North and West Ends as well as in the South End and Roxbury where German Jews had long been settled and where Russian Jews moved, as they climbed to more middle-class status. Except for the original hospital founded after the Civil War, Philadelphia Jews followed the same pattern as Boston, and branches of Mt. Sinai Hospital were founded at Second and Pine and at Fifth and Wilder, both in the heart of the Russian Ghetto; also within the ghetto was the Lebanon Hospital on North Fourth Street.

While the needs and the patterns of hospital founding in the two cities were more or less parallel in the early, and especially the immigrant days from 1880 to the First War, the final consolidation of the Albert Einstein in Philadelphia and the Beth Israel Hospital in Boston were significantly different. Thus Boston consolidated its major hospital effort in the Beth Israel Hospital, in Roxbury and then at its present site on Brookline Avenue, in the heart of medical and educational Boston. Due largely to the leadership of Louis Kirstein who would have only the very best and held that Harvard University in general and the Medical School in particular symbolized the best in the nation if not the world, he insisted that Beth Israel be located next to the Harvard Medical School and for a quarter of a century it was the only teaching Jewish hospital in the nation.

Philadelphia Jewry, on the other hand, did not centralize its hospital structure in the Einstein Medical Center until 1951, and it is still today located in two places: the Daroff Center in South Philadelphia, as well as at Old York and Tabor Roads in North Philadelphia. Only recently have these two branches been recognized as teaching hospitals, in the north, affiliated with Temple University Medical School and in South Philadelphia, associated with Thomas Jefferson University Medical School. Once again the Philadelphia-Quaker pattern of letting institutions and people do their own thing contrasted with the Puritan Boston emphasis on quality and organization.

As far as Jewish educational institutions are concerned, the two cities were approximately similar, with the older Philadelphia community's in-

The first building of Jewish Hospital, Old York Road, 1873. *Courtesy of Albert Einstein Medical Center.*

stitutions being founded earlier. Thus Gratz College was the first Hebrew teachers college in the nation. Dropsie College, though concentrating on a non-theological graduate school leading to a Ph.D. in Hebrew and related studies, was unique and fitting to more Conservative and Orthodox Philadelphia, while Brandeis University, the only nonsectarian institution of higher learning in America to be founded and supported by Jews, was, appropriately enough, located in the Boston area at its founding in 1948.

Perhaps nothing better symbolizes or sums up the differences between Quaker Philadelphia and Puritan Boston than the attitudes of the University of Pennsylvania and Harvard toward Jews. The egalitarian tolerance of Quakerism was characteristic of Penn, and produced there a laissez-faire kind of cultural pluralism; at Harvard, on the other hand, the characteristic hierarchical intolerance of Puritanism, ambivalent at first, eventually produced a kind of Brahmin hegemony highly conducive to assimilation. Philadelphia Jews have been students at Penn ever since the eighteenth century, whereas the first Boston Jew graduated from Harvard College in 1870.[38] More indicative, however, was Harvard and Penn's reaction to the rising tide of antisemitism in America in the first part of the twentieth century, especially as it reached the college level in the interwar years.

As we have already seen above, Presidents Eliot and Lowell of Harvard, both Brahmin-bred to the core, held very different views of the hoards of immigrants from Southern and Eastern Europe who came to America in the years before the First World War. Eliot, as a reaction to both his Puritan heritage and upbringing, was an extreme Unitarian liberal, while Lowell acted more in accord with his Puritan roots; Eliot vigorously opposed the ideals of the Immigration Restriction League, while Lowell supported the League of Nations and was a vice-president after 1912. Finally, while Eliot once said that as a Unitarian he would be glad to be followed in the Harvard presidency by Brandeis, a Jew, Lowell wrote to Woodrow Wilson after the election in 1912 that Brandeis "did not stand very high in the opinion of the best judges in Massachusetts." In brief, Eliot believed in individualism, diversity and cultural pluralism, and built the finest graduate schools in the nation, at the same time atomizing life at the College with his famous elective system. Lowell believed in paternalism, hierarchy and community, and concentrated his energies on the College where he built new halls for freshmen in 1914, and after the Harkness gifts in 1928, constructed colleges for upperclassmen, all in an effort to create an atmosphere of "intellectual and social cohesion." Above all, Lowell believed in assimilation to some sort of traditional Harvard ideal. What he once wrote of the Irish, who were coming increasingly to Harvard in his day, applied to all minorities: "What we need is not to dominate . . . but to absorb. . . . Their best interests and ours are, indeed, the same in this matter. We want them to become rich, and send their sons to our colleges, to share our prosperity and our sentiments. We do not want to feel that they are among us and not really a part of us."[39]

And Lowell applied these assimilationist sentiments to Jewish students at Harvard, whose number had grown from less than 10 percent when he took office to more than 20 percent by the early 1920s. He even tried to establish a formal quota for Jews but was turned down by the Overseers ("howled down by men who preferred hypocrisy"). In his judicial discussion of antisemitic sentiments in the Harvard philosophy department, Bruce Kuklick wrote of Lowell's position as follows:

> In the early 1920s, when he tried to establish a formal quota for Jews, he did so not because he felt any prejudice against the Jews per se, but because Harvard could not assimilate the Jews if their number became too large. One of Harvard's goals was to produce the "pure American" Jew. Harvard had to give "special consideration" to the Jews just as it did to alumni children: the nation would be strong only if both groups received Harvard socialization.[40]

The long tradition of laissez-faire cultural pluralism which marked Philadelphia as a whole and also the University of Pennsylvania, carried into the interwar years at Penn when many other of the leading Eastern institutions were becoming more and more restrictive. All during the 1920s and 1930s, Penn remained a largely commuter school and tended to accept any students, regardless of ethnicity or race, especially if their parents could afford to pay the tuition bills. As Lawrence R. Vesey wrote in *The Emergence of the American University*, "the University of Pennsylvania welcomed commuters, immigrants, and socialites alike;" it was said to have "the democracy of the street car."[41] Just as in the city as a whole, however, this cultural pluralism at Penn during the interwar years led to a campus social life which was more or less rigidly divided as between Jew and Gentile, between fraternity members and the rest. With perhaps the largest proportion of Jews in the Ivy League, Penn was dominated socially by a large number of fraternities, rigidly divided into "A" or Gentile houses and "B" or Jewish houses. One wonders whether Jewish alumni have been more loyal to the democratic but segregated pluralism of Penn, or the discriminating but assimilating class values of Harvard. Theodore H. White, who entered Harvard as a freshman from the Jewish ghetto of Dorchester, a year after Lowell's retirement in 1933, has made some interesting observations on this point. White noted that when he entered Harvard it still "combined the best of the old warmth and the new strivings."[42] While the new strivers surely enriched the mind of Harvard Yard, White saw that it was the still hegemonic values of Lowell and his overwhelmingly, old-stock faculty which supplied the warmth. But White also noted that President Conant, of New England lineage as ancient as Lowell's, was more sympathetic to the values of Charles W. Eliot and proceeded to make "Harvard the most competitive school in American scholarship, a meritocracy in which students and professors vied for honors with little mercy or kindness."[43] Thus, by the time White wrote these words in the late 1970s, *both* Penn and Harvard were highly competitive, intellectual meritocracies and far more democratic than ever before in their histories. The class authority and ideal of assimilation of prewar Harvard had now lost out to the values of democracy and cultural pluralism which had always been more characteristic of Penn and the Quaker City as a whole. White's reaction to these changes at Harvard were as follows:

> I have, in the years since, served as an overseer of that majestic institution Harvard University, a member of the Honorable and Reverend Board of the most ancient corporation in the Western World, the chosen thirty who tip their silk hats as they file, two by two, past the statue of John Harvard on Commencement Day in the Yard. But it was a better Harvard I entered in the 1930s than it was later, when I sat on the Board of Overseers, or than it is today.[44]

The central difference between Jewish Boston and Jewish Philadelphia, at least in the early part of this century, can also be seen in the life and career of Louis D. Brandeis. If Theodore White is one of the more distinguished American Jews of this generation, surely Louis D. Brandeis was the most distinguished Jew in American history; and both men shared a loving admiration for the values of Old New England Puritanism and its proudest progeny, Harvard University. Brandeis once said that his years at the Harvard Law School were "the happiest of my life . . . For me the world's center

Louis D. Brandeis with Rabbi Stephen S. Wise, 1917. *(Library of Congress) Reproduced by courtesy of the Museum of American Jewish History.*

was Cambridge."[45] And his Brahmin law partner, Samuel D. Warren, once told him: "In many ways you are a better example of New England virtues that the natives."[46] But in Brandeis's generation as we have already seen, the Brahmin Bostonian's attitude toward the Jew was at best ambivalent. At any rate, a brief outline of Brandeis's Boston career between his coming to the Law School in 1875 and his going on the Supreme Court in 1916 should highlight the values of class authority and assimilation, on the one hand, and the more democratic values of cultural pluralism, on the other. For Brandeis began as an assimilationist, but slowly became a cultural pluralist, and finally an active Zionist when he came to feel that his own generation of Boston Brahmins had betrayed their Puritan heritage, among other things for surrendering their economic independence to the New York monopolists. For Brandeis, finally, the Zionists among his own people were the "New Puritans."[47]

While Jacob Hecht, the leader of Boston Jewry, had provided security for his tuition at the law school, and his wife had invited him to her Sunday afternoon at homes on Commonwealth Avenue, young Brandeis avoided active membership in the Jewish society of Temple Israel and the Elysium Club.[48] This was especially so after he had been asked to form a law partnership with his best Yankee friend, Samuel D. Warren, in 1879. Warren, a prosperous paper manufacturer's son and a member of Porcellian at Harvard, provided an ideal entree into Boston Society, and Brandeis was soon listed in the *Blue Book* and later in the *Social Register* when it first appeared in the 1890s. Though he was not a member of The Country Club in Brookline, nor the Somerset in Boston, he was soon taken into the respectable Union Club in the city, and the suburban Dedham Polo Club (Sam Warren was a founder and president).

Even though overtly accepted in Boston's best social circles, Brandeis soon realized that it was through Warren's social and family connections that most of the State Street clients came to the partnership. He consequently turned to a small group of prosperous Jewish firms such as Hecht Brothers and Company in order to contribute his share of clients. Unfortunately, his relationship to Warren cooled somewhat after Warren married in 1883, and his caste-conscious wife refused to include Brandeis among the hundred or so invited guests. When Brandeis married Alice Goldmark in 1891, the wedding was held in New York, a small and very private family affair. Only a few of the prominent clients of the law firm sent wedding gifts or left calling cards when the newlyweds settled in Boston. Brandeis bought a country place in Dedham in 1900; few of the neighbors were friendly, according to his daughter, who remembers solitary walks and canoeing with her father; at the Polo Club, Brandeis was allowed to "flock by himself," as a member once rather callously put it. At any rate, by 1910 the doors were pretty firmly closed to elite Jews in Boston; the eccentric bachelor and reformer, Edward Filene, in a bitter battle to avoid being classified as a Jew, founded the Boston City Club where liberal businessmen, Gentile and Jew, lunch together to this day; his more conservative brother, Lincoln Filene, even after becoming a Congregationalist to please his wife, finally joined the Kernwood Country Club in order to play golf. For Brandeis the final turning point in his relationship with Yankee Boston was probably the suicide of his friend Warren in February 1910. Though hardly intimate with the family, it was Brandeis who took charge and prevented the scandal reaching the press; then, a week after the suicide, the Dedham Polo Club partially burned, and, rather than restoring the clubhouse, the membership merged with the Norfolk Country Club, in Weston, to form the present Dedham Country and Polo Club. Members of the Brandeis family were not asked to join.

In the meantime, Brandeis gradually rejected the ideal of assimilation and embraced cultural pluralism, rediscovering his Jewish heritage after first publicly identifying himself as a Jew in 1905. His movement back to Judaism was of course quite complicated; but it was in Woodrow Wilson's campaign for the presidency that he came to know Jacob De Haas, later his biographer and at one time the secretary and forever a hero-worshiper of Theodore Herzl. De Haas had taken over the editorship of Boston's *Jewish*

Advocate which vigorously supported Wilson in 1912. After the Democratic victory, the *Advocate* reported that Wilson had received an unusual amount of Jewish financial and political support, especially from such prominent Jews as Henry Morgenthau and the well-known lawyer, Samuel Untermyer. Brandeis now worked closely with De Haas in ethnic politics, finally making him his private secretary and "instructor in the history of Zionism."

The New Century Club in Boston was founded in 1900 by a rapidly rising group of Russian-Jewish professional men, many of whom had gone to the Boston University Law School where they had been members of the Century Club. It is indicative of the mind and heart of Louis D. Brandeis that he made his first public statement on Zionism at the parvenu New Century Club rather than at the stolid and conservative Elysium Club. On March 22, 1913, according to De Haas, "In the privacy of the monthly dinner . . . Brandeis made his first serious utterance on Zionism. He unfolded his deep solicitude for the spiritual welfare of the Jews. He explained his interest in Zionism and identified himself in unqualified terms with the cause."[49]

Notes

Chapter 1

1. *History of the Jews of Philadelphia* (Philadelphia: Jewish Publication Society, 1956, 1975). Henry Samuel Morais, *The Jews of Philadelphia: Their History from the Earliest Settlements to the Present Time* (Philadelphia: The Levytype Co., 1894) is largely a source book. A typewritten manuscript by Charles S. Bernheimer, *Historical Sketch of the Jewish Community of Philadelphia, 1703–1926,* is available at the Library Company of Pennsylvania.
2. Jeffrey Gurock, *When Harlem Was Jewish, 1870–1930* (New York, 1979), pp. 198–99, n. 6.
3. *American Jewish Year Book, 1981* (Philadelphia: American Jewish Committee and Jewish Publication Society, 1980), pp. 180, 290–291.
4. Bertram W. Korn, "1655–1901" in *75 Years of Continuity and Change: Our Philadelphia Jewish Community in Perspective, Jewish Exponent,* Supplement, May 12, 1976, p. 10.
5. Melvin I. Urofsky, "American Jewish Leadership," *American Jewish History,* June 1981, Vol. 70, No. 4, pp. 401–19.
6. Diane King, *A History of Gratz College, 1893–1928* (Ph.D. dissertation, Dropsie College, 1979), p. 3.
7. *Community and Polity: The Organizational Dynamics of American Jewry* (Philadelphia: Jewish Publication Society, 1976), p. 105.
8. Elazar, *Community and Polity,* p. 105.
9. As quoted by Bertram Korn, *Eventful Years and Experiences: Studies in Nineteenth Century American Jewish History* (Cincinnati: American Jewish Archives, 1954), p. 35.
10. Korn, "1655–1901," *Jewish Exponent,* p. 6, 11. But compare Hyman B. Grinstein, *The Rise of the Jewish Community of New York, 1654–1860* (Philadelphia: Jewish Publication Society, 1945), p. 413.
11. Bernheimer, *Historical Sketch of the Jewish Community of Philadelphia,* p. 23; see also Dixon Wecter, *The Saga of American Society: A Record of Social Aspiration, 1607–1937* (Charles Scribner's Sons, New York, 1937), p. 153; and Nathaniel Burt, *The Perennial Philadelphians: The Anatomy of an American Aristocracy* (Boston: Little, Brown, 1963), p. 566.
12. Korn, *Eventful Years and Experiences,* p. 63.
13. *Philadelphia: Patricians and Philistines, 1900–1950* (New York: Farrar, Straus & Giroux, 1980), pp. 6–7.
14. On the response of Leeser and Philadelphia Jews to nativism, see Korn, *Eventful Years and Experiences,* p. 63.
15. W. E. B. DuBois, *The Philadelphia Negro* (New York: Schocken Books, 1967), pp. 27–32.
16. When Mikveh Israel was founded and plans made to build it next to a German Reformed Church, vigorous protests caused congregational leaders to purchase a new lot north of High (Market) Street where the synagogue was erected in 1792. See Jacob Radar Marcus, *Early American Jewry: The Jews of New York, New England and Canada, 1649–1794,* Vol. 2 (Philadelphia: Jewish Publication Society, 1951), pp. 125–31.
17. Strong animosities, for example, existed in the New York City financial quarter against German Jewish manufacturers and retail merchants following the Civil War. See Maxwell Whiteman, *Copper for America: The Hendricks Family and a National Industry, 1755–1939* (New Brunswick, N.J.: Rutgers University Press), pp. 204–05.

18. Morais, *The Jews of Philadelphia*, p. 57.
19. Arthur A. Goren, "Jews," in Stephen Thernstrom, ed., *Harvard Encyclopedia of Ethnic Groups* (Cambridge, Mass.: Harvard University Press, 1980), p. 579.
20. E. Digby Baltzell, *Philadelphia Gentlemen: The Making of a National Upper Class* (Glencoe, Ill.: The Free Press, 1958), pp. 285–87.
21. Maxwell Whiteman, "A History of the Jewish Exponent," *Jewish Exponent*, June 8, 1962, p. 25.
22. "A Century of Jewish History, 1881–1981: The View from America," *American Jewish Year Book, 1982*, Vol. 82, p. 21.
23. Korn, "1655–1901," p. 14; Bernheimer, *Historical Sketch of the Jewish Community of Philadelphia*, p. 17.
24. *History of the Jews of Philadelphia.*
25. Lukacs, *Philadelphia: Patricians and Philistines*, pp. 22–23.
26. Ande Manners, *Poor Cousins* (New York: Coward, McCann & Geoghegan, 1972), p. 157.
27. See King, *History of Gratz College*, p. 11.
28. Maxwell Whiteman, "Western Impact on East European Jews," in Randall M. Miller and Thomas D. Marzik, *Immigrants and Religion in Urban America* (Philadelphia: Temple University Press), p. 124.
29. Whiteman, "Western Impact on East European Jews," p. 120.
30. Korn, "1655–1901," p. 15.
31. This description of cultural life is taken mainly from Albert Mordell, "Life Among the Philadelphia Russian Jews in the Nineties," *Jewish Exponent*, June 8, 1962.
32. David Halberstam, *The Powers That Be* (New York: Dell), pp. 35–37.
33. Quoted by Maxwell Whiteman, "History of the Jewish Exponent," *Jewish Exponent*, June 8, 1962.
34. *History of the Jews of Philadelphia*, pp. 234–5.
35. John Higham, "Social Discrimination Against Jews in America, 1830–1930," *American Jewish Historical Society*, Vol. 47, No. 1, September 1957, pp. 1–33; John Higham, "Anti-Semitism in the Gilded Age: A Reinterpretation," *Mississippi Valley Historical Review*, March 1957, pp. 3–22.
36. Her full statement is: "When I think how mere wealth is taking possession of Chestnut, Walnut, Spruce and Pine, how uptown is marrying into it, how the Jew and alien are forcing their way in, I see in loyalty to the traditions of the Assembly the Philadelphian's strongest defense of the social rights which are his by inheritance." (Lukacs, *Philadelphia: Patricians and Philistines*, p. 46.)
37. E. Digby Baltzell, "The Development of a Jewish Upper-class in Philadelphia: 1782–1940," in Marshall Skare, ed., *The Jews: Social Patterns of an American Group* (Glencoe, Ill.: The Free Press, 1958), pp. 282–3.
38. On biographical materials on Philadelphia Jewish leaders, see the notes for Chapter 9, "The Philadelphia Group."
39. *Solomon Schechter* (Philadelphia: Jewish Publication Society, 1938), p. 122.
40. Abraham A. Neuman, "Cyrus Adler, A Biographical Sketch," *American Jewish Yearbook*, Vol. 42, (Philadelphia: Jewish Publication Society, 1941), p. 69.
41. Neuman, "Cyrus Adler," p. 49.
42. Baltzell, *The Protestant Establishment*, p. x.
43. Cyrus Adler, *I Have Considered the Days* (Philadelphia: Jewish Publication Society, 1941), p. 245.
44. Oscar Handlin, "Introduction," in Charles Reznikoff, ed., *Louis Marshall, Champion of Liberty*, Vol. I (Philadelphia: Jewish Publication Society, 1957), pp. xiv–xvi.
45. Adler, p. 245.
46. Naomi W. Cohen, *Not Free to Desist: A History of the American Jewish Committee, 1906–1966* (Jewish Publication Society, 1972), pp. 8–9, 25–28.
47. Aaron Rothkoff, *Bernard Revel, Builder of American Orthodoxy* (Jewish Publication Society, 1972), p. 35. Levinthal recognized the young, immigrant scholar, Bernard Revel and invited him to come to Philadelphia as his secretary and assistant. Revel lived with Levinthal for two years, during which he received "his first intimate glimpse of the complex world of American Jewry." Revel was later named to head Yeshiva University,

where he came to be the "Builder of American Orthodoxy." There is no full-scale biographical treatment of Levinthal's life and career.

48. Manners, *Poor Cousins,* p. 194. "Although the Jewish Theological Seminary was situated in New York, the inspiration of its policies continued to emanate from Philadelphia," Abraham A. Neuman wrote of the period when Dr. Morais headed it. ("Cyrus Adler, A Biographical Sketch," p. 69.)

49. Marshall Skare, *Conservative Judaism: An American Religious Movement* (Schocken Books, New York, 1972, p. 165; Bentwich, *Solomon Schechter,* p. 169; Neuman, "Cyrus Adler," p. 69; Moshe Davis, *The Emergence of Conservative Judaism* (Jewish Publication Society, 1963), pp. 322–23; Seymour Siegel, "Mordecai M. Kaplan in Retrospect," *Commentary,* July 1982, pp. 59–60.

50. I am indebted for most of the information in this paragraph to Rabbi Robert Tabak. See his comprehensive proposal, "The Transformation of Jewish Identity: The Philadelphia Experience, 1920–1945."

51. Baltzell, "The Development of a Jewish Upper-Class in Philadelphia," p. 284.

52. Jerald S. Auerbach, *Unequal Justice* (New York: Oxford University Press, 1976), pp. 120–129.

53. Baltzell, *Philadelphia Gentlemen,* pp. 263, 325.

54. Adler, p. 54.

55. Roman Slobodin, "1918–1956," in *Jewish Exponent,* Supplement, p. 29.

56. Jewish Employment and Vocational Service *40th Anniversary Report.*

57. Slobodin, "1918–1956," p. 29; Hurwitz, "1956–1976," *Jewish Exponent* Supplement, pp. 36–37.

58. Sheldon Marcus, *Father Coughlin: The Tumultuous Life of the Priest of the Little Flower* (Boston: Little, Brown, 1973), pp. 146, 158; Maxwell Whiteman, "Human Rights and Civil Rights," in *A History of the First Twenty-Five Years of the Philadelphia Fellowship Commission,* 1969.

59. Stern, pp. 175–176.

60. Whiteman, *History of the First Twenty-Five Years of the Fellowship Commission,* p. 8.

61. Dale Phalen, *Samuel Fels of Philadelphia* (Samuel S. Fels Fund, Philadelphia, 1969), p. 42.

62. Paul Lyons, *Publishing Communists* (Ph.D. dissertation, Temple University), p. 94.

63. Margaret Brenman-Gibson, *Clifford Odets, American Playwright: The Years from 1906 to 1940* (Atheneum, New York, 1981), pp. 122–124; Kenneth Aaron Kanter, "The Jews in Tin Pan Alley, 1910–1940," *American Jewish Archives,* April 1982.

64. For an excellent discussion of the important support given by German-Jewish leaders "without which there would have been no living settlements to incorporate statehood," see Barbara W. Tuchman, "The Assimilationist Dilemma: Ambassador Morgenthau's Story," *Commentary,* May 1977, pp. 58–62.

65. Maxwell Whiteman, "Zionism Comes to Philadelphia," in Isidore S. Meyer, *Early History of Zionism in America* (American Jewish Historical Society and Theodor Herzl Foundation, New York, 1958), pp. 193–195; Melvin I. Urofsky, *We Are One!* (Garden City, N.Y.: Anchor/Doubleday, 1978), p. 85.

66. Stanley Feldstein, *The Land That I Show You: Three Centuries of Jewish Life in America* (Anchor Press/Doubleday, Garden City, N.Y., 1978), p. 368; Naomi Wiener Cohen, "The Reaction of Reform Judaism in America to Political Zionism," in Abraham J. Karp, ed., *The Jewish Experience in America,* Vol. 5 (New York: American Jewish Historical Society and Ktav Publishing House, 1969), p. 180.

67. This account of the founding of the American Council of Judaism is based on Elmer Berger, "Memoirs of an Anti-Zionist Jew," *Journal of Palestinian Studies* (Institute for Palestine Studies and Kuwait University), Autumn 1975/Winter 1976, pp. 3–55.

Chapter 2

1. Mayer Sulzberger was the first to assemble material for a biography of Leeser based on the latter's correspondence given to him by the Cozzens family in 1913. The work was never

completed, but his notes were used by Henry Englander, "Isaac Leeser, 1806–1868," *Central Conference of American Rabbis Yearbook*, Vol. 28 (Cincinnati, 1918), pp. 213–252; Maxwell Whiteman, "Isaac Leeser and the Jews of Philadelphia," *Publication of the American Jewish Historical Society*, Vol. 48, No. 4 (June 1959), pp. 207–244.

2. Ben C. Truman, *The Field of Honor* (New York, 1884), p. 301; Herbert I. Ezekiel and Gaston Lichtenstein, *The History of the Jews of Richmond* (Richmond, 1917), p. 55.

3. Edwin Wolf 2nd and Maxwell Whiteman, *The History of the Jews of Philadelphia from Colonial Times to the Age of Jackson* (Philadelphia, 1975), p. 372.

4. See Wolf and Whiteman, pp. 352–353; 377 and 478, for Abraham Hart.

5. Jacob Leeser died in Philadelphia on March 15, 1834.

6. Leeser's *Moreh derekh . . . The Hebrew Reader. Designed as an Easy Guide to the Hebrew Tongue, for Jewish Children and Self-Instruction* (Philadelphia, 1839) went into six editions by 1868. *Catechism for Younger Children* (Philadelphia, 5599 [1839]) reached a third edition by 1863.

7. *Discourses, Argumentative and Devotional, on the Subject of the Jewish Religion* (Philadelphia, 5597 [1836]) contains the first two volumes of sermons. A third under the same title appeared in 1841, and seven additional volumes were published in 1867.

8. See Whiteman, "Isaac Leeser and the Jews of Philadelphia," p. 214.

9. Leeser, *Discourses*, Vol. 3, pp. 248–260; *The Philadelphia Inquirer and Daily Courier*, October 23, 1840.

10. *Philadelphia, Ab, 5601, July 1841*, a three-page folio circular representing the first call for a union of Hebrew congregations; Abraham Moise to the Rev. Isaac Leeser, August 12, 1841 (author's collection).

11. Leeser first announced his plans for a journal in the *Allgemeine Zeitung des Judenthums*, October 1842, pp. 618–619. A prospectus in English was released at the same time.

12. The first issue of the *Occident* appeared in April 1843. In August 1843, a German periodical, *Israelite*, appeared in Philadelphia of which two numbers are known to have been published; a second German journal appeared in New York *Israels Herold* on March 30, 1849. It lasted until June 15, 1849 and was published by Isidor Busch. Another journal made its appearance in New York on October 26, 1849, Robert Lyon's *Asmonean*, and it lasted until 1858. Meanwhile, in July 1854 Wise began the publication of the *Israelite* in Cincinnati.

13. Max Lilienthal (1814–1882) came to the United States late in 1845. Isaac Mayer Wise (1819–1900) arrived on July 23, 1846. Isaac Mayer Wise, *Reminiscences* (Cincinnati, 1901), p. 13. *Occident*, Vol. 5 (1847), pp. 109–111; (1848), pp. 431–435, which is a printing of *Circular, To the Ministers and other Israelities . . . Albany, the Ninth day of Marcheshvan, 5609, A.M. 1848*. It is prefaced by ten pages of comment by Leeser and has the following note appended, "Dr. Wise has in the above responded to our request to give his views concerning the proposed meeting of Jewish ministers in the course of the ensuing spring."

14. *The Law of God. Edited and with Former Translations Diligently compared and Revised* (Philadelphia, 5605 [1845]). Five volumes with Hebrew and English on facing pages.

15. Solomon Grayzel, "The First American Jewish Publication Society," *Jewish Book Annual* (New York, 5795, 1944–1945), pp. 42–44. A more detailed study of this society is needed.

16. Bibliographical data are to be found in A. S. W. Rosenbach, *An American Jewish Bibliography* (Baltimore, 1926), pp. 155, 431, 443, 451–452. The work was done with Joseph Jaquett.

17. *Constitution and By-Laws of the Hebrew Education Society of Philadelphia. Adopted at a Town Meeting of Israelites on Sunday, Sivan 3, 5608 (June 4, 1848)* (Philadelphia, 5608 [1848]). *Fifty Years Work of the Hebrew Education Society of Philadelphia, 1848–1898* (Philadelphia, 1899).

18. *Occident*, Vol. 6 (1849), p. 473. M. A. Mitchell, A. Hart, Isaac Leeser, H. deBoer and Edward H. Weil to the congregation Mikveh Israel, Philadelphia, April 16, 1856, Mikveh Israel Archives. Hyman B. Grinstein, *The Rise of the Jewish Community of New York* (Philadelphia, 1945), p. 155.

19. Maxwell Whiteman, *Mankind and Medicine: A History of Philadelphia's Albert Einstein Medical Center* (Philadelphia, 1966), pp. 1–18.

20. See *Occident*, Vol. 5 (1847), p. 214, for Julius Stern and Keneseth Israel.

21. Timothy Flint, *Western Review*, Vol. 3 (May 1830), p. 579.
22. *Occident*, Vol. 3 (1845), p. 169.
23. *A Review of the Late Controversies between the Rev. Isaac Leeser and the Congregation Mikveh Israel* (Philadelphia, 1850); *A Review of "The Review" of the late Controversy between the Rev. Isaac Leeser and the Philadelphia Congregation "Mickve Israel" by an Israelite* (New York, 1850); *Deutsch-Amerikanische Skizzen für jüdische Auswanderer und Nichtauswanderer* (Leipzig, 1857), p. 74.
24. Joseph Schwartz, *A Descriptive Geography and Brief Historical Sketch of Palestine. Translated by Isaac Leeser* (Philadelphia, 5610 [1850]); *Occident*, Vol. 7 (1849), p. 379.
25. Frank Fox, "Quaker, Shaker, Rabbi: Warder Cresson, the Story of a Philadelphia Mystic," *Pennsylvania Magazine of History and Biography*, Vol. 95, No. 2 (Philadelphia, April 1971), pp. 147–194.
26. Maxine S. Seller, "Leeser on the Restoration of a Jewish Palestine," *American Jewish Historical Quarterly*, Vol. 58, No. 1 (September 1968), pp. 118–135; *Occident*, Vol. 7 (October 1849), pp. 344.
27. For a summary of Leeser's travels, see Jacob R. Marcus, *Memoirs of American Jews, 1775-1865*, Vol. 2 (Philadelphia, 1955), pp. 58–87.
28. *Occident*, Vol. 14 (1856), pp. 72–81, 353–355.
29. *Occident*, Vol. 16 (1859), pp. 541–542, and Vol. 17 (1859), pp. 218–219.
30. Beth El-Emeth was organized in 1857 and also was known as the Franklin Street Synagogue.
31. *Occident*, Vol. 25 (1867), pp. 324–325.
32. Whiteman, *Mankind and Medicine*, pp. 1–18.
33. See Bertram W. Korn, "The First American Jewish Theological Seminary: Maimonides College, 1867–1873," in *Eventful Years and Experiences* (Cincinnati, 1954), pp. 151–213, for the only detailed study of this college.

Chapter 3

1. Population estimates are from Edwin Wolf 2nd, "By the people and for the people," typescript history of the Federation of Jewish Charities, Philadelphia Jewish Archives Center (PJAC), p. 21.
2. Shubert Spero, "Orthodox Judaism," in Bernard Martin, ed., *Movements and Issues in American Judaism: An Analysis and Sourcebook of Developments Since 1945* (Westport, Conn., 1978), p. 84.
3. See for example Charles Liebman, "Orthodoxy in American Jewish Life," *American Jewish Year Book* 66 (1965), pp. 27–30. See also Zvi Halevy, "Were the Jewish Immigrants to the United States Representative of Russian Jews?" *International Migration* 16, (1978), pp. 66–73.
4. See Leon Jick, *the Americanization of the Synagogue, 1820–1870* (Hanover, N.H., 1976).
5. See Maxwell Whiteman, "The Eastern European Jew comes to Philadelphia," in *The Ethnic Experience in Pennsylvania*, John Bodnar, ed. (Lewisburg, Pa., 1973); and Moses Freeman, *Fuftzig yohr geshikhte fun yidishen leben in Philadelphia*, Vol. 1 (Philadelphia, 1929–34), pp. 24–35.
6. On immigrant neighborhoods, see Maxwell Whiteman, "Philadelphia's Jewish Neighborhoods," and Caroline Golab, "The Immigrant and the City: Poles, Italians, and Jews in Philadelphia, 1870–1920," both in *The Peoples of Philadelphia*, Allen F. Davis and Mark H. Haller, eds. (Philadelphia, 1973). See also Golab's *Immigrant Destinations* (Philadelphia, 1979). On the influence of Yiddishist schools on Talmud Torahs, see the Workmens Circle *Shul Almanakh* (New York, 1935); H. Sigal, "Fuftzen yor arbeter ring shul tetikeyt in Philadelphia, 1920–35," p. 103. See also *ATT Parent-Teachers Bulletin*, May 1940 (PJAC).
7. Survey materials of the Council on Jewish Education (ca. 1936) with ATT records. Survey for 1939 shows a larger number in 1939 attending one day a week (56% of enrollment in non-congregational schools; of the remainder, 63% were in five-day a week programs). Most in non-Reform congregational schools were in multi-day programs. "Report of the

Study Committee of the Philadelphia Council on Jewish Education," March 1940 (PJAC, United Hebrew Schools Collection).

8. *Geshikhte fun Yeshivas Mishkan Yisroel-Central Talmud Torah* (Philadelphia, 1934), p. 32. (Copies at PJAC and in the Levinthal Papers, American Jewish Archives, Cincinnati.)

9. For an appeal by Levinthal for the yeshivas and Central Talmud Torah, see *Jewish World (Yidishe velt)*, March 13, 1932, p. 1. On the Kosher chicken "tax," see *Jewish Exponent* August 5, 1932, particularly David J. Galter, "Shall we pay a tax on kosher chickens to aid the Talmud Torahs?"

10. See Norma Fain Pratt, "Transitions in Judaism: The Jewish American Woman Through the 1930's," *American Quarterly* 30 (Winter 1978), pp. 681–702. The Neziner synagogue formed a sisterhood in 1928, at about the same time a younger leadership took over the synagogue presidency. (Interviews with David Kraftsow, July 1982, and Sybil Richmond Margolis, August 1982.) In fraternal landsmanshaftn, many women's groups were also founded in the 1920s.

11. *Jewish Times* March 26, 1937, pp. 26, 33; April 2, 1937, p. 12.

12. Brief biographies of Levinthal are included in *Encyclopedia Judaica; Toldot Anshe Shem*, Vol. 1, Z. Rand, ed., (New York, 1950); and the festschrift presented to Levinthal, *Kavod Hahamim* (Philadelphia, 1934). A full biography of Levinthal would be of considerable interest. Work on this is difficult because his papers are divided between the American Jewish Archives in Cincinnati and the Philadelphia Jewish Archives Center. A paper by Lewis M. Barth, "The Bernard L. Levinthal Papers" (1962), describes without much analysis some of the Hebrew and English (but not the Yiddish) materials in Cincinnati. Besides obituaries, articles on Levinthal by his son, Israel, appeared in the *Jewish Exponent*, March 2, 1956; December 7, 1956; and March 15, 1957. See also Aaron Rothkoff, *Bernard Revel: Builder of American Orthodoxy* (Philadelphia, 1972), pp. 32–35, for a description of Levinthal's home.

13. Correspondence of Cyrus Adler to Louis Marshall, reprinted in Aaron Rakeffet-Rothkoff, "The Attempt to Merge the Jewish Theological Seminary and Yeshiva College, 1926–27," *Michael* 3 (1975).

14. Biography of Levinthal by Rabbi Moshe Shapiro of Atlantic City (one of his former students), in *Kavod Hahamim*, p. 77. The statement quoted was taught in the name of Rabbi Zvi Hirsh of Vilna, but it clearly was a significant part of Levinthal's own philosophy.

15. Correspondence with Treasury Department, October 24; November 10, 18, 1927 (Levinthal Papers, PJAC).

16. Levinthal to Sen. J. McGuffey on meeting with Secretary of State Cordell Hull, May 20, 1941 (Levinthal Papers, PJAC).

17. While one article in the *Jewish Times* (September 19, 1930, p. 78) referred to him as "Chief Rabbi of America," Levinthal never used such a title. He did serve as president of the Union of Orthodox Rabbis and was referred to by others as *Rav kollel d'Philadelphia* (chief rabbi of Philadelphia).

18. Russian War Relief, letters in PJAC collection and program for April 22, 1945 rally, J. Billikopf Papers, AJA, Cincinnati. Levinthal also spoke at the June 22, 1942 meeting.

19. On the American Jewish Congress elections, see *Jewish Times,* June 24, 1938 (pp. 4, 5, 9), and July 8, 1938 (p. 11).

20. Controversy and conflict have often been part of kashrut in North America. See H. Gastwirt, *Fraud, Corruption, and Holiness* (New York, 1974); "Kashruth and the Law in New York," *Michael* 3 (1975); Arthur Goren, *New York Jews and the Quest for Community: The Kehillah Experiment, 1908–1922* (New York, 1970), pp. 76–85; Stephen Speisman, *The Jews of Toronto: A History to 1937* (Toronto, 1979), pp. 276–292; and Moshe Stern, "Communal Problem Solving: The Winnipeg Vaad Hair, 1946" *Canadian Jewish Historical Society Journal* 4 (1980), pp. 4–24. On economic aspects of kashrut, see Stanley Shapiro, "Can the Kosher Butcher Remain Competitive in a Changing Market?" (M.B.A. thesis, University of Pennsylvania, 1958).

21. Legal deposition between Herman Sack and the Vadd Hakashruth Levinthal Papers, PJAC, June 16, 1939; and letter to Edward Culter, June 28, 1939. Cutler apparently operated a kosher shop in West Philadelphia and one "under investigation" as to kashrut in Elkins Park.

22. Circular "Oifruf" from the Vaad Hahashruth and Orthodox rabbis on need for kosher tags on all chickens (November 1935; copy in personal collection of Rabbi Sherman Novoseller).
23. Letter from Rabbi Levinthal to Station WRAX, January 7, 1931. Levinthal ordered meat packers not to deliver to the non-kosher Baranafsky store (Levinthal Papers, PJAC).
24. The Jewish Community of Philadelphia has not been studied. This kehillah published annual reports from 1912 to 1916; some records are at Dropsie University.
25. On the 1928 kehillah attempt, see David J. Galter, "550 Delegates Attempt to Form a Kehillah," *Jewish Exponent* March 2, 1928. See also "The Great Philadelphia Kehillah," *Jewish Times,* March 2, 1928; the editorial in the same issue of the *Times,* p. 6; and *Jewish World*'s editorial call for a democratic Vaad Hair to include kashrut control, March 18, 1928. Galter's article makes kashrut controversy a major reason for the kehillah's formation. Levinthal mentions "changes in the alignment of kosher slaughtering in this city" (Letter to Rev. S. Cherry, Consolidated Dressed Beef Co., November 1, 1928; on December 14, 1927 he wrote to the Wilson Meat Company, warning against "outsiders' inquiry . . . I cannot permit interference . . ." (Levinthal Papers, PJAC).
26. "The New Philadelphia Jewish kehilla is no longer a dream!" *Morgen Zhurnal,* August 4, 1933, p. 1; on Barishanski, *Morgen Zhurnal,* August 15, 1933, p. 1; on shochtim, August 24, 1933, p. 1 (all in Yiddish; Balch Institute for Ethnic Studies, Philadelphia). See also "Thirty Synagogues Unite Here for Kashrut Regulation," *Jewish Exponent,*August 25, 1933, p. 2.
27. On koshering Mt. Sinai Hospital kitchen, see *Jewish Exponent,* April 11, 1930, p. 12.
28. *Kavod Hahamim,* p. 82.

Chapter 4

1. Maxwell Whiteman, "Western Impact on East European Jews," in Randall M. Miller and Thomas D. Marzik, eds., *Immigrants and Religion in Urban America* (Philadelphia, 1977), pp. 117–137, provides the only account of the strikes of 1889–90.
2. Elden LaMar and J. B. S. Hardman, *The Clothing Workers in Philadelphia* (Philadelphia, 1940), pp. 68, 73, 85, 121.
3. See collection of broadside circulars in Yiddish, Italian, Latvian and Polish from 1915–1923; Urban Archives, Temple University.
4. A. Silver, ed., *Third Anniversary Historical Edition: Waist, Silk, Suit and Children's Dressmakers' Union, Local 15, ILGWU* [in Yiddish] (Philadelphia, 1918) is the only contemporary account of any of the unions in which Jews played a dominant role in Philadelphia and which recognized the position of women.
5. U. S. Congress, House, *Report of the Committee on Manufactures on the Sweating System,* 52nd Cong., 2d sess., 1893, H. Rept. 2309, XVII and 218.
6. Joseph Cohen, *The Jewish Anarchist Movement in the United States* (Philadelphia, 1945), p. 149 [in Yiddish].
7. I. M. Bodish, *Geshikhte fun di klot, het, kep un milineri arbeter* (New York, 1926), pp. 293–299, deals exclusively with the Philadelphia Jewish workers.
8. Silver, *Third Anniversary Historical Edition,* pp. 33–34.
9. LaMar and Hardman, *The Clothing Workers in Philadelphia,* pp. 50–51.
10. Henry J. Tobias, *The Jewish Bund in Russia: From its Origins to 1905* (Stanford, 1972), p. 241.
11. Silver, *Third Anniversary Historical Edition,* p. 39.
12. Silver, 40–43.
13. Silver, p. 42.
14. See *Jewish Exponent,* August 24, 1906, for an editorial, news report and statement of justification by Tutelman Brothers and Fagan.
15. *Jewish American,* September 4, 1908, for a retrospective account of the shirtmakers' struggle for bread and dignity.
16. See *Jewish American* and Silver, pp. 44–49.
17. Statistics on Italian workers are not available. However, by the mid-1930s they had their

own coatmakers' local, numbering 1912 members. The Yiddish-speaking coatmakers, Local 148, had a membership of 1010. The total number of coatmakers for 1939 was 6,774. Meetings were conducted in Italiam and Yiddish and calls for meeting prior to 1920 were bilingual. See LeMar and Hardman, p. 140.

18. Paul Avrich, *An American Anarchist: The Life of Voltairine de Cleyre* (Princeton, 1978), pp. 190–212, recounts the Broad Street riot, but additional details are given in *Public Ledger*, February 21, 1908. An differing account is given in Cohen, *The Jewish Anarchist Movement*, pp. 215–225.

19. *Public Ledger*, February 21, 1908.

20. See Elias Tcherikower, ed., *The Early Jewish Labor Movement in the United States* (New York, 1961), pp. 226, 265–77, for this and subsequent references to Weinberg.

21. *Public Ledger*, February 21, 1908.

22. For details on the early careers of Staller, Gordon and Prenner, see Maxwell Whiteman, *Mankind and Medicine, A History of Philadelphia's Albert Einstein Medical Center* (Philadelphia, 1966), p. 237; Benjamin L. Gordon, *Between Two Worlds* (New York, 1952), pp. 154–183; and Whiteman, "Western Impact on East European Jews," Miller and Marzik, pp. 117–137.

23. *Jewish American*, September 4, 1908.

24. Silver, pp. 49–51.

25. Silver, p. 52; Patrick Renshaw, "Rose of the World: The Pastor-Stokes Marriage and the American Left, 1905–1925," in *New York History* (Vol. 62, No. 4), October 1981, pp. 415–438, for the most recent account of Rose Pastor Stokes.

26. Silver, pp. 54–60.

27. Hyman Berman, "The Cloakmakers' Strike of 1910," in *Essays on Jewish Life and Thought* (New York, 1959), pp. 90–94.

Chapter 5

1. Edwin Wolf 2nd, and Maxwell Whiteman, *The History of the Jews of Philadelphia from Colonial Times to the Age of Jackson* (Philadelphia, 1975), pp. 130–131; Sidney M. Fish, *Aaron Levy of Aaronsburg* (New York, 1951), p. 78.

2. Other publishers of Yiddish almanacs included Emanuel & Son, 528 South Street; Seelig & Son, 722½ South Street; and J. H. Spielman, 44 North Seventh Street. For Magil, see I. L., Malamut, *Filadelfier idishe anshtaltn un zayer feerer* (Philadelphia, 1943), pp. 290-91.

3. Zalman Shneour, *Restless Spirit* (translated by M. Spiegel) (New York, 1963), p. 42.

4. Moses Freeman, *Fifty Years of Jewish Life in Philadelphia 1879–1929* (Philadelphia, 1929), pp. 128–135; Dov Ber Tirkel, "Bibliography of the Yiddish Press in Philadelphia," in *Pinkos* Vol. 1, No. 3 (New York, 1928), pp. 260–262 in Yiddish. *Geklibene shriftn fun Prof. G. Selikovitch* (New York, 1913), pp. 3–14.

5. Moses Freeman, *Fifty Years of Jewish Life in Philadelphia, Part II* (Philadelphia, 1934), pp. 250–265, gives an account of the early years of the *Yidishe velt*. See A. Frumkin and Hayyim Feinman, *M. Katz Zamelbukh* (Philadelphia, 1925); M. Katz, *Geklibene shriftn* (New York and Philadelphia, 1939); and Malamut, pp. 322–325, for brief sketches of Leaf and Ginzburg.

6. Malamut, pp. 326–27.

7. Gerald H. Wilk, "The Bohemian Who Wrote 'Hatikvah'," in *Commentary* (January 1951), pp. 48–60. The references to Imber's appearance in the *Jewish Exponent* are hitherto unnoted.

8. Ozer Smolenskin, *Geklibene lider* (Philadelphia, 1933).

9. J. S. Prenowitz, *Gedikhte* (Philadelphia, 1911); *Lider* (Philadelphia, 1921).

10. Louis Harap, *The Image of the Jew in American Literature* (Philadelphia, 1974), p. 450.

11. Henry Samuel Morais, *The Jews of Philadelphia* (Philadelphia, 1894), pp. 353–54.

12. Morais, pp. 219–20.

13. Naphtali Herz Imber, *Hakus. . . The Rubaiyat of Omar Khayyam* (New York, 1905), contains an introduction by Joseph Jacobs and a dedicatory poem in Hebrew and English by George A. Kohut in addition to Imber's dedication to Sulzberger.

14. See Jacob Zausmer, *Bayikvay Hador (Footprints of a Generation)* (Philadelphia, 1957), pp. 171–76, for S. L. Blank; *Who's Who in American Jewry* (New York, 1928), p. 498, for the Hebrew philologist Phineas Mordell and Moses Klein, *Migdal Zophim* (Philadelphia, 1889).

15. See S. L. Citron, *M'shumdim . . . tsvayter tile* (Warsaw, 1923), pp. 92–117, for a biographical account of Gershoni.

16. Max Green, *The Jewish Question and the Key to its Solution* (Philadelphia, 1909). A Yiddish edition appeared simultaneously.

17. Yehoash and Hayyim Spivack, *Idishe Verterbukh* (New York, 1911). A second edition appeared in 1926.

18. Joshua Bloch, of *Making Many Books* (Philadelphia, 1953), provides an excellent bibliographical record, although it does not concern itself with the history of the society.

19. Solomon J. Silberstein to Meyer Sulzberger, February 8, 1910; Abraham Cahan to Mayer Sulzberger, April 3, 10 and May 2, 1901, on the stationery of *The Commercial Advertiser.*

20. Leo Wiener to Henrietta Szold, September 16, 1898; January 4, 1899; Charles Scribner's Sons to Mayer Sulzberger, February 9, 1899; and Sulzberger to Scribner's, February 14, 1899.

21. Bernard Harris to Mayer Sulzberger, March 10, 1897, and Bernard Harris to Zvi H. Masliansky, March 2, 1897, in Yiddish.

22. Henrietta Zsold to Mayer Sulzberger, February 19, 20, March 12, 13, 1906.

23. Paul Avrich, *An American Anarchist. The Life of Voltairine de Cleyre* (Princeton, 1978), pp. 79, 94.

24. Emily Wayland Dinwiddie; *Application: The Board of Foreign Missions of the Presbyterian Church in the U.S.A.* (1917).

25. John Foster Carr, *Vegviizer fun di farainigtn staatn far dem idishn imigrant* (New York, 1912); English edition: *Guide to the United States for the Jewish Immigrant* (New York, 1913).

Chapter 6

1. B. M. Wood, *Who's Who in the Motion Picture World,* 1910, as quoted in M. J. McCosker, "Philadelphia and the Genesis of the Motion Picture," *The Pennsylvania Magazine of History and Biography,* October 1941, p. 418.

2. Robert Sklar, *Movie-Made America: A Cultural History of American Movies* (New York, 1975), p. 46.

3. Norman Zierold, *The Moguls* (New York, 1969), p. 254.

4. "Lubin: Movie King, Business Genius, Yet an Altruist," *The Philadelphia Ledger,* November 9, 1913.

5. Eugene Pharo, "Gave World Moving Pictures; Made and Lost Millions," *The Philadelphia Press,* May 6, 1917, p. 8.

6. Irving Howe, *World of Our Fathers* (New York, 1976), p. 77.

7. Handwritten family history notes of Emily Lubin Lowry, Lubin's daughter, Lubin Archive in the Theater Collection, Free Library of Philadelphia.

8. Pharo, "Gave World Moving Pictures," p. 8; Interview by the authors with Marguerite Sessler Goldsmith, October 6, 1980.

9. "Mark Dintenfass, Film Pioneer, Passes at 55," *Motion Picture Herald,* undated and unpaginated clipping provided by the Dintenfass family. Mark Dintenfass was actually 63 at the time of his death, November 23, 1933.

10. Zierold, *Moguls,* p. 223; George F. Worts, "As Clear As A Bell," *The World's Advance* (September 1915), p. 307.

11. Terry Ramsaye, *A Million and One Nights; A History of the Motion Picture Through 1925* New York, 1926), p. 270.

12. M. J. McCosker, "Philadelphia and the Genesis of the Motion Picture," *The Pennsylvania Magazine of History and Biography,* October 1941, pp. 401–02; For information on Lubin's song slides, see John W. Ripley, "Old Lantern Slides, the Song Plugger's Best Friends," *Hobbies; The Magazine for Collectors,* December 1969, pp. 98–99; Lubin's advertisements in *The New York Clipper,* 1897–1903.

13.	Pharo, "Gave World Moving Pictures," p. 8.

14.	McCosker, "Philadelphia Genesis," p. 415.

15.	McCosker, pp. 415–16; George Pratt, "Firsting the Firsts," *Image: The Quarterly Journal of the Eastman House,* December 1971.

16.	*The New York Clipper: The Oldest American Theatrical Journal,* was published in New York City by the Frank McQueen Publishing Company between 1853 and 1924 before being absorbed into *Variety.*

17.	*The Sears, Roebuck Catalogue,* No. 111 (Chicago, 1902), p. 170, states: "The slightly increased cost will . . . prevent incompetent persons from entering the field. . . ." It is safe to infer that this was a consideration that never entered Lubin's mind at this early stage of the business. He consistently priced his offerings lower than Edison or Edison representatives—like Sears—as a means of undermining the competition.

18.	Ramsaye, *Million,* p. 251.

19.	Ramsaye, p. 308.

20.	Ramsaye, pp. 269–80.

21.	Ramsaye, p. 272.

22.	Ramsaye, pp. 279–80.

23.	Arthur Hotaling, "Arthur Hotaling Recalls the 'Gold Old Days,'" *The Moving Picture World,* July 15, 1916, p. 380.

24.	Hotaling, p. 381.

25.	Lubin also advertised this package deal in *Billboard,* October 15, 1904. See Ramsaye, *Million,* p. 419.

26.	McCosker, "Philadelphia Genesis," p. 418.

27.	The authors are grateful for information about Lubin's theaters provided by Irvin R. Glazer, President of the International Theater Historical Society; Robert K. Headly, *Exit: A History of Movies in Baltimore* (Baltimore, 1974), pp. 92–93; Robert K. Headley, "The First Mini-Movie Complex?—Lubin's I, II, III," Marquee, Vol. 4, No. 1, 1972.

28.	"The Lubin Theater, Philadelphia," *The Moving Picture World,* January-June 1911, p. 185.

29.	May, *Screening,* p. 42; Zierold, *Moguls,* p. 328.

30.	Fred J. Balshofer and Arthur C. Miller, *One Reel a Week* Berkeley, 1967), pp. 4–9.

31.	Hotaling, "Recalls," *The Moving Picture World,* p. 380.

32.	Ramsaye, *Million,* pp. 286–89.

33.	Ramsaye, p. 381.

34.	Ramsaye, pp. 327–38.

35.	Balshofer and Miller, *One Reel,* pp. 5–9.

36.	Besides the weekly *Clipper* ads for these films, another source of Lubin film titles for these years is Kemp R. Niver, *Motion Pictures from the Library of Congress Paper Print Collection, 1894–1912* (Berkeley, 1967).

37.	Pharo, "Gave World Moving Pictures," p. 8. In this interview Lubin told Eugene Pharo: "We had a colored man who translated nearly all our titles and he was good."

38.	Balshofer and Miller, *One Reel,* pp. 9–10.

39.	Thomas Roy Smith, *Drexel Hill, 1875–1912* (privately printed, 1980), p. 33.

40.	Robert Conot, *A Streak of Luck: The Life and Legend of Thomas Alva Edison* (New York, 1979), p. 426.

41.	Kevin Brownlow and John Kobal, *Hollywood, the Pioneers* (New York, 1979), p. 54.

42.	Sklar, *Movie-Made America,* p. 46.

43.	Zierold, *The Moguls,* p. 321.

44.	Charles E. Nixon, "Lubin of Lubinville," *Movie Pictorial,* July 1915, p. 24.

45.	Pharo, "Gave World Moving Pictures," p. 8; Ramsaye, *Million,* p. 495; Zierold, *Moguls,* pp. 116–126.

46.	Letter to the authors from Charles Tarbox, October 29, 1981.

47.	Interviews by the authors with Thomas McMahon and James V. Riley, long-time residents of the 20th and Indiana neighborhood.

48.	" 'Movie King' Lubin, His workshop and an Actress," *The Philadelphia Evening Ledger,* November 9, 1914.

49.	"Lubin Manufacturing Co., Philadelphia, Pa. and Everywhere, Producers of Photoplays," *United Labor Journal,* August 31, 1915; "Welcome Back" address for Lubin written by H. A. D'Arcy, unidentified clipping in Lubin's 1915 scrapbook, Lubin Archive, Free Library of Philadelphia.

50. W. Stephen Bush, "A Day with Siegmund Lubin," *The Moving Picture World*, July 1, 1914, p. 210.
51. "S. Lubin, Philosopher," *The Moving Picture World*, March 1, 1913, p. 877.
52. Zierold, *The Moguls*, p. 358.
53. Many of the clippings in the Lubin scrapbooks from 1914 and 1915 concern the various duties and activities of Lubin's sons-in law.
54. Bush, "A Day," p. 209. The benevolent industrial patriarch was a Philadelphia tradition, other examples of which include John B. Stetson of the Stetson Hat Company, and Philip J. Baur and Herbert C. Morris of the Tasty Baking Company.
55. Zierold, *Moguls*, p. 272.
56. Unpaginated clipping from *The Moving Picture World*, January 20, 1912.
57. "Lubin Banquet," *The Moving Picture World*, February 1, 1913, p. 452.
58. Unpaginated clipping from *Motion Picture News*, September 25, 1915. Clipping provided by Marc Wanamaker of Bison Archives, Los Angeles.
59. Pharo, "Gave World Moving Pictures," p. 8.
60. "Seventy Five Years of Continuity and Change," supplement to the *Jewish Exponent*, March 12, 1976, p. 22.
61. Zierold, *Moguls*, p. 222.
62. "Great Progress in Educational Films the World Over," *New York Morning Telegraph*, February 18, 1912.
63. Unpaginated clippings of February and March 1912, in Lubin scrapbooks.
64. Fritz Stern, *Gold and Iron; Bismarck, Bleichröder, and the Building of the German Empire* (New York, 1977), pp. 479–81.
65. Charles E. Nixon, "Lubin of Lubinville," *Movie Pictorial*, July 1915, p. 7.
66. "Lubin Hall Presented," *Hartford Post*, June 9, 1915.
67. From a brief profile of Joseph Krauskopf which aired on KYW radio in 1982, produced by the Atwater Kent Museum to commemorate famous Philadelphians.
68. "Evelyn Nesbit at Lubin," *The Moving Picture World*, August 1915. The film was *Threads of Destiny.*
69. Krauskopf radio program, Atwater Kent Museum.
70. Interview by the authors with Emily Lowry Armstrong, granddaughter of Siegmund Lubin, November 17, 1981.
71. Unpaginated clipping in the 1913 Lubin scrapbook.
72. Pharo, "Gave World Moving Pictures," p. 8.
73. Betzwood was the subject of many articles in early motion picture trade journals. The articles quoted here are "S. Lubin Buys $100,000 Estate," *The Moving Picture World*, August 31, 1912; "Get Off at Lubin," *The Moving Picture World*, August–September 1913; "Betzwood the Great," The *Moving Picture World*, July 11, 1914; "Betzwood, the 500-Acre Studio," *The New York Dramatic Mirror*, March 18, 1914, pp. 28–29.
74. "Betzwood Film Company Buys Lubin's Betzwood Plant," *The Moving Picture World*, February 16, 1918.
75. Stern, *Gold and Iron*, pp. 171–74.
76. "S. Lubin Buys $100,000 Estate," p. 864.
77. "Film War Scene on Lubin Estate," *The Moving Picture World*, August 23, 1913, p. 825.
78. Pharo, "Gave World Moving Pictures," p. 8; Interviews by the authors with former Betzwood employee, John C. Comfort, 1979–81.
79. Bush, "A Day," p. 210; Pharo, "Gave World Moving Pictures," p. 8. By odd coincidence, the suggestion that Lubin's Indians were Jews finds a parallel years later at the Columbia studios where mogul Harry Cohn asserted, "the only Jews we put into pictures play Indians." The suggestion was finally rendered surreal when Mel Brooks appeared in *Blazing Saddles* as a Yiddish-speaking Indian chief.
80. Zierold, *Moguls*, p. 81.
81. Sklar, *Movie-Made America*, pp. 35–41; May, *Screening*, p. 61, pp. 209–10.
82. Stern, *Gold and Iron*, especially Chapter 17, "The Jew as Patriotic Parvenu."
83. Samuel Goldwyn, "The Best Advice I Ever Had," *Reader's Digest*, unpaginated clipping from the papers of Emily Lubin Lowry. Brownlow and Kobal, *Hollywood: The Pioneers,*

p. 56, relate this episode and attempt to explain Lubin's motive by suggesting that he was perhaps secretly duping a print of *The Squaw Man.* By 1914, however, Lubin had no reason to dupe anything, let alone a film which he had been given the exclusive contract to print.

84. Ramsaye, *Million,* p. 626.
85. Interviews by the authors with former Lubin laboratory technician Ida Hanneman Breuninger, October and November 1980. Mrs. Breuninger, who worked at both 20th and Indiana and Betzwood, recalls developing and printing being done for "lots of little companies that none of us recognized."
86. In January 1914, Lubin released a four-reel Civil War spectacular, *The Battle of Shiloh.* See "Film War Scene," p. 825. While D. W. Griffith had begun production of *Judith of Bethulia* early in 1913, Patents Company member Biograph was annoyed that he had gone beyond the limits they had set on his work and refused to release it until March 1914. See Sklar, *Movie-Made America,* pp. 56–57.
87. Ramsaye, *Million,* pp. 566–68.
88. "S. Lubin, Philosopher," p. 877.
89. Interview by the authors with Emily Lowry Armstrong, November 17, 1981.
90. Pharo, "Gave World Moving Pictures," p. 8; Terry Ramsaye, "A Gallant Figure Passes— Lewis J. Selznick," *Motion Picture Herald,* February 4, 1933, p. 12.

Chapter 7

1. Henry Samuel Morais, *The Jews of Philadelphia* (Philadelphia: The Levytype Company, 1894), pp. 207–208; Edwin Wolf 2nd, "1901–1918," in *75 Years of Continuity and Change* (Philadelphia: Federation of Jewish Agencies, 1976), p. 18.
2. Charles S. Bernheimer, ed., *The Russian Jew in the United States* (Philadelphia: John C. Winston, 1905), p. 80.
3. *Statistics of the Jews of the United States, Compiled under the authority of the Board of Delegates of American Israelites and The Union of American Hebrew Congregations* (Philadelphia: Union of American Hebrew Congregations, 1880), p. 15, stated the Jewish population of Philadelphia was "About 12,000;" Bertram W. Korn, "1655–1901," in *75 Years of Continuity and Change,* p. 14, "12,000 to 15,000 in 1875."
4. Morais, pp. 60–63. It is generally forgotten that the Gratzes came from Silesia in the Austrian part of dismembered Poland, and Hyam Salomon from the Prussian part.
5. *Fifty Years' Work of the Hebrew Education Society of Philadelphia* (Philadelphia, 1899), p. 21.
6. B'nai B'rith District Grand Lodge No. 3, *Hospital for Israelites in Philadelphia* (Philadelphia, 1864), small broadside in English and German, dated August 18, 1864.
7. *Dedication of the Jewish Hospital of Philadelphia* (Philadelphia: Jones & Thacher, 1867), pp. 3–5, 22–28.
8. Morais, pp. 112–113, 143; Korn, "1655–1901," p. 15.
9. *Constitution and By-Laws of the Society of the United Hebrew Charities of Philadelphia* (Philadelphia: Siddall Brothers, 1869), p. 5.
10. Morais, pp. 121–122; S. M. Fleischman, *The History of the Jewish Foster Home and Orphan Asylum of Philadelphia* (Philadelphia: Board of Managers, 1905), pp. 21–27.
11. William R. Langfeld, *The Young Men's Hebrew Association of Philadelphia: A Fifty-Year Chronicle* (Philadelphia: The Young Men's and Young Women's Hebrew Association, 1928), p. 8–9.
12. *Fifty Years' Work,* pp. 31–40.
13. E. Digby Baltzell, "The Social Defense of Caste," in *The Protestant Establishment* (New York: Random House, 1964), pp. 109–142.
14. Morais, pp. 53–58; Louis Ginsberg, *A. Hart, Philadelphia Publisher* (Petersburg, Va., 1972).
15. Morais, pp. 250–252.
16. *Income Tax of the Residents of Philadelphia and Bucks County for the Year Ending April 30, 1865* (Philadelphia, 1865), p. 5, actually the tax for 1864; *Income Tax of the Residents of Philadelphia Income of 1865 and 1866* (Philadelphia, 1867), pp. 14 and 59.

17. *Souvenir Journal of the Hebrew Charity Ball* (Philadelphia, 1899), pp. 155–157; Myer Solis-Cohen, *The American Descendants of Samuel Binswanger* (mimeographed monograph, 1957), pp. 19–20.
18. Morais, pp. 309–310.
19. Morais, pp. 245–246.
20. *Income Tax for 1865*, p. 5.
21. Morais, pp. 301–304; *Souvenir Journal*, pp. 51–53.
22. *Addresses Delivered in Memory of Mayer Sulzberger, Memorial Day, May 30, 1923* (Philadelphia, 1924), p. 26.
23. *Addresses*, p. 20.
24. Alexander Marx, "M. Sulzberger," in *Essays in Jewish Biography* (Philadelphia: Jewish Publication Society, 1947), pp. 223–228.
25. Abraham A. Neuman, "Cyrus Adler, A Biographical Sketch," in *The American Jewish Year Book 5701* (Philadelphia: Jewish Publication Society, 1940), pp. 23–144.
26. Neuman, p. 86.
27. Morais, pp. 273–276; *Souvenir Journal*, pp. 65–67.
28. Morais, pp. 331–333.
29. Maxwell Whiteman, "The Eastern European Jew Comes to Philadelphia," *Jewish Exponent*, March 31, 1972, pp. 24–25.
30. Morais, pp. 281–282.
31. *Fifty Years' Work*, p. 84; Maxwell Whiteman, "Philadelphia's Jewish Neighborhoods," in Allen F. Davis and Mark H. Haller, eds., *The Peoples of Philadelphia* (Philadelphia: Temple University Press, 1973), pp. 232–236.
32. *Fifty Years' Work*, pp. 84–86.
33. *Fifty Years' Work*, p. 89.
34. *Fifty Years' Work*, p. 95.
35. Bernheimer, *The Russian Jew*, pp. 52n and 43.
36. *The History of the Young Women's Union of Philadelphia, 1885–1910* (Philadelphia, 1910), p. 3.
37. *The History*, p. 3.
38. *The History*, p. 3.
39. *Souvenir Journal*, pp. 143–145, noted that Muhr "was of much assistance to this society [the Association of Jewish Immigrants] in its succor of the needy victims of Russian injustice and tyranny" (*History of the Young Women's Union*, p. 7).
40. *Fifty Years' Work*, pp. 99–104.
41. Morris U. Schappes, ed., *A Documentary History of the Jews in the United States 1654–1875* (New York: The Citadel Press, 1950), pp. 333–341.
42. *Fifty Years' Work*, pp. 104–107.
43. *Souvenir Journal*, pp. 161–162.
44. *History of the Young Women's Union*, p. 4.
45. Morais, pp. 267–68.
46. Morais, p. 114.
47. Morais, p.115.
48. *Constitution and By-Laws of the Society of the United Hebrew Charities of Philadelphia* (Philadelphia: Rudolph Stein, 1869), p. 5; Philadelphia Society for Organizing Charitable Relief and Repressing Mendicancy, *Manual for Visitors Among the Poor* (Philadelphia: J. B. Lippincott, 1879).
49. *Manual for Visitors*, pp. 131–133.
50. Bernheimer, pp. 84–85.
51. *Souvenir Program*, pp. 101–103. Levy wrote the chapter on Philadelphia philanthropy in Bernheimer's *The Russian Jew in the United States*.
52. Neuman, "Cyrus Adler," p. 73.
53. Stephen Birmingham, *"Our Crowd": The Great Jewish Families of New York* (New York: Harper & Row, 1967), p. 8.
54. Nathaniel Burt, *The Perennial Philadelphians: The Anatomy of an American Aristocracy* (Boston: Little, Brown, 1963), p. 43. Burt erroneously stated that in the mid-nineteenth century members of the Binswanger, Rosenbach, Polock, Solis-Cohen and Wolf families "knew and mingled with the Christian upper class on boards and institutions," but was

correct in continuing: "but they belonged to their own clubs, supported their own charities and lived in their own residential area on North Broad Street."

55. E. Digby Baltzell, *Philadelphia Gentlemen: The Making of a National Upper Class* (Glencoe, Ill.: The Free Press, 1958), pp. 273–287.
56. It is amusing that an old Philadelphian on the board of the Library Company always spoke of me as a "Hebrew," not wishing to seem to insult me by calling me "Jewish."
57. Zosa Szajkowski, "The Attitude of American Jews to East European Jewish Immigration (1881–1893), *Publications of the American Jewish Historical Society*, 40 (1951), p. 240.
58. *The Jewish Exponent*, September 9, 1887.
59. *Souvenir Journal*, p. 2ff.
60. *Souvenir Journal*, pp. 23–25.
61. *Souvenir Journal*, pp. 35–37; Morais, pp. 305–307.
62. *Souvenir Journal*, pp. 45–57.
63. *Souvenir Journal*, pp. 55–103.
64. Bernheimer, *The Russian Jew*, p. 55.
65. Morais, p. 133.
66. Wolf, "1901–1918," pp. 18–19.
67. Wolf, unpublished manuscript history of Federation, p. 6.
68. Wolf, "1901–1918," pp. 20–21.
69. Wolf, unpublished manuscript, p. 10.
70. Bernheimer, *The Russian Jew*, pp. 84–85.
71. Henry N. Wessel, *History of the Jewish Hospital Association of Philadelphia* (Philadelphia: Edward Stern, 1915), pp. 20–27. Mt. Sinai Hospital (now the Daroff branch of the Albert Einstein Medical Center) was founded by and for Russian Jews and Russian Jewish doctors in 1899 with Jacob Lit as president.
72. Henrietta Szold, "The Year 5660," in *The American Jewish Year Book 5661* (Philadelphia: Jewish Publication Society, 1900), p. 32.

Chapter 8

1. Annual Report, November 4, 1857, *Minute Books of the Female Hebrew Benevolent Society, 1845–1858*.
2. For a list of Philadelphia female-run societies, see Thomas J. Scharf and Thompson Westcott, *History of Philadelphia 1609–1885*, Vol. II (Philadelphia: L.H. Everts & Co.), pp. 1449–56.
3. Gerda Lerner, *The Female Experience* (Indianapolis: Bobbs-Merrill, 1977), pp. 191–92.
4. E. Digby Baltzell, *Philadelphia Gentlemen: The Making of a National Upper Class* (Glencoe, Ill.: Free Press, 1958), pp. 273–89.
5. For the general education of immigrant girls, see Stanley Brav, "The Jewish Woman, 1861–1865," *American Jewish Archives*, Vol. 17 (1965), p. 41; Rudolf Glanz, *The Jewish Woman in America: Two Female Immigrant Generations, 1820–1929* (New York: Ktav Publishing House and National Council of Jewish Women, 1976), Vol. 2, No. 62, p. 195; James Pyle Wickersham, *History of Education in Pennsylvania: Private and Public, Elementary and Higher—From the Time of the Swedes to the Present Day* (Lancaster, Pa.: Inquirer Publishing Company, 1886), p. 389; and Joseph R. Rosenbloom, *And She Had Compassion: The Life and Times of Rebecca Gratz* (Cincinnati: Hebrew Union College, 1957), pp. xiv–xv.
6. Baltzell, *Philadelphia Gentlemen*, p. 181.
7. Edwin Wolf 2nd and Maxwell Whiteman, *The History of the Jews of Philadelphia From Colonial Times to the Age of Jackson* (Philadelphia: Jewish Publication Society, 1975), p. 271.
8. For a description of the philanthropic activities of Gratz's nieces and sister-in-law and their own accounts of the life of Rebecca Gratz, see Henry Samuel Morais, *The Jews of Philadelphia: Their History from the Earliest Settlements to the Present Time* (Philadelphia: Levytype Co., 1894), p. 151; Rosa Mordecai, *Hebrew Watchword and Instructor* (February, March, April 1897); Miriam Gratz Mordecai, "Rebecca Gratz," *The Hebrew*

Sunday School Society of Philadelphia, 1838–1913, Celebration of the Seventy-Fifth Anniversary, Philadelphia Jewish Archives Center (Philadelphia, 1913); and Joshua Block, "Rosa Mordecai's Recollection of the¨st Hebrew Sunday School," *Publications of the Jewish Historical Society*, Vol. 42 (1953), pp. 397–406.

9. *The Constitution of the Female Hebrew Benevolent Society of Philadelphia* (Philadelphia: Lydia R. Bailey, 1836).

10. *Constitution of the Female Hebrew Benevolent Society.*

11. Rosenbloom, *Rebecca Gratz*, pp. 205–6.

12. See Mary P. Ryan, *Womanhood in America: From Colonial Times to the Present* (New York: Franklin Watts, 1975), p. 107; Lerner, pp. 191–200.

13. *Annual Report of the Female Hebrew Benevolent Society*, 1848.

14. *Constitution of the Female Hebrew Benevolent Society.*

15. Rosenbloom, *Rebecca Gratz*, p. 243. For accounts of the school, see Rosenbloom, *Rebecca Gratz*, pp. 222–279; Sidney Fish, "The Hebrew Sunday School Society of Philadelphia: Five Generations of Pioneering in Communal Service," Address on the Seventy-Fifth Anniversary, Philadelphia Jewish Archives Center; Abraham S. Wolf Rosenbach, "The History of the Society," Anniversary Materials of the Hebrew Sunday School Society, PJAC; Solomon Solis-Cohen, "The Hebrew Sunday School Society," *Judaism and Science with other Addresses and Papers* (Philadelphia: privately printed, 1940).

16. Rosenbloom, *Rebecca Gratz*, pp. 246–8.

17. Fish claims the school was partial to the needs of girls.

18. February, 23, Philipson, 275. Though the letter is not dated as to year, internal evidence places in in 1840.

19. *First Minute Book of the Hebrew Sunday School Society*, 1838.

20. Rosenbloom, *Rebecca Gratz*, p. 245.

21. See *Watchword*, December 1896, pp. 3–5; and Morais, *The Jews of Philadelphia*, pp. 150–51.

22. *Jewish Exponent*, March 7, 1913, p. 1; Harold Jeffrey Kravits, "Developments in the History of the Hebrew Sunday School Society," Philadelphia Jewish Archives Center (unpublished manuscript).

23. Joseph R. Rosenbloom, "Rebecca Gratz and the Jewish Sunday School Movement in Philadelphia," *Publications of the American Jewish Historical Society*, 48 (December 1958), p. 77.

24. Sim'ha Peixotto to the Board of Managers of the Hebrew Sunday School Society, October 8, 1885, Philadelphia Jewish Archives Center. She retired the following year.

25. Maxwell Whiteman, *Scrapbook of Newspaper Cuttings* (London: Marcus Ward, n.d.).

26. Rosenbloom, *Rebecca Gratz*, p. 249.

27. *Annual Report of the Female Hebrew Benevolent Society*, 1848.

28. *The Occident and American Jewish Advocate*, Vol. 8 (1850), pp. 1–2.

29. For a complete history of the Home, see S. M. Fleishman, *The History of the Jewish Foster Home and Orphan Asylum, 1855–1905.*

30. *Constitution and Bylaws of the Jewish Foster Home* (Philadelphia, 1856).

31. Morais, *The Jews of Philadelphia*, p. 156.

32. Jacob Rader Marcus, *The American Jewish Woman: A Documentary History* (New York: Ktav, 1981), p. 87.

33. *Constitution and Bylaws of the Jewish Foster Home.*

34. Fleishman, *The History of the Jewish Foster Home*, pp. 93–99.

35. *Charter and Constitution and Bylaws of the Jewish Foster Home* (Philadelphia, 1866).

36. *Annual Report of the Female Hebrew Benevolent Society, 1862*, in *The Occident* (December 1862), p. 413.

37. *The Second Minute Book of the Hebrew Sunday School Society*, Philadelphia Jewish Archives Center.

38. See *The Occident* (June 1863, p. 143) for both meetings. For a description of the work of the women, see Bertram Wallace Korn, *American Jewry and the Civil War* (Philadelphia: Jewish Publication Society, 1951), pp. 100–01; and Brav, p. 57. See Morais, *The Jews of Philadelphia*, pp. 254–55 for Matilda Cohen's Biography.

39. *Philadelphia Public Ledger*, June 26, 1863.

40. Korn, *American Jewry and the Civil War*, p. 101.

41. Korn, *American Jewry and the Civil War,* p. 103.
42. *Memorial of the Great Central Fair Held at Philadelphia,* June 1864 (Philadelphia: United States Sanitary Commission, 1864).
43. For a history of the Association, see Maxwell Whiteman, *Mankind and Medicine: A History of Philadelphia's Albert Einstein Medical Center* (Philadelphia, 1966).
44. Morais, *The Jews of Philadelphia,* p. 113.
45. *Annual Report of the Jewish Hospital Association,* January 7, 1866 (Philadelphia: Archives of the Albert Einstein Medical Center, 1866).
46. *Annual Report of the United Hebrew Charities,* Philadelphia Jewish Archives Center, 1872.
47. *Annual Report of the United Hebrew Charities,* 1870.
48. Fleishman, *The History of the Jewish Foster Home,* p. 23.
49. Fleishman, *The History of the Jewish Foster Home,* pp. 22–23; and *Constitution and Bylaws of the Jewish Foster Home and Orphan Asylum* (Philadelphia, 1874), Philadelphia Jewish Archives Center.
50. See Ira Harkavy, "Reference Group Theory and Group Conflict in Advanced Capitalist Societies: Presbyterians, Workers, and Jews in Philadelphia, 1790–1968" (unpublished Ph.D. dissertation, University of Pennsylvania, 1979), p. 489.
51. Kravits, p. 11.
52. *Directory of the Charitable, Social Improvement Educational and Religious Associations and Churches of Philadelphia* (Philadelphia, 1903), pp. 347–352.
53. Emilie S. Van Beil, "Report of the Rebecca Gratz Sewing School, 1876," *Second Minute Book,* Hebrew Sunday School Society, Philadelphia Jewish Archives Center.
54. Van Beil, "Report of the Rebecca Gratz Sewing School."
55. Ruth Braude Sarner, *The Hebrew Sunday School Society of Philadelphia: Perspective and Promise* (Philadelphia, 1964), p. 6.
56. *Jewish Record,* September 20, 1883, p. 1.
57. S. Belle Cohen, "A History of the Jewish Maternity Hospital," *Fortieth Annual Report of the Jewish Maternity Association* (Philadelphia, 1914), p. 30.
58. Original Charter, Philadelphia Jewish Archives Center.
59. *Annual Report of Jewish Maternity Association* (Philadelphia, 1900).
60. *Constitution and Bylaws* (Philadelphia, 1891), Philadelphia Jewish Archives Center.
61. *Constitution and Bylaws* (Philadelphia, 1893).
62. *Constitution and Bylaws* (Philadelphia, 1892).
63. *Constitution and Bylaws* (Philadelphia, 1892). The quotations and philosophy are embodied in president Amram's report, significantly entitled "The Influence of the Home."
64. See Introduction to Robert Morris and Michael Freund, *Trends and Issues in Jewish Social Welfare, Seen through the Proceedings and Reports of the National Conference of Jewish Communal Service* (Philadelphia: Jewish Publication Society, 1966).
65. *Jewish Exponent,* September 2, 1883, p. 4.
66. *Minute Books* for February and March 1882, give detailed accounts of preparations (Philadelphia Jewish Archives Center). See also David Sulzberger, "The Beginnings of Russo-Jewish Immigration to Philadelphia," *Publications of the American Jewish Historical Society* (1910), pp. 125–150.
67. *Minute Books of the United Hebrew Charities,* May 8, 1890, Philadelphia Jewish Archives Center.
68. Gertrude Berg, Rosena Fels, Leah Abeles, et al., *The History of the Young Women's Union* (Philadelphia, 1911), pp. 3–4.
69. Evelyn Bomeisler, "Work of the Jewish Women of Philadelphia," *Jewish Exponent,* September 8, 1893, pp. 1–4.
70. Berg, Fels, Abeles, et al., *History of the Young Women's Union,* p. 6.
71. Berg, Fels, Abeles, et al., *A History of the Young Women's Union,* p. 7.
72. *Annual Report, Young Women's Union,* 1896, Philadelphia Jewish Archives Center.
73. *Jewish Exponent,* January 4, 1898, p. 7.
74. Berg, Fels, Abeles, et al., *History of the Young Women's Union,* p. 6.
75. "Constitution and Bylaws of the Young Women's Union," *Annual Report, 1906* Philadelphia Jewish Archives Center.
76. *Jewish Record,* November 13, 1885.

77. *Jewish Record*, November 13, 1885.
78. *Jewish Record*, July 10, 1887, p. 7.
79. Mary Cohen, *The Balance of Power Between Industrial and Intellectual Work* (Philadelphia: Philadelphia Social Science Association, 1886).
80. *Jewish Record*, November 2, 1883; Nina Morais, "The Limitations of Sex," *North American Review*, Vol. 132 (1881), pp. 78–95. According to Guidetta's sister, Elinor Solis-Cohen, their father felt it improper for a woman to sign her name. (Interview with Elinor and Bertha Solis-Cohen, July 17, 1981.)
81. *Jewish Exponent*, April 30, 1887, p. 7.
82. *Jewish Exponent*, August 4, 1899, p. 5.
83. *Jewish Exponent*, April 2, 1897, p. 2.
84. Interview with the Solis-Cohens, July 17, 1981.
85. Marcus, *The American Jewish Woman, 1654–1980*, p. 89.
86. *Jewish Exponent*, November 29, 1895, p. 7.
87. Although there is no concrete evidence that the Council was so engaged in its early years, by 1911 it had an Immigrant Aid Committee working with the United Hebrew Charities and the Immigrant Aid Society to save "victims of the 'White Slave Traffic.'" See "Report of the Philadelphia Section," *National Council of Jewish Women: Sixth Triennial Convention, Philadelphia, Pennsylvania, December 11–19, 1911* (Philadelphia, 1911), p. 562; and Charlotte Baum, Paula Hyman, Sonya Michel, *The Jewish Woman in America* (New York: Dial Press, 1976), pp. 170–176.
88. *Proceedings of the First Convention of the National Council of Jewish Women: Held at New York, November 15–19, 1896* (Philadelphia: Jewish Publication Society, 1897).
89. Mordecai mentioned that most of the members were married women, *Proceedings of the First Convention of the National Council of Jewish Women*. For an account of the first meeting, see *Jewish Exponent* October 18, 1895, p. 6.
90. *Jewish Exponent*, June 3, 1895, p. 6; *Jewish Exponent*, September 15, 1895, p. 4; *Jewish Exponent* October 2, 1895, p. 6; and *Jewish Exponent*, January 24, 1896, p. 6.
91. Marcus, *The American Jewish Woman*, 1654–1980, pp. 32–33.
92. See Evelyn Bodek, "Salonieres and Bluestockings: Educated Obsolescence and Germinating Feminism," *Feminist Studies* (Spring-Summer 1976), Vol. 3, pp. 185–199.
93. Will R. Langfeld, *The Y.M.H.A. of Philadelphia: A Fifty-Year Chronicle* (Philadelphia, 1928), pp. 15, 31, 41–42; and *Jewish Exponent*, June 10, 1895, p. 4.
94. *Papers of Congress*, 1897, Vol. 226, p. 43.
95. *The American Jewess* became the official organ of the Council in 1895.
96. *Papers of Congress*, 1897, pp. 134–35.
97. See Glantz, Vol. I, for a history of the Russian immigrant's experience.
98. See *Seventy-Five Years of Continuity and Change* for a brief history of the Federation.
99. See Rela Geffen Monson, *Bringing Women In: A Survey of the Evolving Role of Women in Jewish Organizational Life in Philadelphia* (Philadelphia: American Jewish Committee, 1977); and "Status Report of the Combined Women's Long-Range Planning Committee" (Philadelphia: Federation of Jewish Agencies, 1981).

Chapter 9

1. Louis Edward Levy (1846–1919) has been the subject of limited study in Jewish history. For a brief introduction to his scientific work, see Louis Edward Levy, *Recollections of Forty Years: A Photoengraving Retrospect* (Atlantic City, 1912). The personal correspondence and the bulk of the records of the Association for the Protection of Jewish Immigrants are in the possession of the author. Subsequent references to Levy are based on this material.
2. Sabato Morais (1823–1897) also has been the subject of fleeting attention. His *Dictionary of American Biography* entry (New York, 1934), prepared by Cyrus Adler, contains the principal sources which are commemorative memoirs and necrologies. See also Moshe Davis, "Sabato Morais: A Selected and Annotated Bibliography of His Writings" in *Publications of the American Jewish Historical Society* (New York, 1947), Vol. 37, pp. 55–93.

3. Mayer Sulzberger (1843–1923) is unquestionably the most neglected of the Philadelphians, although the customary tributes at the time of his death are extensive. See *Dictionary of American Biography* (New York, 1936), Vol. 18, pp. 205–206; Moshe Davis, *The Emergence of Conservative Judaism* (Philadelphia, 1963); Meir Ben-Horin, "Solomon Schechter to Judge Mayer Sulzberger," in *Jewish Social Studies* (October 1963), Vol. 25, pp. 249–286; Louis Marshall, "Mayer Sulzberger," in *The American Jewish Yearbook,* 5685 (Philadelphia, 1924), pp. 373–403.

4. Cyrus Adler (1863–1940) is well established in the literature of American Jewish history. See A. A. Neuman in *Dictionary of American Biography Supplement Two* (New York, 1958) and A. A. Neuman, *Cyrus Adler* (New York, 1942).

5. Solomon Solis Cohen (1857–1948), physician, poet and communal leader, was a prolific writer on a variety of subjects. See Edward D. Coleman, *Bibliography of the Writings and Addresses of Solomon Solis-Cohen* (Phildelphia, 1940); Solomon Solis-Cohen, "How a National Organization was Formed," *Jewish Exponent,* May 27, 1892; Solomon Solis-Cohen, "Tuberculosis: A Social Question," *Saturday Evening Post* (April, 1907); Solomon Solis-Cohen in *The Jewish Exponent,* (October 22, 1897 and December 24, 1897); and Solomon Solis-Cohen, "The Philadelphia Group," *Judaism and Science with Other Addresses and Papers* (Philadelphia, 1940), pp. 246–252.

6. See John F. Sutherland, "Rabbi Joseph Krauskopf of Philadelphia: The Urban Reformer Returns to the Land," in *American Jewish Historical Quarterly* (New York, June 1978), Vol. 67, pp. 345–362; and Abraham J. Feldman, "Rabbi Joseph Krauskopf: A Biographical Sketch," in *The American Jewish Yearbook, 5685* (Philadelphia, 1924), pp. 420–447.

7. See Cyrus Adler, *Lectures, Selected Papers, Addresses* (Philadelphia, 1933), pp. 43–64, for the most extensive biographical account of Dropsie.

8. See Barry E. Supple, "A Business Elite: German Jewish Financiers in Nineteenth-Century New York," in *The Business History Review* (Cambridge, Mass., 1957), Vol. 21, pp. 143–178.

9. For an accurate work which treats Jews as Jews and not names, see Maxwell Whiteman, *Gentlemen in Crisis: The First Century of the Union League of Philadelphia* (Philadelphia, 1975).

10. See Morais, pp. 361, 362 and 316–318, for a discussion of the Cohen sisters.

11. See *Pinkos* (New York, 1928), pp. 285–288 [in Yiddish]; Marjorie Hornbein, "Dr. Charles Spivak: Physician, Social Worker, Yiddish Author," in *Western States Jewish Historical Quarterly* (Los Angeles, 1979), Vol. 11, pp. 195–211; and "Eagleville Sanatorium for Consumptives," in *Twenty-Fifth Anniversary of the Jewish Exponent* (Philadelphia, 1912), pp. 46–47, for the involvement of the B'rith Sholom.

12. Abraham Cahan, *Bleter fun main leben II* (New York, 1926), p. 66; Leon Kobrin, *Meine fuftzik yor in Amerika* (Buenos Aires, 1955), pp. 36–46. Phineas (Pinhas ben Bezalel) Mordell made his living as a Hebrew teacher and was the author of *Sefer Yetzirah* (Philadelphia, 1895), and other works. Moses Weinberger became rabbi of Congregation Emunath Israel, the Hungarian synagogue at Fifth and Gaskell Streets, in 1892 and was the author of a number of works in Hebrew, the most important being *Ha-Yehudim veha Yahadut be Nu York* (New York, 1887). For an account of some of Bernard Levinthal's activities, see Aaron Rothkoff, *Bernard Revel, Builder of American Orthodoxy* (Philadelphia, 1972), p. 35.

13. Mark Wischnitzer, *Visas to Freedom: The History of Hias* (Cleveland, 1956), p. 38.

14. *The Annual Reports of the Association for the Protection of Jewish Immigrants* from 1885 to 1919 reveal both the local and national activity of the Association.

15. Maxwell Whiteman, "Western Impact on East European Jews: A Philadelphia Fragment," *Immigrants and Religion in Urban America,* Randall M. Miller and Thomas D. Marzik, eds. (Philadelphia, 1977), pp. 117–137.

16. Davis, *The Emergence of Conservative Judaism,* p. 15.

17. *Chronicle of the Union League of Philadelphia, 1862–1902* (Philadelphia, 1902).

18. Ephraim Deinard, *Or Mayer* (New York, 1896) [In Hebrew]; and Max Radin, "The Sulzberger Collection of Soncino Books in the Library of the Jewish Theological Seminary," in *Bibliographical Society of America Papers* (Princeton, 1912), Vol. 7, pp. 70–89.

19. Naomi W. Cohen, *Not Free to Desist: The American Jewish Committee, 1906–1966* (Philadelphia, 1972), pp. 25–27; 97–98.

20. Rudolf and Clara M. Kirk, "Abraham Cahan and William Dean Howells," in *American Jewish Historical Quarterly*, Vol. 52 (New York, 1962), pp. 27–43.
21. Sulzberger correspondence (Whiteman collection).
22. Governor's correspondence with Mayer Sulzberger, 1890–1905 (Pennsylvania State Archives, Harrisburg).
23. Davis, *The Emergence of Conservative Judaism*, p. 250.
24. Jacob H. Schiff to Mayer Sulzberger, June 16, 1898.
25. See Dropsie, *On Deform in Judaism and on the Study of Hebrew* (Philadelphia, 1895).
26. See Michael Davitt, *Within the Pale: The True Story of Anti-Semitic Persecution in Russia* (Philadelphia, 1903); and Cyrus Adler, *The Voice of America on Kishineff* (Philadelphia, 1904).
27. Cyrus Adler to Mayer Sulzberger, June 2, 1903 (Whiteman collection).
28. Cyrus Adler to Mayer Sulzberger, November 1903 (Whiteman collection).
29. Two major collections of Sulzberger correspondence—one in the hands of Maxwell Whiteman, acquired through the kindness of Solomon Sulzberger Brav, M.D., and the late Abram S. Berg, grandnephews of Sulzberger, and the other at the Dropsie University where it remains uncatalogued—form a remarkable corpus of correspondence which, if published, will revise completely our blurred image of this milieu.
30. Unfortunately, Adler's biographical data is still dependent on the work of A. A. Neuman. Further study of Adler, like Sulzberger, is dependent on the publication of his correspondence.
31. William H. Taft to Mayer Sulzberger, Washington, D.C., April 13, 1909 (Courtesy of Berthold W. Levy, Esq.).
32. Oscar S. Straus, *Under Four Administrations: From Cleveland to Taft* (Boston, 1922), pp. 263–273, which gives a somewhat different account of his reappointment. Julian Mack to Mayer Sulzberger, December 27, 1909 (Whiteman collection).
33. Oscar S. Straus to Mayer Sulzberger, Constantinople, April 29, 1910; and Jacob H. Schiff to Mayer Sulzberger, December 29, 1910 (Whiteman collection).
34. Jacob H. Schiff to Mayer Sulzberger, December 23, 1910 (Whiteman collection).
35. Julian Mack to Mayer Sulzberger, December 20, 1910 (Whiteman collection).
36. Judah L. Magnes to Herbert Friedenwald with marginal notes of H. F. to Mayer Sulzberger, November 11, 1908 (Whiteman collection).
37. Daniel Guggenheim to Mayer Sulzberger, November 25, 1908 (Whiteman collection).
38. *The Year Book of the Pegasus, Number One* (Philadelphia, 1895).
39. Coleman, *Bibliography of the Writings and Addresses of Solomon Solis-Cohen*.
40. Sutherland, "Rabbi Joseph Krauskopf of Philadelphia."
41. Maxwell Whiteman, "Western Impact on East European Jews," in *Immigrants and Religion in Urban America*, R. M. Miller and T. D. Marzik, eds. (Philadelphia, 1977), pp. 117–137.
42. See *Thirty-Fifth Annual Report of the National Farm School* (Philadelphia, 1932) for a retrospective view of the school.
43. Solis-Cohen, "The Philadelphia Group."
44. Cyrus Adler, *Memorandum on the Western Wall* (Philadelphia, 1930).
45. Mayer Sulzberger to Israel Zangwill, October 2, 1895 (Whiteman collection).

Chapter 10

1. Edwin Wolf 2d and Maxwell Whiteman, *The History of the Jews of Philadelphia from Colonial Times to the Age of Jackson* (Philadelphia, 1957), p. 227.
2. Henry Samuel Morais, *The Jews of Philadelphia* (Philadelphia, 1894), p. 84.
3. Joseph L. Blau and Salo W. Baron, *The Jews of the United States, 1790–1840: A Documentary History*, Vol. 2 (Philadelphia, 1963), p. 578; and *The Universal Jewish Encyclopedia*, Vol. 6 (New York, 1939–1943), p. 588.
4. Edward Davis, *The History of Rodeph Shalom Congregation, Philadelphia, 1802–1924* (privately printed), p. 59; also data supplied to the author by Maxwell Whiteman.
5. See William Filby, ed., with Mary K. Meyer, *Passenger and Immigration Lists Index* (Detroit, 1981).

6. Leeser obviously had not met the Reverend Herman Kahn since he printed the name as Cohen. Kahn was elected to Rodeph Shalom in May 1847. See Davis, *The History of Rodeph Shalom*, p. 59.

7. In Baltimore, New York, and Philadelphia, Reform began with an organization of younger men calling themselves "Reform Gesellschaft" (Reform Society). For a description of these organizations, see David Philipson, *The Reform Movement in Judaism* (New York, 1931), p. 335.

8. See Howard W. Fineshriber, *Reform Congregation Keneseth Israel: Its First 100 years, 1847–1947* (privately printed), p. 11.

9. *Occident*, June 1851, p. 224.

10. *Occident*, October 1853; and Davis, *The History of Rodeph Shalom*, p. 72.

11. Fineshriber, *Reform Congregation Keneseth Israel*, p. 10.

12. Davis, *The History of Rodeph Shalom*, p. 70f.

13. Fineshriber, *Reform Congregation Keneseth Israel*, p. 10.

14. Morris U. Schappes, *A Documentary History of the Jews in the United States, 1654–1875* (New York, 1950), p. 444.

15. *Sinai*. Published in Baltimore, February 1856 through May 1861; in Philadelphia, June 1861 to January 1863.

16. For a review of Einhorn's career, see Kaufmann Kohler, *Yearbook of the Central Conference of American Rabbis, 1909*, p. 215; and James G. Heller, *Isaac M. Wise: His Life, Work, and Thought* (New York, 1965), p. 476.

17. *The Jewish Encyclopedia*, Vol. 7 (New York, 1901–1906), p. 77.

18. Bertram Wallace Korn, *Eventful Years and Experiences* (Cincinnati, 1954), Chapter 7.

19. Davis, *The History of Rodeph Shalom*, p. 88.

20. Davis, *The History of Rodeph Shalom*, Chapter 5.

21. Philipson, *The Reform Movement in Judaism*, p. 354; and *Yearbook of the Central Conference of American Rabbis*, 1890, p. 117ff.

22. Heller, *Isaac M. Wise*, p. 394.

23. Hirsch died on May 13, 1889. See *The Jewish Exponent*, May 24, 1889.

24. Philipson, *The Reform Movement in Judaism*, p. 355; and Heller, *Isaac M. Wise*, p. 462. For a description of Krauskopf's role in the Pittsburgh Conference, see Frank J. Adler, *Roots in a Moving Stream: The Centennial History of Congregation B'nai Jehudah of Kansas City, 1870–1970* (Kansas City, 1972), p. 72, and *Proceedings of the Pittsburg (sic) Rabbinical Conference*, November 16–18, 1885.

25. Fineshriber, *Reform Congregation Keneseth Israel*, p. 20.

26. Martin P. Beifield, Jr., "Joseph Krauskopf, 1887–1903" (Cincinnati, unpublished rabbinic dissertation, 1975), Chapter 6.

27. Fineshriber, *Reform Congregation Keneseth Israel*, p. 22.

28. Personal interview with the late Sybil Feineman (Mrs. Joseph) Krauskopf; and Frank J. Adler, *Roots in a Moving Stream*, p. 77.

29. Fineshriber, *Reform Congregation Keneseth Israel*, p. 23.

30. Harlan B. Phillips, "A War on Philadelphia's Slums; Walter Vrooman and the Conference of Moral Workers, 1893," *The Pennsylvania Magazine of History and Biography*, Vol. 76, No. 1 (January 1952), p. 61.

31. Beifield, *Joseph Krauskopf*, Chapter 5.

32. William W. Blood, *Apostle of Reason: A Biography of Joseph Krauskopf* (Philadelphia, 1973), Part 7; and Beifield, *Joseph Krauskopf*, Chapter 7.

33. Fineshriber, *Reform Congregation Keneseth Israel*, p. 24.

34. Abraham J. Feldman, "Rabbi Joseph Krauskopf: A Biographical Sketch," *American Jewish Yearbook*, 5685 (1924–1925), p. 439.

35. See his President's Messages, *Yearbook of the Central Conference of American Rabbis*, 1904, p. 118, and 1905, p. 175.

36. *Keneseth Israel Yearbooks* (copies in Keneseth Israel Archives).

37. Joseph Krauskopf, *Sunday Lectures*, 1897–1898, No. 9; 1904–1905, No. 6; and 1916–1917, No. 24.

38. Personal interview with Madeleine Krauskopf (Mrs. Julian) Hillman.

39. *The Philadelphia Inquirer*, June 13, 1923, p. 2; *Public Ledger*, June 13, 1923, p. 3; and *The Philadelphia Record*, June 13, 1923, p. 8.

40.   Max E. Berkowitz, *The Beloved Rabbi: An Account of the Life and Works of Henry Berkowitz, D.D.* (New York, 1932), p. 22.
41.   Berkowitz was a native of Pittsburgh, born March 18, 1857. See Berkowitz, *The Beloved Rabbi*, p. 2.
42.   Davis, *The History of Rodeph Shalom*, p. 105; Berkowitz, *The Beloved Rabbi*, p. 38.
43.   J. Jacques Stone, "The 70 Years" (Presidential address on the seventieth anniversary of the Society), *American Judaism*, Summer 1963, p. 15.
44.   Berkowitz, *The Beloved Rabbi*.
45.   *Yearbook of the Central Conference of American Rabbis*, 1899, p. 173.
46.   Berkowitz, *The Beloved Rabbi*.
47.   Davis, *The History of Rodeph Shalom*, p. 115; and *Yearbook of the Central Conference of American Rabbis*, 1972, p. 169.
48.   The author's mother, Etta Berkowitz Stern, a long-time teacher in Rodeph Shalom's religious school, was asked by Fineshriber to create the suburban school. For further discussion of the creation of Temple Judea, see the author's memorial tribute to Rabbi Sidney E. Unger, Temple Judea's first rabbi, *Yearbook of the Central Conference of American Rabbis*, 1972, p. 178.
49.   "Wolsey, Louis," *The Universal Jewish Encyclopedia*, Vol. 12, p. 564; and *Yearbook of the Central Conference of American Rabbis*, 1928, p. 17.
50.   Jeanette W. Rosenbaum, "Rodeph Shalom: Philadelphia, 1800–1950," *Liberal Judaism*, September 1950.
51.   "Wolsey, Louis," *The Universal Jewish Encyclopedia*, Vol. 12, p. 564.

Chapter 11

1.   *Minutes of the Board of the Federation of Jewish Charities (FJC Minutes)*, March 12, 1901.
2.   *Fourth Annual Report of the FJC, 1905.*
3.   *Third Annual Report, FJC, 1904; Fourth Annual Report, 1905.*
4.   "Seventy-five Years of Continuity and Change," *Jewish Exponent*, March 12, 1976, p. 22.
5.   Charles Bernheimer, *The Russian Jew in the United States* (Philadelphia: John Winston, 1905), pp. 84–86, 162–167.
6.   Bernheimer, *The Russian Jew*, p. 123; *Seventy-five Years*, p. 14.
7.   Bernheimer, *The Russian Jew*, p. 166.
8.   *Fifty Years Work of the Hebrew Education Society of Philadelphia, 1848–1898* (Philadelphia, 1898), p. 90; Bernheimer, *A Historical Sketch of the Philadelphia Jewish Community, 1714 to 1926* (unpublished manuscript, 1926), p. 66.
9.   *FJC Minutes*, April 19, 1928.
10.   Marilyn Krantz, "People Serving People," *Jewish Exponent*, July 10, 1981.
11.   Krantz, "People Serving People."
12.   *Seventy-five Years*, p. 22; *Philadelphia Inquirer*, March 22, 1939.
13.   "The History of the Young Women's Union," *Fact Sheet of the Philadelphia Jewish Archives Center;* and "Jules Mastbaum on Interlocking Directorates in Communal Work," *Jewish Exponent*, March 19, 1926.
14.   Interview with Julian Greifer, July 6, 1981.
15.   Interview with Julian Greifer.
16.   Joseph L. Kun, "Recollections of the Philadelphia Kehilla," *Jewish Exponent*, January 14, 1955, p. 19.
17.   Kun, "Recollections of the Philadelphia Kehilla"; and "Report of the American Jewish Committee," *American Jewish Yearbook, 1913–14*, p. 451.
18.   *American Jewish Yearbook, 1916–17*, pp. 329–30.
19.   Kun, "Recollections of the Philadelphia Kehilla."
20.   *American Jewish Yearbook, 1913–14*, pp. 450–51.
21.   *American Jewish Yearbook, 1913–14*, pp. 450–51.
22.   Kun, "Recollections of the Jewish Kehilla."
23.   Norman Bentwich, *For Zion's Sake*.
24.   *Jewish Exponent*, January 19, 31, 1919; February 4, 1921, "Fortieth Anniversary of Mischan Israel," p. 40.

25. *Annual Report of FJC, 1919;* and *Seventy-five Years,* p. 23.
26. *Jewish Exponent,* April 18, 1980.
27. *Jewish Exponent,* June 4, 1926.
28. *Jewish Exponent,* May 17, 1935; and *Fact Sheet on the Levinthals,* Philadelphia Jewish Archives Center.
29. *Jewish Exponent,*May 17, 1935; and Rabbi Alex J. Goldman, *Giants of Faith* (New York: Citadel, 1964), pp. 167–69.
30. Goldman, *Giants of Faith.*
31. Interview with Louis Levinthal, July 18, 1971.
32. *Jewish Exponent,* May 17, 1935.
33. Goldman, *Giants of Faith,* pp. 170–73.
34. *Twenty-fourth Annual Report of FJC, 1925; Seventy-five Years,* p. 28; *Jewish Exponent,* April 18, 1980; and interview with Edwin Wolf 2nd, December 23, 1981.
35. *Board Minutes of FJC,* March 16, May 5, and November 9, 1922; E. Digby Baltzell, *The Philadelphia Gentleman,* pp. 287–89; *The Evening Bulletin,* January 5, 1967; and *The Philadelphia Inquirer.* January 5.6, 1967.
36. Interview with Benjamin Sprafkin, July 7, 1981.
37. *Leiberman Fact Sheet,* FJA Publicity Department File; *Jewish Exponent,* August 4, 1947; and Howard Fineshriber and Berthold Levy, *The Birth and Growth of the Jewish Family Service, 1869–1969* (Philadelphia: Federation of Jewish Agencies, 1969).
38. *Leiberman Fact Sheet; Jewish Exponent,* August 3, 1967; and Sprafkin interview.
39. *Seventy-five Years,* p. 29; and *Board Minutes of Allied Jewish Appeal (AJA),* June 7, 1938.
40. *Proceedings of the First Annual Meeting of the AJA,* April 19, 1942.
41. *Jewish Exponent,* May 17, 1935; Bernheimer, *The Russian Jew,* pp. 165, 167; and *Fact Sheet on the Levinthals,* Jewish Archives Center.
42. "Levinthal," *Who's Who in America,* Vol. 33, 1964–65; *Jewish Exponent,* May 28, 1976; interview with Louis Levinthal, October 16, 1972.
43. Interview with Robert Bernstein, July 7, 1981; Levinthal interview, 1972.
44. Howard Sacher, *A History of Israel* (New York: Knopf, 1979), pp. 217–26.
45. *Seventy-five Years,* p. 29; *The Birth and Growth of the Jewish Family,* p. 9.
46. Levinthal interview, 1972.
47. Henry Feingold, *Zion in America,* pp. 291–92; and *Jewish Exponent,* May 15, 1942.
48. Sacher, *A History of Israel,* pp. 725–26; and *The Course of Modern Jewish History* (New York: Schocken, 1958), p. 527.
49. *Daroff Fact Sheet,* FJA Publicity Department File; *Jewish Exponent,* November 26, 1965; and interview with Joseph Daroff by Sis Eisman, March 1974.
50. Daroff interview.
51. Daroff interview.
52. *Daroff Fact Sheet.*
53. *Board Minutes of FJC,* March-October, 1937.
54. Leon Sunstein, "The Structure of the Philadelphia Community," speech given before the Philadelphia Council (Federation of Jewish Agencies, Philadelphia).
55. *Jewish Exponent,* November 26, 1965.
56. Interview with Jacob Gutman, July 9, 1981.
57. Gutman interview.
58. *Board Minutes of FJC,* June 7, 1938.
59. "A Tribute to Tradition," Gifts Dinner Folder, 1976.
60. *Jewish Exponent,* April 18, 1980.

Chapter 12

1. Greenfield's obituary, *New York Times,* January 6, 1967.
2. J. David Stern, *Memoirs of a Maverick Publisher* (New York: Simon & Schuster, 1962), p. 219.
3. *Fortune,* June 1936, p. 192.
4. *Fortune,* June 1936, p. 186.

5. These descriptions and most details regarding the Bankers Trust collapse are taken from *Fortune,* June 1936, p. 67ff.
6. Upton Sinclair, *Upton Sinclair Presents William Fox* (privately published, Los Angeles, 1933), pp. 345–348.
7. The details of Greenfield's origins were provided by his older brother, William, in an interview on October 17, 1975, when he was 93. The spellings of towns may not be correct. Lozovata apparently was located in the state of Podolia, adjoining the state of Kiev to the southwest. However, *Ritters Lexikon* (1906) lists a village named Lozovaia [sic] in the state of Ekaterinoslav, which is southeast of the state of Kiev.
8. Philadelphia *Bulletin,* April 28, 1920.
9. *Bulletin,* December 25, 1921.
10. *Bulletin,* August 25, 1925.
11. Nicholas B. Wainwright, *History of the Philadelphia National Bank* (Philadelphia: William Fell), p. 200.
12. Samuel Barker to Albert M. Greenfield, July 10, 1931. On file among Greenfield's papers at Pennsylvania Historical Society, Philadelphia. Barker to Greenfield, November 7, 1931. Barker to Greenfield, August 10, 1931. Greenfield to Barker, August 11, 1931.
13. *Fortune,* June 1936; also Sinclair, pp. 345–348.
14. *Bulletin,* April 11, 1931.
15. *Bulletin,* June 26, 1931.
16. Sinclair, pp. 86–87.
17. Steven Hopkins, "Stormy Monday," *Philadelphia Magazine,* May 1956, p. 91.
18. Stern, pp. 169–171; also *Fortune,* June 1936, p. 192.
19. Stern, p. 242.
20. Gaeton Fonzi, *Annenberg,* p. 116.
21. *Polk's Philadelphia Blue Book, Elite Directory and Club List* (Philadelphia: R. L. Polk, 1924), p. 624.
22. *New York Times,* May 11, 1939, p. 6.
23. Stern, p. 243.
24. Federation of Jewish Charities, list of annual subscribers, July 15, 1925.
25. U.S. District Court, Chapter XI bankruptcy case 21379, June 21, 1940.
26. *Bulletin,* December 16, 1935.
27. *Fortune,* June 1936, p. 192.

Chapter 13

1. See Bertram Wallace Korn, "1655–1901," in *75 Years of Continuity and Change: Our Philadelphia Jewish Community in Perspective* (supplement), *Philadelphia Jewish Exponent,* March 12, 1976, p. 10.
2. See "Population," in *Encyclopedia Judaica,* Vol. 13 (Jerusalem, 1971), p. 899.
3. Jacob Rader Marcus, *Early American Jewry* (Philadelphia: Jewish Publication Society, 1955), p. 127. This letter is dated May 1, 1782.
4. *Minute Book of Congregation Mikveh Israel,* September 13, 1846.
5. *Minute Book of the Junto of Congregation Mikveh Israel,* special meeting, September 20, 1846.
6. Isadore Margolis, *Jewish Teacher Training School in the United States* (New York: National Council for Torah Education of Mizrachi-Hapoel, 1964).
7. Jeanette W. Rosenbaum, "Rodeph Shalom—Philadelphia, 1800–1950," *Liberal Judaism,* September 1950.
8. For weekly hours of classes, see *Minutes of Congregation Keneseth Israel,* June 3, 1855, and Julius H. Greenstone, *Statistical Data of the Jewish Religious Schools of Philadelphia for 1906–1907* (Philadelphia: Gratz College, 1907).
9. *First Annual Report of the Jewish Community of Philadelphia for the Year 1911–1912* (Philadelphia, 1913). This can be found at the Jewish Archives of Philadelphia.
10. In 1937, when there were 13 Conservative congregational schools, a Board of Jewish Education was established in Philadelphia by the United Synagogue of America to deal

with the educational concerns of these schools and the Conservative Jewish community. One of its prime tasks was to promote standards.

11. Leo L. Honor and Morris Leibman, *Jewish Education in Philadelphia: A Survey* (manuscript, 1943), p. 3.
12. Honor and Leibman, *A Survey*, pp. 68–69.
13. Hyman Grinstein, "In the Course of the Nineteenth Century," *A History of Jewish Education in America,* Judah Pilch, ed. (New York: National Curriculum Research Institute of the American Association for Jewish Education, 1969), p. 31.
14. Oscar and Mary Handlin, "A Century of Jewish Immigration to the United States," *American Jewish Yearbook,* Vol. 50 (Philadelphia: Jewish Publication Society, 1949), p. 55.
15. Grinstein, "In the Course of the Nineteenth Century," p. 55.
16. Greenstone, p. 1; *First Annual Report of the Jewish Community of Philadelphia.*
17. Honor and Leibman, *A Survey*, p. 5.
18. Isaac Leeser had received both a secular and a Jewish education before emigrating. He obtained his secular education at the gymnasium of Muenster and received his Jewish education from Rabbi Benjamin Cohen and Rabbi Abraham Sutro, an ardent opponent of Reform Judaism.
19. Korn, "75 Years, 1655–1901," p. 10.
20. *Minutes of Congregation Mikveh Israel,* September 6, 1829.
21. *Minutes of Congregation Mikveh Israel,* March 27, 1836.
22. Korn, "75 Years, 1655–1901," p. 11.
23. William Chomsky,"Beginnings of Jewish Education in America," *Gratz College Annual of Jewish Studies,* Vol. 5 (Philadelphia: Gratz College, 1976), p. 10.
24. Julius Greenstone, "Jewish Education in the United States," *American Jewish Yearbook* (Philadelphia: Jewish Publication Society, 1916), Vol. 16, p. 98.
25. Morais, *The Jews of Philadelphia,* p. 146.
26. Korn, "75 Years, 1655–1901," p. 11; Jacob Rader Marcus, "Rosa Mordecai," *Memoirs of American Jews 1775–1865,* 3 vols. (Philadelphia: Jewish Publication Society, 1955–1956), Vol. 1, p. 272.
27. Marcus, "Rosa Mordecai," p. 283.
28. Chomsky, "Beginnings of Jewish Education in America," *Gratz College Annual of Jewish Studies,* p. 11.
29. Greenstone, *Statistical Data of Jewish Religious Schools,* p. 1.
30. *First Annual Report of the Jewish Community of Philadelphia.*
31. Honor and Leibman, *A Survey*, p. 5.
32. Isaac Leeser, "Public Religious Education," *The Occident and American Jewish Advocate* (November 1843), Vol. 1, pp. 361–64.
33. Isaac Leeser, "A Plea for Education," *The Occident and American Jewish Advocate* (April 1847), Vol. 4, p. 47.
34. Isaac Leeser, "A General and Hebrew School," *The Occident and American Jewish Advocate* (April 1847), Vol. 4, p. 47.
35. *Fifty Years' Work of the Hebrew Education Society* (Philadelphia: Hebrew Education Society, 1899), p. 12. This school was not connected with any one congregation, but would serve the entire Jewish community.
36. *Fifty Years' Work,* pp. 90–92.
37. *Fifty Years' Work,* p. 19.
38. The building was the hall of the old Phoenix Hose Company on Filbert (then Zane) Street between Seventh and Eighth Streets.
39. *Fifty Years' Work,* pp. 39–44.
40. *Fifty Years' Work,* p. 48.
41. Morais, *The Jews of Philadelphia,* p. 155. Among the students who later became famous in American Jewry was Cyrus Adler.
42. *Fifty Years' Work,* p. 22.
43. Chomsky, "Beginnings of Jewish Education in America," *Gratz College Annual of Jewish Studies,* pp. 8–9.
44. *Fifty Years' Work,*pp. 49–50.
45. *Fifty Years' Work,* p. 50.

46. Abraham Hart was treasurer of the Board of Trustees of the Hebrew Education Society. He was a leading publisher, an associate of the firm of Carey and Hart. He was president of Congregation Mikveh Israel as well as other charitable and educational institutions.
47. *Fifty Years' Work,* pp. 56–57.
48. *Fifty Years' Work,* p. 58.
49. *Fifty Years' Work,* p. 61.
50. Among the faculty of Maimonides College were Isaac Leeser (English literature, logic, and homiletics); Dr. Sabato Morais (Biblical exegesis); Dr. Marcus Jastrow (Talmud, Jewish literature and Hebrew philosophy); Hyman Polano (Hebrew and Mishnah).
51. *Fifty Years' Work,* p. 70. Eliezer Lam, a teacher in the Hebrew School of the Hebrew Education Society, Rev. David Levy, and Rev. Samuel Mendelsohn were the graduates.
52. Greenstone, *Statistical Data of Jewish Religious Schools,* p. 8.
53. In all probability, this was so because it was the only language the teacher knew and the pupils still understood it. The same situation prevailed in many of the *hadarim.*
54. Greenstone, *Statistical Data of Jewish Religious Schools,* p. 6.
55. The Kehilla was established in 1911 under the leadership of Cyrus Adler. The purpose was to further the cause of Judaism and promote concerted action by the Jews of Philadelphia in respect to all matters of Jewish interest. One of its primary spheres of interest was Jewish education. The effort was interrupted by the outbreak or World War I and after the war the effort was not repeated. See the *First Annual Report of the Jewish Community of Philadelphia for the Year 1911–1912* (Philadelphia, 1913).
56. Leo L. Honor, "Jewish Elementary Education in the United States," *Selected Writings of Leo L. Honor,* Abraham P. Gannes, ed. (New York, The Reconstructionist Press, 1965), p. 80.
57. Ben Rosen had been superintendent of one of the largest Talmud Torahs in New York before coming to Philadelphia.
58. Honor, "Jewish Elementary Education in the United States," p. 80.
59. Honor and Leibman, *A Survey,* p. 37.
60. Honor and Leibman, *A Survey,* pp. 55–59.
61. Honor and Leibman, *A Survey,* p. 41.
62. It established a Board of License whose function it was to set up minimum requirements for teachers in regard to Jewish knowledge, secular and professional training as well as teaching effectiveness and personality. Certificates granted by it were recognized by the National Board of License. See Honor and Leibman, *A Survey,* p. 49.
63. Deed of trust recorded in the office of the Recorder of Deeds in the County of Philadelphia on January 29, 1857, in Deed Book R.D.W. No. 117, p. 5.
64. Trust for Portuguese Hebrew Congregation Kaal Kadosh Mikveh Israel under Deed of Trust Hyman Gratz to the Pennsylvania Company for Insurances on Lives and Granting Annuities Court of Common Pleas No. 4 of Philadelphia County, September term, 1906, No. 3983, petition in the matter of 1010 Bainbridge Street.
65. The total value of the estate was between $130,000 and $150,000. This initially yielded an income of about $6,000.
66. *Minutes of the Gratz Trust,* August 29, 1895.
67. Gratz College has the distinction of being the first Hebrew Teacher's College in this country.
68. The Hebrew Education Society was authorized by the terms of its charter to establish a superior seminary within the limits of the Commonwealth of Pennsylvania, which had the power to grant the degrees of Bachelor of Arts, Master of Arts, and Doctor of Law and Divinity.
69. The College course was ten hours per week and extended over four years. It was intended to train teachers for the three-day-a-week Hebrew schools and the Talmud Torahs.
70. A degree program was instituted after 1945. The College now offers both bachelor's and master's degrees. It also has its own high school and an extensive continuing education department.
71. See Diane A. King, "A History of Gratz College, 1893–1928" (Ph.D. thesis, Dropsie University, Philadelphia, 1979). For most of this period the Jewish community was occupied with the dual effort of acculturation and of establishing itself economically.

There was no energy to spare for problems which did not contribute to these all-important tasks. Jewish education was placed in just such a category.
72. Honor and Leibman, *A Survey*, p. 110.
73. Ohel Moshe and Mishkan Israel. The latter had a branch in West Philadelphia.
74. Honor and Liebman, *A Survey*, p. 91.
75. Honor and Leibman, *A Survey*, p. 94. The language of instruction was Yiddish.
76. These schools were sponsored by the Poale Zionists and the Jewish National Workers' Alliance.
77. Honor and Leibman, *A Survey*, pp. 102–103.
78. Honor and Leibman, *A Survey*, p. 106.
79. Honor and Leibman, *A Survey*, p. 107.
80. Honor and Leibman, *A Survey*, p. 97.
81. A majority (about 65%) were girls. See Honor and Leibman, *A Survey*, p. 100.
82. Honor and Leibman, A Survey, p. 97.
83. Frank J. Rubinstein, *The Early Years 1908 to 1919: The Dropsie College for Hebrew and Cognate Learning* (Philadelphia, Dropsie University, 1977), p. 12.
84. Rubinstein, *The Early Years*, p. 7.
85. Honor and Leibman, *A Survey*, p. 13.

Chapter 14

1. Anthony Marmion, *The Ancient and Modern History of the Maritime Ports of Ireland* (London: W. H. Cox, 1860), p. ii.
2. I am indebted to folksinger Maury Callahan for the words to this song.
3. Michael Feldberg, *The Philadelphia Riots of 1844* (Westport, Conn.: Greenwood Press, 1975), pp. 19–161.
4. Dennis Clark, *The Irish in Philadelphia* (Philadelphia: Temple University Press, 1974), pp. 40–55.
5. Henry S. Morais, "Our Jewish Citizens," *The City of Philadelphia As It Appears in the Year 1893* (George S. Harris & Sons, Trades League of Philadelphia, 1893), pp. 146–48; Henry S. Morais, *The Jews of Philadelphia* (Philadelphia: The Levytype Co., 1894), pp. 215–16.
6. Clark, *The Irish in Philadelphia*, Figure 1.
7. James Gopsill, *Gopsill's Philadelphia Business Directory - 1892* (James Gopsill and Co., 1892), pp. 122–28, 240–61. Lists 7 Lynchs and 25 Kellys and dozens of those with "Mc," "Mac" and "O" who began their surnames as grocers, along with Abraham Jacobs and Solomon Jacobs. Irish butchers were common as were tailers and bootmakers. See also Tom Mooney, "Nine Years in America," in John R. Commons, ed., *A Documentary History of American Industrial Society* (Cleveland: A. C. Clark, 1910), Vol. 7, pp. 71–75.
8. Magistrates Court No. 5 (121 S. 7th Street), Criminal Docket 1909–12, Archives of the City of Philadelphia, July 15, 31; August 2, 8, 14; September 2, 9, 11; and October 28.
9. *Jewish Exponent* (Philadelphia), April 21, 1893; June 23, 1893.
10. *Jewish Exponent* (Philadelphia), September 1, 1893.
11. John M. Campbell, *The History of the Friendly Sons of St. Patrick* (Philadelphia: The Hibernian Society, 1892), p. 488.
12. *Boyd's Combined City and Business Directory—1910, 1920, 1930;* Recollections shared with the author by the late Capt. David Roche and Mrs. Anna McGarry; William B. Richter, *North of Society Hill* (North Quincy, Mass.: Christopher Publishing House, 1970), p. 28, affirm the Irish-Jewish affinity.
13. "Irish Voices," a collection of oral history tapes from the Balch Institute, Philadelphia.
14. James F. Connolly, *The History of the Archdiocese of Philadelphia* (Philadelphia: Archdiocese of Philadelphia, 1976), pp. 379–83; Irwin Frank Greenberg, "The Philadelphia Democratic Party, 1911–1934," Ph.D. thesis, Temple University, 1972.
15. Clark, *The Irish in Philadelphia*, p. 147.
16. *"Irish Voices," Balch Institute Collection, interview with Robert V. Clarke.*
17. *Ronald H. Bayor, Neighbors in Conflict: The Irish, Germans, Jews and Italians of New*

York City, 1929–1941 (Baltimore: Johns Hopkins University Press, 1978). Conditions in Philadelphia were more moderate, but the same in general orientation. See also Robert Griffith, *The Politics of Fear: Joseph R. McCarthy and the Senate* (Lexington: University of Kentucky Press, 1970); and the Patrick Stanton Collection, Balch Institute.

18. Thomas C. Cochran, *The Inner Revolution* (New York: Harper & Row, 1964), p. 33.

19. The dour view of American city government held by Lord James Bryce is now seen to have been heavily biased. See Robert C. Brooke, *Bryce's American Commonwealth* (New York: Macmillan, 1939), pp. 56, 95. Zane Miller sees the political machine and its boss performing crucial urban functions. Zane Miller, *Boss Cox's Cincinnati* (New York: Oxford University Press, 1968). For a discussion of the differing interpretations of boss rule see Lyle Dorsett, *The Pendergast Machine* (New York: Oxford University Press, 1968), Introduction; and Lawrence Fuchs, *American Ethnic Politics* (New York: Harper & Row, 1968).

20. Edward Levine, *The Irish and Irish Politicians* (South Bend: University of Notre Dame Press, 1966).

21. Edward P. Hutchinson, *Immigrants and Their Children* (New York: John Wiley & Sons, 1956), pp. 83, 103, 126.

22. Hutchinson, *Immigrants and Their Children*, p. 95; and Maldwyn Allen Jones, *American Immigration* (Chicago: University of Chicago Press, 1960), p. 21.

23. Geoffrey G. Williamson, "Ante-Bellum Urbanization in the American Northeast," *Journal of Economic History*, Vol. 25, No. 4 (October 1965), p. 589.

25. Oscar Handlin, *Boston's Immigrants* (New York: Atheneum, 1968), p. 57. Handlin shows that 48 percent of the Irish were laborers in Boston in the 1840s.

25. For a critique of the Colonial preoccupation of historians of the city, see R. H. Shryock, "Historical Traditions in Philadelphia and in the Middle Atlantic Area," *Pennsylvania Magazine of History and Biography*, Vol. 68, No. 2 (April 1943), pp. 115–41.

26. Sam Bass Warner, "Innovation and Industrialization in Philadelphia, 1800–1850," in Handlin and Burchard, eds., *The Historian and the City* (Cambridge, Mass.: M. I. T. Press, 1963), pp. 65–68; and Edwin T. Freedlay, *Philadelphia and its Manufacturers* (Philadelphia: Edward Young, 1859), pp. 15–43.

27. Sam Bass Warner, *The Private City: Philadelphia* (Philadelphia: University of Pennsylvania Press, 1968), pp. 152–57.

28. Edward C. Kirkland, *Industry Comes of Age* (Chicago: Quadrangle Books, 1961), p. 238. Construction activity has historically been a speculative and economically eccentric field, more sensitive to cycles of boom and bust than most areas of the economy. This has led to a saying in the field that a construction man must of necessity be a gambler. A sudden contraction of credit, a hard rock strata struck in excavation, a laborers' strike could jeopardize not only a single project, but a whole business.

29. Asa Briggs, *Victorian Cities* (New York: Harper & Row, 1970), pp. 16–17.

30. Milton Barron, "Intermediacy: Conceptualization of Irish Status in America," *Social Forces*, Vol. 27, No. 3 (March 1949), pp. 256–63.

31. J. St. George Joyce (ed.), *The Story of Philadelphia* (Philadelphia: Rex Printing House, 1919), p. 474.

32. Interview with James Duffin, grandson of David J. Duffin, June 11, 1970.

33. *Evening Bulletin* (Philadelphia), October 29, 1934.

34. *Evening Bulletin* (Philadelphia), March 10, 1936; June 10, 1962; and February 25, 1968.

35. *Evening Bulletin*, June 10, 1962; and February 25, 1968.

36. See *Evening Bulletin* (Philadelphia), May 29, 1963; and Thomas O'Malley, "John McShain: Builder" *Columbia* (February 1955).

37. *Evening Bulletin* (Philadelphia), May 29, 1963; and October 3, 1962.

38. James Reichley, *The Art of Reform*, (New York: Fund for the Republic, 1959), pp. 9, 20.

39. In their individualism and self-reliance these contractors of the Gilded Age resembled the dynamic boosters of the new cities of the West. See Daniel Boorstin, *The Americans: The National Experience* (New York: Random House, 1965), pp. 115–23. The prevailing spirit is summarized by Thomas C. Cochran and William Miller, *The Age of Enterprise* (New York: Harper & Row), pp. 119–35.

40. For views of the changes in building in the late nineteenth century, see Charles N. Glaab and A. Theodore Brown, *A History of Urban America* (New York: Macmillan, 1967),

p. 146; and Edward C. Kirkland, *Industry Comes of Age* (New York: Harper & Row, 1961), p. 261.

41. Peter Jones, *The Consumer Society* (Baltimore: Penguin Books, 1965), pp. 214–15; and Alfred D. Chandler, "Development, Diversification and Decentralization," in Ross Robertson and James Pate, eds., *Readings in Unted States Economic and Business History* (Boston: Houghton-Mifflin, 1966), pp. 327–48.

42. For an overview of the early history of department stores in Philadelphia, see Frank M. Mayfield, *The Department Store Story* (New York: Fairchild Press, 1949); and Gunther Barth, *City People* (New York: Oxford University Press, 1980).

43. R. C. Moore, *Business Management*, Notes (March 1953), p. 9.

44. Edwin Wolf and Maxwell Whiteman, *History of the Jews of Philadelphia from Colonial Times to the Age of Jackson* (Philadelphia: Jewish Publication Society, 1956), pp. 290–302.

45. Wolf and Whiteman, *History of the Jews of Philadelphia*, p. 37.

46. John William Ferry, *A History of the Department Store* (New York: Macmillan, 1960), pp. 110–11.

47. Ferry, *A History of the Department Store*, p. 11; and Henry S. Morais, *The Jews of Philadelphia* (Philadelphia: The Levytype Company, 1894), p. 300.

48. Ferry, *A History of the Department Store*, pp. 71–72, 102–03; and Tom Mahoney, *The Great Merchants* (New York: Harper & Brothers, 1947), p. 6.

49. Stephen Birmingham, *Our Crowd* (New York: Dell, 1967), p. 24.

50. Ferry, *A History of the Department Store*, pp. 102–11; and Robert Hendrickson, *The Grand Emporiums* (New York: Stein & Day, 1980).

51. Nathaniel Weyl, *The Creative Elite* (Washington, D.C.: Public Affairs Press, 1966).

52. H. C. Adler, *The Jews in Germany from the Enlightenment to National Socialism* (South Bend: University of Notre Dame Press, 1969), pp. 63–72.

53. *Historical Statistics of the United States: Colonial Times to 1957* (Washington, D.C.: Bureau of the Census, 1967), Tables T 183–187; T 1–11; T 359–60; pp. 523, 518, 527.

54. Melech Epstein, *Jewish Labor in the U.S.A.* (New York: Trade Union Sponsoring Committee, 1953), p. 2.

55. *The Hebrew Education Society of Philadelphia* (Philadelphia: Hebrew Education Society, 1899), p. 96.

56. Rufus Learsi, *The Jews in America: A History* (Cleveland: World Publishing Company, 1954), p. 328.

57. John G. Cawelti, *Apostles of the Self-Made Man* (Chicago: University of Chicago Press, 1965), p. 178.

58. Dennis Clark, *Proud Past* (Philadelphia: Catholic Philopatrian Literary Institute, 1976).

59. Bertram Korn, et al., *Continuity and Change* (Philadelphia: Federation of Jewish Agencies, 1976), pp. 15–25; and Milton Goldin, *Why They Give: American Jews and Their Philanthropies* (New York: Macmillan, 1976), pp. 66, 172.

60. Sean Cronin, *The McGarrity Papers* (Tralee, Ireland: The Anvil Press, 1972).

61. Daniel Dougherty, *The Friendly Sons of St. Patrick of Philadelphia, 1892–1951* (Philadelphia: The Friendly Sons of St. Patrick, 1952), pp. 380–81.

62. Maxwell Whiteman, "Zionism Comes to Philadelphia," in Isadore S. Meyers, ed., *Early History of Zionism in America* (New York: American Jewish Historical Society and the Herzl Foundation, 1958), pp. 191–218; and Manuel Lisan Papers, Jewish Archives of Philadelphia.

63. *Philadelphia Inquirer*, October 26, 1936.

Chapter 15

1. John L. Shover, "Ethnicity and Religion in Philadelphia Politics, 1924–1940," *American Quarterly*, Vol. 25, December 1973, pp. 505–506.

2. J. T. Salter, *The People's Choice* (New York: Exposition Press, 1971), p. 71.

3. Edward C. Banfield and James Q. Wilson, *City Politics* (New York: Vintage, 1966).

4. Seymour Martin Lipset, *Political Man* (Garden City, N.Y.: Anchor, 1963), p. 261.

5. *Jewish Exponent*, September 21, 1917, p. 4.
6. *Jewish Exponent*, August 18, 1922, p. 4, and September 1, 1922, p. 4.
7. *Jewish Exponent*, July 31, p. 4.
8. Salter, *People's Choice*, p. 25.
9. Raymond E. Wolfinger, "The Development and Persistence of Ethnic Voting," *American Political Science Review*, Vol. 59, December 1965, pp. 896–908.
10. Raymond E. Wolfinger, *Who Votes* (New Haven: Yale University Press, 1974), p. 76.
11. Salter, *The People's Choice*, pp. 58–59.
12. Salter, *The People's Choice*, p. 54.
13. Shover, p. 513.
14. Salter, pp. 31, 42, 89.
15. *Jewish Exponent*, October 28, 1921, p. 16.
16. Samuel Lubell, *The Future of American Politics*, pp. 44–47.
17. Lubell, *The Future of American Politics, p. 49.*
18. Lawrence H. Fuchs, *The Political Behavior of American Jews* (Westport, Conn.: Greenwood Press, 1980), p. 67.
19. Fuchs, *The Political Behavior of American Jews*, p. 64.
20. Lipset, *Political Man*, pp. 256–257.
21. Fuch, *The Political Behavior of American Jews*, p. 64.
22. *Readers Digest Almanac*, 1981; *Bulletin Almanac*, 1929, 1933, 1949; *Manual of City Council*, Philadelphia, 1928, 1932, 1936, 1948.

Chapter 16

1. E. Digby Baltzell, *Puritan Boston and Quaker Philadelphia: Two Protestant Ethics and the Spirit of Class Authority and Leadership*, (New York: Free Press, 1979), p. 7.
2. Jacob R. Marcus, *The Colonial American Jew: 1492–1776* (Detroit: Wayne State University Press, 1970), Vol. 1, p. 299.
3. Marcus, *The Colonial American Jew*, p. 297.
4. Baltzell, *Puritan Boston and Quaker Philadelphia*, p. 419.
5. E. Digby Baltzell, *Philadelphia Gentlemen: The Making of a National Upper Class*, (Glencoe, Ill.: The Free Press, 1958), p. 277.
6. Baltzell, *Philadelphia Gentlemen*, pp. 277–99.
7. Henry Samuel Morais, *The Jews of Philadelphia: Their History from the Earliest Settlement to the Present Time* (Philadelphia: The Levytype Co., 1894), pp. 402–404, 27–29.
8. Joseph P. Sims, ed., *The Philadelphia Assemblies, 1748–1948* (Privately Printed; n.d.).
9. Edmund Wilson, *A Piece of My Mind* (New York: Anchor Books, 1958), pp. 88–89.
10. See Milton M. Gordon, *Assimilation in American Life* (New York: Oxford University Press, 1964), Chapters 4, 5, and 6.
11. Isaac M. Fein, *Boston—Where It All Began: An Historical Perspective of the Boston Jewish Community* (Boston: Boston Jewish Bicentennial Committee, 1976), p. 1.
12. Fein, *Boston—Where It All Began*, pp. 7–8.
13. Nathan Glazer, *American Judaism*, (Chicago: University of Chicago Press, 1957), p. 22.
14. Bertram Wallace Korn, "Isaac Leeser: Centennial Reflections," *American Jewish Archives*, November 1967, pp. 127–141.
15. Stephen Birmingham, *"Our Crowd" The Great Jewish Families of New York* (New York: Harper & Row, 1967), p. 131.
16. See Glazer, *American Judaism*, pp. 36 and *Dictionary of American Biography*, Vol. 20, pp. 426–27.
17. Glazer, *American Judaism*, p. 42.
18. Glazer, *American Judaism*, p. 57. Also see *Dictionary of American Biography:* Sabato Morais, Vol. 13, pp. 149–50; and Marcus Jastrow, Vol. 10, pp. 102.
19. See Adler biography in *Dictionary of American Biography*, Supplement II, pp. 5–6.
20. Glazer, *American Judaism*, p. 75.
21. Glazer, *American Judaism*, pp. 75–78.

22. *Reform Congregation Keneseth Israel, Its First 100 Years 1847–1957* (Philadelphia: Drake Press, 1950).
23. Esther M. Klein, *A Guidebook to Jewish Philadelphia* (Philadelphia Jewish Times Institute, 1965), p. 102.
24. M. A. DeWolfe Howe, *Boston: The Place and Its People* (New York: Macmillan, 1924), p. 225.
25. Arthur Mann, ed., *Growth and Achievement: Temple Israel 1854–1954* (Cambridge: Riverside Press, 1954), p. 7.
26. Mann, *Growth and Achievement*, p. 46.
27. Mann, *Growth and Achievement*, p. 46.
28. For facts about Schindler, see Mann, *Growth and Achievement*, Chapter 4; and *Dictionary of American Biography*, Vol. XVI, pp. 433–34.
29. Mann, *Growth and Achievement*, Chapter 5.
30. For an excellent discussion of Solomon Schindler and the Yankee and Irish reformers in late 19th-century Boston, see Arthur Mann, *Yankee Reformers in an Urban Age* (Cambridge: Harvard University Press, 1954).
31. Barbara Miller Solomon, *Ancestors and Immigrants: A Changing New England Tradition* (Cambridge: Harvard University Press, 1957) is a brilliant discussion of the founding of the Immigration Restriction League.
32. Barbara Miller Solomon, *Pioneers in Service: The History of the Associated Jewish Philanthropies of Boston* (Boston: Associated Jewish Philanthropies, 1956), p. 4.
33. For Jewish community leadership, see Baltzell, *Philadelphia Gentlemen*, Chapter 11.
34. Baltzell, *Philadelphia Gentlemen*, p. 284.
35. Solomon, *Pioneers in Service*, p. 21.
36. Solomon, *Pioneers in Service*, p. 10.
37. Maxwell Whiteman, *Mankind and Medicine* (Philadelphia: Albert Einstein Medical Center, 1960); and Solomon, *Pioneers in Service*.
38. For the University of Pennsylvania, see Morais, *The Jews of Philadelphia*, pp. 431–443 and for Harvard see Albert Ehrenfreid, *A Chronicle of Boston Jewry: From the Colonial Settlement to 1900*, (Copyright 1963 by Irving Bernstein). Also see Samuel Eliot Morison, *Three Centuries of Harvard* (Cambridge: Harvard University Press, 1963), pp. 57, 198, 203, 417, 422.
39. Bruce Kuklick, *The Rise of American Philosophy: Cambridge, Massachusetts, 1860–1930* (New Haven: Yale University Press, 1977), p. 407.
40. Kuklick, *The Rise of American Philosophy*, p. 407.
41. Lawrence R. Vesey, *The Emergence of the American University* (Chicago: University of Chicago Press, 1965), p. 288.
42. Theodore H. White, *In Search of History*, (New York: Harper & Row, 1978), p. 41.
43. White, *In Search of History*, p. 41.
44. White, *In Search of History*, p. 40.
45. *Dictionary of American Biography*, Supplement III, p. 94.
46. Allon Gal, *Brandeis of Boston* (Cambridge: Harvard University Press, 1980), p. 83.
47. Gal, *Brandeis of Boston*, p. 180.
48. Gal, *Brandeis of Boston*, Chapter 5.
49. Gal, *Brandeis of Boston*, p. 186.

Index

HOLOCAUST MEMORIAL CENTER
28123 Orchard Lake Road
Farmington Hills, MI 48334-3738

HOLOCAUST MEMORIAL CENTER
AMERICA'S FIRST
Remember
Zachor